DISH OF THE DAY

AUTHOR KATE McMILLAN

PHOTOGRAPHY BY ERIN KUNKEL

weldon**owen**

CONTENTS

JANUARY 8

FEBRUARY 32

MARCH 56

APRIL 80

MAY 104

JUNE 130

JULY 154

AUGUST 180

SEPTEMBER 204

OCTOBER 228

NOVEMBER 252

DECEMBER 278

A DISH FOR EVERY DAY

Inspired by both the seasons and a profusion of fresh, flavorful foods, this calendar-style cookbook is a practical guide to putting different and delicious dishes on your table every day of the year. Each month showcases the seasonal vegetables and fruits that arrive in local markets, such as asparagus, peas, and cherries in spring; peppers, corn, tomatoes, and stone fruits in summer; squashes, artichokes, and apples in fall; and sturdy greens, root vegetables, and citrus in winter. Follow the days' suggestions and you'll be sitting down to new, interesting, healthful dishes—both updated classics and modern creations—at every meal.

In these pages, you'll find recipes for soups, salads, mains, sides, and desserts, for both meat-friendly and meat-free diets. Comfort-food standards like lasagna, chicken with dumplings, corned beef and cabbage, and carrot cake are here, along with such global favorites as paella, fresh corn tamales, curried samosas, butternut squash risotto, ramen with sugar snap peas, and apricot clafoutis. You'll also discover plenty of choices for two hallmarks of casual dining: the burger, including turkey, red lentil, portobello mushroom, lamb, tuna, and more; and the pizza, topped with broccoli rabe in January, asparagus and leeks in May, tomatoes and mozzarella in July, and butternut squash in October. Dinner-party fare appears as well, in dishes such as ravioli stuffed with morels and leeks, duck breast salad with oranges, leg of lamb with fennel, French seafood stew, and chocolate-caramel tartlets.

The cooking methods are as varied as the ingredients and the dining styles, with stir-fries and sautés, stews and braises, curries and casseroles, and roasts and grills all represented. This savvy recipe collection also respects the cook's schedule, offering ideas for busy weeknights, such as Spanish-inspired garlic shrimp, eggplant and tofu stir-fry, spinach and Parmesan frittata, and rice noodles with crabmeat and herbs, and lazy weekends, such as slow-cooked lamb shoulder, traditional osso buco, braised duck legs with figs, and pulled pork with peach-mustard sauce.

Everything about this book makes eating according to the calendar and the farm stand easy, satisfying, and a memorable culinary adventure, with scores of evocative photographs illustrating the journey.

The first weeks of the new year are a time for hearty soups and easy braises, baked pastas and healthy grain dishes. Market produce aisles are filled with winter crops—brussels sprouts, broccoli, kale, fennel, beets, leeks, and more—and menu choices are varied and satisfying, from red beans and chorizo and polenta topped with chard and mushrooms to a coconut-rich chicken curry anchored with sweet potatoes and carrots. The season's much-anticipated citrus fruits turn up as well, in salads, in side dishes, and in a pair of irresistible desserts: grapefruit sorbet and lemon chiffon pie.

1
FENNEL-CRUSTED CHICKEN
WITH FENNEL & HERB SALAD
page 11

2
SPANISH TORTILLA WITH LEEKS
page 11

3
SPICED TRI-TIP WITH ROASTED
BRUSSELS SPROUTS
page 12

8
CHAI TEA CUPCAKES
WITH HONEY CREAM
page 15

9
TUNA IN ESCABECHE
page 15

10
BROCCOLI RABE & OLIVE PIZZA
page 17

15
ROASTED BEETS WITH BABY
ARUGULA & RICOTTA SALATA
page 19

16
SALMON CAKES WITH GINGER
& GREEN ONION
page 21

17
POTATO & BROCCOLI SOUP
WITH BLUE CHEESE
page 21

22
STIR-FRIED SOBA NOODLES
WITH BEEF & CABBAGE
page 25

23
VINEGAR-GLAZED BRUSSELS SPROUTS
WITH CHESTNUTS & WALNUT OIL
page 25

24
NOODLE SALAD WITH PORK
& ASIAN LIME VINAIGRETTE
page 27

29
FENNEL SALAD WITH BLOOD
ORANGES & ARUGULA
page 29

30
SPICED PEAR TARTE TATIN
page 30

31
WARM LENTIL & KALE SALAD
WITH BACON
page 30

4

COCONUT RICE NOODLES
WITH CRAB & CILANTRO
page 12

5

RUBY GRAPEFRUIT SORBET
page 14

6

BAKED PASTA WITH
PROSCIUTTO & PEAS
page 14

7

SAUTÉED POTATOES WITH
CHORIZO & PARSLEY
page 14

11

TOFU SALAD WITH EDAMAME
& SHAVED ROOT VEGETABLES
page 17

12

ITALIAN BRAISED SHORT RIBS
page 18

13

MAC & CHEESE CHILI
page 18

14

CHICKEN & COCONUT CURRY
page 19

18

POLENTA WITH WILD MUSHROOMS,
CHARD & CHEDDAR CHEESE
page 22

19

SPICY RED BEAN & CHORIZO STEW
page 22

20

ASIAN-STYLE CHICKEN SOUP
page 24

21

LEMON CHIFFON GINGERSNAP PIE
page 24

25

BARLEY RISOTTO WITH CHICKEN,
MUSHROOMS & GREENS
page 27

26

KUMQUAT-CARROT PURÉE
WITH TOASTED FENNEL SEEDS
page 28

27

QUINOA TABBOULEH WITH
LEMONY GRILLED SHRIMP
page 28

28

CARAMEL-MACADAMIA TARTLETS
page 29

january

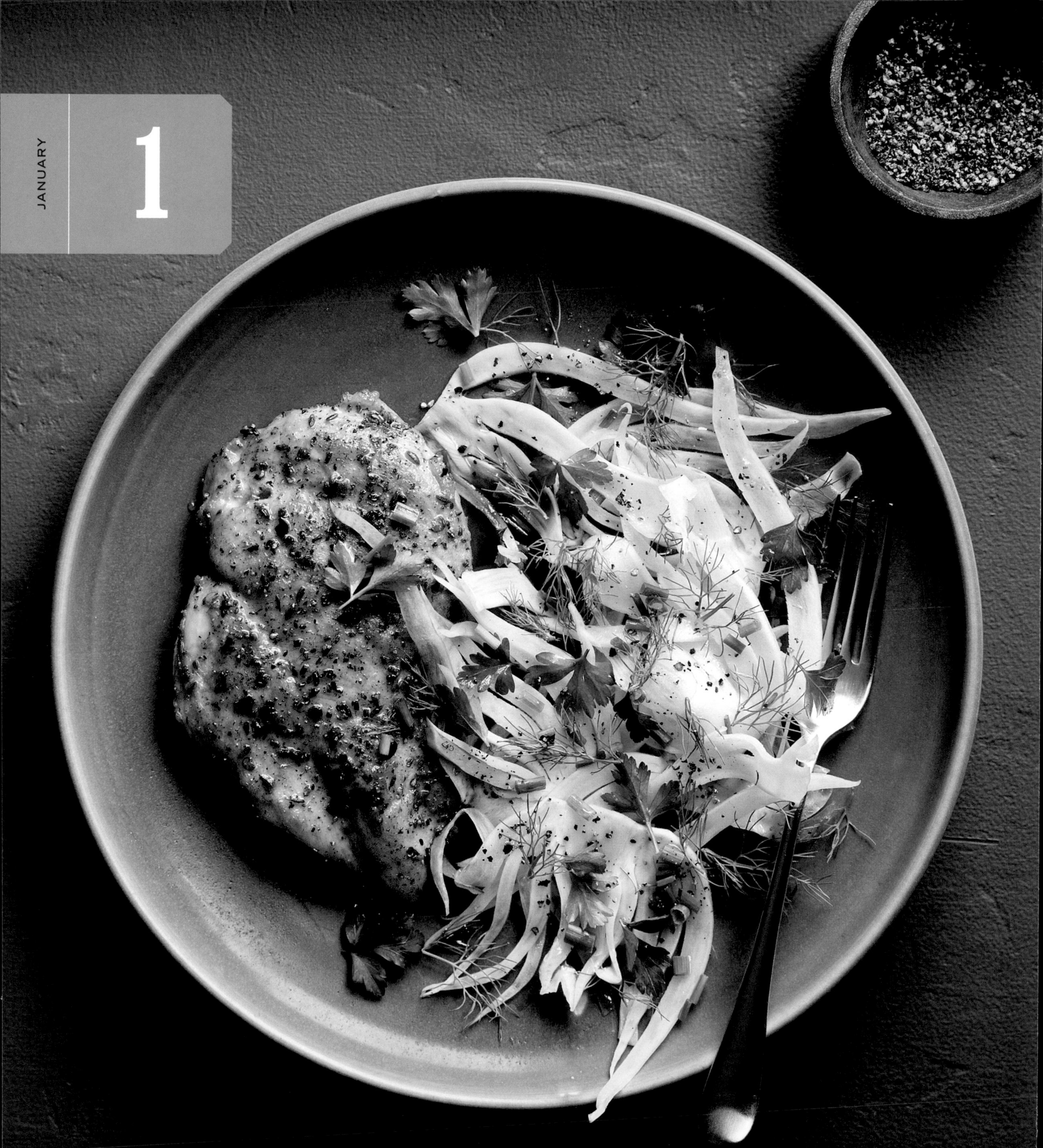

1

FENNEL-CRUSTED CHICKEN WITH FENNEL & HERB SALAD

serves 2

1½ tsp fennel seeds

¼ tsp black peppercorns

Salt and freshly ground black pepper

⅛ tsp red pepper flakes

2 boneless, skinless chicken breast halves

4 tsp extra-virgin olive oil

½ small fennel bulb, shaved (about ½ cup/2 oz/60 g), plus 1 Tbsp fennel fronds

2 Tbsp chopped fresh chives

2 Tbsp fresh flat-leaf parsley leaves

1 Tbsp fresh lemon juice

¼ cup (2 fl oz/60 ml) dry rosé wine

¼ cup (2 fl oz/60 ml) low-sodium chicken broth

An herb and fennel salad is a quick fix for a cool-weather menu that needs color and fresh flavors. A nice break from the more usual lettuce salad, it pairs well here with quickly cooked chicken breasts.

In a mortar using a pestle, grind together the fennel seeds, peppercorns, ¼ tsp salt, and red pepper flakes until coarsely ground.

Place 1 chicken breast half between 2 sheets of plastic wrap and pound lightly with a meat mallet until evenly flattened to ½ inch (12 mm) thick. Repeat with the second chicken breast.

In a large frying pan over medium-high heat, warm 2 tsp of the oil. Sprinkle both sides of the chicken breasts evenly with the fennel seed mixture. Cook, turning once, until golden brown on both sides and just cooked through, 3–4 minutes on each side.

Meanwhile, stir together the shaved fennel, chives, parsley, fennel fronds, lemon juice, and the remaining oil in a medium bowl and season to taste with salt and black pepper.

Transfer the chicken breasts to warmed plates. Add the wine and broth to the frying pan and simmer until reduced by about half, about 1 minute. Pour the pan juices over the chicken and top each with some of the fennel-herb salad, dividing evenly, and serve.

2

SPANISH TORTILLA WITH LEEKS

serves 6

7 Tbsp (3½ fl oz/105 ml) olive oil

1½ lb (750 g) Yukon Gold potatoes, peeled and cut into slices ⅛ inch (3 mm) thick

1 leek, white and pale green parts, thinly sliced

3 eggs, plus 3 egg whites

Salt

Spain's iconic egg-and-potato omelet can be served directly from the frying pan on winter nights or at room temperature on summer days. The tricky part of preparing this dish is flipping the omelet. Iberian cooks typically use a special hinged pan that simplifies the flip. But any large, flat plate or lid, handled carefully, will get the job done.

In a frying pan, warm 5 Tbsp of the oil over medium-high heat. Add the potatoes and leeks and cook, stirring occasionally, until tender, about 20 minutes. Transfer the potato and leek mixture to a colander to drain. Wipe out the pan.

In a large bowl, beat together the eggs, egg whites, and 1 tsp salt. Gently stir in the potatoes and leeks.

In the frying pan, warm the remaining 2 Tbsp oil over medium-high heat. Add the potato-egg mixture, press it into a thick cake with a spatula, and cook until set, about 5 minutes, adjusting the heat to prevent scorching. Loosen the tortilla by working the spatula under it, then continue to cook, shaking the pan occasionally, until the bottom is well browned, about 5 minutes more.

Slide the tortilla onto a large, flat plate. Invert the pan over it and carefully turn the pan and plate together. Return the pan to the stove top and continue to cook the tortilla until the second side is browned, about 5 minutes.

Slide the tortilla onto a platter and let stand for at least 10 minutes. Cut into wedges and serve.

3

SPICED TRI-TIP WITH
ROASTED BRUSSELS SPROUTS

serves 4–6

Tri-tip is a full-flavored cut that remains juicy and moist even when trimmed of fat. Brussels sprouts boast an equally bold flavor to complement the beef. To round out your plate, roast baby potatoes at the same time as the vegetables.

2 lb (1 kg) beef tri-tip, trimmed of fat

Salt and freshly ground pepper

2¼ tsp sweet paprika

2 tsp caraway seeds

2 tsp dried marjoram

1 tsp dry mustard

½ tsp cayenne pepper

3½ Tbsp olive oil, plus more for brushing

1 lb (500 g) brussels sprouts,
halved lengthwise

¾ lb (375 g) small shallots, halved
lengthwise, plus 1 large shallot, minced

1 Tbsp low-sodium soy sauce, plus 2 tsp

½ cup (4 fl oz/125 ml) dry vermouth

½ cup (4 fl oz/125 ml) low-sodium beef
or chicken broth

2 tsp unsalted butter

Preheat the oven to 450°F (230°C). Season the beef with salt and pepper, and place on a baking rack set in a shallow roasting pan.

Mix together 2 tsp of the paprika, 1 tsp of the caraway seeds, ½ tsp of the marjoram, the mustard, and cayenne. Mix in 1 Tbsp of the oil, then rub the mixture all over the beef. Oil a large baking pan and add the brussels sprouts, halved shallots, the 1 Tbsp soy sauce, plus the remaining 2½ Tbsp oil, 1 tsp caraway seeds, and 1 tsp marjoram. Mix to coat. Roast the beef and vegetables until an instant-read thermometer inserted in the thickest part of the beef registers 120°F (49°C) for rare, about 20 minutes, or until cooked to your liking. Roast the vegetables until tender and browned, about 25 minutes. Remove the beef from the oven, transfer to a warmed platter, tent with foil, and let rest for 15 minutes.

Spoon 1 Tbsp fat from the roasting pan into a saucepan over medium heat; discard the remaining fat. Add the minced shallot to the saucepan and sauté until it begins to soften, about 1 minute. Add the vermouth to the roasting pan, set it over medium-high heat, and bring to a boil, scraping up the browned bits on the pan bottom. Pour the mixture ⤳

into the saucepan and boil until syrupy, about 3 minutes. Add the broth, remaining ¼ tsp paprika, and 2 tsp soy sauce to the pan. Boil the sauce until syrupy, about 5 minutes. Remove the pan from the heat and pour in any juices from the platter. Whisk in the butter and the remaining ½ tsp marjoram. Season with salt and pepper. Slice the beef and arrange on a warmed platter with the vegetables. Serve with the sauce.

4

COCONUT RICE NOODLES
WITH CRAB & CILANTRO

serves 4

Using coconut milk is a great way to add natural creaminess and nutrients to a meal. It's easier to digest than dairy milk and imparts an authentic flavor to Asian noodles. Lime juice and coconut milk are a timeless combination that brings fresh flavor to this dish.

Salt

½ lb (250 g) dried flat rice noodles,
about ¼ inch (6 mm) wide

¼ cup (2 fl oz/60 ml) unsweetened
coconut milk

2–3 Tbsp Asian fish sauce

2 Tbsp fresh lime juice

Grated zest of 1 lime

2–4 Thai chiles, sliced (optional)

1 cup (1 oz/30 g) mung bean sprouts

½ English cucumber,
cut into paper-thin slices

½ lb (250 g) fresh lump crabmeat,
picked over for shell fragments and
cartilage and flaked

½ cup (½ oz/15 g) fresh cilantro leaves

In a large pot, bring 4 qt (4 l) water to a rapid boil. Add 1 tablespoon salt and the noodles, stir well, and cook, stirring occasionally, until just tender, 3–5 minutes. Drain in a colander, place under cold running water to cool, and drain again thoroughly.

In a bowl, stir together the coconut milk, fish sauce to taste, lime juice, lime zest, and chiles to taste, if using. Add the bean sprouts, cucumber, and crabmeat and toss gently to mix.

Transfer the noodles to a large, shallow serving bowl. Arrange the crab mixture over the noodles. Scatter the cilantro on top. Serve at room temperature, or cover and refrigerate for up to 3 hours and serve chilled.

5

Put vibrant ruby grapefruit to good use in this light dessert, which makes a refreshing finish to a hearty winter meal. For an elegant presentation, serve in glasses topped with a splash of prosecco.

RUBY GRAPEFRUIT SORBET

makes about 1 qt (32 fl oz/1 l)

1½ cups (12 fl oz/375 ml) fresh grapefruit juice

1⅓ cups (9 oz/290 g) superfine sugar

1 large ruby or pink grapefruit

In a blender, combine 2 cups (16 fl oz/500 ml) cold water, the grapefruit juice, and sugar.

Finely grate the zest from the grapefruit and add to the blender. Peel and segment the grapefruit (see page 37), reserving the juices.

Add the grapefruit segments and juice to the blender. Purée until smooth. Pour into a nonreactive bowl, cover, and refrigerate for 2–3 hours until well chilled.

Pour the chilled grapefruit mixture into an ice-cream maker and freeze according to the manufacturer's directions. If desired, pack it into a freezer-safe container and freeze until very firm before serving.

6

Big pasta tubes are a favorite for tossing with a handful of flavorful ingredients and baking into one-dish meals. Here, the more common ragù is replaced with strips of prosciutto, peas, and Parmesan mixed into an easy white sauce.

BAKED PASTA WITH PROSCIUTTO & PEAS

serves 4–6

½ cup (4 oz/125 g) unsalted butter, plus more for greasing

1 lb (500 g) ziti, penne, or other tubular pasta

½ cup (2½ oz/75 g) all-purpose flour

4 cups (32 fl oz/1 l) milk

⅛ tsp grated nutmeg

2 cups (8 oz/250 g) grated Parmesan cheese

1 cup (5 oz/155 g) frozen petite peas

¼ lb (125 g) prosciutto or ham, chopped

½ cup (1 oz/30 g) fresh bread crumbs

Preheat the oven to 425°F (220°C) and butter a 2-qt (2-l) baking dish. Bring a large pot of salted water to a boil. Add the pasta and cook, stirring occasionally, until not quite al dente, about 2 minutes less than the package directions. Drain, rinse with cold water, drain again, and set aside.

In the same pot, melt the ½ cup butter over medium heat. Add the flour and cook, stirring, for 30 seconds. ⤳

Slowly whisk in the milk, and cook, whisking, until the sauce is thick and creamy, 5–10 minutes. Stir in the nutmeg, cheese, peas, and prosciutto. Add the pasta and toss to combine.

Transfer the pasta and sauce to the prepared dish. Sprinkle with the bread crumbs. Bake until the crumbs are golden and the sauce is bubbling, about 20 minutes. Let cool for about 10 minutes before serving.

7

Humble potatoes are enlivened with a wine reduction, bright parsley, and dry-cured Spanish chorizo. To peel the chorizo, lightly run a sharp knife down its length, then, with your fingers, peel away the skin as if unwrapping the sausage.

SAUTÉED POTATOES WITH CHORIZO & PARSLEY

serves 4

1½ lb (750 g) large waxy potatoes, quartered

½ cup (2 oz/60 g) peeled, thinly sliced mild or hot dry-cured chorizo

¼ cup (1½ oz/45 g) finely chopped red onion

¼ cup (2 fl oz/60 ml) dry white wine

2 Tbsp chopped fresh flat-leaf parsley

In a saucepan, combine the potatoes with water to cover and bring to a boil. Reduce the heat to medium and cook until the potatoes are fork-tender, about 20 minutes. Drain and keep warm.

Heat a frying pan over medium-high heat. Add the chorizo and sauté until most of the fat is rendered, about 2 minutes. Pour off the fat and continue cooking the chorizo until lightly browned, 1–2 minutes. Add the onion and sauté for 1 minute. Add the potatoes and wine and cook until most of the liquid evaporates, about 1 minute.

Transfer to a bowl, toss with the parsley, and serve.

8

CHAI TEA CUPCAKES WITH HONEY CREAM

makes 12 cupcakes

3 chai tea bags

1¼ cups (6½ oz/200 g) all-purpose flour

¾ cup (6 oz/185 g) firmly packed light brown sugar

1 tsp baking soda

¼ tsp kosher salt

¼ cup (3 oz/90 g) plus 2 Tbsp honey, plus more for drizzling

4 Tbsp (2 oz/60 g) unsalted butter, melted

¼ cup (2 fl oz/60 ml) buttermilk

1 large egg

1 cup (8 fl oz/250 ml) cold heavy cream

Traditional chai is a warming cup of milky tea spiked with ginger, cinnamon, cloves, cardamom, and other aromatic spices. This recipe folds those seasonings into a buttermilk batter for cupcakes with a tender crumb and complex flavor. Start with a high-quality tea for the best results.

Preheat the oven to 350°F (180°C). Line 12 standard muffin cups with paper liners or grease with butter and dust with flour.

In a small bowl, steep the tea bags in ⅔ cup (5 fl oz/160 ml) boiling water for 5 minutes. Discard the bags and let the tea cool to room temperature.

In a bowl, whisk together the flour, brown sugar, baking soda, and salt. In a large bowl, using an electric mixer, beat together the ¼ cup honey, butter, buttermilk, and egg. Add the dry ingredients and beat just until incorporated, then add the cooled tea and beat just until combined. Divide the batter among the prepared cups, filling them about three-fourths full.

Bake until a toothpick inserted into the center of a cupcake comes out clean, about 18 minutes. Let cool in the pan on a wire rack for 5 minutes. Transfer the cupcakes to the rack and let cool completely, about 1 hour.

To make the honey cream, in a chilled bowl, combine the cream and remaining 2 Tbsp honey. Using an electric mixer, beat on low speed until slightly thickened, 1–2 minutes. Gradually increase the speed to medium-high and continue to beat until the cream holds medium peaks, 2–3 minutes. Spread the cupcakes with the honey cream and drizzle with additional honey.

9

TUNA IN ESCABECHE

serves 4–6

3 Tbsp olive oil

1½ lb (750 g) albacore or yellowfin tuna fillet, about 1 inch (2.5 cm) thick, cut into 6–8 pieces

1 red bell pepper, seeded and thinly sliced

½ red onion, thinly sliced

1 cup (8 fl oz/250 ml) dry white wine

¾ cup (6 fl oz/180 ml) sherry vinegar

2 cloves garlic, crushed

½ tsp black peppercorns

1 tsp grated orange zest

1 tsp sugar

½ tsp red pepper flakes

Salt

½ cup (2½ oz/75 g) pitted olives

This popular room-temperature Mediterranean dish pairs meaty fish with a slightly sweet, vinegary sauce. Fragrant with orange zest and garlic, it is finished with just enough red pepper flakes to give it a pleasant bite.

In a large frying pan, warm 2 Tbsp of the oil over medium-high heat. Add the tuna and cook, turning once, until browned on both sides but still translucent in the center, 5–8 minutes. Transfer to a 2-qt (2-l) baking dish.

Add the remaining 1 Tbsp olive oil to the pan. Add the bell pepper and onion and sauté until softened, 3–5 minutes. Add the wine, vinegar, garlic, peppercorns, orange zest, sugar, and red pepper flakes. Season with ¾ tsp salt, pour in ¼ cup (2 fl oz/60 ml) water, and bring to a boil.

Pour the hot liquid and vegetables over the fish and scatter the olives over the top. Let stand until cooled to room temperature. Cover and refrigerate for at least 8 hours or up to 24 hours.

Lift the tuna from the marinade and transfer to a platter. Drain the marinade, reserving the vegetables and olives, and arrange them over the tuna. Let stand for about 15 minutes before serving.

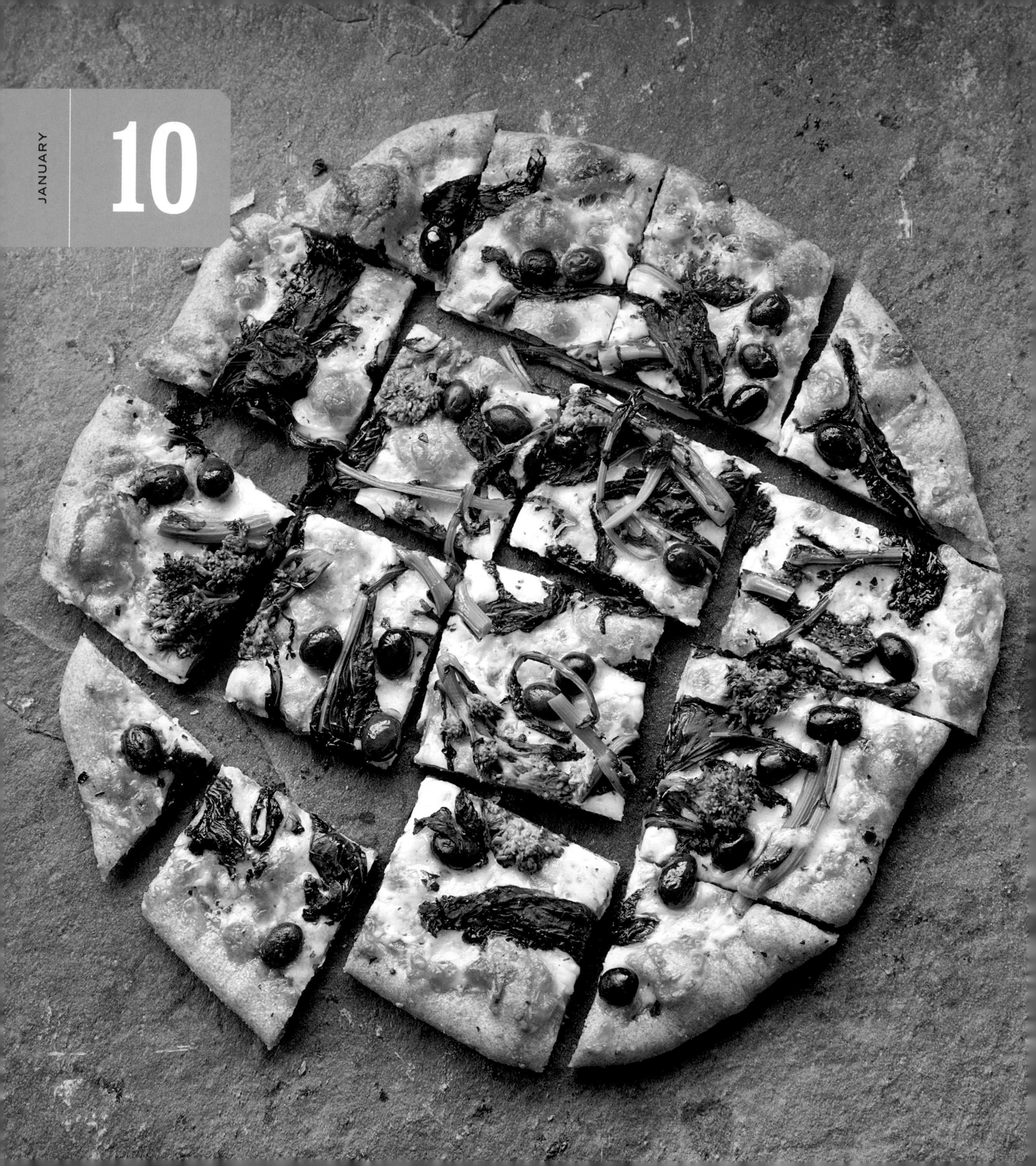

10

BROCCOLI RABE & OLIVE PIZZA

serves 2–3

1 lb (500 g) purchased whole-wheat pizza dough, at room temperature

2 Tbsp extra-virgin olive oil

1 large clove garlic, minced

¼ tsp red pepper flakes

Pinch of salt

1 bunch broccoli rabe, about ¾ lb (375 g), thick stems removed

Flour and cornmeal, for dusting

½ lb (250 g) part-skim mozzarella cheese, coarsely shredded

¼ cup (2 oz/60 g) pitted niçoise olives

Calorie-laden pizza gets a makeover in this healthy rendition. Part-skim mozzarella keeps the topping creamy but low in fat, and cool-weather broccoli rabe is packed with vitamins and minerals but not calories. Nutty niçoise olives develop a pleasing leathery texture in the oven. The pizza is perfect for lunch or dinner, but, cut into small squares, it also makes an appealing shared snack or appetizer.

Position a rack in the bottom of the oven. Place a baking stone on the rack. Preheat the oven to 550°F (290°C), or the highest setting, for at least 45 minutes. Punch the dough down and turn it out onto a work surface. Shape it into a ball. Cover with a clean kitchen towel and let rest for 30 minutes.

In a small bowl, combine the oil, garlic, red pepper flakes, and salt. Let stand for 30 minutes to marry the flavors.

Bring a large pot three-fourths full of salted water to a boil over high heat. Add the broccoli rabe and cook until tender, 2–3 minutes. Drain and cool under running cold water. Gently squeeze out the excess water. Roughly chop the broccoli rabe.

To assemble the pizza, lightly flour a work surface. Roll out the dough into a round 13–14 inches (33–35 cm) in diameter. Generously dust a pizza peel or rimless baking sheet with cornmeal and transfer the dough round to it. Working quickly, spread the cheese evenly over the dough, leaving a ¾-inch (2-cm) rim uncovered. Top evenly with the broccoli rabe and the olives. Brush the rim with some of the seasoned oil, then drizzle more oil evenly over the pizza.

Immediately slide the pizza from the peel onto the baking stone. Bake until the crust is crisp and browned, about 8 minutes. Remove from the oven. Brush the rim of the crust with any remaining oil, and serve.

11

TOFU SALAD WITH EDAMAME & SHAVED ROOT VEGETABLES

serves 4

¾ lb (375 g) firm silken tofu, cut into slices 1 inch (2.5 cm) thick

2 Tbsp light soy sauce

2 tsp toasted sesame oil

2 green onions, including tender green parts, minced

1-inch (2.5-cm) piece fresh ginger, peeled and grated

2 watermelon radishes or 6 red radishes

1 small celery root (about ¾ lb/375 g), peeled and halved lengthwise

2 carrots, peeled and halved crosswise

Salt

2 cups (12 oz/375 g) frozen shelled edamame

2 Tbsp sesame seeds, toasted

A wonderful mix of contrasting colors, textures, and flavors, this vivid salad is not only fast and simple to make but also healthful and delicious. If you are using boxed tofu, be careful when removing it from the container, as you want the block to remain intact so it can be neatly cubed.

Place the tofu in a shallow baking dish. In a small bowl, whisk together the soy sauce, oil, green onions, and ginger. Pour over the tofu and marinate at room temperature for at least 1 hour or up to 3 hours.

Meanwhile, using a mandoline or a very sharp knife, shave the radishes and celery root crosswise. Reserve a few whole shavings for garnish and cut the rest into smaller pieces. Using a vegetable peeler, shave the carrots lengthwise, then cut each ribbon into 3 or 4 pieces. Set aside.

In a saucepan, bring 4 cups (32 fl oz/1 l) water to a boil over medium-high heat. Add ½ tsp salt and the edamame. Reduce the heat to medium and cook until just tender, 5–6 minutes. Drain and rinse with cold water.

Divide the edamame among individual plates. Cut the tofu into 1-inch (2.5-cm) cubes. Using a spatula, carefully remove the cubes from the marinade (they are fragile) and place on top of the edamame. Pour a little of the marinade over them. Top with the radish, celery root, and carrot pieces and sprinkle with the sesame seeds. Garnish with the reserved whole vegetable shavings and serve right away.

12

Meaty short ribs go well with the robust flavors of traditional Italian cooking, and slow cooking coaxes them to fall-off-the-bone tenderness. For an extra flourish, garnish each serving with some of the gremolata traditionally sprinkled over osso buco (page 256), and serve atop polenta (page 22).

ITALIAN BRAISED SHORT RIBS
serves 6–8

3 Tbsp all-purpose flour

Salt and freshly ground pepper

5½–6 lb (2.75–3 kg) beef short ribs, English cut

¼ cup (2 fl oz/60 ml) olive oil

2 oz (60 g) pancetta, chopped

2 yellow onions, finely chopped

4 cloves garlic, minced

1 tsp red pepper flakes

2 carrots, finely chopped

2 Tbsp tomato paste

1 Tbsp sugar

1 cup (8 fl oz/250 ml) dry red wine

1 can (14½ oz/455 g) diced tomatoes

1 cup (8 fl oz/250 ml) beef broth

¼ cup (2 fl oz/60 ml) balsamic vinegar

2 bay leaves

2 sprigs *each* fresh rosemary and thyme

1 Tbsp dried oregano

On a plate, stir together the flour, 1 tsp salt, and ½ tsp pepper. Turn the ribs in the seasoned flour, shaking off any excess. In a large, heavy pot, heat the oil over medium-high heat. Working in batches, sear the ribs, turning occasionally, until evenly browned, about 10 minutes. Transfer to a plate.

Add the pancetta to the pot and sauté until mostly crisp, 4–5 minutes. Add the onions and sauté until beginning to soften, about 3 minutes. Stir in the garlic and red pepper flakes and sauté until fragrant, about 30 seconds. Add the carrots, tomato paste, and sugar and cook, stirring often, until well blended, about 1 minute. Add the wine, bring to a boil, and stir to scrape up any browned bits on the pan bottom. Stir in the tomatoes and their juices, broth, and vinegar and bring to a boil.

Preheat the oven to 350°F (180°C). Return the ribs to the pot with the tomato mixture. Add the bay leaves, rosemary and thyme sprigs, and oregano. Cover and cook in the oven until the ribs are very tender, about 2 hours.

Skim as much fat as possible from the cooking liquid and discard the bay leaves. Season with salt and pepper and serve.

13

Here's a dish that can be prepared a couple of days in advance and stored, tightly covered, in the refrigerator. You can experiment with the flavors by using crumbled spicy sausage or ground turkey in place of the beef or by trading out the Monterey jack for pepper jack. Pasta-based dishes tend to absorb any liquid they contain when they sit, so be sure to have extra broth on hand to adjust the consistency as needed. To add vegetables to this meal, serve the chili atop a bed of sautéed kale in shallow bowls.

MAC & CHEESE CHILI
serves 4–6

2 Tbsp olive oil

½ yellow onion, chopped

2 cloves garlic, chopped

¾ lb (375 g) lean ground beef

1 Tbsp chili powder

1½ tsp ground cumin

Salt and freshly ground pepper

1 can (14½ oz/455 g) fire-roasted diced tomatoes with juices

1 can (16 oz/500 g) pinto beans, drained

4 cups (32 fl oz/1 l) chicken broth

2 cups (7 oz/220 g) elbow macaroni

½ cup (2 oz/60 g) shredded sharp Cheddar cheese

½ cup (2 oz/60 g) shredded Monterey jack cheese

3 green onions, white and tender green parts, chopped

In a large, heavy pot, warm the oil over medium-high heat. Add the yellow onion and cook, stirring occasionally, until translucent, about 6 minutes. Add the garlic and cook, stirring occasionally, until soft, about 2 minutes. Add the ground beef and cook, breaking it up with a wooden spoon, until browned, about 5 minutes. Stir in the chili powder, cumin, and ¼ tsp salt. Add the tomatoes with their juices, the beans, and broth and bring to a boil. Add the macaroni, cover, and reduce the heat to medium. Cook until the pasta is al dente, about 10 minutes.

Stir in half of the Cheddar and Monterey jack cheeses and all of the green onions. Season with salt and pepper. Serve, topped with the remaining cheese.

14

With the infused flavors of ginger, lemongrass, and basil, this traditional yellow curry is both fragrant and sweet and will appeal to milder palates. Choose a hotter curry powder if you like more of a kick. Serve the curry over steamed jasmine rice.

CHICKEN & COCONUT CURRY

serves 6–8

3 Tbsp canola oil

3 lb (1.5 kg) skinless, bone-in chicken thighs

3 cloves garlic, minced

2 shallots, minced

3 Tbsp Madras-style curry powder

1 Tbsp firmly packed dark brown sugar

1 tsp red pepper flakes

Freshly ground black pepper

2 lemongrass stalks, center white part only, cut into 1-inch (2.5-cm) pieces

1-inch (2.5-cm) piece peeled fresh ginger, cut into 4 slices

1 cup (8 fl oz/250 ml) chicken broth

1 can (13½ fl oz/420 ml) unsweetened coconut milk

2 Tbsp Asian fish sauce

3 carrots, cut into 1-inch (2.5-cm) chunks

1 sweet potato, about ¾ lb (375 g), peeled and cut into 1-inch (2.5-cm) chunks

3 Tbsp finely sliced fresh basil

In a large, heavy pot, heat the oil over medium-high heat. Working in batches, sear the chicken until nicely browned, about 4 minutes per side. Transfer to a plate.

Add the garlic and shallots to the pot and sauté just until fragrant, about 30 seconds. Add the curry powder, brown sugar, red pepper flakes, 1 tsp black pepper, the lemongrass, and the ginger and sauté until the spices are fragrant and well blended with the garlic and shallots, about 30 seconds. Add the broth and stir to scrape up any browned bits on the pot bottom. Stir in the coconut milk and fish sauce and bring to a boil. Add the chicken, carrots, and sweet potato, and stir to cover them in the mixture. Partially cover and cook over low heat until the chicken is opaque throughout and the vegetables are very tender, about 1 hour. Garnish with the basil and serve.

15

A mix of colorful beets, deep green arugula, and snowy white cheese can brighten the usually cool, gray days of January. Be careful when working with red beets, as their juice can stain your fingers, countertop, and cutting board. Rinse fingers or work surfaces immediately with water, and use lemon juice to remove persistent stains.

ROASTED BEETS WITH BABY ARUGULA & RICOTTA SALATA

serves 4

3 beets of any color, about 1 lb (500 g) total

4 Tbsp (2 fl oz/60 ml) olive oil

2 Tbsp fresh orange juice

1 Tbsp fresh lemon juice

¼ tsp Dijon mustard

Salt and freshly ground pepper

2 cups (2 oz/60 g) wild or baby arugula, tough stems removed

4–5 oz (125–155 g) ricotta salata cheese, crumbled

Preheat the oven to 350°F (180°C).

If the greens are still attached to the beets, remove them, leaving 1 inch (2.5 cm) of the stem intact. Place the beets in a small roasting pan and rub with 1½ Tbsp of the oil. Roast the beets, turning once or twice, until tender when pierced with a fork, 1–1¼ hours. Let cool. Peel the beets and cut into thin wedges.

In a bowl, using a fork, mix together the orange and lemon juices, the remaining 2½ Tbsp oil, the mustard, ½ tsp salt, and ¼ tsp pepper. Add the sliced beets to the bowl and turn gently to coat with the dressing. Add the arugula and toss until well mixed. Top with the ricotta salata and serve.

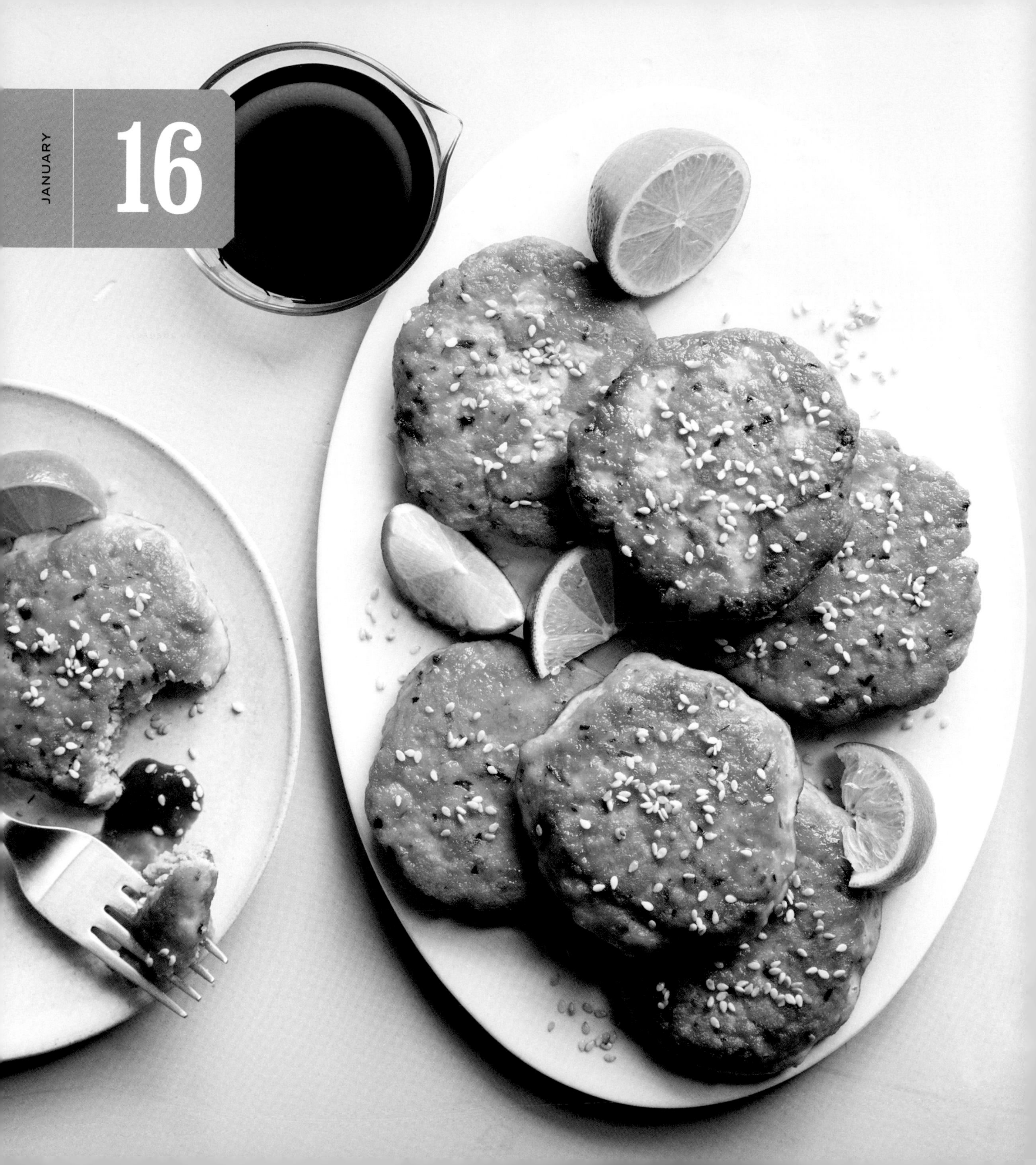

16

SALMON CAKES WITH GINGER & GREEN ONION

serves 4

2 Tbsp coarsely chopped fresh ginger

2 green onions, white and pale green parts, coarsely chopped

1 lb (500 g) wild salmon fillet, skin removed, cut into small pieces

1 tsp cornstarch

1 large egg white

Salt

1 tsp Asian fish sauce

1 Tbsp canola oil, or as needed

1 Tbsp sesame seeds, toasted

Low-sodium soy sauce, for serving

Sriracha sauce, for serving

1 lime, cut into wedges

Unlike many fish cakes that are loaded with fillers, these crisp salmon patties are nearly all fish, with just a little ginger and green onions for flavor. Serve them with steamed bok choy and brown rice for a healthy weeknight dinner.

In a food processor, combine the ginger and green onions and process until finely chopped, stopping once or twice to scrape down the sides of the work bowl. Sprinkle the salmon with the cornstarch and add to the processor with the egg white, a pinch of salt, and the fish sauce. Using quick pulses, process until the mixture resembles coarsely ground meat. Do not overprocess or the cakes will be heavy.

Divide the salmon mixture into 8 equal portions. With moistened hands, gently shape each portion into a patty about ½ inch (12 mm) thick. Transfer to a plate, cover with plastic wrap, and refrigerate for 5–10 minutes.

In a large frying pan over medium heat, warm the 1 Tbsp oil. Add the salmon cakes and cook until golden brown on the first side, about 3 minutes. Turn, adding more oil if needed, and cook until the cakes are slightly springy to the touch and have lost their raw color in the center, 2–3 minutes longer. Transfer to plates and sprinkle with the sesame seeds. Serve, passing the soy sauce, Sriracha sauce, and lime wedges at the table.

17

POTATO & BROCCOLI SOUP WITH BLUE CHEESE

serves 4

3 Tbsp unsalted butter

½ cup (2½ oz/75 g) chopped shallots

1 lb (500 g) Yukon Gold potatoes, cubed

1½ lb (750 g) broccoli, tough stems peeled, florets and stems coarsely chopped

Salt and freshly ground pepper

3 Tbsp all-purpose flour

4 cups (32 fl oz/1 l) chicken broth

¼ lb (125 g) blue cheese, crumbled

Broccoli is often combined with potatoes to make a thick, flavorful soup, and cheese, especially Cheddar, is a favorite addition. Using blue cheese instead of Cheddar shifts the flavor slightly toward the tangy side but keeps the creamy texture. This is a good soup for serving with crackers, including breaking a few into the pot to make it even thicker and richer.

In a large, heavy pot, melt the butter over medium-high heat. When it foams, add the shallots and cook, stirring occasionally, until limp, about 1 minute. Stir in the potatoes and broccoli. Sprinkle with ½ tsp salt, ¼ tsp pepper, and the flour and stir until the flour is incorporated, about 1 minute. Add about ½ cup (4 fl oz/125 ml) of the broth, stirring to make a paste, then gradually add the remaining broth and bring to a boil. Reduce the heat to medium-low and simmer until the potatoes and broccoli stems are fork-tender, about 15 minutes. Let cool slightly.

Working in batches, purée the soup in a food processor or blender. Return the soup to the pot, place over medium-high heat, and bring to a simmer. Sprinkle in half of the cheese and stir until it melts, about 1 minute. Serve with the remaining cheese on the side.

18

Both vegetarians and carnivores will find this meatless main dish a satisfying choice for a cool winter evening. You can use any mushrooms in the mix and substitute spinach or kale for the chard. The Cheddar cheese infuses the polenta with a nutty flavor; Parmesan or fontina would be a good choice, as well.

POLENTA WITH WILD MUSHROOMS, CHARD & CHEDDAR CHEESE

serves 6–8

Sea salt and freshly ground pepper

1½ cups (10½ oz/330 g) polenta

2 bunches chard, tough stems removed

1 fresh rosemary sprig, about 6 inches (15 cm) long

1 Tbsp extra-virgin olive oil

4 Tbsp (2 oz/60 g) unsalted butter

1 Tbsp minced shallots

1 lb (500 g) assorted wild mushrooms such as chanterelles, porcini, morels, or lobster mushrooms, coarsely cut or left whole depending on size

1 cup (4 oz/125 g) shredded or crumbled white Cheddar cheese

In a saucepan over high heat, bring 8 cups (64 fl oz/2 l) water and 1½ tsp salt to a boil. Slowly add the polenta, stirring constantly. Reduce the heat to low and cook, stirring often, until the polenta pulls away from the sides of the pan, about 40 minutes.

Meanwhile, bring a large pot of water to a boil over high heat. Add the chard leaves and rosemary sprig. Reduce the heat to medium and cook until the chard ribs are easily pierced with a fork, about 10 minutes. Drain well. Chop coarsely and squeeze dry. Set aside.

In a frying pan over medium-high heat, warm the oil with 1 Tbsp of the butter. Add the shallots and mushrooms and cook until the mushrooms are tender, 8–10 minutes. Using a slotted spoon, transfer to a bowl. Reserve the juices.

When the polenta is ready, stir in the remaining 3 Tbsp butter, all but ¼ cup (1 oz/30 g) of the cheese, 1 tsp salt, and 1 tsp pepper and cook until the butter and cheese have melted, 3–4 minutes longer. Return the frying pan used for the mushrooms to medium-high heat. Warm the reserved juices, then add the chard and mushrooms and cook, stirring, until hot and well coated. Season with salt and pepper.

Spoon the polenta into a large serving bowl, top with the chard and mushrooms, sprinkle with the remaining cheese, and serve.

19

Warm up on cold days with spicy Latin flavors. Spanish-style chorizo adds robust flavor to this stew, which is extra satisfying because of the double dose of protein from the beans and the meat.

SPICY RED BEAN & CHORIZO STEW

serves 6–8

2¼ cups (1 lb/500 g) dried red kidney beans, picked over and rinsed

2 Tbsp canola oil

1 large yellow onion, finely chopped

3 celery ribs, finely chopped

1 green bell pepper, seeded and chopped

6 cloves garlic, minced

Salt and freshly ground black pepper

4 cups (32 fl oz/1 l) beef or chicken broth

2 tsp red wine vinegar

½–¾ tsp red pepper flakes

3 bay leaves

1 lb (500 g) cured Spanish-style chorizo, cut into slices ¼ inch (6 mm) thick

Hot-pepper sauce, such as Tabasco

Cooked white rice for serving

Place the beans in a large bowl with cold water to cover and soak for at least 4 hours or up to overnight. (For a quick soak, combine the beans and water to cover in a large pot, bring to a boil, remove from the heat, cover, and soak for 1 hour.) Drain and rinse the beans.

In a large, heavy frying pan, heat the oil over medium-high heat. Add the onion, celery, and bell pepper and sauté until softened and just beginning to brown, about 6 minutes. Add the garlic, season with salt and black pepper, and cook for 1 minute. Pour in 1 cup (8 fl oz/250 ml) of the broth and stir to scrape up any browned bits on the pan bottom. Transfer the contents of the pan to a slow cooker and stir in the drained beans, remaining 3 cups (24 fl oz/750 ml) broth, the vinegar, red pepper flakes to taste, bay leaves, and chorizo. Cover and cook on the low setting for 6–8 hours, stirring once or twice. The beans should be very tender.

Discard the bay leaves. Season with salt, black pepper, and Tabasco. If desired, using the back of a spoon, mash some of the beans against the inside of the cooker to thicken the stew.

Spoon rice into shallow bowls, top with the stew, and serve.

20

Here, chicken, vegetables, and rice noodles are cooked in a clear, spice-infused broth. An abundance of bright green garnishes liven up this one-dish meal. The more of them you add, the healthier and more flavorful this soup becomes.

ASIAN-STYLE CHICKEN SOUP
serves 4

8 cups (64 fl oz/2 l) low-sodium chicken broth

1 bunch green onions, plus thinly sliced green onions for serving

2-inch (5-cm) piece fresh ginger, peeled and sliced

2 Tbsp Asian fish sauce

1 Tbsp sugar

6 *each* star anise pods and cloves

1–1¼ lb (500–625 g) skinless, boneless chicken breasts

3 Thai chiles, or 1 serrano chile, thinly sliced

Bean sprouts, basil sprigs, cilantro sprigs, and lime wedges for serving

Hoisin sauce (optional)

4 heads baby bok choy

6–7 oz (185–220 g) dried rice stick noodles

Salt and freshly ground pepper

In a large pot over high heat, combine the broth and 2 cups (16 fl oz/500 ml) water. Cut the green onion bunch in half crosswise and add to the pot; add the ginger, fish sauce, and sugar. In a tea ball, combine the star anise and cloves; add to the pot. Bring the broth to a boil. Add the chicken breasts, return to a boil, reduce the heat to medium-low, and simmer until the chicken is cooked through, 10–15 minutes. Using tongs, transfer the chicken to a plate. Continue to simmer the broth to develop the flavor, 15–30 minutes.

Place the sliced green onions, sliced chiles, bean sprouts, herb sprigs, lime wedges, and hoisin sauce, if using, on a platter and set on the table.

Slice the bok choy crosswise about ½ inch (12 mm) thick. Thinly slice the chicken breasts crosswise. In a large bowl, soak the noodles in very hot water for 3 minutes.

Remove the green onions and ginger from the broth and discard. Season the broth to taste with salt and pepper. Add the bok choy, raise the heat to high, and bring to a boil. Drain the noodles, add them to the broth, and cook until just tender, about 2 minutes.

Using tongs, divide the noodles and bok choy among 4 warmed deep bowls. Divide the chicken among the bowls. Ladle the broth over the top. Serve, allowing diners to add the condiments to taste.

21

Filled with a rich, tangy lemon pudding lightened up with whipped cream, lemon chiffon pie is a timeless dessert that will brighten any winter table. Here, it has been updated with a spicy gingersnap crust. A sealable plastic bag and a rolling pin make short work of crushing the cookies into crumbs.

LEMON CHIFFON GINGERSNAP PIE
serves 6–8

1¼ cups (4 oz/125 g) gingersnap cookie crumbs

5 Tbsp (2½ oz/75 g) unsalted butter, melted

¾ cup (6 oz/185 g) plus 3 Tbsp granulated sugar

2¼ tsp (1 package) unflavored powdered gelatin

⅛ tsp kosher salt

¾ cup (6 fl oz/180 ml) fresh lemon juice, strained

1 Tbsp finely grated orange zest

4 large egg yolks, lightly beaten

1¼ cups (10 fl oz/310 ml) heavy cream

¼ cup (1 oz/30 g) confectioners' sugar

Preheat the oven to 350°F (180°C). In a bowl, stir together the crumbs, butter, and 3 Tbsp granulated sugar until the crumbs are evenly moistened. Pat the crumb mixture firmly and evenly into the bottom and all the way up the sides of a 9-inch (23-cm) pie pan or dish. Bake until the crust is firm, 5–7 minutes.

Pour ¼ cup (2 fl oz/60 ml) cold water into a saucepan and sprinkle with the gelatin. Let stand until the gelatin softens and swells, 5–10 minutes. Stir in the ¾ cup granulated sugar, salt, lemon juice, orange zest, and egg yolks; the mixture will be lumpy. Cook over medium heat, stirring continuously, until the gelatin melts and the mixture thickens, 6–8 minutes. Do not allow the mixture to boil. Set the saucepan in an ice bath until the mixture is cool to the touch.

In a large bowl, using an electric mixer, whip the cream and confectioners' sugar on medium-high speed until thick, soft peaks form. Spoon the whipped cream into the gelatin mixture and fold together with a rubber spatula until smooth. Pour into the prepared crust, smoothing the top.

Refrigerate the pie until chilled and firm, 3–4 hours. Let stand at room temperature for 20 minutes before serving.

22

The nutty flavor and delicate texture of soba noodles pair particularly well with mild napa cabbage. If napa cabbage is not in the market, bok choy or green cabbage can be substituted.

STIR-FRIED SOBA NOODLES WITH BEEF & CABBAGE

serves 4

1 lb (500 g) boneless beef sirloin or tenderloin, partially frozen

¼ cup (2 fl oz/60 ml) toasted sesame oil

¼ cup (2 fl oz/60 ml) soy sauce

¼ cup (2 fl oz/60 ml) plus 1 Tbsp peanut oil

2 Tbsp peeled and grated fresh ginger

¾ lb (375 g) dried soba noodles

2 large cloves garlic, minced

4 green onions, including 3 inches (7.5 cm) of green tops, thinly sliced on the diagonal

1 head napa cabbage, about 2 lb (1 kg), cored and shredded

2 cups (16 fl oz/500 ml) chicken or beef broth

1 Tbsp cornstarch

½ lb (250 g) snow peas, trimmed and halved crosswise

Salt

¼ cup (1 oz/30 g) sesame seeds, lightly toasted

Using a sharp knife, cut the beef across the grain into thin slices, then cut the slices into matchsticks. In a bowl, whisk together the sesame oil, soy sauce, ¼ cup peanut oil, and ginger. Add the beef and stir to coat evenly. Cover and refrigerate, stirring occasionally, for at least 1 hour or up to 3 hours.

Bring a large pot of water to a rapid boil. Add 2 Tbsp salt and the noodles, stir well, and cook, stirring occasionally, until just tender, 5–7 minutes. Drain the noodles.

Meanwhile, in a wok or large frying pan, heat the 1 Tbsp peanut oil over medium-high heat. Add the garlic and green onions and stir-fry until lightly colored, about 1 minute. Raise the heat to high, add the beef and its marinade, and stir-fry until lightly browned, about 8 minutes. Add the cabbage and 1½ cups (12 fl oz/375 ml) of the broth and toss to combine. Cover, reduce the heat to medium-high, and cook until the cabbage wilts, about 4 minutes.

In a small bowl, whisk the cornstarch into the remaining ½ cup (4 fl oz/125 ml) broth. Add the cornstarch mixture to the pan, and stir and toss to incorporate. ↠

Add the snow peas, stir and toss to combine, cover, and cook until just tender, about 2 minutes. Take care not to overcook; the snow peas and cabbage should remain crisp.

Add the noodles to the pan and stir and toss until well combined. Garnish with the toasted sesame seeds and serve.

23

In this dish, the rich walnut oil, sweet brown sugar, and tart wine vinegar work together to temper the cabbagey taste of brussels sprouts, while the chestnuts add texture and flavor. Look for vacuum-packed roasted and peeled chestnuts in gourmet shops and well-stocked supermarkets.

VINEGAR-GLAZED BRUSSELS SPROUTS WITH CHESTNUTS & WALNUT OIL

serves 4

1 Tbsp olive oil

1 lb (500 g) brussels sprouts, trimmed

Salt and freshly ground pepper

1 Tbsp unsalted butter

1 cup (8 fl oz/250 ml) chicken broth

3 oz (90 g) vacuum-packed chestnuts, coarsely chopped

1 Tbsp firmly packed golden brown sugar

2 Tbsp red wine vinegar

2 tsp toasted walnut oil

In a large frying pan, warm the oil over medium heat. Add the brussels sprouts in a single layer and sprinkle lightly with salt. Cook, stirring once or twice, until the sprouts are golden brown and caramelized on all sides, about 4 minutes.

Raise the heat to medium-high and add the butter, broth, and chestnuts. Bring the broth to a boil and stir to scrape up any browned bits on the bottom of the pan. Reduce the heat to medium-low, cover partially, and simmer until the sprouts are just tender when pierced with a knife and most of the liquid has evaporated, 20–22 minutes.

Add ¼ cup (2 fl oz/60 ml) water to the pan, stir in the sugar and vinegar, and raise the heat to medium-high. Cook, stirring occasionally, until the liquid reduces to a glaze, 2–3 minutes. Remove the pan from the heat and stir in the walnut oil. Season with salt and pepper. Transfer to a bowl and serve.

24

Pale yellow Chinese egg noodles, sometimes labeled lo mein, are ideal for tossing with meat and/or vegetables and a brightly flavored vinaigrette for a hearty main-course salad. If fresh Chinese noodles are unavailable, substitute dried, or used dried vermicelli from the Italian pasta shelf at the market.

NOODLE SALAD WITH PORK & ASIAN LIME VINAIGRETTE

serves 6

2 pork tenderloins, about ¾ lb (375 g) each, trimmed

1 Tbsp peanut oil

Salt and freshly ground pepper

FOR THE ASIAN LIME VINAIGRETTE

2 Tbsp peanut oil

1 Tbsp soy sauce

Juice of 1 lime

2 tsp sherry vinegar

1 tsp peeled and minced fresh ginger

⅛ tsp sugar

2 or 3 drops Sriracha or other hot sauce

1 lb (500 g) fresh Chinese egg noodles

1 red bell pepper, seeded and thinly sliced

1 small red serrano chile, seeded and thinly sliced crosswise (optional)

¼ cup (⅓ oz/10 g) *each* chopped fresh flat-leaf parsley and cilantro leaves

Prepare a charcoal or gas grill for direct-heat cooking over high heat, or preheat the broiler. Brush the pork tenderloins with the 1 Tbsp oil and season with salt and pepper. Place on the grill rack or on a broiler pan 4 inches (10 cm) from the heat source and cook, turning occasionally, until an instant-read thermometer inserted into the thickest part registers 150°F (65°C) or the pork is pale pink when cut in the thickest portion, about 12 minutes. Transfer to a cutting board and let rest for 2–3 minutes before carving. Cut crosswise into slices ¼ inch (6 mm) thick.

Meanwhile, to make the vinaigrette, in a blender, combine the 2 Tbsp oil, soy sauce, lime juice, vinegar, ginger, sugar, and Sriracha to taste. Purée until smooth.

Bring a pot three-fourths full of salted water to a boil. Add the noodles, stir, and cook until just tender, according to package directions. Drain well and transfer to a large bowl. Add the bell pepper, chile (if using), vinaigrette to taste, and half each of the parsley and cilantro, and toss to mix well.

Transfer the noodles to bowls and arrange the pork and remaining herbs over the top. Serve warm or at room temperature.

25

Barley has a pleasantly chewy texture and a sweet, nutty flavor. When stirred into broth over low heat, it cooks into a creamy risotto-style dish. The addition of meaty mushrooms, shredded chicken, and slightly bitter greens to the barley creates a balanced one-dish dinner.

BARLEY RISOTTO WITH CHICKEN, MUSHROOMS & GREENS

serves 4

6 cups (48 fl oz/1.5 l) chicken broth

1½ Tbsp olive oil

1 yellow onion, chopped

1 clove garlic, minced

2 cups (6 oz/185 g) sliced cremini mushrooms

Salt and freshly ground pepper

½ cup (4 fl oz/125 ml) dry white wine

1 cup (7 oz/220 g) pearl barley

3 cups (4 oz/125 g) bite-sized pieces Swiss chard leaves

2 cups (¾ lb/375 g) shredded cooked chicken

½ cup (2 oz/60 g) grated Parmesan cheese

In a saucepan, bring the broth to a simmer over medium-high heat. Turn off the heat, cover, and keep warm.

In a large saucepan, heat the oil over medium-high heat. Add the onion and garlic and cook, stirring frequently, until the onion is soft, about 5 minutes. Add the mushrooms, ¼ tsp salt, and a few grindings of pepper. Cook, stirring frequently, until the mushrooms release their liquid and start to brown, 4–5 minutes. Add the wine, bring to a boil, and cook for 1 minute.

Add 5 cups (40 fl oz/1.25 l) of the hot broth and the barley. Cover and simmer over medium-low heat, stirring occasionally and adding more broth ¼ cup (2 fl oz/60 ml) at a time if the barley becomes dry, until the barley is tender, about 45 minutes.

Stir in the Swiss chard and more broth, if necessary. Cook, uncovered, until the greens are wilted, about 2 minutes. Stir in the chicken and cook for 1 minute to heat through. Stir in the Parmesan, season with salt and pepper, and serve.

26

Kumquats, tiny oval citrus fruits packed with flavor, are usually in season from December to March. You eat the peel as well as the flesh, as the peel is sweet and balances the tartness of the flesh. Here, kumquats are paired with the season's sweet carrots in a puréed soup suitable for a family supper or a dinner party.

KUMQUAT-CARROT PURÉE WITH TOASTED FENNEL SEEDS

serves 4

2 tsp fennel seeds

4 Tbsp (2 oz/60 g) unsalted butter

1 small yellow onion, chopped

2 cloves garlic, minced

1 cup (6 oz/185 g) kumquats, unpeeled, chopped, plus kumquat slices for garnish

2 lb (1 kg) carrots, peeled and thinly sliced

5 cups (40 fl oz/1.25 l) chicken broth

Salt and freshly ground pepper

In a small frying pan, toast the fennel seeds over medium heat just until fragrant, about 3 minutes. Transfer to a spice grinder and grind finely.

In a large, heavy pot, melt the butter over medium-high heat. Add the onion and garlic and sauté until translucent, about 5 minutes. Add the kumquats and carrots and sauté for 10 minutes. Add the broth and bring to a boil. Reduce the heat to low and simmer, uncovered, until the carrots and kumquats are very soft, 35–40 minutes. Remove from the heat and let cool slightly.

Working in batches, purée the soup in a blender. Return to the pot and stir in the ground fennel. Season with salt and pepper and serve, garnished with kumquat slices.

27

Quinoa, a gluten-free, protein-packed, grain-like seed, replaces bulgur wheat in this new riff on a Mediterranean classic. The addition of grilled shrimp makes this dish hearty enough to serve as a main course. This recipe would also be delicious with other proteins, such as grilled salmon or leftover shredded rotisserie chicken.

QUINOA TABBOULEH WITH LEMONY GRILLED SHRIMP

serves 4–6

1 lb (500 g) shrimp, peeled and deveined

Grated zest and juice of 1 lemon

1 tsp olive oil

Salt and freshly ground pepper

1 cup (8 oz/250 g) quinoa, rinsed

1 English cucumber, cut into ½-inch (12-mm) pieces

1 pint (12 oz/375 g) cherry tomatoes, halved

2 green onions, chopped

1 cup (1½ oz/45 g) chopped fresh flat-leaf parsley

FOR THE LEMON-GARLIC DRESSING

2 cloves garlic, minced

Juice of ½ lemon

¼ cup (2 fl oz/60 ml) extra-virgin olive oil

Salt and freshly ground pepper

Place the shrimp in a nonreactive bowl with the lemon zest and juice and the oil. Season with salt and pepper and toss to combine. Cover and refrigerate for 1 hour.

Bring 2 cups (16 fl oz/500 ml) water to a boil in a saucepan over medium-high heat. Add ½ tsp salt and the quinoa and reduce heat to low. Cover the saucepan and cook until the water is absorbed and the quinoa is tender, 15–20 minutes. Transfer the quinoa to a bowl and let cool.

Warm a stove-top grill pan over high heat. Remove the shrimp from the marinade and place on the grill pan; discard the marinade. Cook just until the shrimp are bright pink and opaque throughout, about 2 minutes per side. Transfer the shrimp to the bowl with the quinoa. Add the cucumber, tomatoes, green onions, and parsley and mix to combine.

To make the dressing, place the garlic and lemon juice in a small bowl. Whisk in the extra-virgin olive oil and season to taste with salt and pepper.

Stir the dressing into the quinoa. Season to taste with salt and pepper and serve at room temperature, or refrigerate and serve cold.

28

CARAMEL-MACADAMIA TARTLETS

makes 6 tartlets

A creamy caramel sauce fills these individual tartlets. When making the caramel, be sure to watch it carefully to ensure it doesn't burn. The addition of macadamia nuts gives these tartlets an incomparable richness. The deep golden caramel sauce is also excellent poured over ice cream or drizzled over cake.

FOR THE CREAM CHEESE TARTLET DOUGH

½ cup (4 oz/125 g) unsalted butter

3 oz (90 g) cream cheese

1 cup (5 oz/155 g) all-purpose flour, sifted

½ cup (4 fl oz/125 ml) heavy cream

⅔ cup (5 oz/155 g) sugar

½ tsp fresh lemon juice, strained

⅛ tsp kosher salt

¾ cup (4 oz/125 g) unsalted roasted macadamia nuts, roughly chopped

In the bowl of a stand mixer fitted with the paddle attachment, beat the butter and cream cheese on low speed until smooth and blended, about 45 seconds. Add the flour and mix until a smooth dough forms. Transfer the dough to a work surface and shape into a thick log. Wrap with plastic wrap and store in the refrigerator until ready to use, up to 3 days.

Cut the dough into 6 equal portions. Roll each portion into a 2-inch (5-cm) ball. Place a ball in each of six 3½-inch (9-cm) tartlet pans. Press the dough evenly over the bottom and up the sides of each pan until it is even with the rim. Remove any overhang. Freeze until the dough is firm, about 30 minutes.

Preheat the oven to 400°F (200°C). Line the tartlets with foil and fill with pie weights. Place on a baking sheet and bake until the crusts start to look dry, about 15 minutes. Remove the weights and foil. Reduce the oven temperature to 350°F (180°C) and continue to bake until the crusts are lightly browned, about 5 minutes. Let cool on the sheet.

Meanwhile, in a small saucepan, warm the cream over low heat until it registers 150°F (65°C) on an instant-read thermometer. Keep the cream over very low heat to maintain this temperature.

In a large, heavy saucepan, stir the sugar, lemon juice, and 3 Tbsp water over medium heat until the sugar dissolves. ⇥

Stop stirring and wash down the pan sides with a pastry brush dipped in water. Raise the heat to medium-high and bring the mixture to a boil. Boil until the sugar melts and turns a dark golden color, about 4 minutes. Watch carefully, swirling the pan occasionally to ensure that the sugar cooks evenly. Remove from the heat.

Slowly pour the warm cream into the hot caramelized sugar. The mixture will bubble up. Return the pan to low heat, add the salt, and stir until the caramel completely dissolves and is smooth, about 1 minute. Set aside to cool and thicken slightly, about 30 minutes.

Stir the nuts into the caramel. Pour the mixture into the cooled tartlet shells, dividing it evenly and filling them to just below the rim. Bake until the filling begins to bubble, 10–15 minutes. Transfer the baking sheet to a wire rack and let the tartlets cool completely before unmolding and serving.

29

FENNEL SALAD WITH BLOOD ORANGES & ARUGULA

serves 6–8

To make this crisp salad even more refreshing, slice the fennel no more than a few minutes in advance of serving, and keep the bulbs cold until just before slicing. If fennel is sliced and left undressed, it will discolor within about 20 minutes.

2 fennel bulbs, trimmed

2 Tbsp red wine vinegar

Salt and freshly ground pepper

6 Tbsp (3 fl oz/90 ml) extra-virgin olive oil

4 cups (4 oz/125 g) loosely packed arugula leaves

4 blood or navel oranges, peeled with a knife and sliced crosswise into thin slices

Halve the fennel bulbs lengthwise and, using a mandoline or a very sharp knife, cut the halves crosswise into paper-thin slices.

In a large bowl, whisk together the vinegar, ¼ tsp salt, and ¼ tsp pepper. Add the oil in a thin stream, whisking constantly until the dressing is smooth. Add the arugula and fennel and toss to coat evenly with the vinaigrette. Mound the mixture on a platter, distribute the orange slices over and around the salad, and serve.

30

Traditional tarte tatin *uses apples and a classic pastry crust, but this delicious variation substitutes pears and flaky puff pastry. Crystallized ginger packs a gentle heat and plays against the pears' sweet, floral flavor. Serve wedges of this festive tart with dollops of crème fraîche.*

SPICED PEAR TARTE TATIN

serves 6–8

½ sheet frozen puff pastry
(about ½ lb/250 g), thawed

4 Tbsp (2 oz/60 g) unsalted butter,
at room temperature

¼ cup (2 oz/60 g) granulated sugar

6 firm, ripe pears, peeled, halved, and cored

½ cup (3½ oz/105 g) firmly packed light
brown sugar

2 Tbsp finely chopped crystallized ginger

½ tsp ground cinnamon

¼ tsp freshly grated nutmeg

1 Tbsp fresh lemon juice

Preheat the oven to 400°F (200°C). On a lightly floured work surface, roll out the pastry into an 11-inch (28-cm) round about ¼ inch (6 mm) thick. Trim the edges, then chill until ready to use.

Spread 2 Tbsp of the butter over the sides and bottom of a 10-inch (25-cm) round ovenproof frying pan. Sprinkle the granulated sugar evenly over the bottom, then place the pears, cut side up, in a tight layer in the pan. Cook over medium heat until the pears start to release their juices, about 10 minutes. In a bowl, stir together the brown sugar, ginger, cinnamon, and nutmeg. Sprinkle over the pears along with the lemon juice. Dot the top with the remaining 2 Tbsp butter.

Top the pears with the pastry, tucking the edges into the pan to form a rim that encircles the pears. Prick the top with a fork.

Bake until the crust is golden brown, the pears are tender, and a thickened golden syrup forms in the pan, about 45 minutes. Let stand for 5 minutes. Run a knife around the inside edge of the pan. Invert the tart onto a plate, dislodging and replacing any pears that may have stuck to the pan. Serve.

31

Woodsy thyme pairs beautifully with the hearty flavors of winter ingredients. Here, it seasons brown lentils, which star in a richly textured and colored salad that also features thinly sliced kale, roasted carrots, sautéed onions, and crisp bacon.

WARM LENTIL & KALE SALAD WITH BACON

serves 6

6 small carrots, finely chopped

4 Tbsp (2 fl oz/60 ml) olive oil

Salt and freshly ground pepper

1 large red onion, thinly sliced

1 large bunch kale, ribs removed,
leaves thinly sliced

4 large cloves garlic

10 fresh thyme sprigs

1 cup (7 oz/220 g) brown lentils,
picked over and rinsed

4 cups (32 fl oz/1 l) chicken broth

6 slices bacon

1 tsp sherry vinegar

Preheat the oven to 400°F (200°C). Line a baking sheet with foil. Place the carrots on the prepared sheet, drizzle with 2 Tbsp of the oil, sprinkle with ¾ tsp salt and ¼ tsp pepper, and toss to coat. Spread the carrots out evenly. Roast, stirring once or twice, until tender, about 15 minutes. Let cool to room temperature.

Meanwhile, in a frying pan, warm the remaining 2 Tbsp oil over medium heat. Add the onion, ¼ tsp salt, and several grinds of pepper and sauté until the onion is soft and lightly caramelized, about 15 minutes.

Bring a saucepan of water to a boil. Add 1 Tbsp salt and the kale and cook until tender, about 6 minutes. Drain.

Place the garlic and thyme on a square of cheesecloth, bring the corners together, and secure with kitchen string. In the same saucepan used to cook the kale, combine the lentils, broth, ½ tsp salt, ¼ tsp pepper, and the cheesecloth bundle. Bring to a boil, reduce the heat to medium, and simmer, uncovered, until the lentils are tender but not mushy, 15–20 minutes. In a frying pan, cook the bacon over medium heat, turning once, until crisp and browned, about 7 minutes. Transfer to paper towels to drain. Let cool and then coarsely chop.

Drain the lentils and discard the cheesecloth bundle. Transfer to a bowl. Stir in the cooked kale, the vinegar, and ½ tsp salt. Top with the carrots, onion, and bacon, and serve.

30 JANUARY

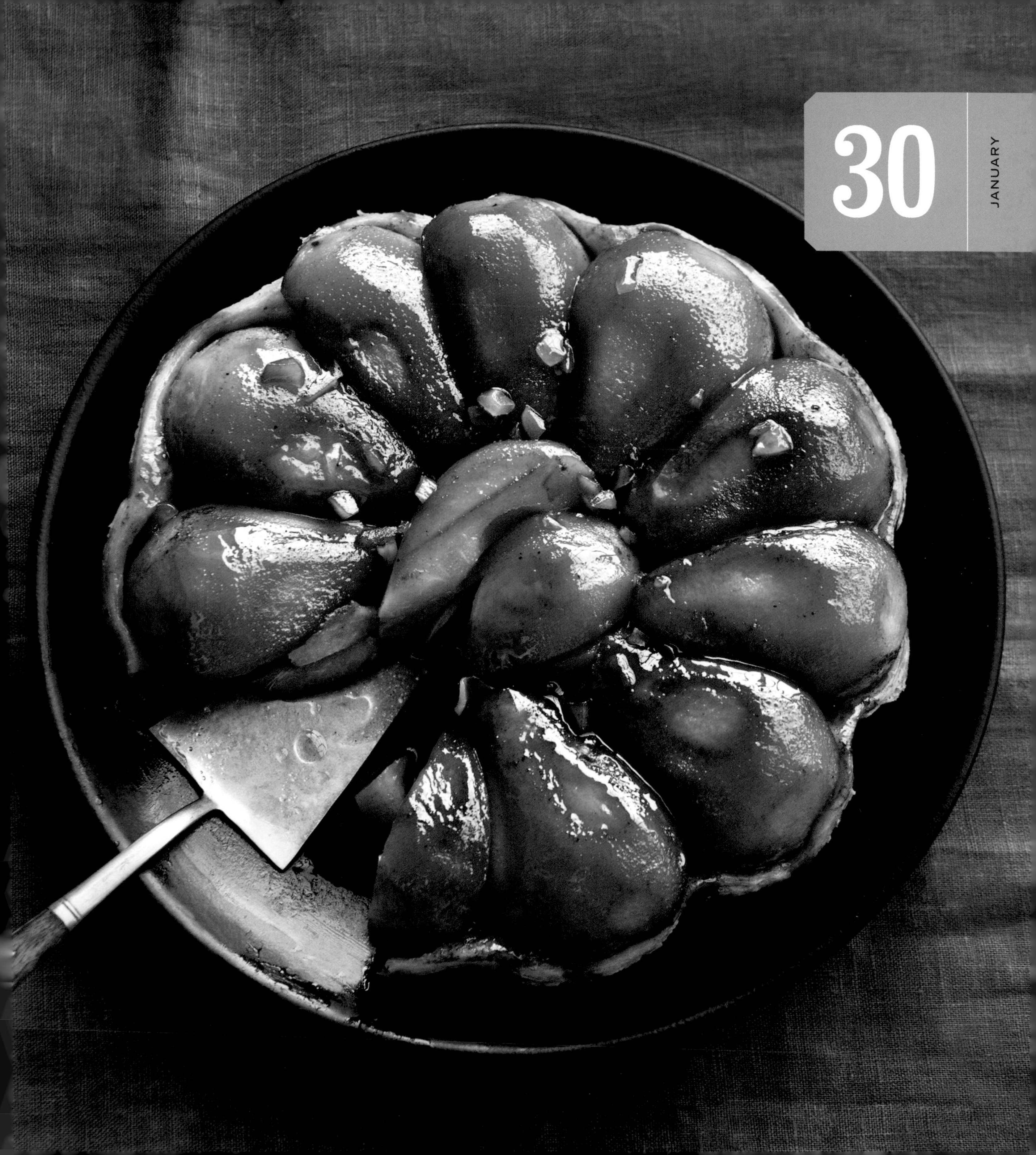

The short days and cold nights of February call for big flavors and robust fare, like zesty fennel-infused seafood spaghetti, Korean-inspired noodles with beef and kimchi, and macaroni and cheese dressed up with bacon. The brassicas and chicories—cabbage, brussels sprouts, broccoli, radicchio—remain popular cool-weather choices, along with two Beta genus favorites, Swiss chard and beets. Citrus continues to star at dessert time, in lemon squares, in warm lemon sugar–coated doughnuts, and in orange curd–filled tartlets.

1
THAI BEEF SALAD
page 34

2
SWEET POTATO & GREEN CHILE
QUESADILLAS WITH ARUGULA
page 34

3
GINGER RICE WITH CHICKEN,
CHARD & SHIITAKES
page 37

8
ROASTED BROCCOLI WITH SOY,
RICE VINEGAR & SESAME SEEDS
page 39

9
CREAMY BRUSSELS SPROUT SOUP
WITH MAPLE BACON
page 40

10
TURKEY BURGERS WITH
RADICCHIO SLAW
page 40

15
SAUTÉED SOLE WITH FENNEL
& LEMON COMPOTE
page 46

16
OATMEAL–CHOCOLATE CHIP
COOKIES WITH ALMONDS
page 46

17
CHICKEN STEW WITH
BUTTERMILK-CHIVE DUMPLINGS
page 47

22
MOROCCAN-SPICED ROASTED
VEGETABLES & QUINOA
page 50

23
POTATO GALETTES WITH
SMOKED SALMON
page 52

24
LEG OF LAMB WITH ROASTED FENNEL
& PAN SAUCE
page 52

4

ROASTED SALMON WITH
AVOCADO-GRAPEFRUIT SALSA
page 37

5

RAINBOW CHARD GRATIN
WITH RICOTTA & GRUYÈRE
page 38

6

LENTIL & CHARD SOUP
WITH DUCK CONFIT
page 38

7

SPINACH & BLACK BEAN
ENCHILADAS
page 39

11

KOREAN-STYLE NOODLES WITH
MARINATED STEAK & KIMCHI
page 43

12

MACARONI WITH FARMSTEAD
CHEDDAR & BACON
page 43

13

MEYER LEMON SQUARES
page 44

14

SPINACH SALAD WITH ORANGES
& ROASTED BEETS
page 44

18

PEANUT-BRAISED TOFU WITH NOODLES
page 47

19

BUTTERMILK DONUTS WITH
LEMON SUGAR
page 49

20

GARLICKY SHRIMP SCAMPI
page 49

21

CHICKEN TAGINE WITH PRESERVED
LEMONS & OLIVES
page 50

25

SPAGHETTI WITH SHRIMP, FENNEL,
TOMATOES & OLIVES
page 53

26

BLOOD ORANGE TARTLETS
page 53

27

SALAD OF ASIAN GREENS WITH
TAMARI-GLAZED PORK BELLY
page 55

28

SPICY SIMMERED EGGS WITH KALE
page 55

february

1

THAI BEEF SALAD

serves 4

This Asian-inspired salad tosses fresh herbs, crisp cucumber and bell pepper, and briefly seared flank steak in a chile-laced dressing of lime juice and fish sauce. To round out the menu, accompany the salad with freshly cooked regular or sticky rice and cold Asian beer.

FOR THE SPICY DRESSING

3 Tbsp Asian fish sauce

3 Tbsp fresh lime juice

2 tsp sugar

1–2 tsp minced Thai chiles with seeds

1 flank steak, ¾–1 lb (375–500 g)

Salt and freshly ground pepper

2 tsp peanut oil

1 large head butter lettuce, torn into bite-sized pieces

1 cup (5 oz/155 g) thinly sliced English cucumber

½ cup (2 oz/60 g) thinly sliced sweet onion or red onion

½ cup (2½ oz/75 g) red bell pepper strips

½ cup (¾ oz/20 g) lightly packed torn fresh mint leaves

½ cup (¾ oz/20 g) lightly packed torn fresh cilantro leaves

¼ cup (⅓ oz/10 g) lightly packed torn fresh Thai or regular basil leaves

To make the dressing, in a large bowl, stir together the fish sauce, lime juice, sugar, and chiles until well blended. Set aside.

Preheat the broiler or prepare a charcoal or gas grill for direct-heat cooking over high heat. Sprinkle the steak evenly with salt and pepper and rub into the meat. Brush lightly on both sides with the oil.

To cook the steak, place it on a broiler pan and slide it under the broiler about 4 inches (10 cm) from the heat source, or place it on the grill rack. Cook, turning once, until the meat is seared on the outside and cooked rare to medium-rare in the center, about 4 minutes per side. Transfer the steak to a cutting board and let rest for 20 minutes.

Cut the steak across the grain into very thin slices, then cut each slice in half lengthwise if needed. Add the slices of meat to the dressing and toss to coat. Add the lettuce, cucumber, onion, bell pepper, mint, cilantro, and basil, toss to coat, and serve.

2

SWEET POTATO & GREEN CHILE QUESADILLAS WITH ARUGULA

serves 4

A perfect balance of flavors, these easy quesadillas combine mild jack cheese and sweet and spicy vegetables with crisp, cool arugula leaves. If you have leftover roasted sweet potatoes, this recipe is a great way to use them up. Serve with a crisp white wine or Mexican beer.

2 sweet potatoes, about 1 lb (500 g) total, peeled and cut into ½-inch (12-mm) pieces

4 Tbsp (2 fl oz/60 ml) olive oil, plus 2 tsp

8 flour or corn tortillas, about 9 inches (23 cm) in diameter

3 cups (12 oz/375 g) shredded Monterey jack cheese

1 can (4 oz/125 g) roasted green chiles, drained

⅓ cup (½ oz/15 g) fresh cilantro leaves

4 oz (125 g) baby arugula

Juice of ½ lemon

Salt and freshly ground pepper

Preheat the oven to 450°F (230°C). Line a baking sheet with parchment paper. Place the sweet potato pieces on the prepared baking sheet, drizzle with 2 Tbsp of the oil, and spread out in a single layer. Roast, stirring once, until the potatoes are caramelized and very tender, about 25 minutes. Let cool, transfer to a bowl, and, using a potato masher or a fork, mash slightly.

Place 4 tortillas on a work surface. Cover each tortilla with one-fourth of the sweet potatoes, cheese, green chiles, and cilantro. Cover with the remaining 4 tortillas.

In a large frying pan, warm about ½ tsp of the oil over medium heat. Fry 1 quesadilla, turning once, until the cheese is melted and the tortilla is golden brown, about 3 minutes. Repeat with the remaining 3 quesadillas, using ½ tsp oil for each. Transfer the quesadillas to a cutting board and cut into quarters.

Put the arugula in a bowl and drizzle with the remaining 2 Tbsp oil and the lemon juice. Season with salt and pepper and toss to combine. Serve the quesadillas topped with the arugula.

FEBRUARY

4

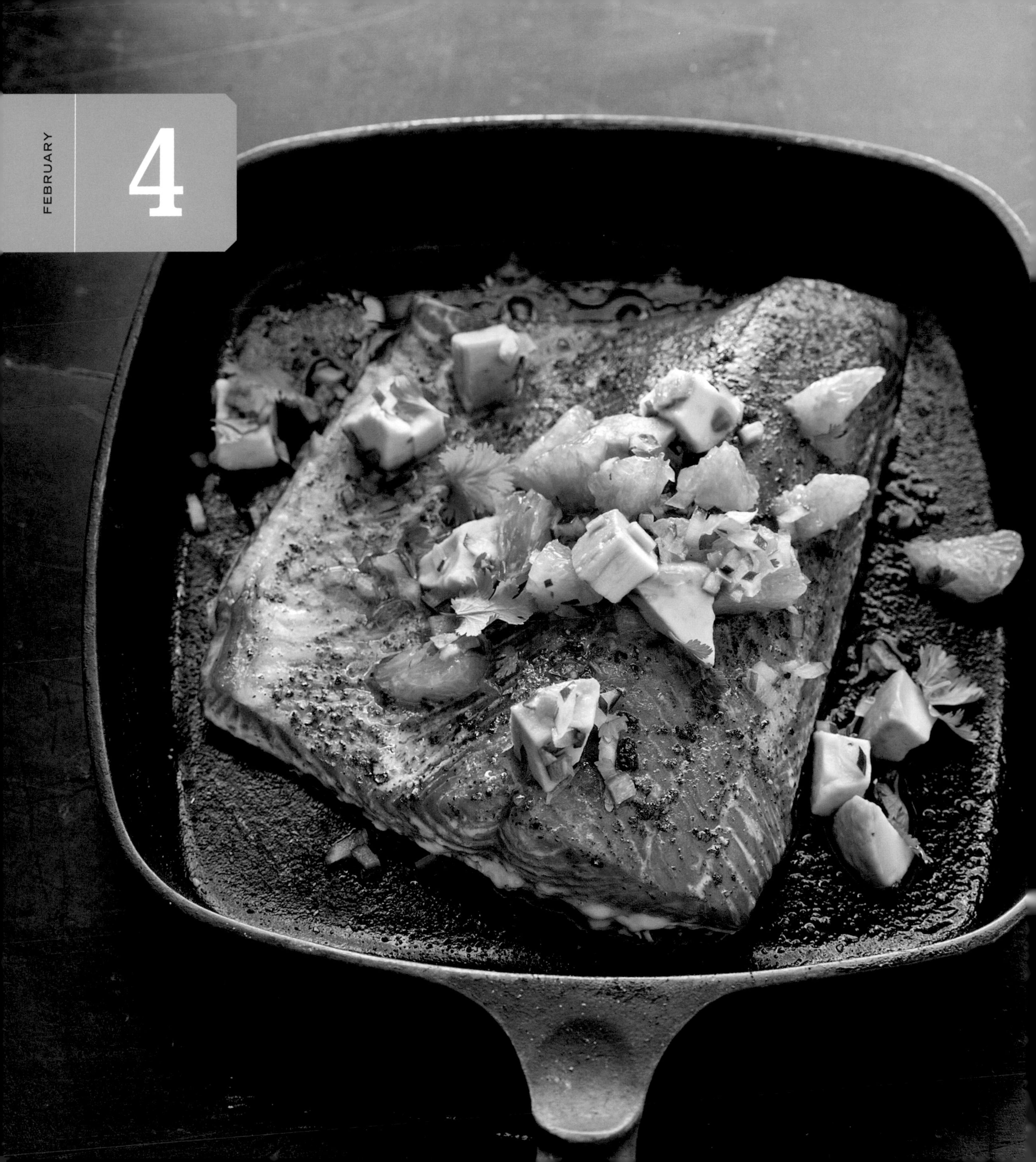

3

GINGER RICE WITH CHICKEN, CHARD & SHIITAKES

serves 4

This health-savvy rice casserole features jasmine rice, tender chicken, meaty mushrooms, and dark winter greens. For added flavor, whisk together a quick Asian sauce: In a small bowl, stir together 2 Tbsp oyster sauce, 1 tsp Asian sesame oil, 1 Tbsp rice vinegar, and 1 tsp hot water. Drizzle over the dish before serving.

2 skinless, boneless chicken thighs, cut into bite-sized pieces

1 tsp peeled and grated fresh ginger

1 Tbsp oyster sauce

1 Tbsp soy sauce

1 Tbsp rice wine or dry sherry

1 tsp toasted sesame oil

¼ tsp sugar

Ground white pepper

1½ cups (10½ oz/330 g) jasmine rice

1 bunch Swiss chard, tough stems removed and leaves chopped

6 oz (185 g) shiitake mushrooms, stems discarded and caps thinly sliced

1 green onion, white and tender green parts, thinly sliced

In a bowl, combine the chicken, ginger, oyster sauce, soy sauce, rice wine, oil, sugar, and a pinch of pepper, and mix well. Let stand for 10 minutes.

In a heavy saucepan, combine the rice, chard, mushrooms, chicken and its marinade, and 3 cups (24 fl oz/750 ml) water. Bring to a boil over high heat, cover, reduce the heat to low, and cook until the rice has absorbed the water and the chicken is opaque, about 20 minutes. Remove from the heat and let stand, covered, for 10 minutes. Fluff the rice with a fork, transfer to a serving bowl, garnish with the green onion, and serve.

Alternatively, to prepare in an electric rice cooker, combine the rice, chard, mushrooms, chicken and its marinade, and 3 cups (24 fl oz/750 ml) boiling water in the cooker, cover, and turn on the cooker. The rice should be ready in about 30 minutes. Let stand undisturbed for 10 minutes before garnishing with green onion and serving.

4

ROASTED SALMON WITH AVOCADO-GRAPEFRUIT SALSA

serves 2

Tangy grapefruit combined with silky avocado, sharp red onion, and bright fresh cilantro makes a lively topping for wild Alaskan king salmon—a great sustainable fish choice. Both salmon and avocados are full of omega-3 fatty acids, which are especially important for good brain and heart health. This recipe can be doubled for a family meal or dinner party and served with rice pilaf and sautéed cabbage.

¾ lb (375 g) wild salmon fillet, about 1½ inches (4 cm) thick

Olive oil, for brushing

Salt and freshly ground pepper

Ancho chile powder

1 large grapefruit

1 small, firm but ripe avocado, pitted, peeled, and cubed

½ large jalapeño chile, seeded and minced

3 Tbsp red onion, minced

2 Tbsp minced fresh cilantro

1 Tbsp fresh lime juice

Preheat the oven to 375°F (190°C). Place the fish in a small baking pan and brush on both sides with oil. Season lightly with salt, pepper, and chile powder. Roast until the salmon is almost opaque in the center, about 18 minutes.

Meanwhile, using a sharp knife, cut off the peel and all of the white pith from the grapefruit. Working over a medium bowl, use a paring knife to cut between the membranes to release the grapefruit segments into the bowl. Squeeze the juice from the membranes into the bowl. Remove the grapefruit segments from the bowl and cut crosswise into ½-inch (12-mm) pieces; return to the bowl. Gently stir in the avocado, jalapeño, onion, cilantro, and lime juice. Season the salsa with salt and pepper.

Cut the fish in half and divide between 2 warmed plates. Spoon the salsa over the top, and serve.

5

This contemporary gratin takes advantage of rainbow chard, with its beautiful tricolored stems and flavorful crinkled leaves. Ricotta and Gruyère melt and bind the ingredients together, sparing you from whisking over a hot stove.

RAINBOW CHARD GRATIN WITH RICOTTA & GRUYÈRE

serves 4–6

Unsalted butter, for greasing

3 lb (1.5 kg) rainbow chard

1 Tbsp olive oil

1 yellow onion, thinly sliced

1 clove garlic, minced

1½ tsp minced fresh thyme

Salt and freshly ground pepper

2 cups (1 lb/500 g) ricotta cheese

1 cup (4 oz/125 g) shredded Gruyère cheese

1 Tbsp Dijon mustard

1 cup (2 oz/60 g) fresh bread crumbs

Preheat the oven to 375°F (190°C). Butter a 12-inch (30-cm) oval gratin dish.

Cut the chard leaves from the stems. Keeping the leaves and stems separate, cut both into 1-inch (2.5-cm) pieces. In a large frying pan, warm the oil over medium heat. Add the chard stems and sauté for 2 minutes. Add the onion, garlic, and thyme and sauté until the onion softens, about 6 minutes. Add the chard leaves and cook, stirring, until wilted, about 4 minutes. Season with salt and pepper. Transfer the chard leaves and stems to a colander and drain well, pressing with a spoon to remove excess liquid.

In a bowl, stir together the cheeses and mustard. Add the chard and stir to mix well. Spread the chard mixture in the prepared dish and scatter the bread crumbs on top. Bake until the bread crumbs are golden and the gratin is heated through, about 20 minutes, then serve.

6

The inspiration for this full-bodied soup comes from southwestern France, where duck confit and lentils are a classic combination. Duck confit can be purchased ready to use in well-stocked supermarkets and butcher shops. Each bowl is finished with a crusty baguette crouton topped with a bit of the preserved duck.

LENTIL & CHARD SOUP WITH DUCK CONFIT

serves 8

2 tsp olive oil, plus 2 Tbsp

1 yellow onion, minced

1 clove garlic, minced

1 carrot, peeled and minced

2 cups (14 oz/440 g) lentils, picked over and rinsed

1 bay leaf

4 thyme sprigs

Salt and freshly ground pepper

6 large chard leaves, chopped, including ribs

2 duck legs confit

8 baguette slices, cut on the diagonal

In a large, heavy pot, warm the 2 tsp oil over medium heat. Add the onion and cook, stirring occasionally, until translucent, about 2 minutes. Add the garlic and carrot and cook, stirring occasionally, for 2 minutes. Stir in the lentils and 10 cups (80 fl oz/2.5 l) water and bring to a boil, then reduce the heat to low. Add the bay leaf, thyme, 1 tsp salt, and ½ tsp pepper and simmer for 15 minutes. Add the chard and duck legs and cook until the lentils are almost tender, 20–25 minutes.

Transfer the duck legs to a cutting board and, when they are cool enough to handle, remove and discard the skin. Cut off the meat, discarding the bones. Coarsely chop the meat and stir all but about ¼ cup (1½ oz/45 g) into the soup. Cook until the lentils are tender but not mushy, about 10 minutes longer. Remove and discard the bay leaf and thyme sprigs. Stir in ½ tsp salt.

Meanwhile, in a large frying pan, warm the 2 Tbsp oil over medium-high heat. Add half of the baguette slices and fry until golden, about 3 minutes. Turn and fry until golden on the other side, about 2 minutes. Transfer to a paper towel–lined plate. Repeat with the remaining baguette slices.

Ladle the soup into bowls. Garnish each with a fried crouton topped with a bit of the reserved duck meat.

SPINACH & BLACK BEAN ENCHILADAS

serves 4–6

Enchiladas originated in Mexico, where they are typically made with corn tortillas and filled with a seemingly endless variety of meats, cheeses, or vegetables. For this vegetarian version, use soft flour tortillas in place of the usual corn tortillas. If you like, trade out the black beans for pinto beans and the jack cheese for queso blanco, *a good melting cow's milk cheese. For extra richness, pass a bowl of crema (tangy, lightly thickened cream) or sour cream at the table.*

12 tomatillos, husked and halved

3 poblano chiles, halved lengthwise and seeded

1½ white onions, chopped

2 cloves garlic

1½ cups (1½ oz/45 g) fresh cilantro leaves

Salt and freshly ground pepper

3 Tbsp canola oil

½ red bell pepper, seeded and chopped

1 Tbsp plus 1 tsp ground cumin

10 oz (315 g) spinach, tough stems removed

2 cans (15 oz/470 g each) black beans, drained and rinsed

2 cups (8 oz/250 g) finely shredded Monterey jack cheese

10 flour tortillas

2 avocados, halved, pitted, peeled, and sliced, for garnish (optional)

Preheat the broiler. Arrange the tomatillos and poblanos, cut side down, on a baking sheet. Broil until charred, about 7 minutes. Let cool briefly.

Working in batches, place the tomatillos, poblanos, two-thirds of the onions, the garlic, and 1 cup (1 oz/30 g) of the cilantro in a blender and purée. Transfer to a bowl and season with salt and pepper.

Preheat the oven to 350°F (180°C).

In a frying pan, heat the oil over medium-high heat. Add the remaining onions and the bell pepper and sauté until the onions are translucent, about 5 minutes. Add the cumin, season generously with salt, and stir to combine. Add the spinach in batches and cook, stirring occasionally, until wilted. Remove from the heat, tilt the pan, and using a spoon, press against the spinach and discard as much liquid as possible. Let the spinach cool slightly and transfer to a large bowl. Add the beans, 1 cup (4 oz/125 g) of the cheese, and ¾ cup (6 fl oz/180 ml) of the tomatillo sauce. Roughly chop the remaining cilantro leaves, add to the bowl, and stir to combine.

Cover the bottom of a 9-by-13-inch (23-by-3-cm) baking dish with a few ⇥

tablespoons of the tomatillo sauce. Place ½ cup (2 oz/65 g) of the spinach mixture on each tortilla, roll up tightly, and arrange, seam side down, in the dish. Cover the enchiladas with the remaining tomatillo sauce and sprinkle with the remaining 1 cup cheese.

Cover the dish with foil and bake for 30 minutes. Uncover and continue baking until the cheese is lightly browned, about 10 minutes. Top the enchiladas with the avocado slices, if using, and serve.

ROASTED BROCCOLI WITH SOY, RICE VINEGAR & SESAME SEEDS

serves 4

Roasting brings out the best in broccoli. The tips of the florets char lightly, while the stems stay nicely crisp. To vary the flavors, use garlic oil in place of the sesame and soy sauce: Omit the peanut and sesame oils, sesame seeds, soy sauce, and rice vinegar. In a small bowl, stir together 3 Tbsp olive oil and the garlic. Arrange the broccoli on the baking sheet. Season with salt and pepper and brush with the garlic oil. Roast for about 15 minutes. Drizzle 2 tsp fresh lemon juice over the broccoli and serve.

1 lb (500 g) broccoli stalks with florets, tough ends trimmed

Salt and freshly ground pepper

2 Tbsp peanut oil

1 Tbsp Asian sesame oil

1 large clove garlic, finely chopped

1 Tbsp sesame seeds

1 Tbsp soy sauce

1 Tbsp rice vinegar

Preheat the oven to 475°F (245°C).

If the broccoli stalks are large, split them in half or thirds lengthwise. Arrange the broccoli stalks in a single layer on a rimmed baking sheet. Season lightly with salt and pepper. In a small bowl, stir together the peanut and sesame oils and the garlic. Brush the broccoli stalks on all sides with the oil mixture.

Roast the broccoli, turning once, until the stems are nearly tender-crisp and the florets are beginning to brown, about 10 minutes. Remove the broccoli from the oven and sprinkle with the sesame seeds. Continue to roast until the seeds are toasted, the stems are tender-crisp, and the florets are browned, about 5 minutes.

Remove from the oven and arrange the broccoli on a platter. Drizzle with the soy sauce and vinegar, and serve warm or at room temperature.

9

CREAMY BRUSSELS SPROUT SOUP WITH MAPLE BACON

serves 4–6

8 slices thick-cut applewood-smoked bacon

3 Tbsp pure maple syrup

1 small yellow onion, chopped

1 lb (500 g) brussels sprouts, halved

1 russet potato (about ¾ lb/375 g), peeled and cut into ½-inch (12-mm) pieces

Salt and freshly ground pepper

2 cloves garlic, chopped

2 thyme sprigs

4 cups (32 fl oz/1 l) chicken broth

Here's a great way to introduce brussels sprouts to a young, fussy eater. This is a creamy and healthful soup topped with a familiar crowd-pleaser: bacon! And it's hard to think of a dish that isn't better with the addition of candied bacon. Be sure to look for pure maple syrup, passing up any bottle that lists artificial sweeteners.

Preheat the oven to 400°F (200°C).

Working in batches if necessary, in a large, heavy pot, fry the bacon over medium-high heat, flipping once, about 6 minutes total (the bacon will not be fully cooked). Using tongs, transfer the bacon to a baking sheet and let cool slightly. Brush the bacon slices on one side with the maple syrup and bake until cooked through, 8–10 minutes. Let cool, then cut into bite-sized pieces. Set aside.

Pour off all but 2 Tbsp of the fat from the pot and return to medium-high heat. Add the onion, brussels sprouts, and potato, and season with salt and pepper. Cook, stirring frequently, until the vegetables begin to soften, about 8 minutes. Add the garlic and thyme sprigs and cook, stirring frequently, until the garlic is soft, about 2 minutes. Add the broth, raise the heat to high, and bring to a boil. Reduce the heat to low and simmer until the brussels sprouts are tender, 8–10 minutes. Remove and discard the thyme sprigs. Let cool slightly.

Working in batches, purée the soup in a food processor or blender. Return to the pot and season with salt and pepper. Serve, topped with the maple bacon.

10

TURKEY BURGERS WITH RADICCHIO SLAW

serves 4

3 Tbsp olive oil mayonnaise

1½ Tbsp whole-grain Dijon mustard

3 Tbsp capers, rinsed and minced

1¼ lb (625 g) ground turkey

1 Tbsp fresh thyme, minced

4 Tbsp (2 fl oz/60 ml) extra-virgin olive oil, plus more for brushing

1 large shallot, minced

Salt and freshly ground pepper

4 whole-grain rolls, split

1 head radicchio, cut into quarters, then thinly sliced

1½ Tbsp balsamic vinegar

The wine-red color and bitter flavor of leafy radicchio come from its high concentration of healthful antioxidants. Here, this popular chicory is used to make a quick slaw for topping turkey burgers. Double the recipe for the creamy mustard-mayonnaise sauce and use the extra sauce as a dip for raw vegetables served on the side. For the best flavor and juiciness, purchase ground dark-meat turkey or ground turkey that is no more than 90 percent lean.

In a small bowl, combine the mayonnaise, mustard, and 1½ Tbsp of the capers. Refrigerate until ready to serve.

In a bowl, combine the turkey, thyme, and remaining 1½ Tbsp capers. In a small frying pan over medium heat, warm 1 Tbsp of the oil. Add the shallot and sauté until tender, about 4 minutes. Add to the turkey along with ¾ tsp salt and a generous amount of pepper. Mix gently to combine. Form the mixture into 4 patties, each about ½ inch (12 mm) thick. Brush the cut surface of the rolls with oil, and sprinkle with pepper.

Preheat the broiler. Heat a large frying pan over medium heat; brush with oil. Add the patties and cook until cooked through, about 5 minutes on each side.

Meanwhile, in another bowl, toss the radicchio with the vinegar and the remaining 3 Tbsp oil. Season to taste with salt and pepper.

Place the rolls, cut side up, on a rimmed baking sheet. Broil until golden-brown, about 4 minutes.

To serve, divide the roll bottoms among 4 warmed plates. Top them with the patties, sauce, and slaw, and cover with the roll tops. Spoon the remaining slaw alongside the burgers, and serve.

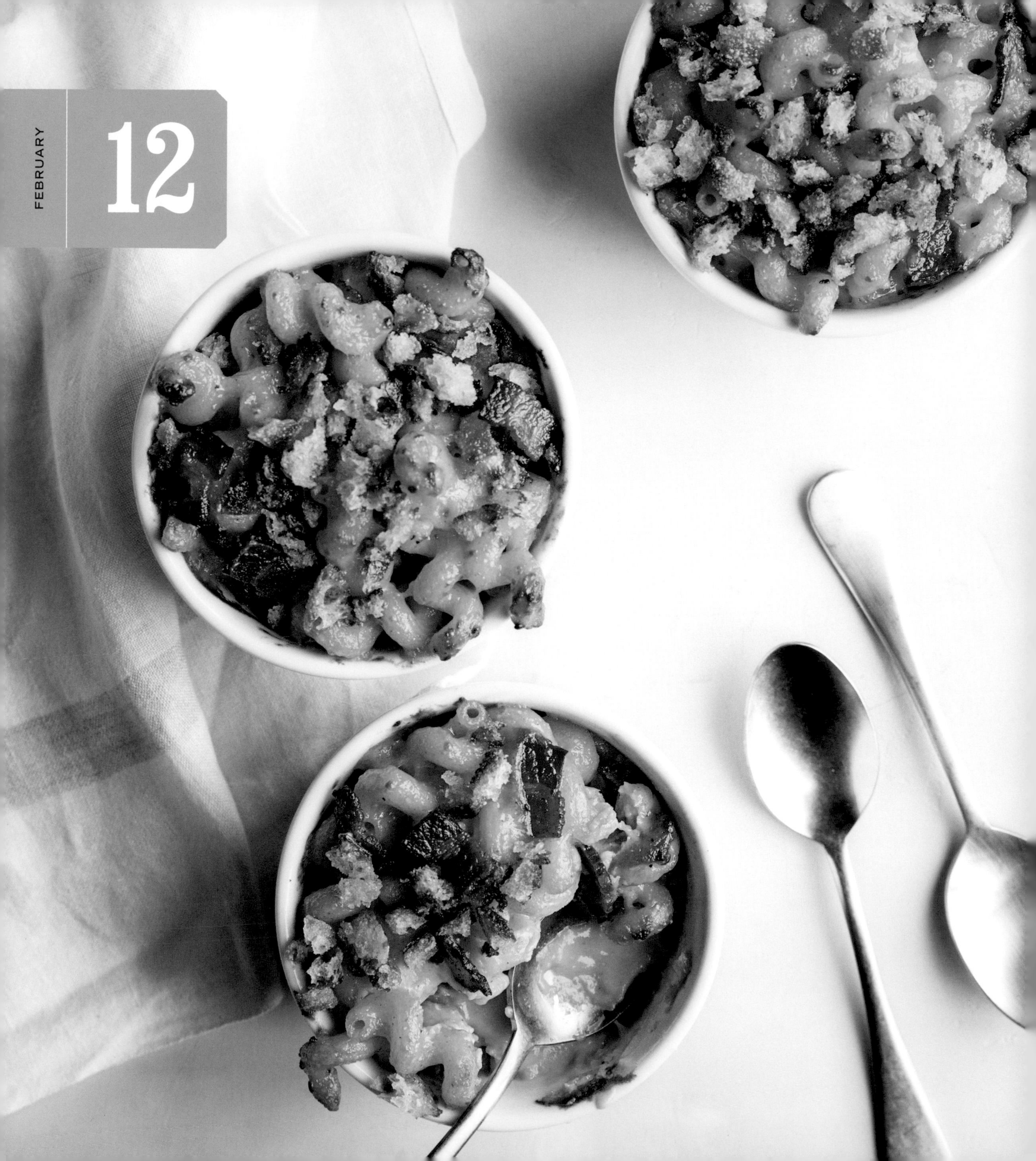

11

Kimchi, the spicy fermented cabbage condiment found on nearly every Korean table, is used as a generous garnish for this highly seasoned noodle dish. Look for bean thread noodles, dried transparent noodles made from mung bean starch, in well-stocked supermarkets or Asian groceries. Or you can omit the noodles and serve the beef-and-vegetable stir-fry atop steamed brown or white rice.

KOREAN-STYLE NOODLES WITH MARINATED STEAK & KIMCHI

serves 4

3 Tbsp Asian sesame oil

1 Tbsp *each* low-sodium soy sauce and mirin

1 Tbsp light brown sugar

1 tsp minced garlic

1 tsp Korean chile bean paste (such as gochujang) or Sriracha sauce

¼ cup (40 g) toasted sesame seeds

12 oz (375 g) flank steak, sliced against the grain into thin strips

½ lb (250 g) bean thread noodles

2 Tbsp canola oil

½ lb (250 g) shiitake mushrooms, stemmed and thinly sliced

1 cup (3½ oz/105 g) thinly sliced onions

1 cup (5 oz/155 g) julienned carrots

¼ cup (1 oz/30 g) thinly sliced green onion

½ cup (2 oz/60 g) kimchi, coarsely chopped

In a baking dish, stir together the sesame oil, soy sauce, mirin, brown sugar, garlic, chile bean paste, and 2 Tbsp of the sesame seeds until the sugar dissolves. Set half of the mixture aside. Add the sliced steak to the remaining mixture. Cover and marinate in the refrigerator for at least 30 minutes or up to 4 hours. Remove the dish from the refrigerator 30 minutes before cooking.

Place the noodles in a heatproof bowl and cover with very hot tap water. Let the noodles soak until they become tender and opaque, about 10 minutes. Drain well.

Warm a wok over medium-high heat and add 1 Tbsp canola oil. Remove the meat from the marinade, letting any excess liquid drain off. Add the steak to the wok and stir-fry just until it begins to brown, 2–3 minutes. Transfer the steak to a plate. Warm the remaining 1 Tbsp canola oil in the wok, then add the mushrooms and onions. Stir-fry until the vegetables begin to soften, 2–3 minutes. Add the carrots and green onion and stir-fry until the onions are soft and lightly browned, 4–5 minutes. Stir in the noodles. Add the reserved sauce and the beef, stirring well to coat.

Transfer the noodles to a warm serving dish, garnish with the kimchi, and serve.

12

Aged Cheddar gives this hearty baked pasta a richness that is nicely balanced by the addition of salty, smoky bacon. A layer of toasted coarse bread crumbs provides a crunchy contrast to the creamy casserole.

MACARONI WITH FARMSTEAD CHEDDAR & BACON

serves 4–6

4 Tbsp (2 oz/60 g) unsalted butter, plus more for greasing

4 slices baguette or other firm bread, crusts removed and bread torn into bread crumbs

4 slices thick-cut bacon, cut crosswise into ½-inch (12-mm) strips

¼ cup (1½ oz/45 g) all-purpose flour

Salt and freshly ground black pepper

¼ tsp cayenne pepper

3 cups (24 fl oz/750 ml) milk, heated

¾ lb (375 g) Cheddar cheese, preferably farmstead, shredded

½ lb (250 g) elbow macaroni

Butter a shallow 1½-qt (1.5-l) baking dish or 4 individual ramekins. In a frying pan, melt 1 Tbsp of the butter over medium-high heat. Add the bread crumbs and fry until golden, about 4 minutes. Transfer to a plate.

In the frying pan, fry the bacon over medium heat until cooked but not crisp, 3–5 minutes. Drain on paper towels. In a saucepan, melt the remaining 3 Tbsp butter over medium-high heat. Add the flour, ½ tsp salt, ¼ tsp black pepper, and the cayenne and whisk until a smooth paste forms. Slowly whisk in the hot milk, reduce the heat to medium, and cook, whisking constantly, until the sauce thickens, about 15 minutes. Add two-thirds of the cheese and stir until melted, about 2 minutes. Remove from the heat.

Preheat the oven to 375°F (190°C). Bring a large pot of salted water to a boil. Add the macaroni, stir well, and cook until al dente, according to package directions. Drain, add to the prepared dish(es), and toss with the bacon. Pour in the cheese sauce and stir to mix well. Top with the remaining cheese and then the bread crumbs. Bake until the sauce is bubbling and the top is golden, about 30 minutes. Let stand for a few minutes before serving.

13

The filling for these squares is a homemade lemon curd—thick, smooth, lemony, and buttery. It can also be spread on flaky scones or layered in cakes. Meyer lemons, which are appreciated for their sweet flavor and flowery fragrance, are used in this recipe, but common lemons, such as Eureka, can be substituted. Although the lemon filling remains soft even when cold, it holds its shape when the squares are cut.

MEYER LEMON SQUARES
makes 9–12 squares

¾ cup (4 oz/125 g) all-purpose flour

¼ cup (1 oz/30 g) confectioners' sugar, plus more for dusting

⅛ tsp kosher salt

12 Tbsp (6 oz/185 g) cold unsalted butter, cut into pieces

2 Tbsp pine nuts, lightly toasted

3 large whole eggs, plus 3 large egg yolks

¾ cup (6 fl oz/180 ml) fresh Meyer lemon juice, strained (about 5 lemons)

1 cup (8 oz/250 g) granulated sugar

1 tsp grated Meyer lemon zest

Preheat the oven to 350°F (180°C). Butter an 8-inch (20-cm) square baking pan. To make the crust, combine the flour, ¼ cup confectioners' sugar, and the salt in a food processor and pulse a few times until blended. Add 6 Tbsp (3 oz/90 g) of the butter and pulse 6–8 times until the mixture forms large, coarse crumbs the size of small peas. Stir in the pine nuts.

Press the crumb mixture into the bottom and 1 inch (2.5 cm) up the sides of the prepared pan. Bake the crust until golden and the top feels firm when lightly touched, about 15 minutes. Reduce the heat to 325°F (165°C).

In the top of a double boiler, whisk together the whole eggs, egg yolks, lemon juice, and granulated sugar until the sugar dissolves. Place over (not touching) barely simmering water and add the remaining 6 Tbsp butter. Using a large spoon, stir constantly until the butter melts and the mixture is thick enough to coat the back of the spoon and registers 160°F (71°C) on an instant-read thermometer, about 12 minutes. Remove from over the water and strain the lemon curd through a medium-mesh sieve placed over a bowl. Stir in the lemon zest. Let cool for 10 minutes.

Pour the lemon curd over the baked crust. Bake until the center is set, 13–17 minutes. Transfer to a wire rack and let cool for about 20 minutes, then cover and refrigerate until chilled, at least 3 hours or up to overnight. The filling will thicken as it cools.

Just before serving, sift a thick layer of confectioners' sugar over the top. Cut into squares and serve.

14

Plump, sweet navel oranges turn up frequently in winter salads—and not just fruit salads. They add appealing color and a tart-sweet flavor to this mix of beets and spinach, a good prelude to a main course of pork chops or duck. Red-fleshed blood oranges, at their delicious peak during winter, can be used in place of the navel oranges.

SPINACH SALAD WITH ORANGES & ROASTED BEETS
serves 6

4 small beets (about ½ lb/250 g total weight)

FOR THE SHALLOT DRESSING

1 Tbsp fresh lemon juice, plus more as needed

1 shallot, minced

Salt and freshly ground pepper

3 Tbsp extra-virgin olive oil

2 large navel oranges

6 cups (6 oz/185 g) baby spinach

Preheat the oven to 375°F (190°C). Trim off the leafy beet tops. Wrap the beets in foil and roast on a baking sheet until easily pierced with the tip of a knife, 45–60 minutes. Remove from the oven and let cool in the foil.

Meanwhile, to make the dressing, in a small bowl, combine the lemon juice and shallot. Season with salt and pepper. Let stand for 30 minutes to allow the shallot flavor to mellow, then add the oil in a thin stream, whisking constantly until the dressing is well blended.

Cut a slice off the top and bottom of each orange. Stand each upright and, following the contour of the fruit, cut away all the peel and white pith. Cut along both sides of each segment to free it from the membrane.

When the beets are cool enough to handle, peel and cut them into wedges about the size of the orange segments. Put the beet wedges in a bowl and toss with just enough of the dressing to coat them lightly.

Put the spinach in a large bowl and add the orange segments. Add the remaining dressing and toss to coat. Taste and adjust the seasoning with salt, pepper, and lemon juice.

Divide the spinach and oranges among individual plates. Arrange the beets on top and serve.

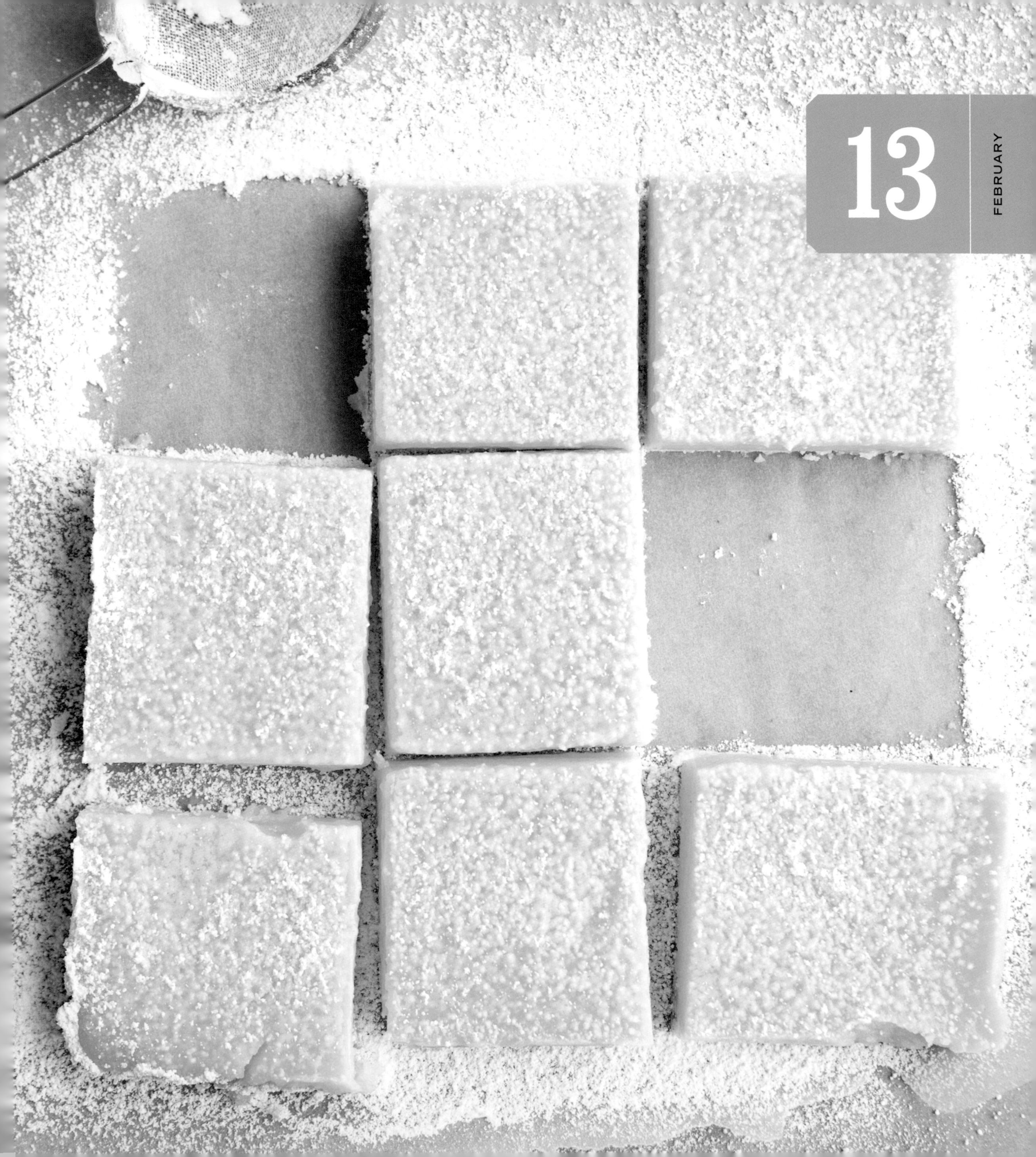

15

SAUTÉED SOLE WITH FENNEL & LEMON COMPOTE

serves 4

3 Tbsp olive oil

2 large fennel bulbs, fronds reserved, trimmed, cored, and cut into thin slices

Salt and freshly ground pepper

¼ cup (2 fl oz/60 ml) dry white wine

Finely grated zest of 1 lemon and 1 Tbsp lemon juice

2 tsp sugar

⅓ cup (3 fl oz/80 ml) grapeseed oil

1 egg

2 or 3 drops hot red-pepper sauce

1¾ cups (2½ oz/75 g) whole-wheat panko bread crumbs

2 Tbsp all-purpose flour

4 fillets of sole, about 6 oz (185 g) each

2 Tbsp chopped fresh flat-leaf parsley

Delicate sole forms a delicious crust and turns out tender and flaky when seared over high heat. Grapeseed oil is the perfect fat to use, as it has a high smoke point and a neutral flavor. Whole-wheat panko ensures a particularly crispy crust and is a more healthful choice than the typically used flour. Accompany the sole with steamed small potatoes and wilted greens.

In a saucepan over medium heat, warm the olive oil. Add the fennel slices and ½ tsp salt and sauté until lightly browned, 3–4 minutes. Stir in the wine, lemon zest and juice, and sugar. Cover the pan, reduce the heat to low, and cook until the fennel is very soft, 5–6 minutes. Keep warm.

Warm a very large sauté pan over medium-high heat and add the grapeseed oil. Meanwhile, in a large, shallow dish, whisk together the egg, pepper sauce, ¼ tsp salt, and a few grinds of pepper. Add the panko and flour to separate shallow dishes. Lightly flour a fish fillet on both sides, dip it into the egg mixture, and then into the panko, coating both sides evenly. Gently place the breaded fillet into the hot oil and, working quickly, repeat with the remaining fillets. Sauté the fillets until nicely browned on the first side, about 3 minutes. Turn the fillets and sauté until the second side is browned and the fish is opaque throughout, about 2 minutes longer.

Transfer the fillets to warmed plates and spoon the compote alongside. Sprinkle with the parsley and serve.

16

OATMEAL–CHOCOLATE CHIP COOKIES WITH ALMONDS

makes about 60 cookies

1 cup (8 oz/250 g) unsalted butter

¾ cup (6 oz/185 g) granulated sugar

¾ cup (6 oz/185 g) firmly packed light brown sugar

2 large eggs

1 tsp pure vanilla extract

1½ cups (7½ oz/235 g) all-purpose flour

1 tsp baking soda

¼ tsp kosher salt

2 cups (6 oz/185 g) rolled oats

2 cups (12 oz/375 g) semisweet chocolate chips

1 cup (4 oz/125 g) whole almonds, toasted and chopped

Oatmeal cookies don't have to be boring, nor do they have to contain raisins. Throw in a handful of chocolate chips instead, and then take them one step further by folding in some toasted almonds. The nuts will bolster the flavor of the brown sugar and butter in the dough.

Preheat the oven to 350°F (180°C). Line 2 baking sheets with parchment paper.

In a large bowl, using an electric mixer on medium speed, beat the butter and granulated and brown sugars until creamy. Add the eggs and vanilla and beat until smooth. In another bowl, stir together the flour, baking soda, and salt. Add the dry ingredients to the butter mixture and beat on low speed until smooth. Stir in the oats, chocolate chips, and almonds.

Drop rounded tablespoonfuls of the dough onto the prepared sheets, spacing them about 1½ inches (4 cm) apart. Bake until the cookies are golden brown, 10–12 minutes. Transfer the cookies to wire racks and let cool completely.

17

CHICKEN STEW WITH BUTTERMILK-CHIVE DUMPLINGS

serves 4

This is a great way to use up leftover cooked chicken; just skip the first step and substitute chicken broth for the poaching liquid. Feel free to change up the vegetables: add spinach, sweet potatoes, or frozen peas.

2 skinless, boneless chicken breast halves

2 skinless, boneless chicken thighs

1 bay leaf

3 peppercorns

Salt and freshly ground pepper

4 Tbsp (2 oz/60 g) unsalted butter

2 leeks, white parts only, chopped

2 carrots, peeled and sliced

3 celery ribs, sliced

2 Tbsp all-purpose flour

4 cups (32 fl oz/1 l) chicken broth

1 russet potato, peeled and cut into ½-inch (12-mm) dice

2 Tbsp heavy cream

FOR THE DUMPLINGS

1¼ cups (6½ oz/200 g) all-purpose flour

1 tsp baking soda

½ tsp salt

1 Tbsp chopped chives

Large pinch of cayenne pepper

3 Tbsp cold unsalted butter, cut into bits

½ cup (4 fl oz/125 ml) buttermilk

Put the chicken breasts and thighs, bay leaf, peppercorns, and ¼ tsp salt in a saucepan and add cold water to cover by 1 inch (2.5 cm). Bring to a boil, then reduce the heat to medium-low. Simmer until the chicken is cooked through, 15–20 minutes, skimming off any foam on the surface. Remove the chicken, shred the meat, and set aside. Reserve 2 cups (16 fl oz/500 ml) of the poaching liquid.

In a large saucepan, melt the butter over medium-high heat. Add the leeks, carrots, and celery and sauté until they begin to soften, about 5 minutes. Add the flour and cook for 2 minutes, stirring. Add the broth and the reserved poaching liquid and bring to a boil. Add the potato and reduce the heat to medium-low. Cook until the potato begins to soften, about 10 minutes.

Add the chicken and cream and continue to cook until the soup thickens and the ⟩⟩→

potatoes are very tender, 5 minutes. Season with salt and pepper.

To make the dumplings, sift together the flour, baking soda, and salt into a bowl. Stir in the chives and cayenne. With a pastry blender, cut in the cold butter until it resembles coarse cornmeal. Add the buttermilk and stir just to combine. Use your hands to form small dumplings and add them to the soup, cover, and let steam for 20 minutes. Serve.

18

PEANUT-BRAISED TOFU WITH NOODLES

serves 4

Fresh Chinese noodles and tofu come together quickly on weeknights, and a sauce of coconut milk and creamy peanut butter brings richness and flavor to this vegetarian main course. Serve with steamed broccoli or bok choy on the side.

1 lb (500 g) firm tofu, cut into ¾-inch (2-cm) cubes

1 cup (4 oz/125 g) trimmed and halved snow peas

½ lb (250 g) thin fresh Chinese egg noodles

½ cup (4 fl oz/125 ml) unsweetened coconut milk

½ cup (5 oz/155 g) creamy peanut butter

1 Tbsp chile paste

1 tsp sugar

¼ cup (2 fl oz/60 ml) vegetable broth

2 Tbsp soy sauce

2 Tbsp fresh lime juice

Line a baking sheet with a double thickness of paper towels. Arrange the tofu in a single layer on the towels. Top with another layer of towels and pat the tofu dry.

Bring a large saucepan of water to a boil. Add the snow peas, cook for 30 seconds, and remove with a slotted spoon and set aside. Add the noodles to the boiling water and cook according to the package directions. Drain the noodles, rinse well with cold water, and drain again.

In the saucepan, stir together the coconut milk and peanut butter until well combined. Stir in the chile paste, sugar, broth, soy sauce, and lime juice. Add the tofu. Cook over medium heat, stirring occasionally, until the sauce is hot and the tofu is heated through, about 2 minutes. Stir in the peas and the noodles and serve.

19

BUTTERMILK DONUTS WITH LEMON SUGAR

makes about 10 donuts and 10 donut holes

1¼ cups (6½ oz/200 g) all-purpose flour

1 cup (4 oz/125 g) cake flour

1 tsp baking powder

½ tsp baking soda

½ tsp freshly grated nutmeg

½ tsp kosher salt

1 large egg

1 cup (8 oz/250 g) sugar

½ cup (4 fl oz/125 ml) buttermilk

1 Tbsp unsalted butter, melted

1 tsp pure vanilla extract

Canola or peanut oil for deep-frying

Finely grated zest of 2 lemons

These old-fashioned buttermilk donuts recall childhood visits to a favorite bakery. The dough takes just minutes to mix and then fry to a golden finish. For a more traditional sugared donut, omit the lemon zest and add 1 tsp ground cinnamon to the sugar for coating.

Sift the flours, baking powder, baking soda, nutmeg, and salt into a bowl. In another bowl, using an electric mixer, beat the egg and ½ cup (4 oz/125 g) of the sugar on low speed until creamy and pale in color. Add the buttermilk, butter, and vanilla and beat until blended. Add the dry ingredients and beat on low speed just until a soft dough forms. Cover and refrigerate the dough until firm, at least 30 minutes or up to 1 hour.

Line a baking sheet with paper towels. Pour oil to a depth of 2 inches (5 cm) into a deep, heavy frying pan and warm over medium-high heat until it reaches 360°F (182°C) on a deep-frying thermometer.

On a generously floured work surface, roll out the dough into a round 10 inches (25 cm) in diameter and ½ inch (12 mm) thick. Using a 3-inch (7.5-cm) round donut cutter, cut out as many donuts as possible. Gather the scraps and repeat the rolling and cutting.

Working in batches, carefully lower 2–5 donuts or holes into the hot oil and deep-fry until dark golden, about 1½ minutes. Turn and cook until dark golden on the second side, about 1 minute longer. Using a slotted spoon, transfer to the paper towels to cool. Allow the oil to return to 360°F between batches.

In a bowl, stir together the remaining ½ cup sugar and the lemon zest. While the donuts and holes are still warm, coat both sides with the lemon sugar. Serve right away.

20

GARLICKY SHRIMP SCAMPI

serves 4

½ cup (2½ oz/75 g) all-purpose flour

Salt and freshly ground pepper

2 Tbsp olive oil, plus more as needed

1½ lb (750 g) jumbo or extra-large shrimp, peeled and deveined, tails intact

12 Tbsp (6 oz/185 g) unsalted butter

3 cloves garlic, minced

¼ cup (2 fl oz/60 ml) dry white wine

Grated zest of 1 lemon

2 Tbsp fresh lemon juice

2 Tbsp finely chopped fresh flat-leaf parsley

Lemon wedges

American cooks use the term scampi *to describe sautéed jumbo shrimp in a buttery white wine sauce. Scallops are good with this sauce, too. Small bay scallops will cook in about the same amount of time as the shrimp. If you like, serve the saucy scampi over fresh pasta.*

In a shallow bowl, stir together the flour, ½ tsp salt, and ¼ tsp pepper. In a large frying pan, heat the 2 Tbsp oil over medium-high heat. Toss half of the shrimp in the flour mixture to coat evenly, shaking off the excess. Add to the pan and cook, turning occasionally, until opaque throughout, about 3 minutes. Transfer to a plate and tent with foil. Repeat with the remaining shrimp, adding more oil as needed.

Reduce the heat to medium-low, add 2 Tbsp of the butter and the garlic, and cook, stirring frequently, until the garlic softens and is fragrant but not browned, about 2 minutes. Add the wine and the lemon zest and juice and bring to a boil over high heat. Cook until reduced by half, about 1 minute. Reduce the heat to very low. Whisk in the remaining 10 Tbsp butter, 1 Tbsp at a time, letting each addition soften into a creamy emulsion before adding more.

Return the shrimp to the sauce and mix gently to coat well. Remove from the heat and season with salt and pepper. Transfer to a serving dish and sprinkle with the parsley. Serve, passing the lemon wedges at the table.

21

CHICKEN TAGINE WITH PRESERVED LEMONS & OLIVES

serves 4–6

This colorful Moroccan stew is richly spiced, but stays light and bright with tart citrus, briny green olives, and fresh cilantro. Serve the tagine atop a bed of couscous, just as a North African cook would.

¼ tsp saffron threads

2 large yellow onions, chopped

½ cup (¾ oz/20 g) coarsely chopped fresh cilantro, plus more for garnish

½ cup (¾ oz/20 g) coarsely chopped fresh flat-leaf parsley, plus more for garnish

4 Tbsp (2 fl oz/60 ml) fresh lemon juice

1 tsp ground cumin

½ tsp ground ginger

½ tsp ground turmeric

Salt

2 large cloves garlic, crushed

6 Tbsp olive oil

6 skin-on, bone-in chicken thighs

2 preserved lemons, thinly sliced

½ cup (4 fl oz/125 ml) chicken broth

1½ cups (8 oz/250 g) green olives

In a small bowl, soak the saffron in 2 Tbsp warm water for 10 minutes.

In a food processor, combine the onions, the ½ cup cilantro, ½ cup parsley, and 2 Tbsp of the lemon juice. Add the cumin, ginger, turmeric, and the saffron and its soaking liquid. Season with 1 tsp salt and process to a pulpy purée. Transfer to a large resealable plastic bag. Add the garlic and 3 Tbsp of the oil. Add the chicken pieces, seal the bag, and massage to coat the chicken with the mixture. Refrigerate for at least 8 hours or up to 24 hours.

In a large, heavy pot, warm 1 Tbsp of the oil over medium-high heat. Add the lemon slices and sear until browned, 3–5 minutes. Transfer to a plate. Add the remaining 2 Tbsp oil to the pot. Remove the chicken pieces from the marinade, shaking off the excess and reserving the marinade. Working in batches, sear the chicken pieces, skin side down, until golden brown, 5–6 minutes. Transfer to another plate.

Pour the broth into the pot, stirring to scrape up any browned bits from the pot bottom. Stir in the reserved marinade and add the chicken and any juices. ⤳

Bring to a boil, cover, reduce the heat to medium-low, and simmer until the chicken is opaque throughout, about 40 minutes.

Simmer the olives in a saucepan of boiling water for 5 minutes. Add the strained olives, the seared lemon, and the remaining 2 Tbsp lemon juice to the pot. Cover and simmer until the chicken is falling-off-the-bone tender, 10–15 minutes.

Garnish the stew with chopped cilantro and parsley and serve.

22

MOROCCAN-SPICED ROASTED VEGETABLES & QUINOA

serves 4–6

Moroccan spices, such as cumin, turmeric, and cinnamon, infuse this delicious and aromatic main course. Quinoa, which is both gluten-free and high in protein, has a light and fluffy texture that makes a nice counterpoint to the tender root vegetables. Dried fruit and nuts, which are common in Moroccan cuisine, lend sweetness and crunch.

3 parsnips, cut into ½-inch (12-cm) pieces

2 carrots, peeled and cut into ½-inch (12-cm) pieces

6 Tbsp (3 fl oz/90 ml) olive oil

1 Tbsp ground cumin

2 tsp ground turmeric

1 tsp ground cinnamon

Salt and freshly ground pepper

2 cups (16 fl oz/500 ml) low-sodium chicken or vegetable broth

1 cup (8 oz/250 g) quinoa, rinsed

¼ cup (1½ oz/45 g) dried apricots, quartered

3 Tbsp slivered almonds, toasted

2 Tbsp chopped fresh flat-leaf parsley

Preheat the oven to 400°F (200°C). Toss the parsnips and carrots with 2 Tbsp of the oil, the cumin, turmeric, and cinnamon. Spread in a single layer on a baking sheet lined with parchment paper and season well with salt and pepper. Roast, stirring a couple of times, until the vegetables are very tender and caramelized, 35–40 minutes.

Bring the broth to a boil in a saucepan over high heat. Add the quinoa, cover, and reduce the heat to medium-low. Cook until all the broth is absorbed, about 12 minutes.

Transfer the quinoa to a large bowl and add the roasted vegetables, apricots, almonds, and parsley. Stir in the remaining 4 Tbsp (2 fl oz/60 ml) oil, season with salt and pepper, and serve.

23

POTATO GALETTES WITH SMOKED SALMON

serves 4

2 russet potatoes, about ¾ lb (375 g) total, peeled

2 Tbsp canola or olive oil

Salt and freshly ground pepper

3 oz (90 g) thinly sliced smoked salmon, cut into 2-inch (5-cm) squares

1 Tbsp snipped fresh chives

1–2 Tbsp sour cream for garnish (optional)

Panfried potatoes are a welcome vehicle for smoky cured fish, especially with a spoonful of sour cream and a sprinkle of chives. After shredding the potatoes, press out as much moisture as possible. This both firms the texture of the galettes and protects you from spatters while working over a hot pan.

Shred the potatoes on the large holes of a grater-shredder to make long shreds. Squeeze the potatoes dry, one handful at a time, with a kitchen towel.

In a frying pan, warm 2 tsp of the oil over medium-high heat. For each galette, put 1 heaping Tbsp potato shreds in the pan, making 4 at a time. Using a spatula, firmly flatten the potatoes into 3-inch (7.5-cm) pancakes, repeatedly pressing to compact the potatoes and pushing in the loose edges to prevent them from burning. Work the spatula under each galette to keep it from sticking. Continue pressing and lifting the galettes until the tops look translucent, about 3 minutes longer. Turn and cook, continuing to press and lift, until the galettes are well browned, about 3 minutes. Season with salt and pepper. Remove the galettes from the pan and keep warm.

Wipe out the pan. Add the oil 1 tsp at a time as needed, and repeat to cook the remaining galettes in 2 more batches. As the pan gets hotter, the potatoes will cook more quickly; reduce the heat if necessary.

Top each galette with a square of smoked salmon and a sprinkle of chives. Dot with sour cream, if desired, and serve.

24

LEG OF LAMB WITH ROASTED FENNEL & PAN SAUCE

serves 4

2 Tbsp *each* minced shallot, minced fresh thyme, and grated orange zest

2¼ tsp fennel seeds, crushed

1¼ lb (625 g) boneless leg of lamb, trimmed

Salt and freshly ground pepper

1 Tbsp olive oil, plus more for brushing

1 large fennel bulb, trimmed, cored, and cut lengthwise into wedges about ¼ inch (6 mm) thick

1 large red onion, cut lengthwise into thin wedges

⅓ cup (3 fl oz/80 ml) dry vermouth

⅓ cup (3 fl oz/80 ml) low-sodium chicken broth

To save time on serving day, make the seasoning mixture, spread half of it on the lamb, and refrigerate the lamb for up to 1 day. Then, when you are ready to cook, all you need to do is slip the lamb under the broiler. For a complementary side dish, toss fingerling potatoes with olive oil and rosemary and roast them in the oven.

Preheat the broiler. In a small bowl, mix together the shallot, thyme, orange zest, and fennel seeds. Place the lamb on a broiler pan and season it with salt and a generous amount of pepper. Rub half the shallot mixture all over the lamb, and then brush it with oil.

Broil the lamb until a thermometer inserted in the thickest part registers 125°–130°F (52°–54°C) for medium-rare, about 8 minutes on each side. Transfer the lamb to a warmed platter and tent loosely with foil.

In a large bowl, combine the fennel and onion. Add the 1 Tbsp oil and toss to coat. Set aside 1 Tbsp of the shallot mixture for the sauce; add the remaining mixture to the vegetables and toss to coat. Season with salt and pepper. Brush a large, heavy baking sheet with oil; transfer the vegetables to the sheet and arrange in a single layer. Broil the vegetables until they start to brown, about 7–8 minutes, stirring halfway through.

De-fat the juices in the broiler pan. Set the pan on the stove top over medium heat. Add the vermouth and bring to a boil, stirring up the browned bits on the pan bottom. Boil until syrupy, about 3 minutes. Add the broth and boil until it thickens slightly, about 2 minutes. Mix in the reserved shallot mixture and any lamb juices from the platter. Taste and adjust the seasoning.

Slice the meat thinly and serve with the vegetables and sauce.

25

When looking for a healthy main course, turn to this easy pasta dish, which calls for nutrient-rich fennel, multigrain spaghetti, and low-fat shrimp. Kalamata olives and San Marzano tomatoes add lots of flavor but not many calories. If friends unexpectedly drop by, you can easily double this recipe to serve four.

SPAGHETTI WITH SHRIMP, FENNEL, TOMATOES & OLIVES

serves 2

Salt and freshly ground black pepper

1½ Tbsp olive oil

½ tsp fennel seeds

1 large fennel bulb, cored and thinly sliced lengthwise, fronds chopped and reserved

1 yellow onion, halved and thinly sliced

Red pepper flakes

1 can (28 oz/875 g) Italian tomatoes, preferably San Marzano

¼ cup (1 oz/30 g) pitted Kalamata olives, quartered lengthwise

3 Tbsp dry white wine

7–8 oz (220–250 g) spaghetti, preferably multigrain

½ lb (250 g) shrimp, peeled and deveined

Bring a large pot three-fourths full of salted water to a boil.

Meanwhile, in a large frying pan over medium-high heat, warm the oil. Add the fennel seeds and stir until fragrant, about 10 seconds. Add the fennel bulb, onion, and a large pinch of red pepper flakes. Season with salt and black pepper. Sauté, stirring frequently, until the fennel and onion are tender and browning on the edges, about 10 minutes. Add the tomatoes with their juices, the olives, and wine. Simmer, breaking up the tomatoes with a wooden spoon, until the sauce thickens, about 5 minutes.

While the tomatoes are simmering, add the pasta to the boiling water, stir well, and cook until al dente, about 11 minutes.

After the tomatoes have simmered for 5 minutes, add the shrimp to the frying pan and simmer until they are just opaque at the center, about 3 minutes; do not overcook.

Drain the pasta, add to the sauce, and stir to coat the pasta. Taste and adjust the seasonings. Transfer to a large warmed bowl, sprinkle with the fennel fronds, and serve.

26

If you cannot find blood oranges, the juice of regular oranges can be substituted. Blood orange juice is typically more tart than the juice of other varieties, so reduce the amount of sugar in the filling to ⅔ cup (5 oz/155 g). To make the whipped cream, in a bowl, using an electric mixer fitted with the whisk attachment, whip 1 cup (8 fl oz/250 ml) heavy cream, 2 Tbsp sugar and ½ tsp pure vanilla extract on medium speed until medium peaks form. Use right away or cover with plastic wrap and refrigerate until ready to use, up to 4 hours. Whisk the cream briefly before using.

BLOOD ORANGE TARTLETS

serves 6

Cream Cheese Tartlet Dough (page 29)

2 large whole eggs, plus 3 large egg yolks

½ cup (4 fl oz/125 ml) fresh blood orange juice, strained

2 Tbsp fresh lemon juice, strained

¾ cup (6 oz/185 g) sugar

½ cup (4 oz/125 g) unsalted butter, cut into pieces

2 tsp grated blood orange zest, plus more for garnish (optional)

Whipped cream (*left*)

Cut the dough into 6 equal portions, and place one portion in each of six 4-inch (10-cm) tartlet pans. Press the dough evenly over the bottom and up the sides of each pan until it is even with the rim. Trim any overhang. Freeze until the dough is firm, about 30 minutes.

Preheat the oven to 400°F (200°C). Line the tartlets with foil and fill with pie weights. Place on a baking sheet and bake until the crusts start to look dry, about 15 minutes. Remove the weights and foil. Reduce the oven temperature to 350°F (180°C) and continue to bake until the crusts are lightly browned, about 5 minutes. Let cool on the sheet.

Reduce the oven temperature to 325°F (165°C). In the top of a double boiler over (not touching) barely simmering water, whisk together the whole eggs, egg yolks, orange juice, lemon juice, and sugar. Whisk constantly until the mixture is thick enough to coat the back of a spoon and registers 160°F (71°C) on an instant-read thermometer, about 12 minutes. Remove from over the water and pour through a medium-mesh sieve into a bowl. Add the butter and orange zest and stir until the butter melts and is incorporated. Let stand for 10 minutes, then spoon into the cooled tartlet shells.

Bake the tartlets until the centers are set, 12–15 minutes. Let the tartlets cool on the sheet on a wire rack for 20 minutes. Cover and refrigerate for at least 3 hours or up to overnight. The filling will thicken further.

To serve, unmold each tartlet and top with a dollop of whipped cream and a sprinkle of zest, if you like.

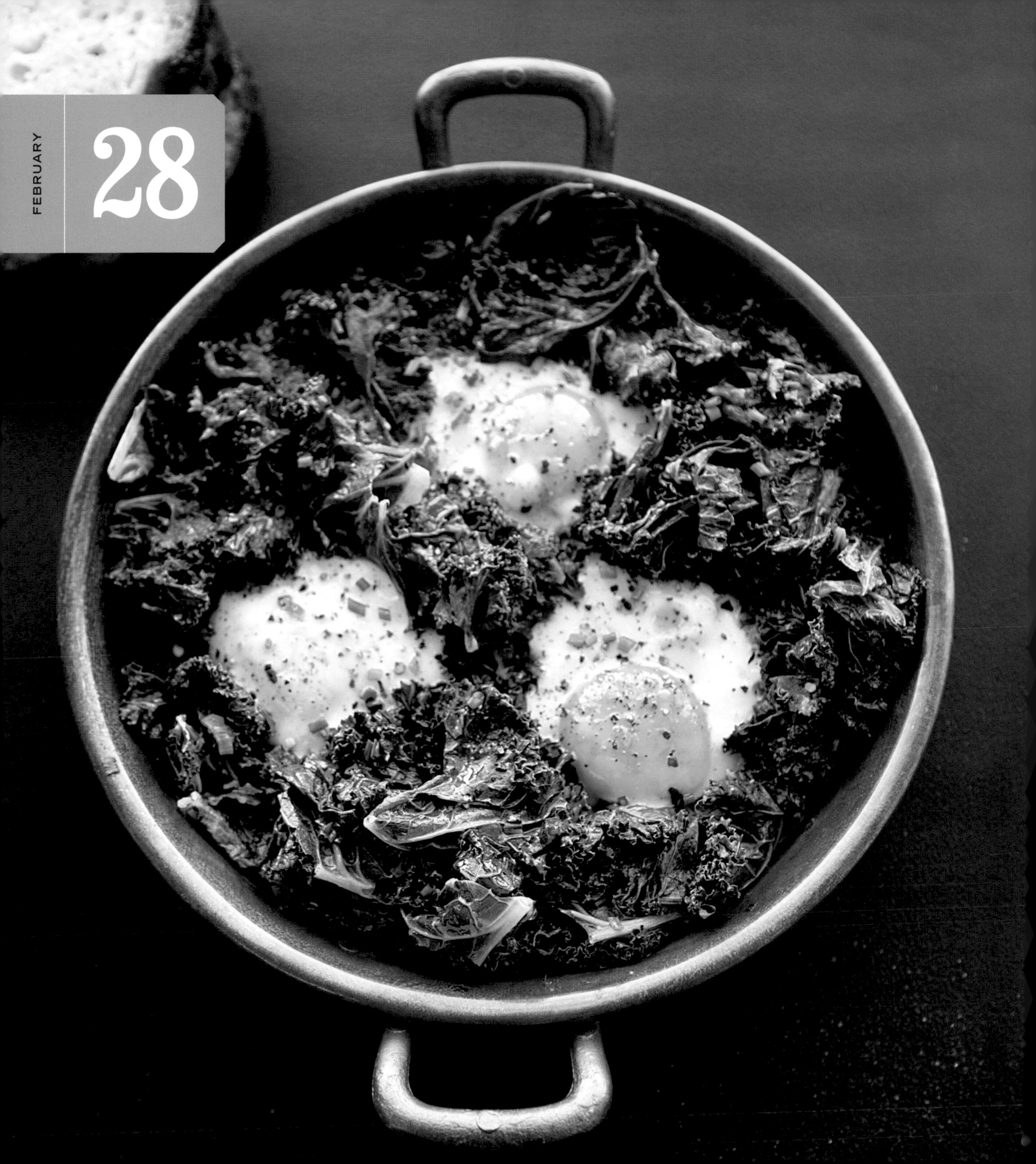
FEBRUARY
28

27

Tamari, a rich, dark, less salty, and sometimes wheat-free Japanese soy sauce, imparts a hint of smokiness to the grilled pork belly. This dish goes together quickly, with the pork belly on the grill for only about 10 minutes and the greens for even less time. To save time, ask the butcher to remove the skin from the pork belly for you.

SALAD OF ASIAN GREENS WITH TAMARI-GLAZED PORK BELLY

serves 6

¼ cup (2 fl oz/60 ml) tamari

½ tsp toasted sesame oil

1 Tbsp honey

2 lb (1 kg) pork belly, skin removed

3 heads small bok choy

¼–⅓ small head green cabbage, shredded

2 celery ribs, minced

Sliced green onion tops for garnish (optional)

FOR THE DRESSING

2 tsp tamari

1 tsp toasted sesame oil

1 tsp honey

1 tsp sherry vinegar

In a small bowl, whisk together the tamari, oil, and honey to make a marinade. Pour into a shallow baking dish, add the pork belly, and turn several times to coat. Cover and refrigerate for 3–4 hours, turning and basting occasionally with the marinade.

Cut off the dark green tops from 2 heads of the bok choy, roll the tops together into a cylinder, and thinly slice crosswise. Transfer to a large bowl. Finely chop the white part and add to the bowl along with the cabbage and celery. Set aside. Cut the other head in half lengthwise and set aside.

To make the dressing, in a small bowl, whisk together the tamari, oil, honey, and vinegar until well blended. Set aside.

Prepare a charcoal or gas grill for direct-heat cooking over medium-high heat. Alternatively, preheat a stove-top grill pan over medium-high heat. Place the bok choy halves on the grill rack or in the grill pan and cook, turning several times, until lightly charred, about 4 minutes. Transfer to a cutting board.

Remove the pork belly from the marinade, reserving the marinade. Place the pork belly on the grill rack or in the pan and cook, turning often and basting occasionally with the reserved marinade, until pork is firm to the touch and is a dark mahogany color, ⟶

about 10 minutes. Transfer to a cutting board and let rest for 5 minutes, then cut crosswise into slices ¼ inch (6 mm) thick.

Chop the grilled bok choy and add to the bowl with the other vegetables. Drizzle with the dressing and toss gently to coat. Mound the salad onto individual plates and arrange the pork belly on top. Sprinkle with green onion, if desired. Serve right away.

28

This easy, rustic dish is both healthy and hearty. Winter kale is first braised with garlic, green onions, and lemon juice. Protein-rich eggs are then nestled in the bed of kale, where they cook gently until nearly done. A finishing garnish of red pepper flakes adds the perfect amount of spice.

SPICY SIMMERED EGGS WITH KALE

serves 4

2 Tbsp unsalted butter

4 green onions, white and light green parts only, chopped

2 cloves garlic, minced

2 bunches kale, tough stems removed, roughly chopped

1 cup (8 fl oz/250 ml) chicken or vegetable broth

Salt and freshly ground black pepper

Grated zest and juice of 1 lemon

4 eggs

Red pepper flakes

In a large skillet over medium-high heat, melt the butter. Add the green onions and garlic and cook, stirring, until fragrant, about 1 minute. Add half of the kale and sauté, stirring frequently until it begins to wilt, about 2 minutes. Stir in the remaining kale and repeat. Add the chicken broth, ½ tsp salt, and ¼ tsp black pepper. Stir in the lemon zest and juice. Let simmer, stirring occasionally, until the kale softens, about 6 minutes.

Using the back of a spoon, create a pocket for each egg in the kale. Crack one egg into each pocket. Reduce the heat to medium-low, and sprinkle the eggs with salt and black pepper. Cover the pan and let the eggs cook until almost opaque, 4–5 minutes. Turn off the heat and let the eggs rest, covered, until done to taste. Sprinkle with red pepper flakes and serve.

With spring arriving midmonth, bright green vegetables begin to show up in markets, taking their place alongside the last of winter's leafy greens. Sugar snap and English peas, fava beans and leaves, asparagus, and artichokes all become players in this month's salads, curries, stir-fries, and sautés. Warm spring rains signal the beginning of mushroom season, with savvy cooks fashioning morel-and-leek-stuffed ravioli or pairing morels and chanterelles with their domestic kin in a big, garlicky sauté. Rhubarb and lavender are appearing now, too, in a fruit crisp and in buttery shortbread cookies.

1
STIR-FRIED PORK & SUGAR SNAPS
WITH SOBA NOODLES
page 59

2
RED QUINOA WITH ASPARAGUS,
PORTOBELLOS & FETA
page 59

3
DARK CHOCOLATE PUDDING
page 60

8
SALMON WITH SPRING VEGETABLES
page 63

9
CHICKPEA & ROASTED TOMATO SOUP
WITH FRIED ROSEMARY
page 65

10
MUSHROOMS WITH GARLIC BUTTER
& PINE NUTS
page 65

15
BAKED COD WITH LEEKS,
MORELS & BACON
page 68

16
BEEF-CHIPOTLE CHILI
page 68

17
FAVA GREENS WITH CHICKEN,
PECANS & KUMQUATS
page 70

22
TANDOORI-STYLE CHICKEN
page 73

23
CORNED BEEF & CABBAGE
page 73

24
ARTICHOKES WITH WARM
CANNELLINI BEAN SALAD
page 74

29
BLACK BEAN–JALAPEÑO BURGERS
WITH AVOCADO MASH
page 77

30
CHICKEN BREASTS WITH FAVA BEANS
page 79

31
GINGERED RHUBARB CRISP
page 79

4
FALAFEL BURGERS WITH
LEMON-TAHINI SAUCE
page 60

5
MOREL & LEEK RAVIOLI
WITH ENGLISH PEA PURÉE
page 62

6
LEMON CRÈME MILKSHAKES
page 62

7
SOBA NOODLE SALAD WITH SUGAR
SNAP PEAS & SOY-PEANUT DRESSING
page 63

11
GARLICKY SHRIMP & CHARD SAUTÉ
page 66

12
LAVENDER SHORTBREAD
page 66

13
LEEK, PANCETTA & GRUYÈRE TART
page 67

14
THAI GREEN CHICKEN CURRY
WITH ASPARAGUS
page 67

18
MISO SOUP WITH SHRIMP & PEA SHOOTS
page 70

19
FOUR SEASONS PIZZA WITH
MUSHROOMS, BELL PEPPERS,
ARTICHOKES & OLIVES
page 70

20
SPICY BRAISED TOFU WITH PORK
page 71

21
BANANA-HONEY CAKE
page 71

25
CHICKEN & WILD RICE SOUP
WITH GINGER
page 74

26
LEEK & YUKON GOLD POTATO SOUP
WITH FRIED PROSCIUTTO
page 76

27
SALAD OF NEW POTATOES,
SPRING PEAS & MINT
page 76

28
THREE-ONION SOUP WITH
CAMBOZOLA GRILLED CHEESE
page 77

march

MARCH

1

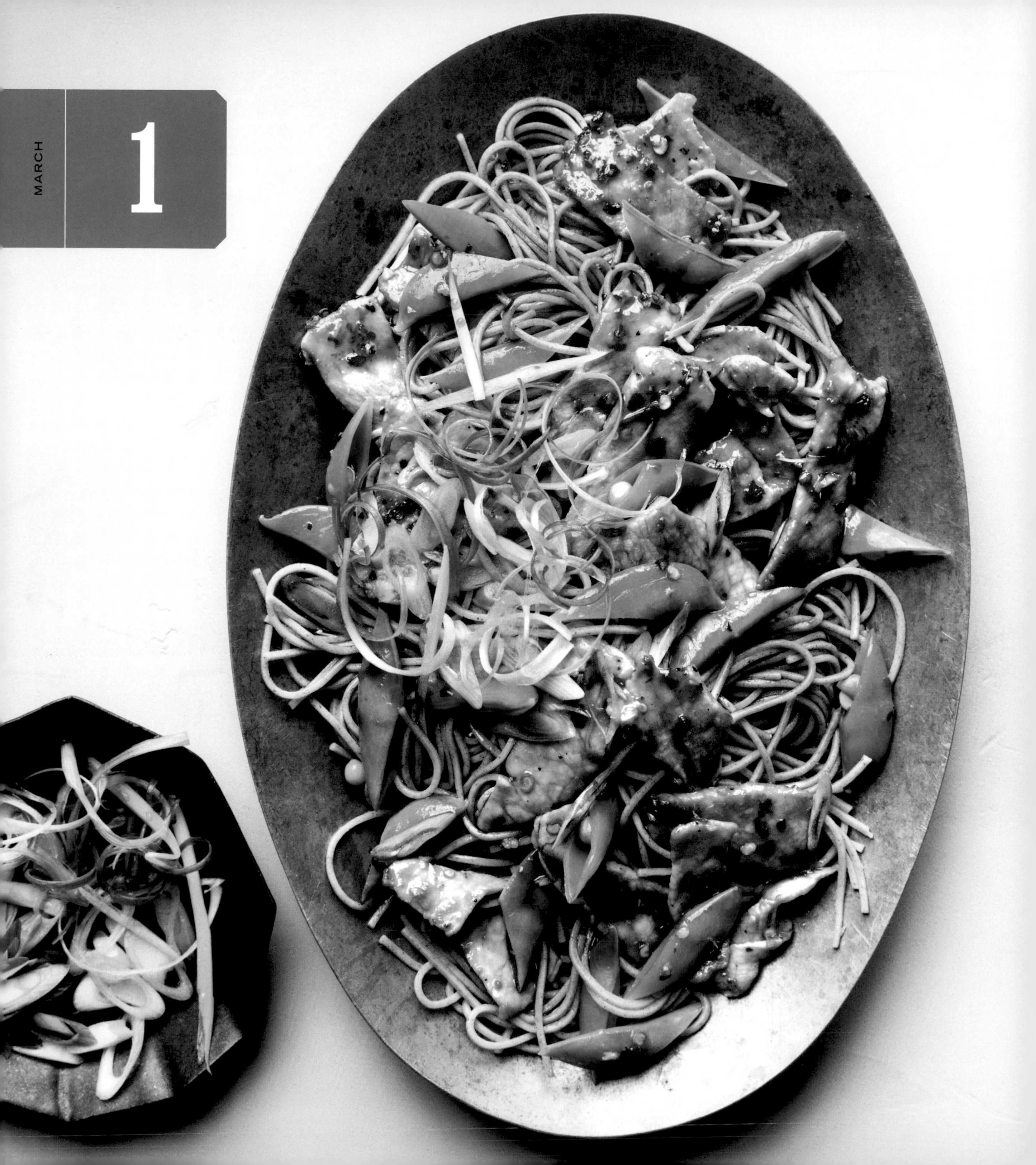

1

STIR-FRIED PORK & SUGAR SNAPS WITH SOBA NOODLES

serves 2

Crunchy sugar snap peas, young green onions, and just a small amount of pork are the basis for this novel dish made with Japanese buckwheat noodles and bold Asian flavors. If you're eating gluten-free, check the label of the soba noodles to make sure they do not contain wheat.

4 Tbsp (2 fl oz/60 ml) low-sodium soy sauce

1½ tsp cornstarch

1½ tsp toasted sesame oil, plus 1 Tbsp

½ lb (250 g) boneless center-cut pork chops, cut across the grain into thin strips

Freshly ground black pepper

2 Tbsp rice wine vinegar

1½ tsp sugar

½ lb (250 g) sugar snap peas, trimmed and halved on the diagonal

6 oz (185 g) soba noodles

1 bunch green onions, thinly sliced

1 Tbsp peanut oil

1 Tbsp minced peeled fresh ginger

¼ tsp red pepper flakes

In a bowl, combine 2 Tbsp of the soy sauce with the cornstarch and stir to dissolve. Mix in the 1½ tsp sesame oil. Add the pork and a generous amount of pepper and stir to coat. Let marinate for 15–30 minutes. Meanwhile, in a small bowl, combine the remaining 2 Tbsp soy sauce and 1 Tbsp sesame oil with the vinegar and sugar, and stir to dissolve.

Bring a large pot of water to a boil. Add the sugar snap peas and cook until just tender-crisp, about 4 minutes. Using a slotted spoon, transfer the peas to a bowl. Add the noodles to the boiling water and cook until just tender, stirring occasionally, about 4 minutes. Drain the noodles and return to the pot along with half the sauce. Stir to coat. Mix in the sugar snap peas and all but 2 Tbsp of the green onions. Cover to keep warm.

In a large nonstick frying pan over medium-high heat, warm the peanut oil. Add the ginger and pepper flakes and stir until fragrant, about 5 seconds. Add the pork with the marinade and separate the pieces. Stir constantly until the pork is just cooked through, 2–3 minutes. Add the remaining sauce and stir until the sauce thickens, about 30 seconds. Immediately add the pork and sauce to the noodles, and then toss to coat. Divide the noodles between 2 warmed plates. Sprinkle with the remaining green onions and serve.

2

RED QUINOA WITH ASPARAGUS, PORTOBELLOS & FETA

serves 4

Nutty quinoa, tangy feta, hearty portobello mushrooms, and earthy asparagus make this a delicious meatless dinner option. It also works well as a side dish to accompany rotisserie chicken or leftover roasted pork, or it can be chilled and served as part of a spring lunch buffet. Accompany with warm garlic bread and a crisp Sauvignon Blanc.

1 cup (5 oz/155 g) red quinoa

2½ cups (20 fl oz/625 ml) chicken or vegetable broth

⅓ cup (1½ oz/45 g) dried currants

¼ cup (2 fl oz/60 ml) olive oil, plus more for drizzling

3 cloves garlic, minced

2 portobello mushrooms, sliced

1 small red onion, halved and sliced

Salt and freshly ground pepper

1 Tbsp balsamic vinegar

1 lb (500 g) asparagus, trimmed and cut into pieces

⅓ cup (½ oz/15 g) chopped fresh flat-leaf parsley

Grated zest of 1 lemon

4 oz (125 g) feta cheese, crumbled

In a saucepan, bring the quinoa and 2 cups (16 fl oz/250 ml) of the broth to a boil over medium-high heat. Add the currants, reduce the heat to a simmer, cover, and cook until the liquid is absorbed, about 15 minutes. Remove from the heat, but keep covered to stay warm.

In a large frying pan, heat the ¼ cup oil over medium-high heat. Add the garlic, mushrooms, and onion and season with salt and pepper. Sauté until the vegetables soften and begin to brown, 4–6 minutes. Stir in the vinegar and cook until absorbed, about 2 minutes. Add the asparagus and toss to coat with the oil. Add the remaining ½ cup (4 fl oz/125 ml) broth and cook, stirring occasionally, until the asparagus is fork-tender, about 4 minutes. Stir in the quinoa, parsley, lemon zest, and half of the feta. Remove from the heat and season with salt and pepper. Garnish with the remaining feta, drizzle with olive oil, and serve.

3

DARK CHOCOLATE PUDDING

serves 6

2 cups (16 fl oz/500 ml) whole milk

6 large egg yolks

¾ cup (6 oz/185 g) sugar

3 Tbsp all-purpose flour

2 Tbsp unsweetened natural cocoa powder

6 oz (185 g) semisweet chocolate, finely chopped

2 oz (60 g) unsweetened chocolate, finely chopped

1 tsp pure vanilla extract

Whipped cream (see page 53; optional)

This bittersweet chocolate pudding is easy to adapt. You can turn it into a parfait with layers of whipped cream and fresh raspberries, or you can stir in a little rum, Amaretto, or Frangelico, then garnish each serving with crushed chocolate wafer cookies or shaved semisweet chocolate.

In a saucepan, warm the milk over medium heat until small bubbles appear along the edge of the pan. Remove from the heat.

In a bowl, whisk together the egg yolks and sugar until smooth. Sift the flour and cocoa powder over the yolk mixture and whisk until smooth. Whisking constantly, slowly pour in the hot milk. Pour the mixture into the pan and cook over medium heat, stirring constantly, until it comes to a boil and thickens, about 4 minutes. Reduce the heat to low and cook, stirring constantly, for 1 minute.

Pour the pudding through a fine-mesh sieve into a bowl. Add the chocolates and stir until melted. Stir in the vanilla. Spoon into serving cups. Refrigerate until chilled, about 2 hours. Serve with whipped cream, if you like.

4

FALAFEL BURGERS WITH LEMON-TAHINI SAUCE

serves 8

FOR THE LEMON-TAHINI SAUCE

⅓ cup (3 oz/90 g) tahini

¼ cup (2 fl oz/60 ml) fresh lemon juice

3 Tbsp plain yogurt

1 clove garlic

Salt and freshly ground pepper

FOR THE FALAFEL BURGERS

2 cans (14 oz/440 g each) chickpeas, drained and rinsed

½ red onion, chopped

2 Tbsp fresh flat-leaf parsley leaves

5 fresh mint leaves

2 cloves garlic

Grated zest and juice of 1 lemon

1 Tbsp ground cumin

2 tsp ground coriander

1 tsp paprika

1 tsp salt

½ tsp freshly ground pepper

1 egg, lightly beaten

½ cup (¾ oz/20 g) whole-wheat panko bread crumbs

Nonstick cooking spray

4 whole-wheat pita breads, toasted, cut in half, and split to form pockets

Thinly sliced red onion, sliced Roma tomatoes, and romaine lettuce, for serving

Falafel is traditionally deep-fried, but here the burgers are cooked on a stove-top grill pan, for a healthier dish. Made from toasted sesame seeds, tahini naturally separates on standing, so be sure to stir together the oil and paste until fully blended before measuring it for the sauce. For a gluten-free dish, serve the patties on a salad of romaine lettuce, tomatoes, olives, and cucumbers and drizzle the lemon-tahini sauce over the top.

To make the sauce, in a blender, combine the tahini, lemon juice, yogurt, and garlic andpurée until smooth. Season with salt and pepper.

To make the burgers, in a food processor, combine the chickpeas, onion, parsley, mint, garlic, lemon zest and juice, cumin, coriander, paprika, salt, and pepper. Process until smooth and transfer to a large bowl. Add the egg and bread crumbs and stir to combine. Form into 8 patties.

Warm a stove-top grill pan over medium-high heat and coat with cooking spray. Cook the burgers, carefully turning once, until golden-brown, about 4 minutes per side.

To serve, put each burger in a pita pocket, top with a generous helping of sauce, and fill with red onion, tomato slices, and lettuce.

MOREL & LEEK RAVIOLI WITH ENGLISH PEA PURÉE

serves 6

2 Tbsp extra-virgin olive oil

2 Tbsp unsalted butter

½ cup (1½ oz/45 g) thinly sliced leeks

Salt and freshly ground pepper

1 lb (500 g) fresh morel mushrooms

1 tsp minced fresh thyme

1 cup (8 oz/250 g) fresh ricotta cheese

½ cup (2 oz/60 g) freshly grated pecorino romano cheese

12 oz (375 g) fresh pasta sheets, 10 by 5 inches (23 by 13 cm)

All-purpose flour, for dusting

2 lb (1 kg) fresh English peas, shelled

1 cup (8 fl oz/250 ml) low-sodium chicken broth

2 tsp fresh lemon juice

¼ cup (2 oz/60 g) minced fresh chives

In this celebration of spring's bounty, earthy morels and oniony leeks are enclosed in delicate pasta pillows and served on a bed of bright green pea purée. Accompany the ravioli with a simple green salad and pour a Rioja from Spain or a Gewürztraminer from the Alsace.

Warm a sauté pan over medium heat. Add 1 Tbsp of the oil and 1 Tbsp of the butter. When the butter melts, add the leeks and a pinch each of salt and pepper. Sauté until translucent, 4–5 minutes. Coarsely chop half of the morels and add them to the pan with another pinch of salt. Sauté until the mushrooms have softened, 3–4 minutes. Add the thyme and sauté for 1 minute. Transfer the mixture to a bowl. When it is slightly cool, stir in the ricotta and half of the pecorino. Season with salt and pepper.

Lay a pasta sheet horizontally on a work surface. Place tablespoonfuls of the filling along the bottom half of the dough, spaced 1½ inches (4 cm) apart and leaving a border of about ½ inch (12 mm) around the edge. Lightly moisten the edges of the dough with water. Fold the top half of the dough over the filled half, pressing down between the mounds of filling to seal the dough and remove any air pockets. Using a fluted cutter or sharp knife, cut the filled pasta into squares and place them on a lightly floured baking sheet. Repeat with the remaining pasta sheets and filling.

Bring a large pot of generously salted water to a boil over high heat and prepare a bowl of ice water. ⟶

When the water comes to a boil, add the peas and cook until tender, 5–6 minutes. Remove the peas with a strainer or slotted spoon and immediately plunge them into the ice water. When the peas are cool, drain and transfer 1 cup to a food processor. Return the water to a boil.

Add the broth, lemon juice, half of the chives and a pinch of salt and pepper to the food processor and purée the mixture until smooth.

Place the sauté pan back over medium heat and add the remaining oil and butter. Sauté the remaining whole morels with salt and pepper, stirring, until lightly browned and tender, 4–5 minutes. Add the pea purée and remaining peas and reduce the heat to low.

When water comes back to a boil, add half of the ravioli and reduce the heat to medium. Cook just until the ravioli float to the top of the water, 2–3 minutes. Remove the ravioli with a slotted spoon and add them to the pan with the pea purée. If needed, add some of the pasta cooking water to the pea purée to loosen the sauce. The sauce should cling nicely to the ravioli without being too thick. Repeat with the remaining ravioli.

Transfer the ravioli and sauce to a warm serving dish and top with the remaining pecorino and chives.

LEMON CRÈME MILKSHAKES

serves 4

1 pt (16 fl oz/500 ml) lemon sorbet

1 pt (16 fl oz/500 ml) vanilla ice cream

⅓ cup (3 fl oz/80 ml) whole milk, plus more if needed

Whipped cream (see page 53)

You won't find these elegant shakes at the local drive-through. For an after-dinner refresher, add a splash of limoncello.

Place the sorbet, ice cream, and ⅓ cup milk in a blender. Blend until smooth, adding more milk if necessary. Pour into 4 chilled tall glasses and garnish each shake with a dollop of whipped cream.

7

SOBA NOODLE SALAD WITH SUGAR SNAP PEAS & SOY-PEANUT DRESSING

serves 4

Pairing the dense, rich character of Japanese soba with finely cut spring vegetables and chopped fresh herbs creates a satisfying balance of textures and flavors. The creamy peanut dressing, which carries a hint of salt, spice, and tartness, binds all of the elements together in a filling main dish.

1 lb (500 g) dried soba noodles or whole-wheat spaghetti

1 cup (⅓ lb/155 g) sugar snap peas, trimmed and cut in half on the diagonal

3 or 4 small carrots, peeled and julienned

½ cup (⅔ oz/20 g) chopped fresh cilantro leaves

½ cup (⅔ oz/20 g) chopped fresh mint leaves

FOR THE SOY-PEANUT DRESSING

1 tsp canola or peanut oil

1-inch (2.5-cm) piece fresh ginger, peeled and minced

2 cloves garlic, minced

1 Tbsp soy sauce

4 tsp rice vinegar

½ tsp red pepper flakes

⅓ cup (3 oz/90 g) chunky peanut butter

½ cup (4 fl oz/125 ml) chicken or vegetable broth

Salt

In a large pot of boiling water, cook the noodles until tender, according to package directions. Two minutes before the noodles are ready, add the snap peas and carrots. After 2 minutes, drain the noodles and vegetables and place in a large bowl along with the cilantro and mint.

To make the dressing, in a saucepan, heat the oil over medium-high heat. Add the ginger and garlic and stir. Add the soy sauce, vinegar, red pepper flakes, peanut butter, broth, and salt to taste. Stir until the mixture is smooth, then reduce the heat to low and simmer until thick, 5–7 minutes.

Pour the dressing over the noodles, vegetables, and herbs and gently turn to coat well. Let cool to room temperature before serving.

8

SALMON WITH SPRING VEGETABLES

serves 4

Here, a trio of spring vegetables— leeks, asparagus, and peas—are sautéed in butter and oil just until tender and then served alongside moist braised salmon, adding both color and garden-fresh flavor to the plate. If leeks are unavailable, substitute 6–8 green onions. Serve with steamed new potatoes, if desired.

1 cup (8 fl oz/250 ml) dry white wine

½ cup (4 fl oz/125 ml) vegetable broth

½ small yellow onion, sliced

3 sprigs fresh tarragon

Salt and freshly ground pepper

4 salmon fillets, about 6 oz (185 g) each

1 lb (500 g) asparagus, trimmed and cut into 2-inch (5-cm) pieces

1 Tbsp unsalted butter

1 Tbsp olive oil

2 leeks, white and pale green parts, cut into 2-inch (5-cm) matchsticks

2 cups (10 oz/315 g) fresh or thawed frozen peas

Grated zest and juice of ½ lemon

Minced fresh chives for garnish

In a slow cooker, combine the wine, broth, onion, and tarragon. Stir in ½ cup (4 fl oz/125 ml) water, ½ tsp salt, and several grindings of pepper. Cover and cook on the low setting for 30 minutes. Add the salmon, re-cover, and cook for 1 hour. The fish should be opaque throughout, firm, and very tender.

About 15 minutes before the fish is ready, bring a saucepan of salted water to a boil. Add the asparagus and cook until just tender, about 6 minutes. Drain and refresh with cold water, and drain again.

In a large frying pan, melt the butter with the oil over medium heat. Add the leeks and sauté for 2 minutes. Add the peas and cook for 1 minute, then add the asparagus and sauté until heated through, 1–2 minutes. Stir in the lemon juice and remove from the heat.

Transfer the salmon to a platter. Use the braising liquid to moisten the fish, if desired. Arrange the vegetables around the salmon. Sprinkle with the lemon zest and chives, and serve.

MARCH 9

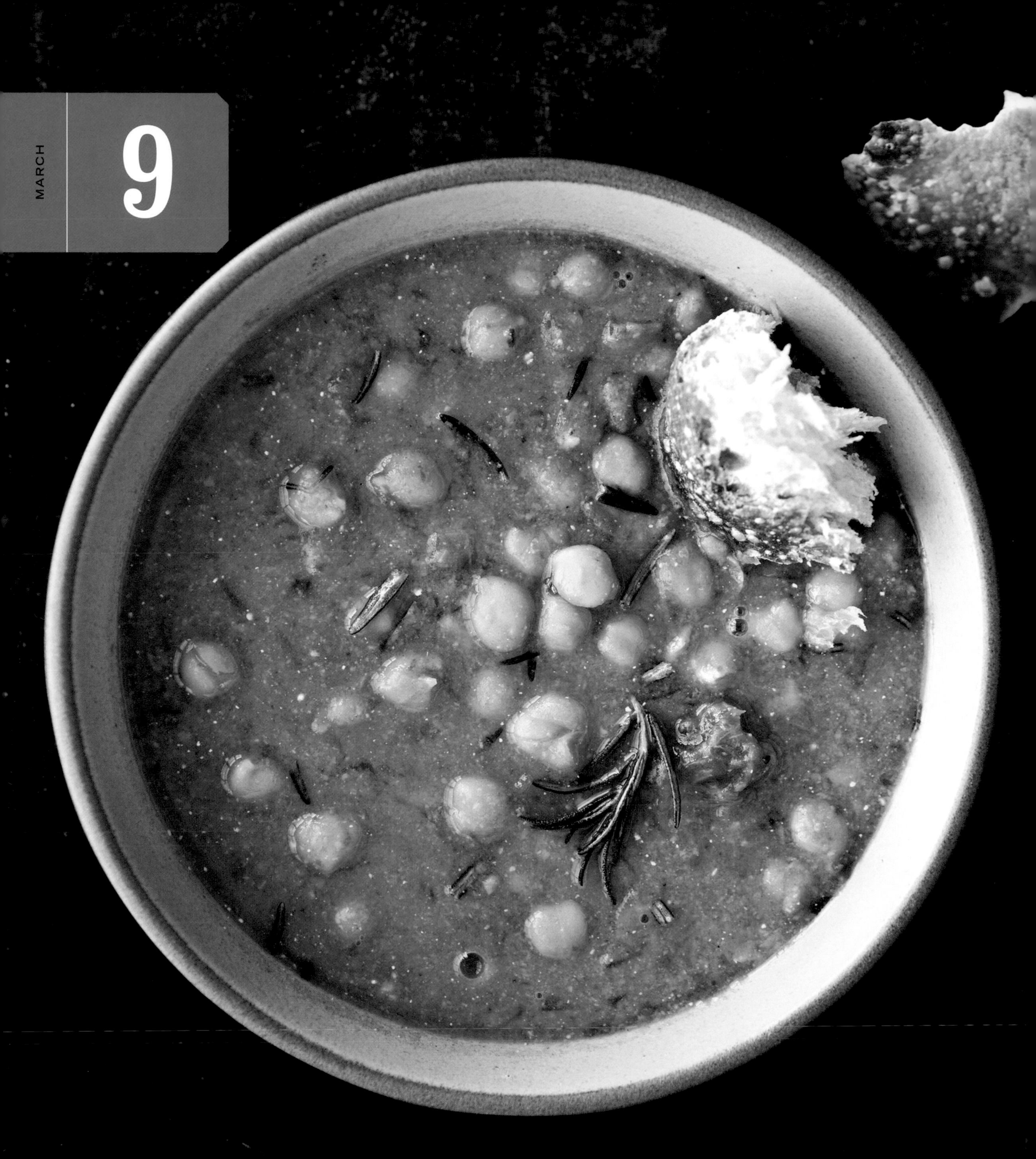

9

CHICKPEA & ROASTED TOMATO SOUP WITH FRIED ROSEMARY

serves 4–6

1 lb (500 g) plum tomatoes

4 Tbsp (2 fl oz/60 ml) olive oil

Salt and freshly ground pepper

1 large yellow onion, chopped

4 cloves garlic, minced

1 tsp ground cumin

½ tsp paprika

1 cinnamon stick

3 cans (15 oz/470 g each) chickpeas, drained

4 cups (32 fl oz/1 l) chicken broth

1 Tbsp sour cream

Fried rosemary for garnish (*left*)

To make the fried rosemary, in a small frying pan, warm 2 Tbsp olive oil over high heat. Add 4 sprigs rosemary, 2 at a time, and fry for 1 minute on each side, then transfer to paper towels to drain. Once the sprigs are cool enough to handle, remove the leaves and chop or leave whole, as desired.

Preheat the oven to 450°F (230°C). Slice the tomatoes in half and place in a single layer on a baking sheet. Drizzle with 2 Tbsp of the oil and season with salt and pepper. Roast the tomatoes until they are soft and caramelized, 25–30 minutes. Set aside.

In a large, heavy pot, warm the remaining 2 Tbsp oil over medium-high heat. Add the onion and the garlic and sauté until soft, about 5 minutes. Add the cumin, paprika, and cinnamon stick and toast the spices, stirring often, for 2 minutes. Add the chickpeas, roasted tomatoes, and broth, stir to combine, and bring to a boil. Reduce the heat to low and simmer until the chickpeas are very tender, about 20 minutes. Remove from the heat and let cool slightly.

Transfer about two-thirds of the chickpeas and broth to a blender and purée. Return to the pot and stir in the sour cream.

Season the soup with salt and pepper and serve, garnished with fried rosemary.

10

MUSHROOMS WITH GARLIC BUTTER & PINE NUTS

serves 4

1 lb (500 g) mixed mushrooms such as morel, portobello, shiitake, oyster, cremini, and white button, stems trimmed

4 Tbsp (2 oz/60 g) unsalted butter, at room temperature

3 cloves garlic, chopped

Salt and freshly ground pepper

2 Tbsp dry white wine

⅓ cup (2 oz/60 g) pine nuts or slivered blanched almonds

1–2 Tbsp chopped fresh chives or flat-leaf parsley

March showers bring wild mushrooms. Explore the season's offerings with a mix of flavors and textures. Oyster, shiitake, portobello, and cremini can all be readily found at the grocery store, but also look for chanterelles, porcini, matsutakes, black trumpets, and musky-flavored morels, all of them favorites of foragers.

Preheat the oven to 450°F (230°C). Cut the larger mushrooms into pieces so that all the mushrooms, whole and cut, are about the same size. Arrange the mushrooms in a single layer in a large roasting pan.

In a bowl, mix together the butter and garlic. Season with salt and pepper. Dot the mushrooms with the butter mixture. Sprinkle the wine over the mushrooms.

Roast the mushrooms until they begin to sizzle and brown, about 15 minutes. Remove from the oven, sprinkle with the pine nuts, and continue roasting until the mushrooms are cooked through and browned in places, about 10 minutes. The total roasting time depends on the types of mushrooms; certain varieties will take longer than others to cook. Adjust the seasoning if necessary.

Transfer the mushrooms to a bowl, sprinkle with the chives, and serve.

11

Chard and shrimp are both complemented by acidic ingredients. In this recipe, the usual lemon juice has been swapped out for the zest and juice of an orange. The orange juice is used to deglaze the pan after sautéing the shrimp, which results in a sweet and savory sauce that is poured over the finished dish.

GARLICKY SHRIMP & CHARD SAUTÉ

serves 4

1 lb (500 g) large shrimp, peeled and deveined

Salt

3 Tbsp extra-virgin olive oil

2 bunches chard, thick ribs removed, chopped

2 Tbsp chopped garlic

½ tsp red pepper flakes

Grated zest and juice of 1 orange

1 bay leaf

2 Tbsp minced fresh flat-leaf parsley

Place the shrimp in a bowl, add 1 tsp salt, and toss to coat. Refrigerate for 15 minutes.

In a frying pan over high heat, heat half of the oil. Add the chard, 1 Tbsp of the garlic, ¼ tsp of the red pepper flakes, and ¼ tsp salt. Sauté until the chard is wilted and tender, about 3 minutes. Transfer to a warmed platter and sprinkle with the orange zest. Cover to keep warm.

Add the remaining oil to the pan. When the oil shimmers, add the shrimp, the remaining 1 Tbsp garlic, the remaining ¼ tsp red pepper flakes, and the bay leaf and sauté until the shrimp starts to turn opaque, about 1 minute. Add the orange juice and continue to sauté, stirring to dislodge the browned bits on the bottom of the pan, until the shrimp is opaque throughout, about 1 minute more.

Arrange the shrimp on top of the chard and drizzle the orange sauce over the top. Garnish with the parsley and serve.

12

Purchase fresh lavender flowers from an organic market or dried lavender in jars from a specialty foods store. Set out these buttery, crumbly shortbreads with tea after lunch, or with a scoop of vanilla ice cream after dinner.

LAVENDER SHORTBREAD

makes 12 shortbreads

2 cups (10 oz/315 g) all-purpose flour

½ cup (2 oz/60 g) cornstarch

¼ tsp kosher salt

1 cup (8 oz/250 g) unsalted butter

½ cup (4 oz/125 g) sugar

2 Tbsp finely chopped unsprayed fresh or dried lavender flowers

Preheat the oven to 350°F (180°C). Have ready a 9½-inch (24-cm) round tart pan with a removable bottom.

Sift the flour, cornstarch, and salt together into a bowl. In a large bowl, using an electric mixer, beat the butter and sugar on medium speed until smooth and creamy, about 4 minutes. Add the lavender and beat well to combine. Slowly add the dry ingredients and beat on low speed just until the dough forms large clumps and pulls away from the sides of the bowl.

Press the dough evenly into the tart pan with a rubber spatula, then smooth the top. Using a fork, prick the entire surface of the dough, making ¼-inch- (6-mm-) deep holes at ½-inch (12-mm) intervals. Place the pan on a baking sheet and bake until the center is very lightly golden, 45–50 minutes.

Using a sharp knife, cut the warm shortbread into 12 wedges, then let cool in the pan. Remove the pan sides and store the shortbread in an airtight container at room temperature for up to 5 days.

13

LEEK, PANCETTA & GRUYÈRE TART

serves 4–8

2 Tbsp olive oil

2 leeks, white and pale green parts, sliced into rounds

2 slices pancetta, coarsely chopped

1 sheet frozen puff pastry, about ½ lb (250 g), thawed

½ cup (2 oz/60 g) shredded Gruyère cheese

Easy, quick, and delicious, this tart goes together with just a handful of ingredients. It makes a wonderful first course, or cut into smaller pieces, an irresistible hors d'oeuvre. Comté, Emmentaler, or fontina can be substituted for the Gruyère. Look for all-butter puff pastry for the best flavor.

In a sauté pan, warm 1 Tbsp of the oil over medium heat. Add the leeks and sauté until softened, about 2 minutes. Transfer to a plate and set aside. In the same pan, warm the remaining 1 Tbsp oil over medium heat. Add the pancetta and cook, stirring occasionally, until browned, about 5 minutes. Using a slotted spoon, transfer to paper towels to drain and set aside.

Preheat the oven to 400°F (200°C). On a lightly floured work surface, roll out the pastry sheet into a 9-by-13-inch (23-by-33-cm) rectangle about ⅛ inch (3 mm) thick. Cut in half lengthwise to form 2 rectangles. Transfer the 2 rectangles to a rimmed baking sheet. Using a fork, prick each rectangle evenly over its entire surface. Fold in ½ inch (12 mm) along all 4 sides of each rectangle to create a border.

Arrange the leeks evenly on top of the pastry rectangles, and then sprinkle evenly with the Gruyère and pancetta. Bake until puffed and golden brown, about 20 minutes. Remove from oven, cut each tart into 4 pieces, and serve.

14

THAI GREEN CHICKEN CURRY WITH ASPARAGUS

serves 4–6

Salt

1½ lb (750 g) asparagus, trimmed and cut into 2-inch (5-cm) pieces

4 skinless, boneless chicken breast halves

2 Tbsp peanut or grapeseed oil

1 yellow onion, cut into 8 wedges

1 small red bell pepper, seeded and cut into matchsticks

½-inch (12-mm) piece fresh ginger, peeled and minced

2 cloves garlic, minced

1 can (13½ fl oz/420 ml) unsweetened coconut milk (unshaken)

3 Tbsp Thai green curry paste

1 cup (8 fl oz/250 ml) chicken broth

2 Tbsp Asian fish sauce

½ cup (¾ oz/20 g) small Thai basil leaves

1 lime, cut into wedges

Thai green curry paste has a bold, concentrated taste and a healthy heat level. Tempered by rich, creamy coconut milk, it makes a fragrant sauce for simmering chicken with springtime's early asparagus and aromatic Thai basil.

Bring a saucepan of salted water to a boil. Add the asparagus and cook just until tender-crisp, about 2 minutes. Drain and refresh with cold water, and drain again. Cut the chicken across the grain on a slight diagonal into slices about ½ inch (12 mm) thick. Season with salt.

In a large frying pan, heat the oil over medium-high heat. Add the onion and bell pepper and sauté until beginning to soften, about 3 minutes. Stir in the ginger and garlic and sauté until fragrant, about 30 seconds. Transfer to a plate.

Open the can of coconut milk (do not shake it) and scoop out 3 Tbsp of the thick cream on the top. Return the pan to medium-high heat. Add the coconut cream and curry paste and stir well. Whisk in the remaining coconut milk, the broth, and the fish sauce. Return the vegetable mixture to the pan, stir in the chicken, and bring to a boil. Reduce the heat to medium-low and simmer, stirring occasionally, until the sauce has reduced slightly and the vegetables are tender-crisp, about 5 minutes. Stir in the asparagus and cook until the chicken is opaque throughout, about 3 minutes. Adjust the seasoning and serve, garnished with the basil and lime wedges.

15

BAKED COD WITH LEEKS, MORELS & BACON

serves 4

¾ oz (20 g) dried morel mushrooms

½ cup (4 fl oz/125 ml) boiling water

3 Tbsp unsalted butter

4 slices bacon

2 cups (6 oz/185 g) thinly sliced leeks, white and pale green parts

Salt and freshly ground pepper

1 tsp champagne vinegar

4 cod fillets, about 6 oz (185 g) each

1 Tbsp minced fresh chives

Here, honeycombed morels partner with smoky bacon and caramelized leeks for a sophisticated baked fish dish. Just a touch of champagne vinegar adds punch, and a few snips of fresh chives contribute color.

Preheat the oven to 375°F (190°C).

In a small heatproof bowl, soak the mushrooms in the boiling water for 20 minutes. Squeeze dry and roughly chop the larger mushrooms into bite-sized pieces. Set aside.

Melt 2 Tbsp of the butter in a large ovenproof frying pan over medium-high heat. Add the bacon and fry until crispy, about 5 minutes. Drain on paper towels. Pour off all but 3 Tbsp fat from the pan. Add the leeks and ¼ tsp salt, stir until evenly coated with the fat, and cook, stirring often, until tender and beginning to brown, about 10 minutes. Crumble the bacon and add half to the leeks along with the reserved morels and the vinegar. Toss to combine well and spread the leek mixture over the bottom of the pan.

Season the cod fillets with salt and pepper and lay them on top of the leeks. Dot with the remaining 1 Tbsp butter. Bake until the fish flakes with a fork, about 12 minutes. Garnish with the remaining bacon and the chives, and serve.

16

BEEF-CHIPOTLE CHILI

serves 6–8

¼ cup (1½ oz/45 g) all-purpose flour

Salt and freshly ground pepper

3 lb (1.5 kg) boneless beef chuck, cut into chunks

4–6 Tbsp (2–3 fl oz/60–80 ml) olive oil

1½ tsp dried oregano

4 cloves garlic, minced

2 red onions, finely chopped

2 cups (16 fl oz/500 ml) beef broth

1 can (7 oz/220 g) chipotle chiles in adobo sauce

Smoky, earthy chipotle chiles are jalapeños that have been dried in a wood-fueled firebox. They are sold dried, both whole and ground, and rehydrated in cans in a vinegary, garlicky red adobo sauce. Here, both the chiles and the sauce add a Southwestern flavor to a simple beef stew. Serve with steamed rice and with a seasonal vegetable, such as Swiss chard or broccoli rabe.

In a resealable plastic bag, combine the flour, 1 tsp salt, and ½ tsp pepper. Add the beef chunks and shake to coat evenly with the flour mixture; reserve the excess flour mixture. In a large frying pan, heat 4 Tbsp (2 fl oz/60 ml) of the oil over medium-high heat. Add half of the beef chunks and cook, turning as needed, until evenly browned on all sides, 10–12 minutes. Drain briefly on paper towels and then transfer to a slow cooker. Repeat with the remaining beef chunks, adding the remaining 2 Tbsp oil if needed. Sprinkle the oregano over the meat.

Return the pan to medium-high heat. Add the garlic and all but about ½ cup (2½ oz/75 g) of the onions and sauté until fragrant, about 1 minute. Sprinkle with the reserved flour mixture and sauté for about 1 minute. Pour in the broth and add the chipotle chiles with their sauce, breaking up the chiles coarsely with your fingers. Raise the heat to high, bring to a boil, and stir to scrape up any browned bits on the pan bottom. Pour the contents of the pan into the slow cooker over the beef.

Cover and cook on the high setting for 3–4 hours or on the low setting for 6–8 hours. The beef should be very tender. Spoon the chili into bowls, sprinkle with the remaining ½ cup chopped onion, and serve.

17

In early spring, start checking your local farmers' market for fava greens, which are the leaves of the fava bean plant. They are a boon to fava bean lovers who often avoid the legume because of its time-consuming prep. They taste milder than the beans and are delicious in salads, contributing a hint of sweetness and acidity.

FAVA GREENS WITH CHICKEN, PECANS & KUMQUATS

serves 4

30 kumquats (½–¾ lb/250–375 g)

¼ cup (2 fl oz/60 ml) blood orange–infused olive oil or extra-virgin olive oil

1 Tbsp honey

½ tsp ground ginger

2 Tbsp champagne vinegar

4 cups (4 oz/125 g) young fava leaves or baby spinach leaves, loosely packed

½ cup (2 oz/60 g) pecans

2 cups (¾ lb/375 g) chopped roasted chicken meat

Cut 20 of the kumquats crosswise into thin slices, removing any seeds as you go. Set aside and quarter the remaining kumquats lengthwise.

In a serving bowl, combine the oil and honey and whisk until the honey dissolves. Stir in the ginger and vinegar. Add the fava leaves, half the pecans, and the chicken and toss to combine. Divide among individual plates. Garnish with the remaining pecans and the sliced and quartered kumquats and serve.

18

Miso soup traditionally contains dried shiitakes, sliced green onions, and tiny cubes of tofu. Here, it gets a springtime profile with shrimp and pea shoots.

MISO SOUP WITH SHRIMP & PEA SHOOTS

serves 2

3-inch (7.5-cm) piece kombu

½ cup (½ oz/15 g) bonito flakes

2 Tbsp white miso

¼ lb (125 g) shrimp, peeled and deveined

⅓ cup (⅓ oz/10 g) pea shoots

In a large saucepan, combine the kombu and 3 cups (24 fl oz/750 ml) cold water. Bring to a boil over medium heat. Remove and discard the kombu. Remove from the heat, add the bonito flakes, and stir gently once. Let stand for 5 minutes. Strain the broth through a fine-mesh sieve, discarding the bonito flakes. Return the broth to the saucepan.

In a small bowl, combine the miso with ¼ cup (2 fl oz/60 ml) of the warm broth. ⤖

Stir until the miso is softened and very smooth. Stir into the broth and warm gently over medium heat, taking care not to boil the soup.

Add the shrimp and simmer just until bright pink, about 3 minutes. Stir in the pea shoots and serve.

19

Because this pizza relies on pantry staples, it's a great, quick option for easy weeknight dinners when your refrigerator is bare. Serve it with a green salad or with room-temperature asparagus dressed in a vinaigrette.

FOUR SEASONS PIZZA WITH MUSHROOMS, BELL PEPPERS, ARTICHOKES & OLIVES

serves 2–4

All-purpose flour and cornmeal, for dusting

1 lb (500 g) purchased whole-wheat pizza dough

½ cup (4 fl oz/125 ml) tomato sauce

1 jarred roasted red bell pepper, cut into strips

2 white mushrooms, brushed clean and thinly sliced

2 jarred artichoke hearts, drained and thinly sliced

6 black olives, pitted and thinly sliced

2 Tbsp olive oil

2 fresh basil leaves, torn into small pieces

Position a rack in the bottom of the oven. Place a baking stone on the rack. Preheat the oven to 550°F (290°C), or the highest setting, for at least 45 minutes.

To assemble the pizza, lightly flour a work surface. Roll the dough into a round 13–14 inches (33–35 cm) in diameter. Generously dust a pizza peel or rimless baking sheet with cornmeal and transfer the dough round to it. Working quickly, spread the tomato sauce on the dough, leaving a ½-inch (12-mm) border uncovered. Visualize the pizza in 4 equal wedges and arrange the pepper strips, mushrooms, artichoke slices, and olives each in their own quadrant. Drizzle with the oil.

Immediately slide the pizza from the peel onto the baking stone. Bake until the crust is crisp and browned, about 8 minutes. Remove from the oven. Sprinkle with the basil and serve.

20

Soft tofu and ground pork are unrivaled partners in this homey Chinese dish inspired by the famed mapo dofou of Sichuan. If you like your food spicy, add a big pinch of red pepper flakes with the green onions.

SPICY BRAISED TOFU WITH PORK

serves 4–6

4 Tbsp soy sauce

2 tsp rice wine or dry sherry

2 tsp toasted sesame oil

¼ lb (125 g) ground pork

14 oz (440 g) soft tofu

½ cup (4 fl oz/125 ml) chicken broth

1 Tbsp chile-bean paste

1 tsp sugar

½ tsp cornstarch

Ground white pepper

2 Tbsp canola oil

3 Tbsp minced green onion, white and tender green parts

1 Tbsp peeled and grated fresh ginger

3 cloves garlic, minced

In a large, nonreactive bowl, stir together 3 Tbsp of the soy sauce, the rice wine, and 1 tsp of the sesame oil. Add the pork and stir to mix well. Set aside.

Bring a small saucepan of salted water to a boil over medium heat. Add the tofu, reduce the heat to low, and simmer gently for 5 minutes to firm up the tofu. Using a slotted spoon, transfer the tofu to a plate. Weight with a second plate to press out the excess water. Set aside for 30 minutes. Just before stir-frying, pour off any water and cut the tofu into ½-inch (12-mm) cubes.

In a small bowl, combine the broth, chile-bean paste, remaining 1 Tbsp soy sauce, the sugar, and cornstarch. Add ⅛ tsp white pepper and the remaining 1 tsp sesame oil and whisk to blend.

In a large wok or frying pan, heat the canola oil over medium-high heat. Add the pork and its marinade and stir-fry just until the meat is no longer pink, about 2 minutes. Add 2 Tbsp of the green onion, the ginger, and garlic and stir-fry until fragrant, about 1 minute. Stir in the broth mixture and simmer until the sauce begins to thicken, 2–3 minutes. Add the tofu, reduce the heat to low, and simmer, uncovered, stirring occasionally and gently so the tofu does not fall apart, until most of the sauce is absorbed, about 10 minutes. Serve garnished with the remaining 1 Tbsp green onion.

21

Everyone will like this simple cake. It follows the same rule as banana bread: the browner the bananas you start with, the sweeter the results. If you like, fold in a handful of chocolate chips or walnuts just before transferring the batter to the pan, or top the cooled cake with cream cheese frosting (see page 102).

BANANA-HONEY CAKE

serves 6–8

2¼ cups (11½ oz/360 g) all-purpose flour, plus more for dusting

1 tsp baking powder

1 tsp baking soda

1 tsp ground cinnamon

½ tsp kosher salt

½ cup (4 oz/125 g) plus 2 Tbsp unsalted butter, at room temperature, plus more for greasing

½ cup (3½ oz/105 g) firmly packed light brown sugar

½ cup (6 oz/185 g) honey

2 large eggs

2 bananas, mashed

Preheat the oven to 350°F (180°C). Butter a 9-inch (23-cm) square baking pan. Sprinkle with flour and tap out the excess.

In a bowl, sift together the flour, baking powder, baking soda, cinnamon, and salt. In another large bowl, using an electric mixer, beat the butter and brown sugar on medium speed until creamy. Add the honey and beat until blended. Add the eggs, increase the speed to medium-high, and beat until smooth. Add the dry ingredients in 2 additions, alternating with the mashed bananas and beating on medium speed after each addition until smooth. Spread the batter evenly in the prepared pan.

Bake until a toothpick inserted into the center comes out clean, 35–40 minutes. Let cool completely in the pan on a wire rack. Cut into squares and serve.

22

Tandoori chicken is traditionally cooked in the high heat of a tandoor, a clay oven fueled by wood or charcoal. Here, it is grilled over a medium-hot fire to mimic that intense heat. The chicken is first marinated in a boldly spiced yogurt mixture, which helps to tenderize it. Serve the chicken with a cooling cucumber-mint sauce (see page 144), basmati rice, and simmered fresh peas.

TANDOORI-STYLE CHICKEN

serves 6

½ tsp *each* cayenne pepper and paprika

Salt and freshly ground black pepper

6 skinless, boneless chicken breasts

Juice of 1 lemon

1 small onion, roughly chopped

2 Tbsp peeled and chopped fresh ginger

2 cloves garlic

½ cup (4 oz/125 g) low-fat plain Greek yogurt

1 tsp garam masala

¼ cup (2 fl oz/60 ml) low-fat milk

Olive oil, for brushing

In a small bowl, stir together ½ tsp each of the cayenne, paprika, salt, and black pepper.

Trim off the tenders from the chicken breasts and reserve for another use. Working with one piece at a time, lay a breast between two pieces of plastic wrap. Use a meat pounder to pound to an even thickness. Place the chicken in a large nonreactive bowl and season with the spice rub, massaging it into the meat. Add the lemon juice and turn to coat. Cover and refrigerate for 30 minutes.

In a food processor, combine the onion, ginger, and garlic. Pulse several times to finely chop. Add the yogurt and the garam masala and continue to pulse until well combined. Add the milk, 1 Tbsp at a time, as needed to thin.

Remove the chicken from the lemon juice and pat dry with paper towels; discard the lemon juice. Return the chicken to the bowl, add the yogurt mixture, and turn to coat. Cover and refrigerate, turning occasionally, for 1–2 hours. Remove from the refrigerator 15 minutes before grilling.

Prepare a grill for direct-heat cooking over medium-high heat. Brush the grill grate with oil. Arrange the chicken breasts on the grill grate, discarding the marinade. Grill, turning once, until grill-marked and charred, 2–3 minutes per side. Move the chicken to the edge of the grill where the heat is less intense. Cover and grill until firm to the touch and cooked through, 3–5 minutes longer. Let rest for 5 minutes.

Slice the chicken and serve.

23

If you like, plan ahead and corn your own brisket: In a bowl, combine 8 cups (64 fl oz/2 l) water, 1½ cups (12 oz/ 375 g) kosher salt, ½ cup (4 oz/125 g) sugar, 3 Tbsp pickling spices, and 3 cloves garlic, crushed. Stir until the salt and sugar are dissolved. Submerge one 4-lb (2-kg) brisket in the mixture, cover, and refrigerate for 5–8 days. Remove the brisket, rinse well under cold water, and then proceed with the recipe.

CORNED BEEF & CABBAGE

serves 6–8

3 sprigs fresh thyme

5 sprigs fresh flat-leaf parsley

3½–4 lb (1.75–2 kg) corned beef brisket (*left*)

2 bay leaves

1 tsp peppercorns

12 white boiling onions or 3 small white onions cut into wedges

6 large or 12 small carrots, cut into large chunks or left whole if small

2 lb (1 kg) small red-skinned or mixed-color new potatoes

1 small head green cabbage, cut into 6–8 wedges

1 cup (8 fl oz/250 ml) heavy cream

3 Tbsp prepared horseradish

Salt

Tie the thyme and parsley sprigs together with kitchen string. Rinse the brisket, put it in a large, heavy pot, and add water to cover by 1 inch (2.5 cm). Bring to a boil over medium-high heat, skimming off any foam from the surface. Add the herb bundle, bay leaves, and peppercorns, reduce the heat to medium-low, cover, and simmer gently until the brisket is almost tender, 2½–3 hours.

Add the onions, carrots, potatoes, and cabbage wedges and return the liquid to a simmer. Cook until the vegetables and brisket are fully tender, about 25 minutes.

Meanwhile, in a bowl, whip the cream until soft peaks form. Fold in the horseradish, then season with salt. Cover and refrigerate the horseradish cream until ready to serve.

Using a slotted spoon, transfer the vegetables to a large platter. Transfer the brisket to a cutting board. Cut the meat across the grain and arrange on the platter with the vegetables. Serve, passing the horseradish cream on the side.

24

During the height of the season, devour artichokes in as many ways as possible. In this salad, the tender hearts are paired with buttery white beans and a quartet of fresh herbs. Artichokes and chicken have a special affinity, which makes this a great dish to serve with a roast bird.

ARTICHOKES WITH WARM CANNELLINI BEAN SALAD

serves 4

1 cup (7 oz/220 g) dried cannellini beans, picked over and rinsed, then soaked overnight in water to cover and drained

6 cups (48 fl oz/1.5 l) chicken broth

4 fresh rosemary sprigs

4 fresh thyme sprigs

4 cloves garlic, crushed

Salt and freshly ground pepper

2 lemons, halved

4 large artichokes, tops trimmed

1 bay leaf

½ cup (4 fl oz/125 ml) extra-virgin olive oil

1 Tbsp white wine vinegar

1 Tbsp minced fresh chives

16 marinated white anchovy fillets

1 cup (3 oz/90 g) shaved pecorino cheese

½ cup (½ oz/15 g) fresh flat-leaf parsley leaves

In a large saucepan, combine the beans, broth, 2 of the rosemary sprigs, 2 of the thyme sprigs, and 2 of the garlic cloves. Season well with salt and pepper. Bring to a boil, reduce the heat to medium-low, cover partially, and simmer until the beans are tender, about 1 hour. Let the beans cool in the cooking liquid and then drain.

Meanwhile, fill a bowl with water and squeeze in the juice from the lemons. Cut off the stem of each artichoke, leaving about 1 inch (2.5 cm) attached to the base. Snap off about 3 layers of the tough outer leaves. Cut the artichokes in half lengthwise. Using a spoon, scoop out and discard the furry chokes. As each artichoke is trimmed, drop it in the lemon water.

Drain the artichokes, transfer to a saucepan, and add water to cover. Add the bay leaf and the remaining rosemary sprigs, thyme sprigs, and garlic cloves. Season with 1 tsp salt. Bring to a boil, reduce the heat to a simmer, and cook until the artichokes are tender when pierced with a knife, 20–30 minutes. Let cool in the cooking liquid.

In a large bowl, whisk together the oil and vinegar. Add the drained beans and chives and toss to combine. ⤏

Season with salt and pepper.

Remove the artichokes from the cooking liquid and pat dry. Divide the bean mixture among 4 plates, top with 2 artichoke halves, garnish with the anchovies, pecorino, and parsley, and serve.

25

White rice and wild rice bring both texture and flavor to this fragrant soup. Full of aromatic cold fighters like ginger, garlic, and cilantro, this comforting dish is ideal for taking to a friend who is feeling under the weather.

CHICKEN & WILD RICE SOUP WITH GINGER

serves 6

½ cup (3 oz/90 g) wild rice, rinsed

1 Tbsp toasted sesame oil

1 Tbsp canola oil

1 yellow onion, chopped

1 Tbsp peeled and grated fresh ginger

2 cloves garlic, minced

4 cups (32 fl oz/1 l) chicken broth

1 carrot, peeled and diced

3 skinless, bone-in chicken breast halves

2 skinless, bone-in chicken thighs

½ cup (3½ oz/105 g) long-grain white rice

¼ cup (¾ oz/20 g) thinly sliced green onion

¼ cup (⅓ oz/10 g) chopped cilantro

Salt and freshly ground pepper

In a small saucepan, bring 2 cups (16 fl oz/500 ml) water to a boil. Add the wild rice, reduce the heat to a simmer, cover, and cook until tender, 45–50 minutes. Drain.

Meanwhile, in a large, heavy pot, warm the sesame and canola oils over medium-high heat. Add the yellow onion and sauté until softened, 3–5 minutes. Add the ginger and garlic and sauté for 2 minutes. Add the broth, carrot, chicken pieces, and white rice. Pour in 2 cups (16 fl oz/500 ml) water and bring to a simmer. Reduce the heat to medium-low, cover, and cook until the chicken is opaque throughout, about 15 minutes.

Transfer the chicken to a plate to cool. Remove the meat from the bones and tear into bite-sized pieces. Stir the chicken back into the soup along with the green onions, cilantro, and wild rice. Season with salt and pepper and serve.

26

LEEK & YUKON GOLD POTATO SOUP WITH FRIED PROSCIUTTO

serves 6–8

8 leeks, about 4 lb (2 kg) total

¼ cup (2 fl oz/60 ml) olive oil

6 slices prosciutto, about 3 oz (90 g) total, cut into ribbons

Salt and freshly ground pepper

1½ tsp minced fresh thyme

2 Tbsp all-purpose flour

8 cups (64 fl oz/2 l) chicken broth

5 Yukon Gold potatoes, about 2½ lb (1.25 kg) total, cut into 1-inch (2.5-cm) chunks

2 bay leaves

¼ cup (½ oz/15 g) minced fresh chives

Although the fried prosciutto pieces that garnish this soup are small, their impact is big. The meaty richness of the famous ham creates chewy-crisp pockets of saltiness. Round out the menu with a tossed green salad, crusty bread, and a selection of two or three cheeses.

Trim off and discard the dark green tops of the leeks. Cut the leeks in half lengthwise and then cut each half crosswise into pieces ½ inch (12 mm) thick.

In a large, heavy pot, warm the oil over medium heat. Add the prosciutto and sauté until crisp, about 6 minutes. Using a slotted spoon, transfer the prosciutto to paper towels to drain. Add the leeks and ½ tsp salt to the pot and stir to coat with the fat. Reduce the heat to medium-low, cover, and cook, stirring occasionally, until the leeks begin to soften, about 10 minutes. Add the thyme and the flour and cook, stirring constantly, until the flour is incorporated.

Raise the heat to medium-high and, stirring constantly, slowly add the broth. Add the potatoes and the bay leaves, season with pepper, cover, and bring to a boil. Reduce the heat to medium-low and simmer until the potatoes just start to become tender, about 6 minutes. Let stand, covered, off the heat until the potatoes are tender all the way through when pierced with a knife, about 15 minutes. Discard the bay leaves and return the soup to a simmer over medium-high heat. If desired, use the back of a large spoon to mash some of the potatoes against the side of the pot and stir them into the soup to thicken it.

Ladle the soup into bowls, garnish with the prosciutto and chives, and serve.

27

SALAD OF NEW POTATOES, SPRING PEAS & MINT

serves 4

¼ cup (2 fl oz/60 ml) extra-virgin olive oil

¼ cup (2 fl oz/60 ml) raspberry vinegar

Salt

4 Tbsp (⅓ oz/10 g) chopped fresh mint, plus sprigs for garnish

12 small new potatoes such as red rose or Yukon Gold (about 1½ lb/750 g total weight)

1 cup (5 oz/155 g) shelled English peas (about 1 lb/500 g unshelled)

½ cup (4 fl oz/125 ml) low-sodium chicken broth

8–12 butter lettuce leaves

Explosive flavors abound in this simple salad. A bouquet of spring mint is combined with raspberry vinegar and olive oil to coat warm new potatoes and peas. More mint, added just before serving, intensifies the vinegar-infused mint of the dressing.

In a small bowl, whisk together the oil, vinegar, ½ tsp salt, and 2 Tbsp of the chopped mint until the vinaigrette is well blended. Set aside.

Put the potatoes in a saucepan and cover with water by 2 inches (5 cm). Bring to a boil over high heat, reduce the heat to medium, and cook until tender when pierced with a knife, about 20 minutes. Drain the potatoes and, when they are cool enough to handle, peel them, if desired. If the potatoes are quite small, leave them whole; if not, halve or quarter them. Transfer to a large bowl.

Meanwhile, in a small saucepan, combine the peas and broth. Bring to a simmer over medium heat and cook just until the peas are warmed through and bright green, about 1 minute. Do not overcook. Drain and add to the bowl with the potatoes.

Drizzle the vinaigrette over the potato salad and let stand for 10–15 minutes, stirring gently several times.

Line individual plates with the lettuce leaves. Mound the potato salad on the lettuce. Sprinkle with the remaining 2 Tbsp chopped mint, garnish each serving with a mint sprig, and serve.

28

THREE-ONION SOUP WITH CAMBOZOLA GRILLED CHEESE

serves 6

2 Tbsp unsalted butter

¼ cup (2 fl oz/60 ml) olive oil

3 large yellow onions, sliced

6 shallots, sliced

3 leeks, white and pale green parts, sliced

1 Tbsp light brown sugar

¼ cup (2 fl oz/60 ml) dry white wine

4 cups (32 fl oz/1 l) chicken broth

Salt and freshly ground pepper

FOR THE GRILLED CHEESE

12 thin slices cranberry-walnut or other fruit-and-nut bread

2 Tbsp unsalted butter, at room temperature

6 oz (185 g) Cambozola or Camembert cheese, at room temperature

Onion soup is nearly always finished with cheese, either a sprinkling of grated cheese or a cheese-crusted crouton. Here, a lighter version of the classic French onion soup skips the typical cheese topping in favor of a creamy, buttery grilled cheese sandwich served on the side.

In a large, heavy pot, melt the butter with the oil over high heat. Add the onions, shallots, and leeks and sauté until the onions soften, 8–10 minutes. Reduce the heat to low and continue to cook, stirring occasionally, for 30 minutes. Sprinkle the brown sugar over the onions, stir, and cook for 10 minutes. Add the white wine and bring to a simmer, stirring to scrape up any browned bits on the bottom of the pan. Cook until the wine is absorbed, 3–4 minutes. Add the broth and bring to a boil over medium-high heat. Reduce the heat to medium and simmer, uncovered, for 10 minutes. Remove from the heat and let cool slightly.

Purée half of the soup in a blender and return to the pot. Season with salt and pepper.

To make the grilled cheese, spread one sideof each slice of bread with the butter. Spread 1 oz (30 g) of the Cambozola on the unbuttered side of each of 6 bread slices and top with another slice of bread, with the buttered sides on the outside of the sandwich. In a frying pan, cook the sandwiches over medium-low heat until the bread is toasted and the cheese is melted, about 4 minutes per side. Cut each sandwich in half.

Ladle the soup into bowls and serve with the grilled cheese on the side.

29

BLACK BEAN–JALAPEÑO BURGERS WITH AVOCADO MASH

serves 4

1 can (14½ oz/455 g) black beans

2 tsp olive oil

¼ cup (1½ oz/45 g) minced yellow onion

1 small jalapeño chile, ribs and seeds removed, minced

1 Tbsp ground cumin

1 tsp dried oregano

1 tsp salt

1 egg, slightly beaten

6 Tbsp (⅔ oz/20 g) whole-wheat panko bread crumbs

FOR THE AVOCADO MASH

2 ripe avocados

1 plum tomato, seeded and diced

Juice of 1 lime

Salt

Nonstick cooking spray

This spicy meatless burger is served without a bun to cut down on carbs and calories, while avocado topping lends color and good-for-you fat. This is an ideal party dish because the burgers can be made ahead and refrigerated overnight. Try serving them in lettuce cups for a portable meal.

Drain and rinse the black beans, then lay them on paper towels and pat dry. Put the beans in a bowl and mash with a fork, leaving the mixture somewhat chunky.

In a small frying pan over medium heat, warm the oil. Add the onion and jalapeño and cook until soft, about 3 minutes. Add the cumin, oregano, and salt and sauté until aromatic, about 1 minute. Transfer to the bowl with the black beans and stir in the egg and panko. Form into 4 patties and transfer to the refrigerator to chill for 30 minutes.

To make the avocado mash, put the avocado in a bowl. Using a fork, mash well. Stir in the tomato and lime juice and season to taste with salt.

Warm a nonstick frying pan to medium-high heat and lightly coat with nonstick cooking spray. Cook the burgers until heated through and golden-brown, about 5 minutes per side.

Arrange the burgers on plates, top with the avocado mash, and serve.

MARCH 30

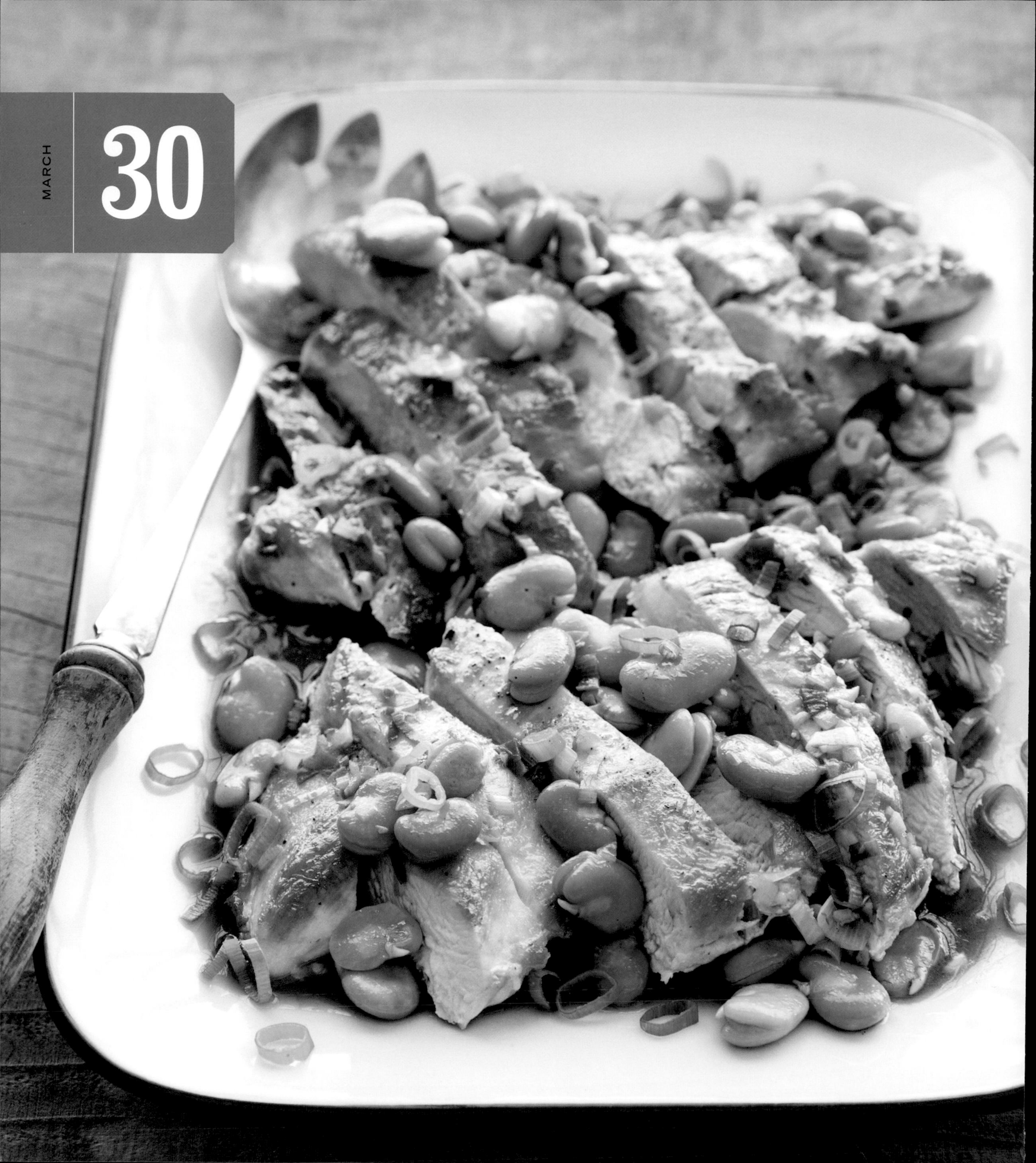

30

CHICKEN BREASTS WITH FAVA BEANS

serves 4

2 lb (1 kg) fava beans, shelled

4 boneless, skinless chicken breast halves, about 6 oz (185 g) each

Salt and freshly ground pepper

2 Tbsp *each* extra-virgin olive oil and unsalted butter

4 green onions, chopped, white and green parts separated

1 clove garlic, minced

¼ cup (2 fl oz/60 ml) dry white wine

¾ cup (6 fl oz/180 ml) low-sodium chicken broth

This light, diet-savvy meal features low-fat skinless chicken and a whole lot of green. If you don't have the time to prepare the fava beans, substitute fresh or frozen peas, adding them after deglazing the pan with wine.

Bring a saucepan three-fourths full of water to a boil and add the favas. Boil for 1 minute, then drain. Squeeze each bean free of its tough outer skin.

Preheat the oven to 200°F (95°C). Using a meat pounder, pound each chicken breast to an even thickness. Season the breasts with 1 tsp salt and ½ tsp pepper.

In a large frying pan, warm the oil over medium-high heat. Add the chicken and cook until golden brown, 3–4 minutes. Turn and cook until the other side is golden and the chicken springs back when pressed, about 4 minutes. Transfer to a rimmed baking sheet and keep warm in the oven.

Pour off the fat from the pan and return it to medium-high heat. Add 1 Tbsp of the butter and allow it to melt. Add the white parts of the green onions and the garlic and sauté until softened, about 2 minutes. Add the wine and cook, scraping up the browned bits from the pan bottom, until almost evaporated, about 30 seconds. Add the fava beans and ¼ cup (2 fl oz/60 ml) of the broth, cover, and cook, stirring occasionally, until tender, about 3 minutes. Stir in the remaining ½ cup (4 fl oz/125 ml) broth and bring to a boil. Remove from the heat and stir in the remaining 1 Tbsp butter. Taste and adjust the seasonings.

Cut each chicken breast across the grain into slices and transfer to warmed plates. Spoon some of the fava beans and sauce over each breast. Sprinkle with the green onion tops and serve.

31

GINGERED RHUBARB CRISP

serves 6

1½ lb (750 g) rhubarb, cut into ½-inch (1.25-cm) slices

1 large orange

¾ cup (6 oz/185 g) granulated sugar

1-inch (2.5-cm) piece fresh ginger, peeled and grated

¾ cup (4 oz/125 g) all-purpose flour

½ cup (3½ oz/105 g) firmly packed light brown sugar

⅓ cup (1 oz/30 g) rolled oats

¼ tsp ground cinnamon

¼ tsp kosher salt

4 Tbsp (2 oz/60 g) unsalted butter, melted and cooled

Vanilla ice cream for serving

Long stalks of tart crimson rhubarb are a welcome treat come springtime. A generous amount of freshly grated ginger adds a warm, spicy bite to this fruit crisp, which is topped with a buttery oatmeal crust.

Preheat the oven to 375°F (190°C). Place the rhubarb in a 9-inch (23-cm) square baking dish. Finely grate 1 tsp zest from the orange and add to the dish. Squeeze ⅓ cup (2½ fl oz/70 ml) juice from the orange and add to the dish along with the granulated sugar. Toss the rhubarb mixture together, then spread out evenly in the dish.

In a bowl, combine the ginger, flour, brown sugar, oats, cinnamon, and salt. Using a fork, toss until blended. Add the butter and stir until the ingredients are evenly moistened. Sprinkle the oat mixture over the rhubarb.

Bake until the topping is golden brown and the juices are thick and bubbling around the edge of the dish, 30–40 minutes. If the top starts to brown too much, loosely cover it with foil. Let the crisp cool, uncovered, on a wire rack for at least 20 minutes. Serve warm, accompanied with scoops of ice cream.

The March vegetable bounty continues in April, with bigger harvests of asparagus, for grilling, for risotto, or for soup, and of English peas, for pairing with spring lamb chops or with crab and ricotta in a frittata. Slim spring leeks are now a regular offering in produce departments, waiting to be baked under a blanket of buttery bread crumbs, and the tender shoots of pea plants, a popular item at farmers' markets, are ideal candidates for stir-frying with shiitakes and noodles. This month's desserts—carrot cake, brownies, citrus mousse—are all timeless choices to please even the fussiest diners.

1
CHICKEN—MATZO BALL SOUP
page 83

2
FAVA BEAN & RICOTTA OMELET WITH SPRING GREENS
page 83

3
KALE, CREMINI MUSHROOM & GOAT CHEESE HAND PIES
page 84

8
GLASS-NOODLE SALAD WITH SHRIMP, CHICKEN & MINT
page 88

9
TORTELLINI IN HERBACEOUS BROTH WITH SNOW PEAS
page 88

10
BROWN BUTTER POUND CAKE WITH STRAWBERRY-RHUBARB COMPOTE
page 89

15
PEA SHOOTS & SHIITAKE MUSHROOMS WITH SOBA NOODLES
page 93

16
FRESH LEMON MOUSSE
page 93

17
SEARED SCALLOP, ORANGE & RED ONION SALAD
page 94

22
BOURBON-GLAZED HAM
page 97

23
ROAST CHICKEN & BREAD SALAD WITH HARICOTS VERTS & STRAWBERRIES
page 99

24
BROCCOLI RABE & PARMESAN FRITTER
page 99

29
CARROT CAKE
page 102

30
ARROZ CON POLLO
page 102

4
CALAMARI & WHITE BEAN SALAD
page 85

5
LENTIL & ANDOUILLE SOUP
page 85

6
GRILLED LAMB CHOPS WITH PEA,
FETA & MINT SALAD
page 86

7
DEVIL'S FOOD LAYER CAKE
page 86

11
CHICKEN TACOS WITH RADISH SLAW
page 91

12
CRAB, PEA & RICOTTA FRITTATA
page 91

13
CREAM CHEESE MARBLE BROWNIES
page 92

14
TUNA BURGERS WITH CREAMY
SMOKED PAPRIKA SAUCE
page 92

18
LAMB TAGINE WITH OLIVES
& PRESERVED LEMON
page 94

19
UDON NOODLES WITH POACHED
SHRIMP, BABY SPINACH & MISO
page 96

20
BAKED LEEKS WITH BREAD CRUMBS
page 96

21
ASPARAGUS RISOTTO
page 97

25
BAKED RIGATONI WITH FENNEL,
SAUSAGE & PEPERONATA
page 100

26
PORK TENDERLOIN WITH
RHUBARB CHUTNEY
page 100

27
GRILLED ASPARAGUS & GREEN ONION
SOUP WITH POACHED EGGS
page 101

28
MUSTARD-CRUSTED SALMON
WITH RED POTATOES
page 101

april

1

Grandmothers may disagree on the exact instructions for this soup, but a richly flavored broth, generous chunks of root vegetables, and light, tender dumplings are common qualities. Matzo is easily found in grocery stores during April for Passover, but you can enjoy this comfort food any time of year.

CHICKEN–MATZO BALL SOUP

serves 6

3–3½ lb (1.5–1.75 kg) assorted chicken pieces, skin on and bone in

2 yellow onions, finely chopped

3 or 4 small carrots, peeled and cut into ½-inch (12-mm) pieces

2 celery ribs, cut into ½-inch (12-mm) pieces

1 parsnip, peeled and cut into ½-inch (12-mm) pieces

Leaves from 1 bunch fresh dill, coarsely chopped

Salt

3 Tbsp finely chopped fresh flat-leaf parsley

FOR THE MATZO BALLS

2 Tbsp canola oil

2 eggs, lightly beaten

½ cup (2¼ oz/67 g) matzo meal

Salt

2 Tbsp seltzer water or sparkling water

In a large pot, combine the chicken pieces, onions, carrots, celery, parsnip, and dill. Add about 2 qt (2 l) water, or enough to cover. Bring to a boil over medium-high heat. Reduce the heat to medium-low, cover partially, and simmer, periodically skimming the foam off the surface, until the soup is full flavored, about 1½ hours. Season with salt. Stir in the parsley and cook for 1 minute.

Meanwhile, make the matzo balls. In a small bowl, whisk together the oil and eggs. In another bowl, combine the matzo meal and 1 tsp salt. Add the egg mixture to the matzo mixture and stir to mix well. Add the seltzer water and stir until blended. Cover and refrigerate for 20 minutes.

Transfer the chicken pieces to a plate, let cool, and then shred the meat, discarding the skin and bones. Return the shredded chicken to the soup.

With lightly oiled hands, shape the matzo dough into balls about 1½ inches (4 cm) in diameter, and place in the simmering soup. Cover the pot and cook until the matzo balls are light and fluffy, 20–30 minutes. Serve.

2

This spring dish is perfect as the centerpiece of a healthy brunch. Fava beans are low in fat and sodium and high in iron and fiber. Here, they are enveloped in creamy, protein-packed eggs and smooth ricotta, for a meal that will satisfy nearly everyone's morning appetite.

FAVA BEAN & RICOTTA OMELET WITH SPRING GREENS

serves 4

2 lb (1 kg) fava beans, shelled

5 Tbsp (3 oz/90 g) part-skim ricotta cheese

¼ cup (¾ oz/20 g) chopped fresh basil

Grated zest and juice of 1 lemon

Salt and freshly ground pepper

8 large eggs

3 Tbsp olive oil

2 cups (2 oz/60 g) spring greens, such as arugula or watercress

Bring a saucepan three-fourths full of water to a boil and add the favas. Boil for 1 minute, then use a skimmer to transfer them to a bowl. Squeeze each bean free of its tough outer skin. Set aside ½ cup (3½ oz/105 g) of the fava beans and transfer the remaining beans to a food processor. Add the ricotta, basil, and lemon zest and process until smooth. Season to taste with salt and pepper.

Preheat the oven to 200°F (95°C). In a bowl, whisk the eggs with 1 Tbsp water until frothy. Season with salt and pepper.

Melt ½ Tbsp oil in a small nonstick frying pan over medium heat. Pour in one-fourth of the egg mixture. Cook until the eggs just begin to set, about 1 minute. Using a spatula, gently lift one side of the eggs while tilting the pan to allow the uncooked egg mixture to drip to the bottom of the pan. Repeat until the eggs are cooked through, about 3 minutes.

Place one-quarter of the puréed fava mixture onto half of the omelet and fold over the other side. Transfer to a plate and keep warm in the oven. Repeat the cooking process 3 more times.

Place the spring greens in a bowl. Drizzle with the remaining 1 Tbsp oil and the lemon juice and season with salt and pepper. Top each omelet with the remaining fava beans and the spring greens, dividing evenly, and serve.

3

You can trade out the kale for chard or spinach and the goat cheese for fontina or Gruyère. Or you can create an entirely different filling, savory or sweet, for tucking inside this versatile dough. Be sure to cook the filling first, as it may not cook through in the oven. Pricking the tops of the pies with fork tines helps prevent them from bursting as they bake. If you have any vegetable filling left over, fold it into an omelet.

KALE, CREMINI MUSHROOM & GOAT CHEESE HAND PIES

makes 22 hand pies; serves 6–8

FOR THE DOUGH

2½ cups (12½ oz/390 g) all-purpose flour

Salt

1 cup (8 oz/250 g) cold unsalted butter, cut into small pieces

4–8 Tbsp (2–4 fl oz/60–120 ml) ice water

2 Tbsp unsalted butter

1 Tbsp olive oil

½ yellow onion, chopped

2 cloves garlic, minced

½ lb (250 g) cremini mushrooms, coarsely chopped

1 bunch kale, ribs removed, leaves chopped into ½-inch (12-mm) pieces

½ cup (4 fl oz/125 ml) chicken or vegetable broth

3 oz (90 g) fresh goat cheese

1 egg

To make the dough, combine the flour and 1 tsp salt in a food processor and pulse to mix. Scatter the butter over the flour and process until the mixture resembles coarse crumbs. With the machine running, add the ice water, 1 Tbsp at a time, and process just until the dough comes together. You will probably use only 4 or 5 Tbsp; do not overmix. Turn the dough out onto a lightly floured work surface and pat it into a disk. Wrap tightly in plastic wrap and refrigerate for at least 30 minutes or up to overnight.

To make the filling, in a large frying pan, melt the butter with the oil over medium-high heat. Add the onion and the garlic and cook, stirring occasionally, until the vegetables soften, about 5 minutes. Add the mushrooms and cook, stirring frequently, until they caramelize, about 7 minutes. Add the kale, toss to coat with the other vegetables, and cook until the kale begins to soften, 3–4 minutes. Add the broth and cook until it is absorbed, about 4 minutes. Transfer to a bowl and let cool completely. ⟶

Position 1 rack in the center and a second rack in the bottom third of the oven and preheat to 400°F (200°C). Line 2 baking sheets with parchment paper. Cut the dough disk in half and rewrap and return half to the refrigerator. On a floured work surface, roll out the dough ⅛ inch (3 mm) thick. Using a 4-inch (10-cm) round cookie or biscuit cutter, cut out as many circles as possible. Gather up the scraps and set aside.

Place a heaping teaspoon of the goat cheese in the center of each circle, top with 1½ Tbsp of the kale mixture, and fold the circle in half to enclose the filling. Using fork tines, crimp the edges firmly to seal and then prick the top. As the pies are formed, transfer them to a prepared baking sheet. Repeat with the remaining dough half, then press together all of the dough scraps, flatten into a disk, and roll out, cut out, and fill more circles.

In a small bowl, whisk the egg with 1 Tbsp water. Using a pastry brush, brush the top of each pie with the egg wash. Bake the pies, switching the pans between the racks and rotating them back to front about halfway through baking, until they are golden brown, about 20 minutes. Let cool briefly before serving.

4

CALAMARI & WHITE BEAN SALAD

serves 4

Eating this mix of tender squid rings, velvety white beans, and roasted sweet peppers tossed in a citrus-and-garlic dressing will have you dreaming of sitting at a seaside table on the sunny Italian coast. Open a bottle of crisp vino bianco to complete the reverie.

Salt and freshly ground pepper

¼ cup (2 fl oz/60 ml) white wine vinegar, or as needed

3 Tbsp fresh lemon juice

1 Tbsp minced garlic

½ cup (4 fl oz/125 ml) extra-virgin olive oil

1 lb (500 g) cleaned squid, cut into bite-sized rings and tentacles

1 can (15 oz/470 g) cannellini beans or other white beans, rinsed and drained

2 jarred roasted red bell peppers, cut into strips

1 cup (4 oz/125 g) thinly sliced red onion

2 Tbsp capers, rinsed

⅓ cup (2 oz/60 g) green olives, pitted and chopped

Fresh flat-leaf parsley leaves for garnish

In a large pot, bring 4 qt (4 l) salted water to a boil over medium-high heat. Have ready a bowl of ice water.

In a large bowl, combine the vinegar, lemon juice, garlic, 1 tsp salt, and ¼ tsp pepper and let stand for 5 minutes. Add the olive oil in a thin stream, whisking constantly until the dressing is well blended.

Add the squid to the boiling water and cook until just tender, about 1 minute. Drain the squid and plunge into the ice water to stop the cooking. Drain well and pat dry.

Add the cooked squid, beans, peppers, onion, capers, and olives to the dressing and mix well. Cover and refrigerate for 2–4 hours to blend the flavors.

Just before serving, taste the salad and adjust the vinegar and seasonings. Divide among individual plates, garnish with parsley leaves, and serve.

5

LENTIL & ANDOUILLE SOUP

serves 8–10

You can make this soup ahead and refrigerate it, but you will need to add more broth when you rewarm it, as the lentils will have absorbed most of the liquid. Kielbasa can be substituted for the andouille.

1 lb (500 g) andouille sausage, cut into ¼-inch-thick (6-mm-thick) slices

2 Tbsp olive oil

2 carrots, peeled and chopped

1 large yellow onion, chopped

4 large cloves garlic, minced

1 lb (500 g) green lentils, picked over and rinsed

8 cups (64 fl oz/2 l) chicken broth, plus more as needed

1 Tbsp heavy cream

¼ cup (⅓ oz/10 g) chopped flat-leaf parsley

Salt and freshly ground pepper

In a large, heavy pot, cook the sausage slices over medium-high heat until browned on both sides, about 8 minutes. Transfer to a plate and set aside.

Add the oil, carrots, onion, and garlic to the same pot and sauté until the vegetables are softened, about 8 minutes. Add the lentils and broth and bring to a boil. Reduce the heat to low and simmer, uncovered, stirring occasionally, until the lentils are tender, 20–30 minutes. Remove from the heat and let cool slightly.

Purée half of the soup in a food processor. Return to the pot and stir to combine. Stir in the sausage, cream, and parsley, and reheat over low heat. Season with salt and pepper and serve.

6

GRILLED LAMB CHOPS WITH PEA, FETA & MINT SALAD

serves 4

Grated zest of 1 lemon

2 Tbsp fresh lemon juice

2 large garlic cloves, minced

3 Tbsp olive oil

8 lamb chops, each 4–5 oz (125–155 g) and 1–1¼ inches (2.5–3 cm) thick

3 cups (15 oz/470 g) shelled English peas

Salt and freshly ground pepper

2 Tbsp minced fresh mint

1 Tbsp red wine vinegar

3 oz (90 g) feta cheese, crumbled

Lean lamb is a good source of protein and minerals. To ensure the best quality and flavor, look for grass-fed, pasture-raised lamb at the butcher shop. Thawed frozen peas can be used in place of fresh and don't need to be blanched.

In a shallow nonreactive dish large enough to hold the chops in one layer, whisk together the lemon zest and juice, garlic, and 1 Tbsp of the oil. Add the lamb chops, turn to coat, and let stand for 30 minutes, turning once halfway through.

Have ready a bowl of ice water. Bring a pot of lightly salted water to a rapid boil. Add the peas and cook until not quite tender, 1–2 minutes. Immediately drain and transfer to the ice water to stop the cooking. Drain well and pat thoroughly dry.

In a bowl, combine the peas, the remaining 2 Tbsp oil, and the mint. Add ½ tsp salt and season with pepper. Toss gently.

Prepare a grill for direct-heat cooking over high heat. Pat the lamp chops dry with paper towels and season both sides generously with salt. Place on the grill rack and cook until dark brown and sizzling, 3–5 minutes. Turn over the chops and continue to cook for 3–5 more minutes for medium-rare, or to your desired doneness. Transfer to a platter, season with pepper, and let rest for 5–10 minutes.

Stir the vinegar and cheese into the pea salad. Serve alongside the chops.

7

DEVIL'S FOOD LAYER CAKE

serves 8–10

¾ cup (2½ oz/75 g) unsweetened natural cocoa powder

1¾ cups (9 oz/280 g) all-purpose flour

1½ tsp baking soda

¼ tsp kosher salt

2 cups (1 lb/500 g) sugar

½ cup (4 oz/125 g) plus 2 Tbsp unsalted butter, at room temperature

3 large eggs

1 tsp pure vanilla extract

1¼ cups (10 fl oz/310 ml) buttermilk

Dark Chocolate Frosting (*left*)

To make the dark chocolate frosting, place ½ lb (250 g) chopped unsweetened chocolate in the top of a double boiler over (not touching) barely simmering water, and warm, stirring often, until melted. Remove from over the water and let cool to room temperature. In the bowl of a stand mixer fitted with the paddle attachment, beat 1 cup (8 oz/250 g) room temperature unsalted butter and 2½ cups (10 oz/315 g) sifted confectioners' sugar on medium speed until light and fluffy, about 3 minutes. Beat in 2 tsp pure vanilla extract. Add the cooled chocolate and beat on low speed until incorporated, then increase the speed and beat until light and fluffy, about 2 minutes. The frosting will keep for up to 3 days.

Preheat the oven to 350°F (180°C). Butter two 9-inch (23-cm) round cake pans. Line the bottom of each pan with a round of parchment paper. Butter the parchment, then dust the pans with flour, tapping out the excess.

In a small heatproof bowl, whisk together the cocoa and 1 cup (8 fl oz/250 ml) boiling water until smooth. Let cool completely. In a bowl, sift together the flour, baking soda, and salt. In a large bowl, using a handheld mixer on medium-high speed, beat together the sugar and butter until the mixture is light in color, about 3 minutes. Beat in the eggs, one at a time, then beat in the vanilla and the cocoa mixture. Reduce the speed to low and add the flour mixture in 3 additions alternately with the buttermilk in 2 additions, stopping to scrape down the bowl as needed, beating until smooth. Divide the batter evenly between the prepared pans.

Bake the cakes until they begin to pull away from the sides of the pans, 35–40 minutes. Transfer to wire racks and let cool in the pans for 15 minutes. Run a knife around the inside of each pan to release the cake. Invert the pans onto the racks, lift off the pans, and peel off the parchment paper. Turn each cake right side up and let cool completely.

Place one layer, top side down, on a flat plate. With an icing spatula, spread about a third of the frosting on top. Place the other cake layer, top side down, on the first layer and press gently. Spread a thin layer of frosting over the entire cake to seal in any crumbs, then thickly coat the cake with the remaining frosting.

8

GLASS-NOODLE SALAD WITH SHRIMP, CHICKEN & MINT

serves 4

½ cup (4 fl oz/125 ml) chicken broth

6 oz (185 g) ground chicken

Salt and freshly ground pepper

6 oz (185 g) shrimp, peeled with tail segments left intact and deveined

¼ lb (125 g) bean thread noodles, soaked in warm water for 15 minutes and drained

FOR THE DRESSING

Juice of 2 limes

3 Tbsp Asian fish sauce

2 tsp sugar

1 Tbsp roasted chile paste

2 large red Fresno or serrano chiles, seeded and finely chopped

1 green onion, including tender green parts, chopped

3 Tbsp coarsely chopped fresh cilantro

1 Tbsp finely shredded fresh mint

4 large red-leaf lettuce leaves, torn into pieces

2 Tbsp fried shallots (*left*)

To make the fried shallots, very thinly slice 4 shallots, then separate the slices. Pour canola oil to a depth of about 1 inch (2.5 cm) into a small frying pan, place over medium heat, and heat to 325°F (165°C) on a deep-frying thermometer. Add the slices and fry until they turn light golden brown, about 5 minutes. Drain and let cool on paper towels.

In a saucepan, bring the broth to a gentle boil over medium heat. Add the chicken and cook, stirring to break up the meat, until the meat turns opaque and has a crumbled texture, about 3 minutes. Using a wire skimmer, transfer the chicken to a bowl. Season with salt and pepper and let cool.

Raise the heat under the boiling broth to medium-high, add the shrimp, and boil until they turn bright orange-pink, about 30 seconds. Drain well and let cool, then add to the bowl with the chicken.

Bring a saucepan three-fourths full of salted water to a boil over high heat. Add the noodles and cook until they are translucent, about 1 minute. Pour into a colander and rinse under cold running water. Drain well and transfer to a bowl. ⇥

To make the dressing, in a large bowl, combine the lime juice, fish sauce, sugar, roasted chile paste, and chiles. Stir together until the sugar dissolves. Add the chicken-shrimp mixture and the noodles to the dressing and toss to mix. Mix in the green onion, cilantro, and mint.

Divide the lettuce among individual salad bowls and mound the noodle salad on top. Garnish with the fried shallots. Serve at room temperature.

9

TORTELLINI IN HERBACEOUS BROTH WITH SNOW PEAS

serves 4–6

2 Tbsp olive oil

2 small leeks, white and pale green parts, halved and thinly sliced

3 cloves garlic, chopped

Salt and freshly ground pepper

6 cups (48 fl oz/1.5 l) chicken broth

1 package (9 oz/280 g) fresh cheese tortellini

½ lb (250 g) snow peas, halved diagonally, trimmed

¼ cup (¼ oz/7 g) loosely packed fresh tarragon leaves, chopped

¼ cup (¼ oz/7 g) loosely packed fresh basil leaves, chopped

2 oz (60 g) Parmesan cheese, grated

Every household should have a few superfast weeknight recipes like this one. Packed with antioxidants, essential oils, and vitamins, fresh herbs are not only nutritional powerhouses but also contribute a heady flavor to this and other soups. Look for flat, crisp, evenly green snow peas, and be careful not to overcook them.

In a large, heavy pot, warm the oil over medium-high heat. Add the leeks and cook, stirring occasionally, until soft, about 6 minutes. Add the garlic, season with salt and pepper, and cook, stirring occasionally, until soft, about 2 minutes. Add the broth and bring to a boil. Add the tortellini and cook for 5 minutes. Add the snow peas, tarragon, and basil and cook until the tortellini is al dente, about 2 minutes.

Serve, garnished with a generous helping of the cheese.

10

Brown butter has the taste and aroma of toasted hazelnuts, with a fuller, deeper flavor and color than plain butter. Here, it enriches a dense, velvety pound cake with a nuttiness that is complemented by a springtime compote.

BROWN BUTTER POUND CAKE WITH STRAWBERRY-RHUBARB COMPOTE

serves 8

FOR THE POUND CAKE

1 cup (8 oz/250 g) unsalted butter

1¼ cups (5 oz/155 g) cake flour

¼ tsp baking powder

½ tsp kosher salt

3 large whole eggs, plus 3 large egg yolks

1 cup (8 oz/250 g) plus 1 Tbsp sugar

1 tsp pure vanilla extract

FOR THE COMPOTE

4 Tbsp (2 fl oz/60 ml) fresh orange juice

⅓ cup (3 oz/90 g) sugar

Kosher salt

8 oz (250 g) rhubarb, cut into ¼-inch (6-mm) slices

2 pt (1 lb/500 g) strawberries, hulled and quartered

1½ tsp arrowroot or cornstarch

To make the pound cake, preheat the oven to 325°F (165°C). Butter a 9-by-5-inch (23-by-13-cm) loaf pan.

In a saucepan, melt the butter over medium heat. Reduce the heat to medium-low and gently simmer, swirling the pan often, until the butter is browned and smells nutty, 12–15 minutes. Strain the butter through a fine-mesh sieve into a small bowl and let cool to room temperature.

Sift the flour, baking powder, and salt into a bowl. In the bowl of a stand mixer, beat the whole eggs and egg yolks, 1 cup (8 oz/250 g) of the sugar, and the vanilla on medium-high speed until pale and thick, 2–3 minutes. Reduce the speed to low and add the dry ingredients in 2 batches, mixing until only a few streaks remain. Increase the speed to medium-low and drizzle in all but 2 Tbsp of the brown butter. Increase the speed to medium and beat until combined. Scrape the batter into the prepared pan. »→

Bake the cake for 40 minutes, rotating it halfway through baking. Brush the top with the remaining brown butter and sprinkle with the 1 Tbsp sugar. Continue baking until a toothpick inserted into the center comes out clean, 10–15 minutes longer. Let cool in the pan on a wire rack for 30 minutes. Turn the cake out onto the rack, turn right side up, and let cool completely.

Meanwhile, make the compote. In a nonreactive saucepan, combine 3 Tbsp of the orange juice, the sugar, and a pinch of salt. Bring to a simmer over medium-high heat. Add the rhubarb, bring to a boil, reduce the heat to medium-low, and simmer, stirring occasionally, until softened, about 5 minutes. Add the strawberries and simmer until softened, about 2 minutes. In a small bowl, mix the arrowroot and the remaining 1 Tbsp orange juice and stir into the rhubarb mixture. Let cool to room temperature.

Serve thick slices of the pound cake topped with the compote.

11

CHICKEN TACOS WITH RADISH SLAW

serves 6

This new take on the taco replaces the usual tomato salsa with a peppery radish slaw dressed with lime juice. The chicken thighs are simmered in a spiced, citrusy liquid until they begin to fall apart, then they are shredded and set atop warm corn tortillas along with the slaw, avocado slices, and a sprinkle of crumbly cotija cheese.

FOR THE CHICKEN

⅔ cup (5 fl oz/150 ml) fresh orange juice

3 Tbsp fresh lime juice

3 Tbsp achiote paste

1 small yellow onion, chopped

2 cloves garlic, chopped

½ tsp dried oregano

2 lb (1 kg) boneless, skinless chicken thighs

Salt and freshly ground pepper

12 small soft corn tortillas, each 4 inches (10 cm) in diameter

FOR THE RADISH SLAW

18 radishes, halved and thinly sliced

⅓ cup (½ oz/15 g) chopped fresh cilantro

2 green onions, thinly sliced

1 Tbsp fresh lime juice

2 large avocados, halved, pitted, and sliced

3 oz (90 g) cotija cheese, crumbled

To prepare the chicken, in a heavy Dutch oven, stir together the orange juice, lime juice, and achiote paste until smooth. Add the onion, garlic, and oregano and mix well. Add the chicken and turn to coat evenly. Sprinkle the chicken with salt. Cover the pot and place over medium heat. Bring to a simmer, then reduce the heat to low and cook, stirring occasionally, until the sauce has thickened and the chicken is opaque throughout, about 40 minutes. Uncover and continue to simmer until the sauce is very thick and the chicken begins to fall apart, about 10 minutes. Let the chicken cool slightly, then shred. Season with salt and pepper.

Wrap the tortillas in foil and seal tightly. Place in a warm oven for 10 minutes.

To make the slaw, in a bowl, combine the radishes, cilantro, green onion and lime juice and toss to mix. Season with salt.

Arrange 2 tortillas on each individual plate. Top the tortillas with the chicken, dividing evenly, and spoon the radish slaw evenly over the chicken. Top with avocado slices and cheese, and serve.

12

CRAB, PEA & RICOTTA FRITTATA

serves 4–6

Sweet fresh crabmeat, creamy ricotta, and tender English peas make this an elegant spring frittata worthy of serving to company. For a special touch, add sliced, toasted brioche to the plate. Frozen peas will work in a pinch; just thaw them for a few minutes before adding them to the eggs.

Salt and freshly ground pepper

1 cup (5 oz/155 g) fresh peas

Ice water

10 eggs

1 Tbsp heavy cream or whole milk

1 Tbsp olive oil

½ lb (250 g) cooked lump crabmeat, picked over for shell fragments, coarsely chopped

½ cup (4 oz/125 g) ricotta cheese

1 Tbsp chopped fresh chives

Bring a saucepan of salted water to a boil. Add the peas and cook until just tender, about 2 minutes. Drain the peas and immediately plunge into a bowl of ice water. Drain again and set aside.

Preheat the oven to 425°F (220°C). In a bowl, whisk together the eggs, cream, and a pinch each of salt and pepper.

In a 10-inch (25-cm) ovenproof frying pan, heat the oil over medium-low heat. Add the egg mixture and cook, stirring gently, until the eggs begin to set but not to scramble. Gently stir in the peas and crabmeat. Cook the eggs, without stirring, until the edges begin to set, 2–3 minutes. Spoon the ricotta evenly over the top of the frittata. Transfer the pan to the oven and bake until the eggs are set around the edges and just firm in the center, about 5 minutes.

Loosen the sides of the frittata with a spatula. Invert a large plate over the top of the pan. Wearing oven mitts, turn both the pan and the plate and invert the frittata onto the plate. Cut into wedges, garnish with the chives, and serve.

13

CREAM CHEESE MARBLE BROWNIES

makes about 16 brownies

½ cup (4 oz/125 g) unsalted butter

4 oz (125 g) unsweetened chocolate, finely chopped

1 cup (5 oz/155 g) all-purpose flour

¼ tsp kosher salt

3 large eggs

1¾ cups (14 oz/440 g) sugar

1 tsp pure vanilla extract

FOR THE CREAM CHEESE FILLING

6 oz (185 g) cream cheese

¼ cup (2 oz/60 g) sugar

1 large egg

1 tsp pure vanilla extract

Here, a fudgy chocolate batter is swirled with a rich cream cheese filling. The result is a chewy, marbled bar, ideal for tucking into a lunch box, packing for a spring picnic, or taking to a potluck.

Preheat the oven to 325°F (165°C). Butter a 9-inch (23-cm) square baking pan, then press a piece of parchment paper across the bottom and up over two sides of the pan. Butter the parchment.

Place the butter and chocolate in the top of a double boiler over (not touching) barely simmering water, and heat, stirring often, until the chocolate is melted and smooth, 3–4 minutes. Remove from over the water and let cool slightly.

Sift the flour and salt into a small bowl. In a large bowl, whisk the eggs and sugar until blended, about 1 minute. Add the chocolate mixture and the vanilla and whisk until combined. Whisk in the dry ingredients just until incorporated.

To make the filling, in a bowl, stir together the cream cheese, sugar, egg, and vanilla until smooth.

Pour two-thirds of the batter into the prepared pan. Spoon the filling over the batter. Pour the remaining batter over the filling. Starting in one corner, swirl a spoon through the batter and filling to create a marble pattern. Repeat, starting from another corner. Bake until a toothpick inserted into the center comes out with moist crumbs attached, 35–40 minutes. Transfer to a wire rack and let cool to room temperature, about 1 hour. Holding the parchment, lift from the pan, then cut into squares.

14

TUNA BURGERS WITH CREAMY SMOKED PAPRIKA SAUCE

serves 4

1 lb (500 g) tuna steak, finely chopped

1 Tbsp Dijon mustard

¼ cup (⅓ oz/10 g) whole-wheat panko bread crumbs

1½ Tbsp chopped green onion

Salt and freshly ground pepper

FOR THE SMOKED PAPRIKA SAUCE

3 Tbsp olive oil mayonnaise

2 Tbsp plain yogurt

1 Tbsp fresh lemon juice

¼ tsp smoked paprika

Salt

Nonstick cooking spray

4 soft whole-grain rolls

These simple burgers come together in minutes, and the raw patties can be made a day ahead of time and refrigerated until just before cooking. Use hot or sweet paprika to match your heat preference.

Put the tuna in a bowl and add the mustard, panko, and green onion. Stir to mix and season with salt and pepper. Shape the mixture into 4 patties and refrigerate for 30 minutes.

To make the sauce, mix together the mayonnaise, yogurt, lemon juice, and smoked paprika in a small bowl and season with salt.

Set a nonstick frying pan over medium-high heat and lightly coat with cooking spray. Fry the burgers until medium-rare, about 4 minutes per side. Serve the burgers on the rolls, with the sauce.

15

PEA SHOOTS & SHIITAKE MUSHROOMS WITH SOBA NOODLES

serves 4–6

Pea shoots, the young, tender leaves and curly, delicate tendrils of the English pea plant, can be eaten raw or cooked and are ideal for fast-cooking dishes like stir-fries. Choose pea shoots that are bright green and show no sign of wilting, and be sure to remove any yellowed or tough stems before using. This simple stir-fry can also be made with rice or udon noodles, or it can be served over steamed brown or white rice.

Salt

½ lb (250 g) dried soba noodles

½ cup (4 fl oz/125 ml) chicken or vegetable broth

3 Tbsp oyster sauce

1 Tbsp plus 2 tsp soy sauce

1 Tbsp plus 2 tsp rice vinegar

1 tsp sugar

½ tsp cornstarch

3 Tbsp canola oil

1 tsp toasted sesame oil

2 cloves garlic, minced

1-inch (2.5-cm) piece fresh ginger, peeled and minced

3 green onions, light green and white parts only, chopped

¾ lb (375 g) shiitake mushrooms, stems removed, caps sliced

3 cups (3 oz/90 g) pea shoots

⅓ cup (⅓ oz/10 g) fresh Thai basil leaves, chopped

Bring a pan of lightly salted water to a boil. Add the soba noodles and cook, stirring occasionally, for 4 minutes. Drain, rinse the noodles under cold water, and set aside.

In a bowl, stir together the chicken broth, oyster sauce, soy sauce, vinegar, sugar, and cornstarch.

In a wok or large frying pan, heat the canola oil and sesame oil over high heat. Add the garlic, ginger, and green onions and cook, stirring constantly, just until aromatic, about 30 seconds. Add the shiitakes and sauté until softened and browned on the edges, about 3 minutes. Add the oyster sauce mixture and bring to a boil. Add the noodles and toss to coat with the sauce. Add the pea shoots and cook, stirring, just until wilted.

Remove from the heat, stir in the basil, and serve.

16

FRESH LEMON MOUSSE

serves 6–8

Lemon, cream, and egg yolks strike the right balance of rich and flavorful in this sunny yellow mousse. It can be made ahead for a dinner party, freeing you up to linger at the table with guests. If you like, top each serving with fresh berries or chopped fresh mint leaves.

2¼ tsp (1 package) unflavored powdered gelatin

1 cup (8 oz/250 g) granulated sugar

⅛ tsp kosher salt

2 tsp finely grated lemon zest

⅔ cup (5 fl oz/160 ml) fresh lemon juice (about 8 lemons)

4 large egg yolks

2 cups (16 fl oz/500 ml) heavy cream

¼ cup (1 oz/30 g) confectioners' sugar

Pour ¼ cup (2 fl oz/60 ml) water into a saucepan and sprinkle with the gelatin. Let stand until the gelatin softens and swells, 5–10 minutes. Stir in the granulated sugar, salt, lemon zest and juice, and egg yolks. Cook over medium heat, stirring constantly, until the mixture thickens and the gelatin melts completely, 6–8 minutes. Do not allow it to boil. Set the saucepan in an ice bath until the mixture is cool to the touch. Remove the pan from the ice bath and let sit at room temperature.

In a bowl, using an electric mixer, beat the cream and confectioners' sugar on medium speed until soft peaks form, 4–6 minutes. Using a rubber spatula, fold in the lemon mixture until smooth. Spoon the mousse into 6–8 custard cups. Refrigerate the mousse until chilled, 2–3 hours. Remove from the refrigerator about 20 minutes before serving.

17

SEARED SCALLOP, ORANGE & RED ONION SALAD

serves 4

½ red onion, thinly sliced

1½ Tbsp rice vinegar

3 oranges

½ cup (2½ oz/75 g) pitted mild green olives

2 Tbsp extra-virgin olive oil

1 lb (500 g) sea scallops, tough muscles removed

Salt and freshly ground pepper

2 Tbsp coarsely chopped fresh mint

This salad, which pairs scallops with late-season oranges, makes a nice main course for lunch or for a light supper. Pass crusty bread or skinny breadsticks and uncork a dry Riesling or a light-bodied red, such as Pinot Noir or Chianti.

Rinse the onion slices under cold running water, then drain. In a bowl, combine them with the rice vinegar and set aside.

Grate the zest of 1 orange to yield 1 tsp zest and reserve. Cut a slice off the top and bottom of each orange. Stand each upright and, following the contour of the fruit, cut away all the peel and white pith. Slice the oranges in half lengthwise, then slice crosswise into thin half-rounds. In a bowl, combine the orange slices with the olives, reserved zest, and 1 Tbsp of the olive oil.

Pat the scallops dry and season them lightly with salt and pepper. In a large nonstick frying pan, warm the remaining 1 Tbsp oil over medium-high heat. Add the scallops and cook, turning once, until browned on both sides and opaque in the center, 4–5 minutes total. Take care not to overcook the scallops, as they go quickly from perfectly tender to overcooked and tough.

Add the onion (including the vinegar), the mint, a pinch of salt, and a few grindings of pepper to the orange mixture and mix gently. Divide the orange salad among dinner plates, top with the warm scallops, and serve.

18

LAMB TAGINE WITH OLIVES & PRESERVED LEMON

serves 4–5

1½ cups (12 fl oz/375 ml) chicken broth

½ tsp saffron threads

2 lb (1 kg) boneless lamb shoulder, cut into 1-inch (2.5-cm) chunks

Salt and freshly ground pepper

2 Tbsp olive oil

1 yellow onion, finely chopped

1 tsp ground ginger

½ tsp sweet paprika

½ tsp ground cumin

2 cloves garlic, minced

1 bay leaf

12 pitted green olives

1 preserved lemon, chopped

2 Tbsp coarsely chopped fresh flat-leaf parsley

The brininess of olives and preserved lemons nicely complement spring lamb. Serve this Moroccan-style stew over a bed of couscous. Instant varieties are easy to steam and fluff right before you sit down to eat.

In a saucepan, heat the broth over medium-high heat until steaming. Remove from the heat, crumble in the saffron, and let steep.

Generously season the lamb chunks with salt and pepper. In a large, heavy pot, warm the oil over medium-high heat. Add the lamb and brown on all sides, about 5 minutes. Transfer to a platter. Add the onion to the pot and cook, stirring occasionally, until softened, about 5 minutes. Add the ginger, paprika, cumin, and garlic and stir for about 1 minute. Return the lamb to the pot and add the saffron broth, the bay leaf, ½ tsp salt, and pepper to taste. Cover and cook over the lowest possible heat—just so the liquid shimmers—until the lamb is tender, at least 1½ hours. If the tagine starts to look a bit dry, add a splash of water.

Transfer the lamb to a platter and tent with foil. Discard the bay leaf and skim the excess fat from the braising liquid. Add the olives and preserved lemon and simmer over medium-high heat until the juices are thickened slightly, about 5 minutes. Return the lamb to the pot and adjust the seasoning.

Garnish with the parsley and serve.

19

UDON NOODLES WITH POACHED SHRIMP, BABY SPINACH & MISO

serves 6

Salt

8 cups (64 fl oz/2 l) low-sodium vegetable broth

4 thin slices fresh ginger

1 bunch green onions, thinly sliced, green tops and white bottoms separated

¼ bunch fresh cilantro, leaves coarsely chopped and stems reserved

¼ cup (2 oz/60 g) white miso

2 tsp low-sodium soy sauce

½ tsp Sriracha sauce

1 lb (500 g) medium shrimp, peeled and deveined

1 lb (500 g) udon noodles

3 cups (3 oz/90 g) baby spinach

Miso paste is full of antioxidants, known to help prevent cancer. Here it pairs with fresh ginger, bright cilantro, and spicy Sriracha sauce for a broth bursting with flavor and health benefits. If you have leftover chicken on hand, you can shred it and use it in place of the shrimp.

Bring a large pot of generously salted water to a boil over high heat.

In a medium saucepan, combine the broth, ginger, green onion tops, and cilantro stems. Bring the mixture to a boil over high heat, then reduce the heat to medium and let the broth simmer until the flavors are infused, 20–25 minutes.

Strain the broth and return it to the pan, discarding the solids. Return the pan to medium heat and whisk in the miso, soy sauce, and Sriracha sauce until smooth. Add the shrimp and cook, stirring occasionally, until they are just pink and opaque, 1–2 minutes. Remove and set aside.

When the water comes to a boil, add the udon and cook just until tender, 2–3 minutes. Drain the noodles well.

Divide the spinach among 6 shallow soup bowls. Top the spinach with the noodles and ladle the broth over the top, adding a few shrimp to each bowl. Garnish with the chopped cilantro and green onion bottoms, and serve.

20

BAKED LEEKS WITH BREAD CRUMBS

serves 6

6 Tbsp (3 oz/90 g) unsalted butter

2 Tbsp minced shallots

6–8 leeks, about 3 lb (1.5 kg) total, white and pale green parts, chopped

Salt and ground white pepper

2 cups (16 fl oz/500 ml) whole milk, plus more as needed

3 Tbsp all-purpose flour

¼ tsp cayenne pepper

½ cup (2 oz/60 g) shredded Gruyère cheese

½ cup (1 oz/30 g) fresh bread crumbs

Springtime leeks are the royalty of the onion family and have pride of place in French cuisine, where they appear with vinaigrettes and in quiches, stews, and gratins, such as this one. This flavorful dish works well as a first course, a main course, or a side, and it can be baked in individual baking dishes or in a single large one. Serve alongside a roast leg of lamb for a special occasion.

Preheat the oven to 400°F (200°C).

In a frying pan, melt 2 Tbsp of the butter over medium-high heat. Add the shallots, leeks, and ½ tsp each salt and white pepper. Reduce the heat to medium and cook, stirring often, until the leeks are translucent and very soft, about 15 minutes.

In a small saucepan, warm the 2 cups (16 fl oz/500 ml) milk over medium heat until small bubbles appear around the edge of the pan. Cover and remove from the heat.

In a saucepan, melt 3 Tbsp of the butter over medium-high heat. Remove from the heat and whisk in the flour, ½ tsp salt, ¼ tsp white pepper, and the cayenne. Return the pan to medium-low heat and cook, stirring often, for 2 minutes. Slowly whisk in the hot milk and simmer, stirring, until the sauce thickens, about 15 minutes. If the sauce is too thin, increase the heat; if it is too thick, whisk in a little more milk. Stir in the leek mixture.

Pour the mixture into a baking or gratin dish. Sprinkle evenly with the cheese and the bread crumbs and dot with the remaining 1 Tbsp butter. Bake until the cheese and bread crumb topping are golden and the gratin is bubbly, 20–30 minutes. Remove from the oven and serve.

21

*Risotto is an
example of the
Italian talent for
turning the simplest
ingredients into
a sublime dish.
Here, springtime
asparagus shines
against the creamy
grains. This light
vegetarian main
is also ideal as
a side dish to meat
or poultry for
a heartier meal.*

ASPARAGUS RISOTTO

serves 6

Salt and freshly ground pepper

12 oz (375 g) asparagus, trimmed
and cut into 2-inch (5-cm) pieces

6 cups (48 fl oz/1.5 l) chicken or
vegetable broth

¼ cup (2 fl oz/60 ml) olive oil

½ cup (2 oz/60 g) finely chopped
yellow onion

2 cups (14 oz/440 g) Arborio or Carnaroli rice

1 cup (8 fl oz/250 ml) dry white wine

1–2 Tbsp unsalted butter

Grated Parmesan cheese

Bring a large saucepan of salted water to
a boil. Add the asparagus and cook until
barely tender, 2–3 minutes. Drain and refresh
with cold water, and drain again.

In the saucepan, bring the broth to a gentle
simmer over medium heat. Reduce the heat
to low and maintain a simmer.

In another large saucepan, heat the oil over
medium heat. Add the onion and sauté until
softened, about 5 minutes. Add the rice and
stir until well coated with oil and translucent,
about 3 minutes.

Add the wine and cook, stirring, until it is
completely absorbed. Add the simmering
broth to the rice a ladleful at a time, stirring
frequently after each addition. Wait until the
broth is almost completely absorbed (but the
rice is never dry on top) before adding the
next ladleful. After about 20 minutes, when
you have added all but ¼ cup (2 fl oz/60 ml)
of the broth, the rice should be tender to
the bite and creamy. If it is not quite done,
continue to cook, adding the remaining broth.

Remove from the heat. Stir in the asparagus
and butter, and Parmesan to taste. Season
with salt and pepper, and serve.

22

*A glistening whole
ham forms a striking
centerpiece for
an Easter dinner
or brunch. Take
inspiration from the
American South and
slip some bourbon
into the glaze for a
hint of sweet and
spice. Accompany
this memorable
main with a basket
of fluffy biscuits
and a green salad.*

BOURBON-GLAZED HAM

serves 12–14, with leftovers

20 lb (10 kg) fully cooked, bone-in ham

2½ cups (17½ oz/545 g) firmly packed
dark brown sugar

⅓ cup (3 fl oz/80 ml) bourbon

15–20 whole cloves

Preheat the oven to 325°F (165°C). Line a
roasting pan with foil and set a roasting rack
in the pan. Cut away and discard any skin
from the ham and trim the fat to ½ inch
(12 mm) thick. Place the ham, fat side up, on
the rack in the pan. Roast until the ham is
fully warmed through and an instant-read
thermometer inserted into the thickest
part of the ham (but not touching the bone)
registers 140°F (60°C), 3–3½ hours.

Remove the ham from the oven. Raise the
oven temperature to 425°F (220°C). In a bowl,
combine the sugar and bourbon and mix to
form a paste. Score the fat on the upper half
of the ham in a diamond pattern, cutting
about ¼ inch (6 mm) deep. Rub the paste over
the surface of the fat, then insert the cloves
at random intersections of the diamonds.
Return the ham to the oven and bake, basting
several times with the pan juices, until the
surface is shiny and beginning to brown,
15–20 minutes.

Transfer the ham to a cutting board and tent
loosely with foil. Let stand for 20–30 minutes.
Remove the cloves. Carve half of the ham,
arrange on a platter, and serve. Carve the
remaining ham as needed.

23

ROAST CHICKEN & BREAD SALAD WITH HARICOTS VERTS & STRAWBERRIES

serves 6–8

APRIL

Ideal for a family dinner, this colorful one-dish meal shows off some of the season's most popular produce, with pump red strawberries alongside slender green haricots verts. You can use a whole chicken, cut into pieces, as suggested here, or you can buy the parts—legs, thighs, breasts—that your family likes best.

1 chicken (3 lb/1.5 kg),
cut into 8 serving pieces

5 Tbsp (3 fl oz/80 ml) olive oil

Salt and freshly ground pepper

8 oz (250 g) haricots verts or thin green beans

½ loaf crusty Italian bread,
cut into 1-inch (2.5-cm) cubes

1 shallot, minced

2 Tbsp red wine vinegar

2 Tbsp dried currants

¼ tsp Dijon mustard

1 pt (8 oz/250 g) strawberries,
hulled and halved

Preheat the oven to 400°F (200°C). Brush the chicken pieces with 2 Tbsp of the oil and place them on a baking sheet. Season well with salt and pepper and roast until an instant-read thermometer inserted into the thickest part of the thigh, not touching bone, reads 170°F (77°C), about 1 hour. Remove from the oven and reduce the oven temperature to 350°F (180°C).

Meanwhile, bring a saucepan of water to a boil over high heat. Add ½ tsp salt and the haricots verts and blanch just until slightly tender, about 2 minutes. Transfer to a colander and run under cold water to stop the cooking. Drain and set aside.

Toss the bread with 1 Tbsp of the oil and season with salt and pepper. Arrange the bread in a single layer on a baking sheet and bake until golden-brown, stirring once or twice, about 12 minutes.

In a small bowl, stir together the shallot, red wine vinegar, currants, and mustard. Slowly whisk in the remaining 2 Tbsp oil and season with salt and pepper to make a vinaigrette.

Place the haricots verts, strawberries, and croutons in a large bowl and add the vinaigrette. Toss to coat well and arrange on a large platter. Nestle the chicken pieces into the bread salad and serve.

24

BROCCOLI RABE & PARMESAN FRITTERS

serves 4–6

APRIL

In these tasty fritters, pleasantly bitter broccoli rabe is mixed with tangy buttermilk and sharp cheese and then panfried until golden. Serve them alongside lamb chops, preferably rubbed with Italian-inspired seasonings.

Ice water

1½ cups (4 oz/125 g) chopped broccoli rabe

2 cups (10 oz/315 g) stone-ground cornmeal

½ cup (2 oz/60 g) grated Parmesan cheese

1 Tbsp all-purpose flour

1 tsp *each* baking soda and baking powder

Salt

⅓ cup (1 oz/30 g) minced green onions,
white and tender green parts only

1 egg, separated, plus 2 egg whites

1½ cups (12 fl oz/375 ml) buttermilk

Canola oil for frying

Bring a pot of salted water to a boil. Have ready a large bowl of ice water. Add the broccoli rabe to the boiling water and cook for 1 minute. Drain and transfer to the ice water. Drain again and spread on paper towels to dry.

In a bowl, combine the cornmeal, cheese, flour, baking soda, baking powder, and 1 tsp salt and mix well. Add the green onions, egg yolk, and buttermilk and stir until well combined. Stir in the broccoli rabe. In a bowl, using an electric mixer, beat the egg whites until stiff peaks form. Fold into the batter.

Pour oil into a large saucepan to a depth of about 2 inches (5 cm) and heat to 325°F (165°C). Working in batches, drop in the batter by the tablespoonful and fry until golden brown, 3–5 minutes. Using a slotted spoon, transfer the fritters to paper towels to drain. Let the oil return to 325°F before frying the next batch. Serve hot.

25

Golden brown and bubbling, this perennial dish is welcome at the table any time of the year. Sweet Italian sausage, colorful peppers, and fragrant fennel add heft to this one-pan baked pasta. A touch of cream finishes the dish and rounds out the tangy tomato sauce.

BAKED RIGATONI WITH FENNEL, SAUSAGE & PEPERONATA

serves 6

2 Tbsp extra-virgin olive oil, plus more for greasing

1 lb (500 g) rigatoni

1 fennel bulb

¾ lb (350 g) sweet Italian sausage, casings removed, crumbled

1 *each* red, yellow, and orange bell pepper, seeded and cut into matchsticks

Salt and freshly ground black pepper

1 tsp sugar

1 Tbsp red wine vinegar

1 cup (8 fl oz/250 ml) prepared tomato sauce

1½ cups (12 fl oz/375 ml) heavy cream

2 cups (8 oz/250 g) shredded fontina cheese

¼ cup (1 oz/30 g) grated Parmesan cheese

Preheat the oven to 425°F (220°C). Lightly oil a 9-by-13-inch (23-by-33-cm) baking dish.

Bring a pot of salted water to a boil. Add the pasta and cook until al dente, 7–8 minutes, or according to the package directions. Drain and place in a large bowl.

Remove and discard the stalks and core from the fennel bulb and dice the bulb. In a frying pan, heat 1 Tbsp of the oil over medium heat. Add the crumbled sausage and cook, stirring occasionally, until lightly browned, 3–4 minutes. Add the fennel and cook, stirring, until tender, 4–5 minutes. Add to the bowl with the pasta.

Add the remaining 1 Tbsp oil to the pan, along with the bell peppers and a pinch each of salt and black pepper. Cook, stirring occasionally, until the bell peppers are tender with a bit of a bite, 3–4 minutes. Add the sugar and vinegar and continue cooking until the vinegar has reduced to a syrup, 1–2 minutes. Add the tomato sauce and cream and cook, stirring, until lightly thickened, 4–5 minutes. Transfer to the bowl with the pasta, add the fontina, and stir well.

Pour the pasta mixture into the prepared dish and top with the Parmesan. Bake until the top is golden brown and the sauce is bubbling around the sides, 10–15 minutes. Serve directly from the dish.

26

Rhubarb is a tart fruit that becomes sweet and tender after cooking. It's important to remove any leaves and green parts of the rhubarb, which can be poisonous. All that should remain is the crimson shaft of the plant, which is rich in vitamin C and fiber. This sweet fruit-and-nut chutney complements juicy pork tenderloin, which is a versatile, lean choice for any meal.

PORK TENDERLOIN WITH RHUBARB CHUTNEY

serves 4

FOR THE RHUBARB CHUTNEY

1 cup (7 oz/220 g) firmly packed light brown sugar

½ cup (4 fl oz/125 ml) cider vinegar

1 Tbsp grated lemon zest

4 rhubarb stalks, cut into 1-inch (2.5-cm) pieces

1 cinnamon stick

2 Tbsp minced fresh ginger

½ cup (3 oz/90 g) golden raisins

¼ cup (1 oz/30 g) chopped walnuts

Salt and freshly ground pepper

1 pork tenderloin, about 1 lb (500 g)

Salt and freshly ground pepper

To make the chutney, in a nonreactive saucepan over low heat, cook the sugar, vinegar, and lemon zest, stirring until the sugar dissolves, about 5 minutes. Add the rhubarb, cinnamon stick, and ginger. Raise the heat to medium and cook, stirring often, until the rhubarb is soft, about 15 minutes. Remove the cinnamon stick. Add the raisins, walnuts, and a large pinch of salt and cook for about 3 minutes. Remove from the heat and set aside to cool.

Preheat the oven to 425°F (220°C). Line a small roasting pan with aluminum foil. Oil a flat roasting rack and place it in the pan.

Season the pork with salt and pepper. Roast the pork on the rack until a thermometer inserted into the thickest part registers 140°F (60°C) for medium, about 40 minutes. Remove from the oven, transfer the pork to a carving board, tent with foil, and let rest for 15 minutes.

Cut the pork into slices ½ inch (12 mm) thick. Arrange on a warmed platter, top with the chutney, and serve.

27

GRILLED ASPARAGUS & GREEN ONION SOUP WITH POACHED EGGS

serves 4

Charring the asparagus and green onions before chopping them and simmering them in broth delivers smoky, complex flavors to the finished soup. Grilling the bread for the poached egg, rather than toasting it in the oven, doubles up on those smoky flavors and makes any brunch or lunch at which this soup is served a special occasion.

2 lb (1 kg) asparagus, trimmed

1 bunch green onions, trimmed

3 Tbsp olive oil

Salt and freshly ground pepper

4 slices baguette, cut on the diagonal

1 Tbsp unsalted butter

½ yellow onion, chopped

5 cups (40 fl oz/1.25 l) vegetable or chicken broth

½ cup (4 oz/125 g) crème fraîche

1 tsp white wine vinegar

4 eggs

Prepare a charcoal or gas grill for direct-heat cooking over medium-high heat. Alternatively, preheat a stove-top grill pan over medium-high heat. In a large bowl, toss together the asparagus, green onions, 2 Tbsp of the oil, ½ tsp salt, and ¼ tsp pepper. Place on the grill rack or in the grill pan and cook, turning often, until lightly golden and tender, about 6 minutes total. Transfer to a cutting board and coarsely chop, keeping the asparagus and green onions separate. Set aside. Brush the baguette slices on both sides with the remaining 1 Tbsp oil. Grill, turning once or twice, until golden, 4–5 minutes total. Transfer to a plate and set aside.

In a large, heavy pot, melt the butter over medium heat. When it foams, add the yellow onion and cook, stirring occasionally, until soft, about 2 minutes. Add the green onions and the broth and bring to a simmer. Reduce the heat to low and simmer for 15 minutes to allow the flavors to blend. Add the asparagus and the crème fraîche and simmer for 2–3 minutes. Let cool slightly.

Working in batches, purée the soup in a food processor or blender. Pour into the same pot, cover, and keep warm over low heat. »→

In a frying pan, heat 1 inch (2.5 cm) of water over medium-high heat. Add the vinegar and reduce the heat to keep the water at a gentle simmer. Break an egg into a small bowl and, using a large spoon, place the egg gently in the water. Repeat with the remaining 3 eggs. Cover and simmer until the whites are firm and opaque and the yolks are cooked but still soft, about 4 minutes.

Ladle the soup into bowls. Top each crouton with a poached egg and place one on each bowl. Sprinkle the eggs with ¼ tsp pepper and serve.

28

MUSTARD-CRUSTED SALMON WITH RED POTATOES

serves 4

Spicy mustard rubbed onto fish imparts a quick infusion of flavor. The whole meal goes into the oven at the same time, as waxy new potatoes roast alongside the salmon. Add a salad of peppery arugula or fresh petite peas, and whisk a dollop of mustard into the vinaigrette to bring it all together.

1 lb (500 g) red-skinned potatoes, quartered

2 Tbsp olive oil

Salt and freshly ground pepper

¼ cup (2 oz/60 g) Dijon mustard

2 Tbsp dry mustard

4 salmon fillets, about 6 oz (185 g) each, skin removed

4 Tbsp (1 oz/15 g) panko or fresh bread crumbs

¼ cup (½ oz/15 g) chopped fresh flat-leaf parsley

Preheat the oven to 375°F (190°C). In a large roasting pan, toss the potatoes with the olive oil and season with salt and pepper. Spread the potatoes evenly in the pan. Roast until the potatoes are golden, about 10 minutes.

Meanwhile, in a small bowl, stir together the Dijon and dry mustard. Coat one side of the salmon fillets with the mustard mixture, then sprinkle evenly with the panko, gently pressing to adhere.

Arrange the fillets in the pan, breaded side up, next to the potatoes. Bake until the fillets are barely opaque, the topping is golden brown, and the potatoes are tender, 15–18 minutes. Arrange the salmon fillets alongside the potatoes on a platter or individual plates, sprinkle with the parsley, and serve.

29

To make the cream cheese frosting, in the bowl of a stand mixer fitted with the paddle attachment, beat ½ lb (250 g) room-temperature cream cheese, ¼ cup (2 oz/60 g) room-temperature unsalted butter, and 2 tsp pure vanilla extract on medium-high speed until light and fluffy, about 2 minutes. Gradually beat in 1 cup (4 oz/125 g) sifted confectioners' sugar and continue to mix until thoroughly combined, scraping down the sides of the bowl as needed. Use right away, or, if the consistency is too soft, refrigerate the frosting until it is spreadable, 10–15 minutes. The frosting will keep in the refrigerator for up to 3 days.

CARROT CAKE

serves 10–12

2 cups (8 oz/250 g) cake flour

2 tsp baking powder

2 tsp baking soda

1 tsp kosher salt

1 tsp ground cinnamon

¼ tsp ground nutmeg

1½ cups (12 oz/375 g) sugar

4 large eggs

1¼ cups (10 fl oz/310 ml) canola oil

Grated zest of 1 orange

4 large carrots, peeled and grated (about 3 cups/1 lb/500 g)

Cream Cheese Frosting (*left*)

Preheat the oven to 350°F (180°C). Butter and flour a 9-by-13-inch (23-by-33-cm) baking pan.

Sift the flour, baking powder, baking soda, salt, cinnamon, and nutmeg onto a sheet of parchment paper. In a large bowl, whisk the sugar, eggs, oil, and orange zest until thoroughly combined. Stir in the carrots. Using a rubber spatula, fold in the dry ingredients just until incorporated. Pour the batter into the prepared pan.

Bake the cake until a toothpick inserted into the center comes out clean, 35–40 minutes. Watch closely at the end so that the cake does not overbake. Let cool in the pan on a wire rack for 15 minutes. Invert the cake onto the rack and let cool completely. Cover with a clean, slightly damp kitchen towel so that the outside does not dry out.

Transfer the cooled cake to a platter. Using an icing spatula, frost the cake with a thick layer of cream cheese frosting and serve.

30

This classic Latin dish of "rice with chicken" is like a simplified version of paella. Saffron-infused rice is simmered with onion, peppers, and tomatoes and topped with pan-seared chicken for a simple and comforting one-pan meal.

ARROZ CON POLLO

serves 6

4 large cloves garlic, minced

2 tsp red pepper flakes

1 Tbsp white vinegar

Salt and freshly ground black pepper

3 lb (1.5 kg) chicken pieces, skin on and bone in

3 Tbsp olive oil

4 cups (32 fl oz/1 l) chicken broth

½ tsp saffron threads

1 red onion, chopped

2 bell peppers, seeded and chopped

1 large jalapeño chile, seeded and minced

4 plum tomatoes, chopped

1 tsp ground cumin

2 bay leaves

2 cups (14 oz/440 g) long-grain white rice

In a large bowl, stir together the garlic, red pepper flakes, vinegar, 1 tsp salt, and ½ tsp black pepper. Add the chicken pieces, toss to coat, and refrigerate for at least 1 hour or up to overnight.

In a large frying pan with a lid, heat the oil over medium heat. Remove the chicken and brush off the marinade, reserving it in the bowl. Arrange the chicken in the pan, skin side down, and cook without turning, until golden brown, 10–15 minutes. Turn the chicken, cover the pan, and cook until golden on the second side, about 10 minutes. Meanwhile, in a saucepan, warm the broth over medium-high heat. Remove from the heat, crumble in the saffron, and let steep.

Transfer the chicken to a plate and pour off all but 2 Tbsp fat from the pan. Add the onion, bell peppers, and jalapeño and sauté until softened, about 3 minutes. Add the tomatoes and cook, stirring, for 1 minute. Add the cumin, bay leaves, and rice and cook, stirring constantly, until the rice has absorbed the pan juices, 3–5 minutes. Pour the reserved marinade and saffron broth into the pan and stir briefly. Place the chicken on top. Raise the heat to medium-high and bring to a boil. Reduce the heat to low, cover, and simmer until the chicken is opaque throughout, the rice is tender, and the liquid has been absorbed, about 25 minutes. Let stand for 5–10 minutes before serving.

Lighter fare is on the calendar this month, as warmer days move salads, grilled vegetables, and simple stir-fries onto the dinner table. Thin, crisp pizza topped with asparagus and leeks, rice-paper rolls filled with shrimp and vegetables, and a chopped chicken salad are all welcome as the days lengthen and the occasional alfresco meal becomes possible. You'll still turn on the oven, of course, to roast end-of-the-season asparagus with morels or to bake a vegetable tart. Both berries and cherries are abundant in May and are perfect choices for such crowd-pleasing desserts as napoleons, clafoutis, and lattice-top pies.

1
FLANK STEAK STUFFED WITH ASPARAGUS PESTO
page 106

2
CHEF'S SALAD WITH SOPRESSATA, FONTINA & PICKLED PEPPERS
page 106

3
STIR-FRIED CALAMARI & PEA SHOOTS
page 109

8
HALIBUT WITH BRAISED ESCAROLE & WHITE BEANS
page 112

9
CARNITAS
page 112

10
DARK CHOCOLATE DONUT HOLES
page 114

15
SQUID SALAD WITH ORANGES, FAVA BEANS & FENNEL
page 116

16
CORN & PEA EMPANADITAS
page 119

17
BRAISED PORK CHOPS WITH CHERRIES
page 119

22
GRILLED ASPARAGUS & ENDIVE WITH FAVAS, ORANGE & MINT
page 123

23
WHITE WINE–BRAISED SALMON WITH TARRAGON
page 123

24
CHOPPED CHICKEN SALAD WITH LEMON-TARRAGON DRESSING
page 124

29
GRILLED BABY ARTICHOKES WITH SPICY GARLIC BUTTER
page 127

30
CHERRY LATTICE PIE
page 129

31
SPANISH GARLIC SHRIMP
page 129

4
ROASTED ASPARAGUS & MORELS WITH SHALLOT BUTTER
page 109

5
CURRIED SAMOSAS WITH TAMARIND CHUTNEY
page 110

6
FROSTED LEMON CUPCAKES
page 111

7
FRESH PEA SOUP WITH CHIVES & CRÈME FRAÎCHE
page 111

11
RAMEN NOODLE SOUP WITH SUGAR SNAP PEAS
page 114

12
LOBSTER & AVOCADO SALAD WITH SHAVED MEYER LEMON
page 115

13
STUFFED PIQUILLO PEPPERS
page 115

14
SPRING VEGETABLE TART
page 116

18
PIZZA WITH ASPARAGUS, LEEKS & HERBED RICOTTA
page 120

19
CHICKEN PARMESAN WITH GREENS
page 120

20
CURRIED CARROT PURÉE
page 121

21
STIR-FRIED RICE VERMICELLI WITH CHICKEN & SHRIMP
page 121

25
STRAWBERRY NAPOLEONS
page 124

26
MEXICAN NACHO CASSEROLE
page 126

27
SHRIMP SUMMER ROLLS
page 126

28
RASPBERRY-ALMOND CLAFOUTIS
page 127

may

FLANK STEAK STUFFED WITH ASPARAGUS PESTO

serves 4–6

Pesto can be made from nearly any green, leafy vegetable or herb and even some stalks, like asparagus. Here, parboiled asparagus blends beautifully into a pesto with bright green color and earthy flavor. The fiber-rich paste is spiraled into a juicy roll of flank steak for a festive presentation. Any leftover pesto is delicious on pasta; spread on whole-grain bruschetta, then topped with fresh mozzarella; or as a filling for an omelet.

FOR THE ASPARAGUS PESTO

½ tsp salt

¾ lb (375 g) asparagus, trimmed

3 Tbsp pine nuts

2 cloves garlic

Grated zest of 1 lemon

½ cup (2 oz/60 g) grated Parmesan cheese

6 Tbsp (3 fl oz/90 ml) olive oil

FOR THE FLANK STEAK

1–1¾ lb (500–875 g) flank steak, butterflied

Salt and freshly ground pepper

2 tsp olive oil

To make the pesto, bring a saucepan of water to a boil over high heat. Add the salt and asparagus and cook just until tender, about 4 minutes. Drain and immediately plunge into a bowl filled with ice water to stop the cooking. Drain well. Transfer the asparagus, pine nuts, and garlic to a food processor and pulse to finely chop. Add the lemon zest, Parmesan, and oil and purée until smooth. Season with salt and set aside.

Preheat the oven to 400°F (200°C). Lay the steak flat on a work surface and season with salt and pepper. Spread a ¼-inch (6-mm) layer of the pesto over the top of the steak, leaving about a ½-inch (12-mm) border around the edges. Roll the steak up with the grain and lay it seam-side down on the work surface. Using kitchen twine, tie the steak roll in 4 different spots, each about 2 inches (5 cm) apart.

In a large frying pan over high heat, warm the 2 tsp oil. Add the flank steak and sear until browned, about 3 minutes per side. Transfer the steak to a baking sheet and place in the oven. Roast until the center of the meat registers about 125°F (52°C) on a meat thermometer, 20–25 minutes. Let the steak rest for 10 minutes.

Remove the strings, slice the steak, and serve.

CHEF'S SALAD WITH SOPRESSATA, FONTINA & PICKLED PEPPERS

serves 6

Think of this as an antipasto platter transformed into a chef's salad with the addition of lettuce and a dressing, and this will help you to create your own variations. Different cured meats, such as salami or bresaola, could be used, or cheeses such as pecorino or mozzarella.

5 thick slices day-old country-style bread

2 Tbsp extra-virgin olive oil

Salt and freshly ground pepper

FOR THE OREGANO VINAIGRETTE

¼ cup (2 fl oz/60 ml) extra-virgin olive oil

1 Tbsp minced shallot

2 Tbsp red wine vinegar

2 Tbsp chopped fresh oregano

12–15 cherry tomatoes, halved

1½ heads romaine lettuce, torn into bite-sized pieces (about 6 cups/6 oz/185 g)

18 slices sopressata or salami, cut into triangles

6 oz (185 g) fontina cheese, thinly sliced and cut into strips ½ inch (12 mm) wide

8 oz (250 g) peperoncini, coarsely chopped

1 Tbsp chopped fresh oregano

Preheat the oven to 400°F (200°C).

Cut the bread into 1-inch (2.5-cm) cubes. Put them on a baking sheet just large enough to hold the cubes in a single layer, drizzle with the 2 Tbsp oil, and toss several times to coat. Sprinkle with ½ tsp salt. Bake, turning several times, until golden, 10–15 minutes. Set the croutons aside.

To make the vinaigrette, in a large bowl, combine the ¼ cup oil, shallot, vinegar, 2 Tbsp oregano, ¼ tsp salt, and ¼ tsp pepper. Mix well with a fork or whisk.

Add the tomatoes to the vinaigrette and press them slightly with the back of a fork to release their juices. Just before serving, add the lettuce and half the croutons and toss.

Divide the dressed salad evenly among individual bowls. Divide and arrange the sopressata, cheese, peperoncini, and remaining croutons on each salad. Sprinkle with the 1 Tbsp oregano and serve.

MAY

3

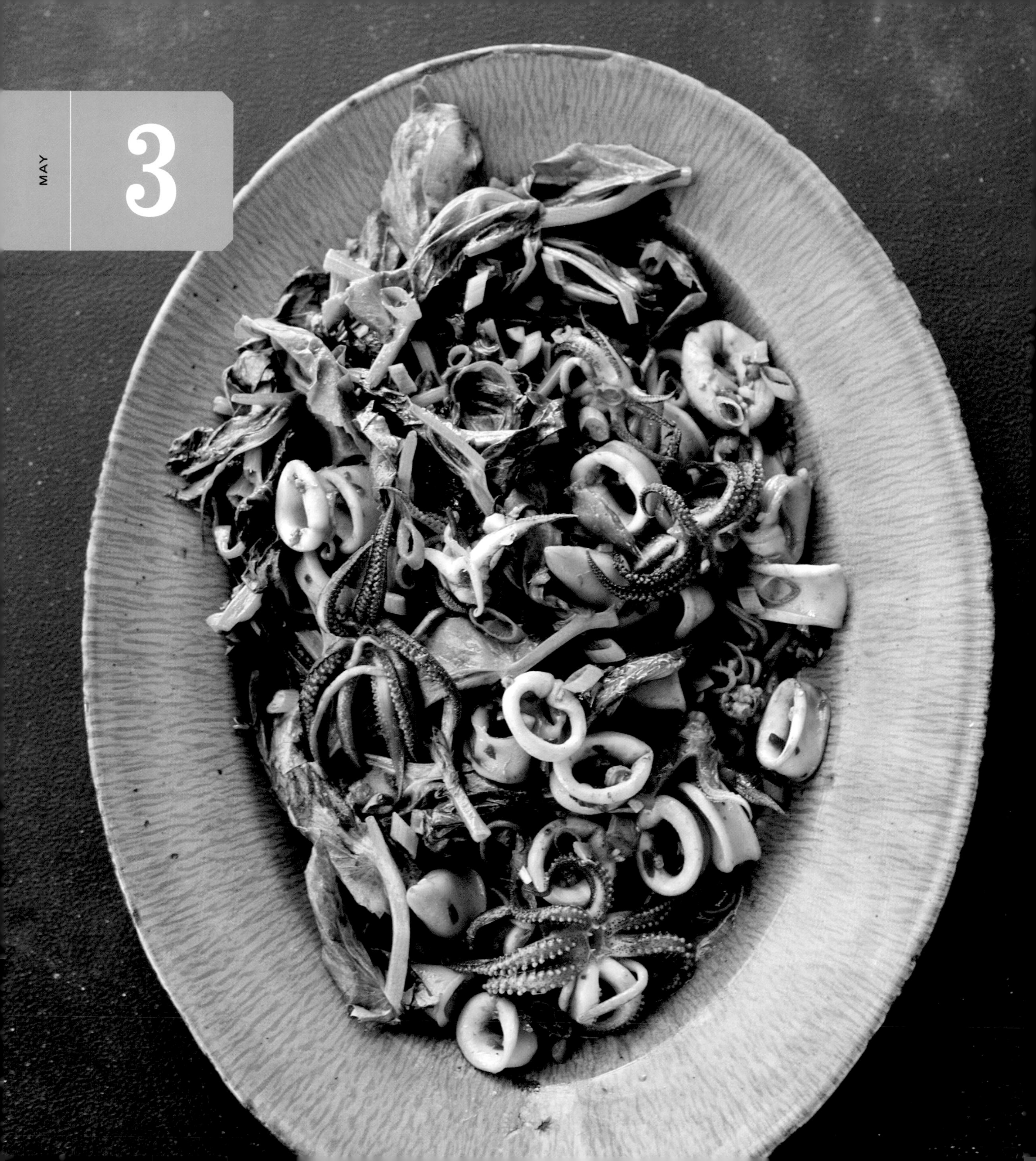

STIR-FRIED CALAMARI & PEA SHOOTS

serves 4

Tender and sweet, pea shoots are delicious when eaten raw or sautéed. Look for them at the farmers' market in the spring and early summer. Here, they are briefly cooked in a hot pan with tender squid rings and tentacles and lots of lemon. If you cannot find pea shoots at the market, substitute spinach leaves.

4 Tbsp (2 fl oz/60 ml) peanut or canola oil

2 Tbsp minced garlic

1 Tbsp peeled and grated fresh ginger

1 lb (500 g) pea shoots, tough parts removed

½ cup (1½ oz/45 g) chopped green onions

¼ cup (2 fl oz/60 ml) chicken broth

Salt and freshly ground pepper

1 Tbsp soy sauce

1 tsp chile paste

1 tsp sugar

1 tsp toasted sesame oil

¾ lb (375 g) cleaned squid, cut into bite-size pieces

Cooked rice for serving (optional)

In a wok or large frying pan, heat 2 Tbsp of the peanut oil over medium-high heat. Add the garlic and ginger and stir-fry until fragrant, about 30 seconds. Add the pea shoots and green onions and stir-fry for 3 minutes. Add the broth, ½ tsp salt, and ⅛ tsp pepper and cook until the shoots are tender-crisp, about 2 minutes. Using a slotted spoon, transfer to a plate. Wipe out the pan.

In a small bowl, mix together the soy sauce, chile paste, sugar, and sesame oil.

Warm the remaining 2 Tbsp peanut oil in the pan over medium-high heat. Add the squid and stir-fry until opaque, about 2 minutes. Return the pea shoots to the pan, add the soy sauce mixture, and stir-fry, tossing to combine and heat through, about 1 minute. Using the slotted spoon, transfer the greens and squid to a platter. Serve over rice, if desired.

ROASTED ASPARAGUS & MORELS WITH SHALLOT BUTTER

serves 6

Look for thin asparagus spears for this dish; they are generally more tender than fat spears, and the stalks do not require peeling before cooking. Morels, with their distinctive conical shape, have a special affinity for asparagus, but if you are unable to find them, oyster or cremini mushrooms can be substituted.

1½ lb (750 g) thin asparagus, ends trimmed

4 oz (125 g) morel mushrooms

4 Tbsp (2 oz/60 g) unsalted butter

2 shallots, minced

1 Tbsp chopped fresh tarragon

Salt and freshly ground pepper

Preheat the oven to 450°F (230°C).

Arrange the asparagus in a single layer on a baking sheet. If the morels are large, cut them crosswise into rings ¼ inch (6 mm) wide. Leave small ones whole. Add the mushrooms to the baking sheet.

In a small saucepan, melt the butter over low heat. Add the shallots and sauté for 1 minute. Drizzle the shallot butter over the asparagus and morels. Scatter the tarragon over the top and season with salt and pepper. Toss the asparagus and morels in the butter and tarragon until evenly coated and then spread in a single layer.

Roast until the asparagus is lightly browned but still crisp and the morels are dark brown, about 10 minutes. Transfer the asparagus and morels to a platter. Drizzle any pan juices over the top and serve.

5

CURRIED SAMOSAS WITH TAMARIND CHUTNEY

serves 8–10

Here, sweet-hot curry powder and pungent garlic and onion contribute their flavors to a creamy butternut squash filling enclosed in a crisp pastry shell. The tart tamarind chutney balances the sweetness of the filling. Serve these savory pastries at a cocktail party or as a starter for a contemporary Indian menu. Look for the tamarind paste in South Asian or Southeast Asian food shops.

FOR THE TAMARIND CHUTNEY

½ tsp ground cumin

½ tsp garam masala

½ tsp ground ginger

¼ cup (2 oz/60 g) seedless tamarind paste

Salt

Sugar

1 butternut squash, about 1½ lb (750 g)

3 Tbsp olive oil

2 Tbsp chopped white onion

2 cloves garlic, chopped

1 Tbsp Madras curry powder

1 tsp sugar

Salt

1 egg

1 package (1 lb/500 g) square wonton wrappers

Canola or rice bran oil for deep-frying

To make the chutney, in a small, dry saucepan, toast the cumin, garam masala, and ginger over medium-low heat, shaking the pan occasionally, until fragrant, 30–60 seconds. Remove from the heat and let cool in the pan for about 2 minutes.

Break up the tamarind paste with your fingers, and remove any errant seeds. Add the tamarind and 2 cups (16 fl oz/500 ml) water to the spice mixture and return to medium heat. Simmer, stirring and mashing the tamarind constantly, until reduced by one-half, about 15 minutes. Taste and adjust the seasoning with salt and sugar. Pour the chutney into a small bowl, let cool, cover, and set aside at room temperature. You should have about 1 cup (8 fl oz/250 ml).

Preheat the oven to 400°F (200°C). Cut the squash in half lengthwise and scoop out and discard the seeds. Place the halves, cut sides up, on a rimmed baking sheet and drizzle with 1 Tbsp of the olive oil. Bake the squash until tender when pierced with a knife, about 40 minutes. Let cool until easy to handle, then scoop the cooled flesh into a bowl and discard the skins. ⇥

In a saucepan, warm the remaining 2 Tbsp olive oil over medium heat. Add the onion and garlic and sauté until the onion is soft, 3–5 minutes. Remove from the heat and stir in the curry powder. Add the squash flesh and mash with a potato masher until almost smooth. Stir in the sugar and 1 tsp salt, then adjust the seasoning if necessary.

In a small bowl, beat the egg with a fork until blended. Lay about 5 wonton wrappers on a work surface; keep the remaining wrappers covered with a slightly damp kitchen towel. Spoon a scant 1 Tbsp of the squash filling in the center of each wrapper and flatten with the bottom of the spoon. Brush the edges of the wrapper with the egg. Fold each wrapper in half on the diagonal, forming a triangle, then press the edges together to seal the filling inside; set aside. Repeat with the remaining wrappers and filling.

Preheat the oven to 200°F (95°C). Set a wire rack on a large baking sheet and place near the stove. Pour oil to a depth of 3 inches (7.5 cm) into a deep, heavy frying pan and heat over medium-high heat until hot but not smoking. Working in batches, add the samosas to the oil and fry, turning once, until golden brown on both sides, about 2 minutes on each side. Using a slotted spoon, transfer to the rack to drain and then keep warm in the oven. Cook the remaining samosas in the same way, adding more oil to the pan if needed. You should have about 40 samosas.

Arrange the samosas on a platter, set the chutney alongside for dipping, and serve.

FROSTED LEMON CUPCAKES

makes 18 cupcakes

2 cups (10 oz/315 g) all-purpose flour

2 tsp baking powder

½ tsp baking soda

½ tsp kosher salt

⅔ cup (5 oz/155 g) unsalted butter, at cool room temperature

1 cup (8 oz/250 g) granulated sugar

1 Tbsp finely grated lemon zest

2 large eggs

1 cup (8 fl oz/250 ml) buttermilk

⅓ cup (3 fl oz/80 ml) strained fresh lemon juice

1 tsp pure vanilla extract

FOR THE LEMON FROSTING

½ cup (4 oz/125 g) unsalted butter, at cool room temperature

3 cups (12 oz/375 g) confectioners' sugar

¼ cup (2 fl oz/60 ml) fresh lemon juice

½ tsp pure vanilla extract

Pinch of kosher salt

These light, tender-crumbed cupcakes boast a double dose of lemon flavor, with finely grated zest and freshly squeezed juice in the buttermilk batter and a healthy measure of juice in the frosting.

Preheat the oven to 375°F (190°C). Line 18 standard muffin cups with paper liners, or grease with butter and dust with flour.

Sift the flour, baking powder, baking soda, and salt into a bowl. In a large bowl, using an electric mixer, beat the butter on medium speed until soft and fluffy. Add the granulated sugar and lemon zest and continue beating until pale. Add the eggs one at a time, beating well after each addition. Add half of the flour mixture and mix on low speed just until blended. Add the buttermilk, lemon juice, and vanilla and beat on low speed until smooth. Add the remaining flour mixture and beat just until blended. The batter will be thick.

Divide the batter between the muffin cups, filling each about three-fourths full. Bake until the edges of the cupcakes are pale golden brown and a toothpick inserted into the center of a cupcake comes out clean, about 17 minutes. Let the cupcakes cool in the pans on a wire rack for 10 minutes, then remove from the pan and let cool completely, about 45 minutes. »→

To make the lemon frosting, in a bowl, using an electric mixer, beat the butter until light and fluffy. Sift the confectioners' sugar over the butter and add the lemon juice, vanilla, and salt. Beat on medium-high speed until smooth and fluffy.

Spread the frosting thickly over the tops of the cupcakes and serve.

FRESH PEA SOUP WITH CHIVES & CRÈME FRAÎCHE

serves 4

3 cups (24 fl oz/750 ml) chicken broth

2½ cups (12½ oz/390 g) fresh peas

Salt and freshly ground pepper

2 Tbsp crème fraîche

2 Tbsp chopped fresh chives or a combination of chopped chives and chive blossoms

Fresh peas are treated delicately here, allowing their inherent sweetness to dominate the flavor of the soup. Chives, with their mild onion flavor, are used as a bright, aromatic garnish, and if their lavender blossoms are available, use them as well. Fresh peas take a bit of work to shell, but the wonderful taste they deliver is worth the time and effort.

In a large saucepan, bring the broth to a boil over medium-high heat. Add the peas, reduce the heat to medium, cover, and cook until the peas are tender, about 10 minutes for young peas and up to 20 minutes for more mature, starchy peas. Let cool slightly.

Working in batches, purée the soup in a food processor or blender. Return to the pot and season with 1 tsp salt and ½ tsp pepper. If you prefer a lighter soup, strain through a fine-mesh sieve lined with cheesecloth, or serve unstrained for a thicker soup. Serve, topped with the crème fraîche and a sprinkling of the chives.

8

A member of the chicory family, escarole, in season in spring and summer, has a pleasantly bitter flavor that holds up well to bold Italian seasonings like garlic and red pepper flakes. Here, it is paired with firm white fish fillets and buttery cannellini beans for a complete meal.

HALIBUT WITH BRAISED ESCAROLE & WHITE BEANS

serves 6

6 halibut fillets, 5–6 oz (155–185 g) each

Salt and freshly ground pepper

4 Tbsp (2 fl oz/60 ml) extra-virgin olive oil, plus more for drizzling

3 cloves garlic, thinly sliced

Pinch of red pepper flakes

1 lb (500 g) escarole, cored and cut into 1½-inch (4-cm) pieces

1 cup (7 oz/220 g) canned white beans such as cannellini, rinsed and drained

Lemon wedges

Season the halibut fillets with salt and pepper. In a large frying pan with a lid, heat 2 Tbsp of the oil over medium-high heat. Add the halibut fillets and sear until golden brown on one side, about 2 minutes. Transfer to a plate.

Warm the remaining 2 Tbsp oil over medium heat. Add the garlic and red pepper flakes and sauté for 1 minute. Add as much escarole as will fit in the pan. As the escarole wilts, continue adding the rest. If the pan gets dry, add a splash of water. Cook until the escarole is slightly wilted, 1–2 minutes. Season with salt and pepper.

Stir in the beans and ½ cup (4 fl oz/125 ml) water. Bring to a simmer, cover, and cook until the escarole is very tender and the liquid has thickened, about 8 minutes. Season with salt and pepper. Nestle the halibut fillets in the escarole, browned side up, cover, and cook until the fish is opaque throughout, about 4 minutes.

Drizzle with a little oil and serve accompanied with lemon wedges.

9

The popular "little meats" of Mexican cooking are traditionally made by simmering chunks of well-seasoned meat in hot lard. This approach drastically diminishes the fat content of the finished dish by simmering the meat in flavorful citrus juices. The results taste marvelously authentic.

CARNITAS

serves 6–8

Salt and freshly ground pepper

1 boneless pork shoulder roast, 3–4 lb (1.5–2 kg)

¼ cup (2 fl oz/60 ml) olive oil

1 white onion, finely chopped, plus more for serving

2 cloves garlic, minced

1 bottle (12 fl oz/375 ml) Mexican lager-style beer

Grated zest and juice of 1 large orange

Grated zest and juice of 1 lime

1 Tbsp dried oregano

Warmed corn or flour tortillas

Lime wedges

Hot or mild salsa

Chopped fresh cilantro

Preheat the oven to 350°F (180°C).

In a small bowl, combine 2 tsp salt and 1 tsp pepper. Season the pork roast with the mixture. In a large, heavy pot, heat the oil over medium-high heat. Add the pork and sear, turning frequently, until browned on all sides, about 10 minutes. Transfer to a plate.

Pour off all but a thin layer of fat from the pot and return it to medium-high heat. Add the chopped onion and the garlic and sauté until they begin to soften, 1–2 minutes. Add the beer and stir to scrape up any browned bits on the pot bottom. Return the pork and any juices to the pot. Add the orange and lime zests and juices and the oregano. Cover and cook over low heat until the pork is very tender, about 2½ hours.

Transfer the pork to a cutting board and cover loosely with foil. Skim the fat from the surface of the cooking liquid. Coarsely cut and shred the pork into small bite-sized pieces. Arrange the meat on a platter, moisten with the cooking juices, and serve with the chopped onion, tortillas, lime wedges, salsa, and cilantro.

10

"Totally chocolate" perfectly describes these chocolate buttermilk donuts dipped in a luscious chocolate glaze. Pleasingly sticky, the glaze is the perfect consistency for taking them over the top: scatter chocolate sprinkles, shaved bittersweet chocolate, or chocolate curls on the glaze before it sets.

DARK CHOCOLATE DONUT HOLES
makes about 40 donut holes

1 cup (5 oz/155 g) all-purpose flour

1 cup (4 oz/125 g) cake flour

¼ cup (¾ oz/20 g) unsweetened cocoa powder

1 tsp baking powder

½ tsp baking soda

½ tsp kosher salt

1 large egg

½ cup (4 oz/125 g) sugar

½ cup (4 fl oz/125 ml) buttermilk

1 Tbsp unsalted butter, melted

1 tsp pure vanilla extract

Canola or peanut oil for deep-frying

FOR THE CHOCOLATE GLAZE

⅓ cup (3 fl oz/80 ml) heavy cream

4 Tbsp (2 oz/60 g) unsalted butter, cubed

3 Tbsp light corn syrup

4 oz (125 g) semisweet chocolate, finely chopped

1 tsp pure vanilla extract

Sift the flours, cocoa, baking powder, baking soda, and salt together into a bowl. In a large bowl, using an electric mixer, beat the egg and sugar on medium speed until creamy and pale. Add the buttermilk, melted butter, and vanilla and beat until smooth. Beat in the dry ingredients on low speed just until the mixture comes together into a soft dough. Cover and refrigerate the dough until firm, about 45 minutes.

To make the glaze, in a saucepan, cook the cream, butter, and corn syrup over medium heat, stirring, until the butter melts and the mixture is hot but not boiling. Remove from the heat and add the chocolate. Let stand for about 30 seconds, then stir until the chocolate is melted and the glaze is smooth. Stir in the vanilla. Let the glaze cool until thickened, about 20 minutes.

Line a baking sheet with paper towels. Pour oil to a depth of 2 inches (5 cm) into a deep, heavy frying pan and heat over medium-high heat until it reaches 360°F (182°C) on a deep-frying thermometer. »→

Drop the dough by heaping teaspoonfuls, about 6 at a time, into the hot oil and deep-fry until brown and crusty, about 2 minutes.

Turn and cook until brown and crusty on the second side, about 1 minute. Transfer to the towel-lined sheet. Repeat to fry the remaining donut holes, allowing the oil to return to 360°F (182°C) between batches.

When the donut holes are cool enough to handle, dip them into the glaze, letting any excess drip back into the bowl. Let stand on a wire rack until the glaze sets slightly, about 10 minutes, before serving.

11

Ramen noodles are a fast, easy, and inexpensive staple to keep on hand. Sugar snap peas and diced tomatoes add depth, flavor, and nutritional value to this perfect weeknight soup.

RAMEN NOODLE SOUP WITH SUGAR SNAP PEAS
serves 4–6

2 Tbsp olive oil

2 shallots, chopped

4 cloves garlic, minced

6 cups (48 fl oz/1.5 l) chicken broth

3 oz (90 g) dried ramen noodles

1 can (14½ oz/455 g) diced tomatoes

1½ cups (5 oz/155 g) sugar snap peas, trimmed and halved diagonally

4 green onions, white and tender green parts, thinly sliced

Salt and freshly ground pepper

Hot sauce, such as Sriracha, for serving

In a large, heavy pot, warm the oil over medium-high heat. Add the shallots and garlic and sauté for 3 minutes. Add the broth and bring to a boil. Add the ramen noodles and tomatoes and cook, stirring occasionally, for 5 minutes. Add the sugar snap peas and green onions and cook for 2 minutes. Season with salt and pepper and serve, passing the hot sauce at the table.

12

Sweet, fragrant Meyer lemons add an intriguing taste to this California-style lobster salad. If you like, use 1 lb (500 g) shrimp, peeled, deveined, and poached just until tender, in place of the lobster tails.

LOBSTER & AVOCADO SALAD WITH SHAVED MEYER LEMON

serves 4

1 very firm Meyer lemon or Valencia orange

¼ cup (2 fl oz/60 ml) extra-virgin olive oil

1 Tbsp minced shallot

2 Tbsp champagne vinegar

Salt and freshly ground pepper

3 cooked, shelled lobster tails,
cut into 1-inch (2.5-cm) chunks

1 head butter lettuce, torn into pieces

1 cup (1½ oz/45 g) fresh flat-leaf parsley leaves

½ cup (¾ oz/20 g) fresh cilantro leaves

½ cup (¾ oz/20 g) fresh chives,
cut into ½-inch (12-mm) lengths

2 avocados, pitted, peeled, and diced

Using a mandoline or a very sharp knife, slice the lemon as thinly as possible. Set aside.

In a large bowl, combine the oil, shallot, vinegar, and ¼ tsp each salt and pepper. Mix well with a fork.

Add the lobster chunks to the vinaigrette, then remove and set aside. Just before serving, add the lettuce and parsley to the vinaigrette. Also add the cilantro and chives, reserving a little of each for garnish. Toss the salad and divide among individual plates. Top each salad with an equal portion of the lobster chunks, Meyer lemon slices, and diced avocado. Garnish with a sprinkling of the reserved cilantro and chives and serve.

13

Spanish piquillo peppers are traditionally handpicked, then roasted in wood-fired ovens, peeled, and packed into jars or cans. The flavor of wood smoke enhances the distinctive, slight spiciness of these small, triangular, intensely red peppers. They are often stuffed with meat or seafood, but here the filling is herbed fresh goat cheese.

STUFFED PIQUILLO PEPPERS

serves 6–8

10 oz (315 g) fresh goat cheese

3–4 Tbsp finely chopped fresh chives,
plus more for garnish

3–4 Tbsp finely chopped fresh basil

Salt and freshly ground pepper

1 jar (12 oz/375 g) roasted piquillo peppers
(about 24 peppers)

1 Tbsp extra-virgin olive oil

FOR THE VINAIGRETTE

⅓ cup (3 fl oz/80 ml) extra-virgin olive oil

3½ Tbsp balsamic vinegar

1 small shallot, minced

Salt and freshly ground pepper

Preheat the broiler.

To make the filling, in a small bowl, use a wooden spoon to mash the goat cheese together with the chives and basil. Season with salt and pepper.

Drain the peppers, but do not rinse them. With your fingers, gently open the stem end of each pepper. Remove any seeds and ribs you can from the insides without cutting or tearing the pepper walls.

With a small spoon or your fingers, carefully stuff about 1 Tbsp of the goat cheese mixture inside each pepper. The cheese mixture should fill the peppers but should not be bursting out.

Arrange the peppers in a single layer on a baking sheet. Brush them with the oil. Slip the pan under the broiler 4–6 inches (10–15 cm) from the heat source and broil until the cheese is soft and bubbly, about 7 minutes. Let cool slightly.

To make the vinaigrette, in a small bowl, whisk together the oil, vinegar, shallot, ½ tsp salt, and ¼ tsp pepper.

Transfer the peppers to a serving dish. Drizzle liberally with the vinaigrette, sprinkle with chives, and serve.

14

SPRING VEGETABLE TART
serves 4

1 sheet frozen puff pastry, about ½ lb (250 g), thawed

1 cup (4 oz/125 g) shredded fontina cheese

15–20 thin asparagus spears, ends trimmed

1 small leek, white part only, halved and thinly sliced

2 eggs

¼ cup (2 fl oz/60 ml) whole milk

Salt and freshly ground pepper

Celebrate the bounty of the season with an all-purpose tart, easy to load with whatever vegetables are stacked highest at the farmers' market. This recipe pairs grassy leeks and sweet, mellow asparagus with pungent fontina cheese. Serve it with a tangle of frisée and a glass of crisp white wine, preferably for a weekend lunch on the deck or patio.

Preheat the oven to 400°F (200°C). Line a baking sheet with parchment paper. Lay the puff pastry on the prepared sheet. Fold over the sides to make a 1-inch (2.5-cm) rim, overlapping the pastry at the corners and pressing it lightly. Inside the rim, prick the pastry all over with a fork.

Sprinkle half of the cheese over the bottom of the pastry inside the rim. Top with the asparagus, laying the spears vertically in a row from one side of the pastry to the other. Sprinkle the leeks over the asparagus. Bake for 15 minutes.

Meanwhile, in a bowl, beat the eggs, milk, ½ tsp salt, and several grinds of pepper until well combined. Remove the pastry from the oven. Pour the egg mixture evenly over the asparagus and leeks and sprinkle on the remaining cheese. Bake until the pastry is puffed and golden brown, about 10 minutes. Let the tart stand for 10 minutes before serving.

15

SQUID SALAD WITH ORANGES, FAVA BEANS & FENNEL
serves 4–6

1½ lb (750 g) fava beans, shelled

Salt and freshly ground pepper

1½ lb (750 g) cleaned squid, bodies cut into ½-inch (12-mm) rings and tentacles coarsely chopped

2 oranges

2 stalks celery, chopped

1 small fennel bulb, halved and thinly sliced

3 Tbsp chopped fresh flat-leaf parsley

Grated zest and juice of 1 lemon

1 Tbsp red wine vinegar

1 tsp Dijon mustard

3 Tbsp extra-virgin olive oil

This make-ahead salad is loaded with fresh flavors, varied textures, plenty of nutrients, and a modest number of calories. Vitamin-rich fennel adds a mild licorice taste and crunch, while juicy, sweet-tart oranges deliver a citrusy aroma and quickly cooked fava beans and squid bring a double dose of low-fat protein.

Bring a saucepan three-fourths full of water to a boil and add the favas. Boil for 1 minute, then use a skimmer to transfer them to a bowl. Squeeze each bean free of its tough outer skin. Put the beans in a bowl.

Bring the water back to a boil. Add 1 tsp salt and the squid and cook until the squid is opaque and just cooked through, about 90 seconds. Drain and immediately plunge into a bowl filled with ice water. Drain again and pat dry with paper towels. Transfer the squid to the bowl with the fava beans.

Grate the zest from 1 orange into a bowl. Cut a slice off both ends of each orange so they will stand upright. Stand them on a cutting board and, using a large, sharp knife, cut away the peel and white pith by slicing from top to bottom, following the contour of the fruit. Using a small knife, and working over the bowl with the zest to capture the juices, cut along either side of each segment to free it from the membrane and let it fall into the bowl. Add the orange segments, zest, and juices to the bowl with the squid. Add the celery, fennel, parsley, and lemon zest and stir to combine.

In a small bowl, combine the lemon juice, red wine vinegar, and Dijon mustard. Slowly whisk in the olive oil. Season with salt and pepper. Pour the mixture over the squid and toss to combine. Season again with salt and pepper, cover, and refrigerate for at least 1 hour before serving.

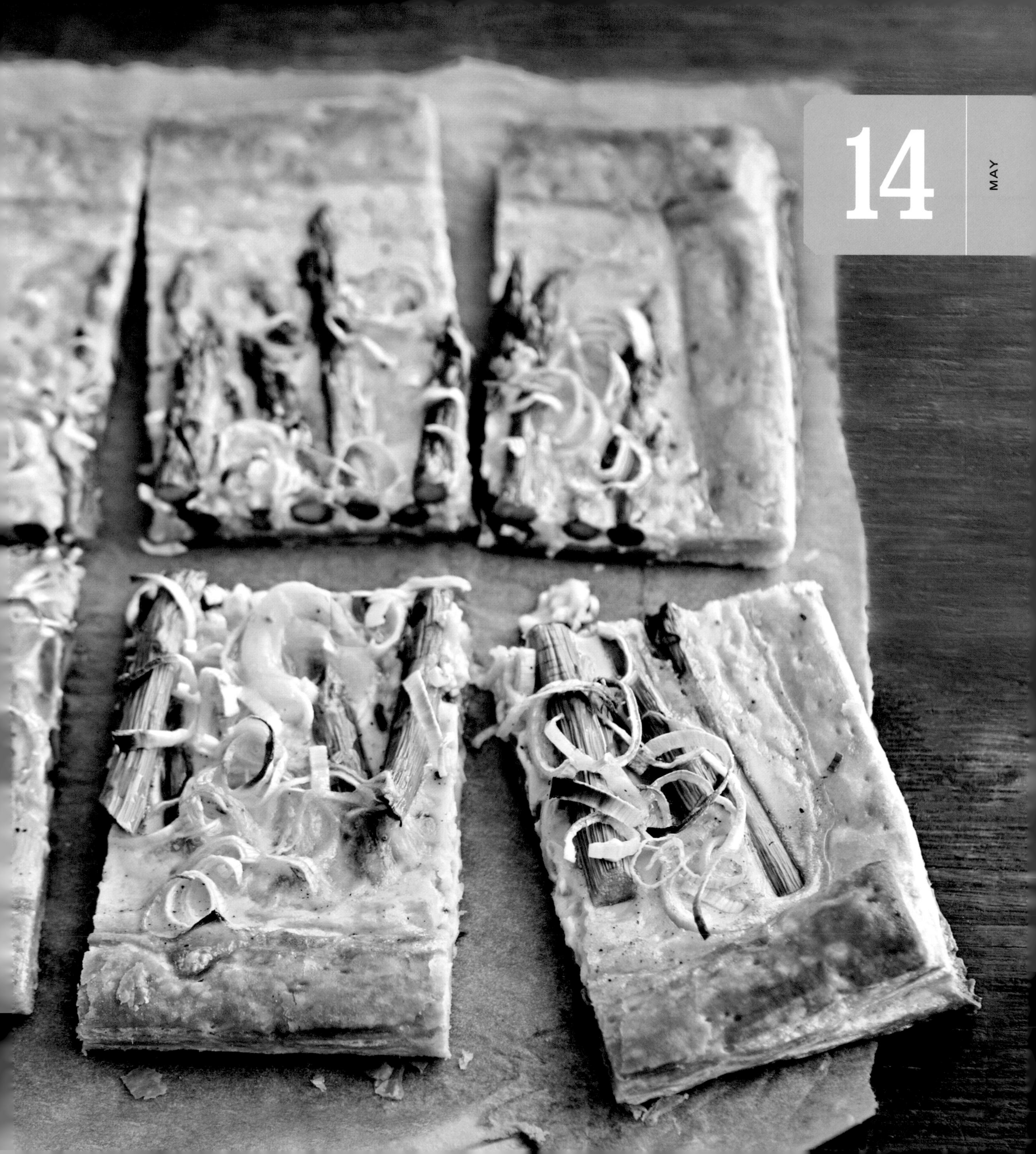

14

MAY

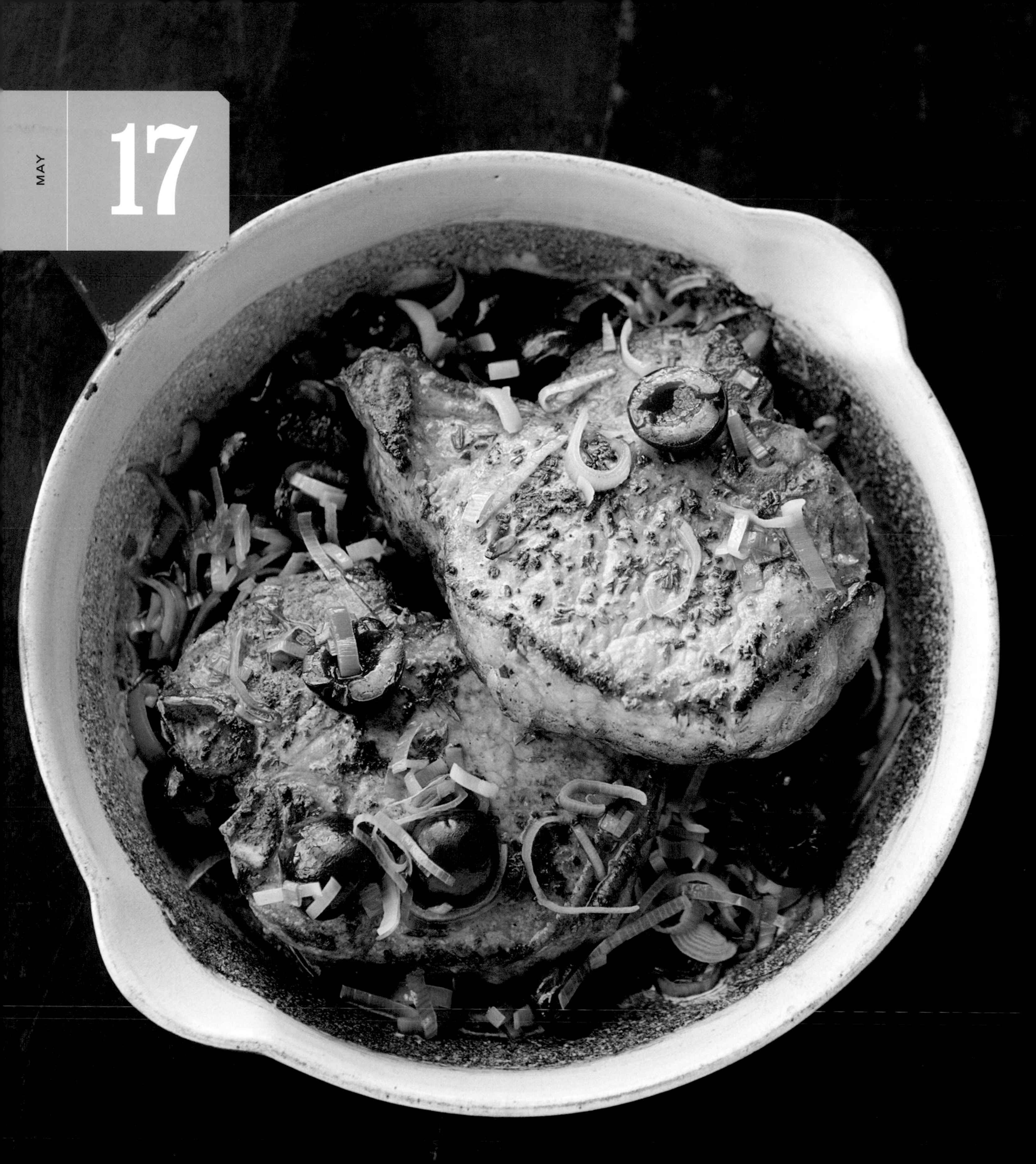
MAY
17

16

Versions of these small, fried or baked pastries are turned out in kitchens throughout South America, where they are filled with everything from seasoned meats, pot beans, or cubed potatoes to pumpkin, cheese, or fruit. Here, a mix of corn, peas, and tomato is spiked with a little jalapeño chile for a satisfying snack or appetizer.

CORN & PEA EMPANADITAS

serves 4–6

FOR THE DOUGH

2 cups (10 oz/315 g) all-purpose flour

1 tsp baking soda

Salt and freshly ground pepper

FOR THE FILLING

1½ Tbsp olive oil

1 white onion, minced

1 small green bell pepper, seeded and minced

1 Tbsp seeded and minced jalapeño chile

2 cloves garlic, minced

1½ cups (9 oz/280 g) frozen corn kernels, thawed

½ cup (2½ oz/75 g) shelled fresh green peas

½ cup (4 fl oz/125 ml) tomato sauce

¼ cup (⅓ oz/10 g) chopped fresh cilantro

Canola oil for frying

To make the dough, in a food processor, combine the flour, baking soda, 1 tsp salt, and ½ tsp pepper and pulse to blend. Add ½ cup (4 fl oz/125 ml) water in a slow stream, pulsing 2 or 3 times until a soft dough forms that sticks together when pinched. If the mixture is still crumbly, drizzle about 2 Tbsp water over the dough and pulse several times. Remove the dough, roll into a log, and wrap tightly in plastic wrap. Refrigerate for 30 minutes.

In a frying pan, warm the olive oil over medium heat. Add the onion, bell pepper, jalapeño, and garlic and cook, stirring, until softened, about 2 minutes. Add the corn and peas and cook, stirring, until tender, about 5 minutes. Add the tomato sauce and cook, stirring frequently, until the mixture thickens, about 5 minutes. Let cool. Stir in the cilantro.

Unwrap the dough, divide into 16 equal pieces, and gently shape each into a ball. On a lightly floured work surface, roll out each ball into a 4-inch (10-cm) circle. Brush the edges of the dough with water. Place about 1 Tbsp of the filling in the center of each circle. Fold the dough in half over the filling and pinch to seal, fluting the edges or crimping them with a fork. »→

Pour oil to a depth of 1 inch (2.5 cm) into a heavy frying pan over medium-high heat and heat to 350°F (180°C) on a deep-frying thermometer. Working in batches, place a few pastries in the hot oil and fry, turning as needed with tongs, until crisp and well browned on all sides, 3–5 minutes. Transfer to paper towels to drain. Serve warm or at room temperature.

17

Cherries have a short season that typically begins in early May. They pair well with duck or pork in savory dishes, bringing out the natural sweetness of the meat. A cherry pitter will make short work of the pits. When fresh cherries aren't in season, use dried cherries.

BRAISED PORK CHOPS WITH CHERRIES

serves 4

4 bone-in, center-cut pork loin chops, each 1 inch (2.5 cm) thick

Salt and freshly ground pepper

1 Tbsp minced fresh rosemary

3 Tbsp unsalted butter

2 leeks, white and pale green parts, halved lengthwise and thinly sliced

1 cup (8 fl oz/250 ml) chicken broth

¼ cup (2 fl oz/60 ml) port

2 Tbsp balsamic vinegar

½ cup (2 oz/60 g) dried cherries or 1 cup (4 oz/120 g) fresh pitted cherries, halved

Season the pork chops with salt and pepper and sprinkle with the rosemary, patting the seasonings firmly to adhere to the meat. In a sauté pan with a lid, melt 2 Tbsp of the butter over medium-high heat. Add the pork chops and cook, turning once, until golden on both sides, about 6 minutes. Transfer to a plate.

In the same pan, melt the remaining 1 Tbsp butter over medium heat. Add the leeks and sauté until softened and beginning to brown, 3–4 minutes. Stir in the broth, stir to scrape up any browned bits on the pan bottom, and cook for 1 minute. Stir in the port, vinegar, and cherries.

Return the pork chops and any juices to the pan and spoon the liquid over them. Cover, reduce the heat to medium-low, and simmer until the pork is tender and barely pink in the center, about 15 minutes. Divide the chops among plates, spoon the cherry mixture over the top, and serve.

18

PIZZA WITH ASPARAGUS, LEEKS & HERBED RICOTTA

serves 4

Use purchased whole-wheat pizza dough for an easy dish you can throw together at the last minute. You won't find any tomatoes on this nontraditional green-and-white pizza. The base is a creamy, low-fat mixture of basil and ricotta. It's topped with a medley of nearly caramelized leeks and asparagus. Pay special attention when cleaning the leeks: it's best to chop them and then let them soak in a bowl of cold water until the dirt embedded between the leaves falls to the bottom.

Flour and cornmeal, for dusting

1 lb (500 g) purchased whole-wheat pizza dough

3 Tbsp olive oil

Salt and freshly ground pepper

1 cup (8 oz/250 g) part-skim ricotta cheese

2 Tbsp chopped fresh basil

3 leeks, white and pale green parts, chopped

3 cloves garlic, chopped

1 bunch thin asparagus, tough ends trimmed, cut into 3-inch (7.5-cm) pieces

Position a rack in the bottom of the oven. Place a baking stone on the rack. Preheat the oven to 550°F (290°C), or the highest setting, for at least 45 minutes.

To assemble the pizza, lightly flour a work surface. Roll out the dough into a round 13–14 inches (33–35 cm) in diameter and ⅛ inch (3 mm) thick. Generously dust a pizza peel or rimless baking sheet with cornmeal and transfer the dough round to it. Brush the top of the pizza with 1 Tbsp of the oil and season all over with salt and pepper. In a small bowl, stir together the cheese and basil. Season with salt and pepper. Spread the ricotta mixture over the dough in a thick, even layer.

In a frying pan over medium-high heat, warm the remaining 2 Tbsp oil. Add the leeks and garlic, season with salt and pepper, and sauté until soft, about 5 minutes. Add the asparagus, stir to coat with the oil, and cook just until the asparagus begins to soften, about 3 minutes. Spread the leeks and asparagus evenly over the ricotta mixture. Immediately slide the pizza from the peel onto the baking stone. Bake until the crust is crisp and browned, 10–12 minutes. Remove from the oven, let cool slightly, and serve.

19

CHICKEN PARMESAN WITH GREENS

serves 4

This Italian American classic takes a healthful turn with the addition of high-fiber, low-calorie kale as well as pan-seared—not fried—then baked chicken breasts. For the best flavor, be sure to purchase fresh, rather than processed, mozzarella, often labeled fior di latte and sold immersed in water.

4 skinless, boneless chicken breast halves, about 1½ lb (750 g) total weight

Salt and freshly ground pepper

2 Tbsp olive oil

1 bunch kale, tough stems removed and leaves torn into large pieces

2 cups (16 fl oz/500 ml) marinara sauce, warmed

8 thick slices fresh mozzarella cheese

½ cup (2 oz/60 g) grated Parmesan cheese

Preheat the oven to 400°F (200°C). Season the chicken generously with salt and pepper. In a large ovenproof frying pan over medium-high heat, warm the oil. Add the chicken and cook, turning once, until golden brown, about 7 minutes total. Transfer to a plate and set aside.

Add the kale to the frying pan and sauté over medium-high heat until wilted, about 1 minute. Add the chicken back to the frying pan with the kale and pour the marinara sauce over the chicken. Place 2 mozzarella slices on each chicken breast. Sprinkle evenly with the Parmesan. Bake until the cheese is golden and the chicken is opaque throughout, about 20 minutes, then serve.

20

CURRIED CARROT PURÉE

serves 4

1 Tbsp olive oil, plus more for drizzling

1 large shallot, minced

1½ lb (750 g) carrots, peeled and coarsely chopped

1 tsp curry powder

6 cups (48 fl oz/1.5 l) chicken broth

2 Tbsp fresh orange juice

Salt and freshly ground pepper

Here, curry powder and orange juice add flavor and vibrancy to an earthy carrot soup. To change the flavor, add ground cinnamon or ginger in place of or in addition to the curry powder. Serve the soup as a first course or accompany it with a green salad for a light lunch.

In a large, heavy pot, warm the 1 Tbsp oil over medium heat. Add the shallot and sauté until translucent, about 2 minutes. Add the carrots, curry powder, and broth. Raise the heat to medium-high and bring to a boil. Reduce the heat to low, cover, and cook until the carrots are tender, about 20 minutes. Remove from the heat and add the orange juice. Let cool slightly.

Working in batches, purée the soup in a blender or food processor. Season with salt and pepper.

The soup can be served warm or chilled. To serve warm, return the purée to the pot and gently warm over medium heat. To serve chilled, let the purée cool, transfer to a covered container, and refrigerate for at least 3 hours or up to overnight. Serve, drizzled with oil.

21

STIR-FRIED RICE VERMICELLI WITH CHICKEN & SHRIMP

serves 4–6

½ lb (250 g) skinless, boneless chicken thighs

¾ cup (6 fl oz/180 ml) chicken broth

3 Tbsp Asian fish sauce

3 Tbsp soy sauce

1 tsp sugar

2 Tbsp canola oil

¼ lb (125 g) medium shrimp, peeled, deveined, and chopped

1 Tbsp peeled and grated fresh ginger

2 cloves garlic, minced

1 small yellow onion, thinly sliced

1 large carrot, shredded

12 oz (375 g) dried rice vermicelli, soaked in warm water for 15 minutes and drained

2 cups (6 oz/185 g) shredded napa cabbage

2 green onions, thinly sliced

1 lemon, cut into wedges

Slender vermicelli noodles and a mixed cast of vegetables, chicken thighs, and plump shrimp combine deliciously in this Philippine-inspired stir-fry. Slicing the vegetables thinly helps to match the delicate structure of the noodles.

Bring a saucepan of water to a boil. Add the chicken and return to a boil. Reduce the heat to medium and simmer, uncovered, until the chicken is opaque throughout, 10–15 minutes. Using tongs, transfer to a plate to cool. Shred the chicken and set aside.

In a small bowl, stir together the broth, fish sauce, soy sauce, and sugar to make a sauce.

Heat a wok or large frying pan over high heat and add 1 Tbsp of the oil. Add the shrimp and stir-fry until just opaque, about 30 seconds. With a slotted spoon, transfer the shrimp to a bowl. Return the pan to high heat and add the ginger, garlic, onion, and carrot and stir-fry until just tender, about 2 minutes. Transfer to the bowl with the shrimp.

Wipe out the pan, return it to high heat, and add the remaining 1 Tbsp oil. Add the noodles and stir-fry until they begin to dry, 2–3 minutes. Return the vegetables and shrimp to the pan, add the cabbage and chicken, and stir-fry until the cabbage begins to wilt and the chicken is heated through, about 5 minutes. Pour in the sauce and stir-fry until most of it has been absorbed, and the noodles have plumped and are translucent, 3–4 minutes. Garnish with the green onions and serve, passing the lemon wedges at the table.

22

Belgian endive has an easy elegance, crunchy texture, and subtle taste, here paired with spring vegetables and shards of bright citrus. You can substitute peas for the fava beans, or grilled fennel for the endive. If it is still too cold to grill outdoors, you can cook these vegetables on a stove-top grill pan with similar results. Pair this dish with a crisp white wine such as Sauvignon Blanc or Pinot Grigio.

GRILLED ASPARAGUS & ENDIVE WITH FAVAS, ORANGE & MINT

serves 4

3 lb (1.5 kg) fava beans, shelled

1 lb (500 g) slender asparagus, ends trimmed

2 heads Belgian endive, preferably red, cut lengthwise into slices about ⅛ inch (3 mm) thick

Salt and freshly ground pepper

1 orange

½ cup (4 fl oz/125 ml) extra-virgin olive oil

½ cup (½ oz/15 g) fresh mint leaves

Bring a pot of lightly salted water to a boil. Add the beans to the boiling water and cook for 1 minute. Drain, rinse under cold running water, and drain again. Pinch each bean to slip it from the skin. Transfer the beans to a bowl.

Preheat a charcoal or gas grill for direct-heat grilling over high heat. Oil the grill rack. Arrange the asparagus and endive slices on the rack perpendicular to the bars. Grill, turning occasionally, until evenly charred, 2–3 minutes. Transfer to a platter and season with salt and pepper.

Working over a bowl, grate the zest from the orange. Cut a thick slice from the top and bottom of the orange. Stand the orange upright and cut off the peel in thick strips, removing the white pith and membrane. Again working over the bowl, cut the segments from the membranes, allowing them and any juices to fall into the bowl. Add the oil and, using a fork, break up the orange segments into bite-sized pieces. Season with salt and pepper.

Scatter the fava beans and mint on top of the grilled vegetables. Drizzle with the oranges and dressing and serve.

23

Here, sweet, anise-like tarragon adds color and garden-fresh flavor to moist, braised salmon. For a perfect side dish, while the fish braises, sauté seasonal fresh green vegetables— asparagus, peas, and leeks—in butter and oil just until tender.

WHITE WINE–BRAISED SALMON WITH TARRAGON

serves 6

½ cup (4 fl oz/125 ml) vegetable broth

1 cup (8 fl oz/250 ml) dry white wine

½ small yellow onion, sliced

3 sprigs fresh tarragon, plus 1 tsp minced

Salt and freshly ground pepper

6 salmon fillets, about 5 oz (155 g) each

In a slow cooker, stir together the broth, wine, onion, and tarragon sprigs. Season with ½ tsp salt and several grindings of pepper. Pour in ½ cup (4 fl oz/125 ml) water and stir to combine. Cover and cook on the low setting for 30 minutes. Add the salmon fillets (they can overlap), cover, and cook for 1 hour. The fish should be opaque throughout, firm, and very tender.

Transfer the salmon fillets to plates and moisten with the braising liquid, if desired. Garnish with the minced tarragon and serve.

24

*This versatile salad
can accommodate
the odds and ends
of raw vegetables
that tend to
accumulate in
the refrigerator
bin. Instead of
fennel, mushrooms,
or radishes,
try cucumber,
zucchini, celery,
or cauliflower.
For a vegetarian
version, omit
the chicken.*

CHOPPED CHICKEN SALAD WITH LEMON-TARRAGON DRESSING

serves 2

1 skinless, boneless chicken breast half,
about ½ lb (250 g)

1½ cups (12 fl oz/375 ml) chicken broth,
or as needed

FOR THE LEMON-TARRAGON DRESSING

1½ Tbsp fresh lemon juice,
plus more if needed

2 tsp minced fresh tarragon

1 tsp Dijon mustard

1 small clove garlic, minced

2½ Tbsp olive oil

Salt and freshly ground pepper

¼ lb (125 g) romaine lettuce heart, chopped

¼ small fennel bulb, trimmed and chopped

6 small fresh mushrooms, chopped

5 radishes, chopped

1 small carrot, peeled and chopped

¼ small head radicchio, chopped

¼ small red onion, chopped

In a small saucepan over medium heat,
combine the chicken breast half and the
1½ cups (12 fl oz/375 ml) broth, using more
broth as needed to cover. Bring to a simmer,
adjust the heat to keep the broth just below a
simmer, and cook, uncovered, until the
chicken is just cooked through, about 10
minutes. Using a slotted spoon, transfer the
chicken breast to a cutting board. When the
chicken is cool, cut it into small, neat pieces.

To make the dressing, in a bowl, whisk
together the 1½ Tbsp lemon juice, tarragon,
mustard, and garlic. Add the olive oil in a
thin stream, whisking constantly until the
dressing is well blended. Season with salt
and pepper to taste. Set aside to allow the
flavors to blend.

In a large bowl, combine the romaine,
fennel, mushrooms, radishes, carrot,
radicchio, and red onion.

Add the chicken to the dressing and stir to
coat. Add the chicken and all the dressing
to the vegetables and toss well. Taste and adjust
the seasoning with lemon juice and serve.

25

*Also known as
mille-feuilles,
literally "thousand
leaves," napoleons
are often artfully
displayed in
patisserie windows.
But they don't
have to be fussy
to create at home.
Use frozen puff
pastry and assemble
and dust the layers
as haphazardly
as you like. The
dessert will be
enticing no matter
how precisely
you stack them.*

STRAWBERRY NAPOLEONS

serves 6

1 sheet frozen puff pastry (about 1 lb/500g),
thawed

1½ cups (6 oz/185 g) hulled and thinly
sliced strawberries

Juice of ½ lemon

1 Tbsp granulated sugar

1 cup (8 fl oz/250 ml) heavy cream

Confectioners' sugar for dusting

On a lightly floured work surface, roll
the puff pastry out into an 8-by-12-inch
(20-by-30-cm) rectangle about ⅛ inch (3 mm)
thick. Use a pastry cutter to cut the pastry
in half lengthwise, then cut each rectangle
crosswise into 6 rectangles. Each piece
should be 2 by 4 inches (5 by 10 cm).

Line a rimmed baking sheet with parchment
paper. Transfer the 12 rectangles to the baking
sheet, spacing them apart, and prick each one
about 4 times with a fork. Refrigerate for
about 30 minutes.

Preheat the oven to 400°F (200°C). Bake the
puff pastry until it is puffed and golden,
about 20 minutes. Set aside to cool.

Meanwhile, in a large bowl, combine the
strawberries, lemon juice, and granulated
sugar and stir to combine. In another bowl,
using an electric mixer or a whisk, beat the
cream until it forms soft peaks. Fold the
cream gently into the strawberry mixture.

Top half of the puff pastry rectangles with
the whipped cream mixture, dividing it evenly.
Top each with one of the remaining puff
pastry rectangles. Dust with confectioners'
sugar and serve.

26

This dish is a brilliant use for leftovers. Stale chips, leftover rotisserie chicken, and any melting cheese can all be put to good use. If you like your Mexican food spicy, use hotter serrano chiles in place of the jalapeños. Keep in mind that the tortilla chips add some salt, so taste as you go and take care not to overseason.

MEXICAN NACHO CASSEROLE

serves 4–6

2 lb (1 kg) plum tomatoes, halved lengthwise

2 jalapeño chiles

6 cloves garlic, unpeeled

1 Tbsp plus 2 tsp olive oil, plus more for greasing

Salt and freshly ground pepper

¼ cup (½ oz/15 g) fresh cilantro leaves

1 white onion, ½ chopped and ½ thinly sliced

6 oz (185 g) corn tortilla chips

1½ cups (9 oz/280 g) shredded cooked chicken

1 can (15 oz/470 g) pinto beans, rinsed and drained

¾ cup (3 oz/90 g) shredded Cheddar cheese

¾ cup (3 oz/90 g) shredded Monterey jack cheese

Sour cream, prepared fresh salsa, and avocado slices

Preheat the broiler.

Combine the tomatoes, chiles, and garlic on a rimmed baking sheet. Drizzle with 2 tsp oil, season with salt and pepper, and toss to coat. Arrange in a single layer, placing the tomatoes cut side down. Broil until the vegetables are lightly charred, about 12 minutes. Let cool, then pull the stems from the chiles and peel the garlic. Put the vegetables and cilantro in a blender and purée.

Preheat the oven to 350°F (180°C). Oil an 8-by-10-inch (20-by-25-cm) baking dish.

In a large frying pan, heat the remaining 1 Tbsp oil over medium-high heat. Add the chopped onion and sauté until translucent, about 5 minutes. Add the puréed vegetables and cook, stirring, for 5 minutes. Season with salt and pepper. Pour half of the purée into the prepared dish. Top with the tortilla chips, laying them flat on each other, breaking them if necessary.

Top the chips evenly with the chicken, then with the beans, the remaining purée, the cheeses, and finally with the sliced onion. Bake until warmed all the way through and the cheese is melted and slightly browned, about 25 minutes. Serve with sour cream, salsa, and avocado.

27

Nuoc cham, a sweet and spicy Vietnamese dipping sauce, adds lively flavor to these fresh vegetable-and-shrimp rolls. Don't skimp on the herbs, as they contribute a bright taste, subtle texture, and a healthy dose of beneficial phytochemicals. The rolls will keep at room temperature for several hours before serving if well covered with plastic wrap.

SHRIMP SUMMER ROLLS

serves 2–4

FOR THE NUOC CHAM

3 cloves garlic, chopped

1½ Tbsp sugar

3 Tbsp Asian fish sauce

2 Tbsp *each* rice vinegar and fresh lime juice

1 serrano chile, seeded and thinly sliced

1 Tbsp *each* grated carrot and daikon

2 oz (60 g) cellophane noodles, soaked in boiling water for 15 minutes

6 rice-paper rounds, each 8 inches (20 cm) in diameter

6 red-leaf lettuce leaves

1 small carrot, shredded

½ small cucumber, peeled, seeded, and shredded

½ cup (½ oz/15 g) mung bean sprouts

6 cooked medium shrimp, cut in half lengthwise

18 *each* fresh mint leaves and cilantro leaves

To make the nuoc cham, put the garlic and sugar in a mini food processor and process until a paste forms. Transfer to a bowl and whisk in the fish sauce, vinegar, lime juice, and ¼ cup (2 fl oz/60 ml) water. Pour through a fine-mesh sieve into a clean bowl and add the chile, carrot, and daikon.

To assemble the rolls, drain the noodles. Fill a wide, shallow bowl with warm water. Soak 1 rice-paper round in the liquid until softened, 5 or 6 seconds. Remove it from the bowl, gently shake off the excess water, and place it on a work surface. Place a lettuce leaf horizontally on the bottom half of the rice paper. In a line across the base of the lettuce, place 1 tsp of the carrot, 1 tsp of the cucumber, several strands of the noodles, and several bean sprouts. Be careful not to overstuff the rolls. Lift the bottom edge of the rice paper and carefully roll up halfway into a tight cylinder. Place 2 shrimp halves and several mint and cilantro leaves tightly along the inside seam of the roll. Fold in the sides of the rice paper and continue to roll the rice paper and filling into a cylinder. Moisten the edge of the roll to seal. Repeat with the remaining ingredients. Cut the rolls in half on the diagonal and serve with the nuoc cham.

28

RASPBERRY-ALMOND CLAFOUTIS
serves 6–8

Unsalted butter, for greasing

¼ cup (1½ oz/45 g) all-purpose flour, plus more for dusting

½ cup (4 oz/125 g) granulated sugar

¼ tsp kosher salt

3 large eggs

1 cup (8 fl oz/250 ml) heavy cream

12 oz (375 g) raspberries

¼ cup (1 oz/30 g) sliced almonds

Confectioners' sugar, for dusting

Clafoutis is an eggy skillet cake punctuated with pieces of fruit. Raspberries pair beautifully with almonds, but you can easily turn this into the more classic cherry clafoutis by replacing the berries with stemmed and pitted cherries. If you like, toss the cherries with 2 Tbsp rum before stirring them into the batter.

Preheat the oven to 375°F (190°C). Butter a shallow 2-qt (2-l) baking dish. Dust with granulated sugar and tap out any excess.

In a large bowl, whisk together the flour, granulated sugar, and salt. Add the eggs and whisk until the batter is smooth. Slowly pour in the cream, whisking constantly. Gently stir the raspberries into the batter until just blended. Pour the batter into the prepared dish. Sprinkle evenly with the almonds.

Bake until puffed and golden, 33–35 minutes. Dust with the confectioners' sugar and serve hot, or let cool to room temperature on a rack. The clafoutis will deflate as it cools but will still be delicious.

29

GRILLED BABY ARTICHOKES WITH SPICY GARLIC BUTTER
serves 4–6

4 Tbsp (2 oz/60 g) unsalted butter

3 cloves garlic, minced

2 Tbsp fresh lemon juice

⅛ tsp red pepper flakes, or more to taste

Hot-pepper sauce

Salt and freshly ground black pepper

20 baby artichokes, about 1 lb (500 g) total

A gently steamed artichoke leaf dipped in melted butter is exquisite, but grilled baby artichokes only improve on a good thing. Don't worry if they are on the grill for what seems like too long. They need time to cook properly. Once you strip away the burnt outer leaves, you'll find a fork-tender center. Grill artichoke halves directly on the grill rack or thread them onto skewers for easy turning.

Prepare a charcoal or gas grill for direct-heat grilling over medium heat. Oil the grill rack. The artichokes can be grilled on skewers. If using wooden skewers, soak in water for at least 30 minutes.

In a small saucepan, melt the butter over medium-low heat. Add the garlic, lemon juice, red pepper flakes, and 1 or 2 dashes of hot-pepper sauce, and stir to mix. Season with salt and black pepper. Reduce the heat to low and keep the mixture warm.

Hit each artichoke on a countertop a couple of times; this will loosen the outer leaves and let the butter mixture penetrate. Cut the artichokes in half lengthwise and trim the stems. Using a small spoon, scoop out the hairy chokes. Slide the artichoke halves onto the skewers, if using, with the cut sides facing the same way.

Place the artichokes, cut sides down, on the grill rack and cook for about 5 minutes. Brush with the butter mixture and cook for another 5 minutes. Turn the artichokes, brush the cut sides with the butter mixture, and continue cooking, turning and brushing with the butter mixture about every 5 minutes, for 20–25 minutes longer, taking care not to burn the artichokes. The artichokes are done when the middle of the cut side gives easily.

Transfer the artichokes to a platter, pour any remaining butter mixture over them, and serve.

This American classic features sour cherries, but because they have a short season and require cooking, most recipes call for jarred sour cherries. If you prefer to use sweet cherries, substitute 4 cups (1½ lb/750 g) pitted fresh sweet cherries for the sour cherries, omit the cherry juice, reduce the amount of sugar to ¾ cup (6 oz/185 g), and add ½ tsp almond extract.

CHERRY LATTICE PIE
serves 6–8

**FOR FLAKY PIE DOUGH
FOR DOUBLE CRUST**

2 cups (10 oz/315 g) all-purpose flour

½ tsp kosher salt

1 Tbsp sugar

¾ cup (6 oz/185 g) cold unsalted butter, cut into pieces

½ cup (4 fl oz/125 ml) ice water, plus more if needed

1 cup (8 oz/250 g) sugar

2 Tbsp tapioca starch

¼ tsp kosher salt

4 cups (1½ lb/750 g) drained jarred or canned pitted sour cherries, plus ⅓ cup (3 fl oz/80 ml) cherry liquid

1 tsp pure vanilla extract

1 Tbsp cold unsalted butter, cut into small pieces

To make the dough, in the bowl of a food processor, combine the flour, salt, and sugar. Sprinkle the butter over the top and pulse for a few seconds, or just until the butter is slightly broken up into the flour but still in visible pieces. Evenly sprinkle the water over the flour mixture, then process just until the mixture starts to come together. Dump the dough into a large zip-top plastic bag and press into a flat disk. Refrigerate for at least 30 minutes or up to 1 day before using, or freeze for up to 1 month.

Transfer the dough to a lightly floured work surface and cut in half. Roll each half into a round at least 12 inches (30 cm) in diameter and about ⅛ inch (3 mm) thick. Transfer one round to a 9-inch (23-cm) pie pan and ease into the pan. Trim the edge, leaving a ¾-inch (2-cm) overhang. Refrigerate the dough-lined pan and dough round until ready to use.

In a small bowl, stir together the sugar, tapioca starch, and salt. Place the cherries in a large bowl, sprinkle with the sugar mixture, and toss to distribute evenly. Add the vanilla and the cherry liquid and mix well. Pour the cherry mixture into the dough-lined pan and dot with the butter. ⇥

Lay the second dough round on a lightly floured work surface and, using a 1-inch (2.5-cm) wide ruler as a guide, cut 9–10 strips of dough. Lay 5 strips of dough evenly across the top, using the longest strips in the center. Lay the remaining 4 or 5 strips perpendicular to the other strips, spacing them evenly. (You can also weave together the strips.) Trim the ends of the strips and tuck the dough under itself to create a rim. Crimp the edges with your fingers or a fork. Refrigerate until the dough is firm, at least 30 minutes.

Preheat the oven to 375°F (190°C). Bake until the crust is golden and the filling is thick and bubbling, 45–60 minutes. Let cool completely on a wire rack to set the filling, then serve.

Inspired by a popular Spanish tapa, this dish requires few ingredients and cooks in only 5 minutes. Serve with a green salad and with grilled whole-grain bread for dipping into in the sauce.

SPANISH GARLIC SHRIMP
serves 4–6

3 Tbsp extra-virgin olive oil

6 cloves garlic, thinly sliced

Pinch of red pepper flakes

1¼ lb (625 g) shrimp, peeled and deveined

½ tsp smoked Spanish paprika

⅓ cup (3 fl oz/80 ml) dry sherry

Salt and freshly ground black pepper

1½ tsp chopped fresh flat-leaf parsley

In a large frying pan over medium-high heat, warm the oil. Add the garlic and red pepper flakes and sauté for 15 seconds. Add the shrimp and paprika and sauté until the shrimp curl and turn pink, about 3 minutes. Add the sherry and cook until the sherry is reduced by half, about 1 minute. Season with salt and black pepper. Transfer the shrimp and the juices to a serving dish, garnish with the parsley, and serve.

Vegetables and fruits become more vibrant as summer unfolds, with cherry and grape tomatoes, avocados, eggplants, tomatillos, sweet peppers, and early-season stone fruits filling market bins and farm stands. Salads of chicken, corn, avocados, and crisp tortillas and of summer squashes, tomatoes, and radishes showcase the rich seasonal palette of colors and flavors. Warmer weather also means burgers, such as lamb patties crowned with a heady yogurt sauce and chickpea and red pepper patties with a paprika mayonnaise. On the dessert menu, summer's stone fruits shine in a deep-dish plum pie, an apricot-studded clafoutis, and mixed roasted fruits atop creamy ricotta.

1
MIXED BERRY GALETTE
page 132

2
FARMERS' MARKET SALAD WITH TOMATO-BASIL VINAIGRETTE
page 132

3
SESAME-CRUSTED SALMON WITH CHERMOULA
page 135

8
GRILLED STEAK TACOS WITH CHIPOTLE SALSA & AVOCADO
page 137

9
CHICKEN TOSTADA SALAD
page 138

10
LAMB BURGERS WITH SPINACH & SPICED YOGURT SAUCE
page 138

15
BUTTERMILK COLESLAW WITH CARROTS & RAISINS
page 143

16
BRINED PORK CHOPS WITH GRILLED STONE FRUIT
page 143

17
GRILLED VEGETABLE GYROS WITH CUCUMBER-MINT SAUCE
page 144

22
MISO-GLAZED GRILLED ASIAN EGGPLANT
page 146

23
FRIED GREEN TOMATOES WITH RÉMOULADE
page 148

24
DEEP-DISH PLUM PIE
page 148

29
GRILLED SUMMER SQUASH PARMESAN
page 152

30
ROASTED SUMMER FRUITS WITH RICOTTA-VANILLA CREAM
page 152

4
ROASTED TOMATO SOUP WITH SERRANO HAM & BURRATA
page 135

5
FARRO SALAD WITH GRAPE TOMATOES & RICOTTA SALATA
page 136

6
APRICOT CLAFOUTIS
page 136

7
AVOCADO SOUP WITH SHRIMP & SALSA
page 136

11
GARLICKY ZUCCHINI SOUP WITH BASIL GREMOLATA
page 140

12
STRAWBERRY-RHUBARB CRISP
page 140

13
PASTA WITH ROSEMARY-LAMB SUGO
page 141

14
VEGETABLE ENCHILADAS
page 141

18
TWO-BEAN & POTATO SALAD
page 144

19
ALBONDIGAS
page 145

20
RISOTTO WITH SAUTÉED SCALLOPS
page 145

21
SPANISH PAELLA
page 146

25
STEAK PIPÉRADE
page 149

26
SPICY PORK KEBABS
page 149

27
CHICKPEA & ROASTED RED PEPPER BURGERS WITH SMOKED PAPRIKA MAYONNAISE
page 151

28
ROASTED POTATO SALAD WITH GREEN ONION DRESSING
page 151

june

1

MIXED BERRY GALETTE

serves 6–8

Flaky Pie Dough for Single Crust (*left*)

2 cups (8 oz/250 g) blackberries

2 cups (8 oz/250 g) blueberries

2 Tbsp lemon juice

¼ cup (2 oz/60 g) granulated sugar

3 Tbsp all-purpose flour

1 large egg, beaten with 1 tsp water (optional)

1 Tbsp turbinado sugar (optional)

Vanilla ice cream for serving

To make the flaky pie dough for single crust, in the bowl of a food processor, combine 1¼ cups (6½ oz/200 g) all-purpose flour, ¼ tsp kosher salt, and 2 tsp sugar. Sprinkle 7 Tbsp (3½ oz/105 g) cold unsalted butter, cut into pieces, over the top and pulse for a few seconds, or just until the butter is slightly broken up into the flour but is still in visible pieces. Evenly sprinkle 5 Tbsp (3 fl oz/80 ml) ice water, plus more if needed, over the flour mixture, then process just until the mixture starts to come together. Dump the dough into a large zip-top plastic bag and press into a flat disk. Refrigerate for at least 30 minutes or up to 1 day before using, or freeze for up to 1 month.

Prepare the dough and chill as directed. Preheat the oven to 425°F (220°C). Line a baking sheet with parchment paper.

On a lightly floured work surface, roll out the dough into a round about 12 inches (30 cm) in diameter and about ⅛ inch (3 mm) thick. Transfer to the prepared sheet.

In a bowl, toss together the berries, lemon juice, granulated sugar, and flour. Spoon the filling onto the dough, leaving a 2-inch (5-cm) border uncovered around the edge. Fold the edge up and over the filling, forming loose pleats. Brush the border with the egg wash and sprinkle with the turbinado sugar, if you like.

Bake until the filling is bubbling and the pastry is golden brown, about 25 minutes. Let cool slightly on a wire rack before serving with scoops of ice cream.

2

FARMERS' MARKET SALAD WITH TOMATO-BASIL VINAIGRETTE

serves 4

FOR THE GARLIC CHIPS (OPTIONAL)

¼ cup (1½ oz/15 g) very thinly sliced garlic

¼ cup (2 fl oz/60 ml) olive oil

Salt

1 plum tomato, peeled, cored, and seeded

1 small clove garlic, minced

1 Tbsp champagne vinegar

¼ cup (2 fl oz/60 ml) extra-virgin olive oil

1½ Tbsp chopped fresh basil

Salt and freshly ground pepper

Pinch of sugar (optional)

2 zucchini, ends trimmed

2 summer squash, ends trimmed

4 radishes, very thinly sliced

1 shallot, very thinly sliced

1 cup (6 oz/185 g) cherry tomatoes, halved

1 cup (5 oz/155 g) crumbled cotija or feta cheese

Although you can serve this salad as is, you can take it up a step with a topping of crispy garlic chips. If you don't have a spiralizer or a mandoline, use a sharp knife: first thinly slice the zucchini and summer squashes lengthwise, then cut again into long julienne strips.

If making the garlic chips, in a small sauté pan, combine the garlic and oil. Place over medium heat and gently fry, stirring occasionally, until the garlic is golden, about 2 minutes. Using a fine-mesh strainer, transfer the chips to a paper towel–lined plate and sprinkle with salt. Reserve the garlicky oil for sautéing or salad dressing.

In a mini food processor, purée the plum tomato. Transfer to a small bowl. Add the minced garlic, vinegar, oil, and basil and whisk until the vinaigrette is well blended. Season with salt and pepper. Taste and add the sugar, if needed.

Using a spiralizer fitted with the small shredder blade, cut the zucchini and squash into spaghetti-like spiral strands, stopping to cut the curls with kitchen shears every 3 or 4 rotations. Alternatively, using a mandoline, slice the zucchini into long julienne strips.

Transfer the zucchini and squash to a large bowl. Add the radishes, shallot, and cherry tomatoes. Drizzle with vinaigrette to taste and toss to coat evenly. Top with the cheese and the garlic chips, if using, and serve.

3

SESAME-CRUSTED SALMON WITH CHERMOULA

serves 4

4 Tbsp (2 fl oz/60 ml) extra-virgin olive oil, plus more for drizzling

½ cup (3 oz/90 g) minced shallots

½ cup (2½ oz/75 g) chopped red bell pepper

3 cloves garlic, chopped

1 tsp *each* ground cumin, ground coriander, and paprika

Salt and freshly ground black pepper

¼ tsp red pepper flakes, plus more if desired

Leaves from 1 bunch fresh flat-leaf parsley, chopped

Leaves from 1 bunch fresh cilantro, chopped

Grated zest and juice of 1 lemon

4 skin-on salmon fillets, each about 6 oz (185 g)

¼ cup (1 oz/30 g) black sesame seeds

Here, sesame seeds form a wonderful crisp coating on pan-seared salmon. Black sesame seeds add a striking color contrast, but the white variety will work well, too. The pungent pepper, shallot, and herb condiment that accompanies the salmon is an adaptation of chermoula, a popular North African marinade or sauce. Serve the salmon with a side of sautéed sugar snap peas or spinach.

To make the chermoula, warm a sauté pan over medium-high heat and add 2 Tbsp of the oil. When the oil is hot, add the shallots and bell pepper. Sauté for about 3 minutes or until the vegetables begin to soften. Add the garlic, cumin, coriander, paprika, ½ tsp salt, and the red pepper flakes. Sauté for 1 minute or until the garlic is fragrant. Transfer to a food processor. Add the parsley, cilantro, and lemon zest and juice to the vegetables and pulse the mixture about 10 times or until blended but still slightly chunky. Scrape down the sides and pulse a few more times. Taste and adjust the seasoning with more salt or pepper flakes.

Arrange the salmon fillets skin-side down on a cutting board. Pat them dry and season with salt and black pepper. Drizzle the fillets with a drop of oil and use your fingers to coat them. Sprinkle the sesame seeds on top and press lightly to adhere.

Warm a large sauté pan over medium-high heat and add the remaining 2 Tbsp oil to the pan. When the oil is hot, add the salmon, sesame seed–side down. Turn the fish after 3 minutes. The sesame seeds should be crisp. Cook the second side for another 3 minutes or until cooked through.

Transfer the fillets to warmed plates and serve with a dollop of chermoula.

4

ROASTED TOMATO SOUP WITH SERRANO HAM & BURRATA

serves 4

4 thin slices serrano ham

2½ lb (1.25 kg) small tomatoes, such as plum or Campari, halved

4 Tbsp (2 fl oz/60 ml) olive oil

Salt and freshly ground pepper

1 yellow onion, chopped

4 cloves garlic, minced

2 cups (16 fl oz/500 ml) chicken broth

6 oz (185 g) burrata or fresh mozzarella cheese, sliced

1 Tbsp finely chopped chives

Tomatoes and mozzarella are a classic combination that only gets better with the addition of Spain's signature cured ham. Make sure the serrano dries out completely in the oven for the best grinding. Slice the burrata, a soft, runny cheese made by filling a shell of mozzarella with thick cream and bits of fresh cheese, just before serving. Don't worry if the slices fall apart, as the chunks will still taste delicious melting into the soup.

Preheat the oven to 200°F (95°C). Place the ham in a single layer on a baking sheet and bake until completely dried, about 1 hour and 45 minutes. Transfer the ham to paper towels and blot it to remove any excess oil. Tear the ham into small pieces, transfer to a spice grinder, and grind into a fine dust. Set aside.

Raise the oven temperature to 450°F (230°C). Arrange the tomatoes in a single layer on a baking sheet, drizzle with 2 Tbsp of the oil, and season with salt and pepper. Roast the tomatoes until very soft and caramelized, 25–30 minutes. Set aside.

In a large, heavy pot, warm the remaining 2 Tbsp oil over medium-high heat. Add the onion and garlic and sauté until translucent, about 5 minutes. Add the tomatoes with all their juices and stir to combine. Using a wooden spoon, break up the tomatoes a bit and sauté for 3 minutes. Add the broth and bring to a boil. Reduce the heat to low and simmer for 20 minutes. Remove from the heat and let cool slightly.

Purée half of the soup in a blender. Return to the pot, stir in the ham dust, and season with salt and pepper.

Ladle the soup into bowls. Garnish each bowl with a slice of burrata and let it sit for a minute or two so that the cheese begins to melt into the soup. Top each bowl with chopped chives and serve.

5

Farro, *an ancient form of wheat, is cultivated primarily in the Italian regions of Tuscany and Umbria. The light brown grains have a full, nutty flavor that is delicious in soups and salads. Dry, crumbly* ricotta salata *and summer's juicy tomatoes and aromatic basil join* farro *in this rustic Italian salad.*

FARRO SALAD WITH GRAPE TOMATOES & RICOTTA SALATA

serves 4

1 cup (6 oz/185 g) farro

Salt and freshly ground pepper

2 Tbsp extra-virgin olive oil

1 Tbsp fresh lemon juice

1 cup (6 oz/185 g) grape or cherry tomatoes, stemmed and halved

½ cup (2 oz/60 g) crumbled ricotta salata cheese

2 green onions, including tender green tops, thinly sliced

¼ cup (⅓ oz/10 g) shredded fresh basil

In a large saucepan, combine the farro and 2 qt (2 l) water. Place the pan over medium-high heat, bring to a boil, and add 1 tsp salt. Reduce the heat to medium or medium-low, so the farro simmers steadily, and cook, uncovered, until tender yet still slightly firm and chewy, about 30 minutes. Remove from the heat and drain well in a fine-mesh sieve.

In a serving bowl, whisk together the olive oil and lemon juice until well blended. Whisk in salt and pepper to taste. Add the farro and toss well. Gently stir in the tomatoes, cheese, green onions, and basil until all the ingredients are evenly distributed. Serve at room temperature.

6

This creamy custard features quartered apricots sprinkled with brandy. The clafoutis is best served warm, with scoops of vanilla ice cream alongside.

APRICOT CLAFOUTIS

serves 4

2 Tbsp unsalted butter

1 lb (500 g) apricots, pitted and quartered

2 tsp brandy or Cognac

2 large eggs

¾ cup (6 fl oz/180 ml) plus 2 Tbsp whole milk

6 Tbsp (3 oz/90 g) granulated sugar

1 tsp finely grated lemon zest

1 tsp pure vanilla extract

⅓ cup (2 oz/60 g) all-purpose flour

2 Tbsp confectioners' sugar

Preheat the oven to 375°F (190°C). In a 9-inch (23-cm) ovenproof frying pan, melt the butter. ⟫→

Arrange the apricots in an even layer in the bottom of the pan and sprinkle with the brandy.

In a blender, process the eggs, milk, granulated sugar, lemon zest, vanilla, and flour until smooth. Pour the batter over the apricots.

Bake until the clafoutis is puffed and golden brown, about 45 minutes. Let cool slightly on a wire rack. Dust with confectioners' sugar and serve.

7

Usually served chilled, this Latin American soup is also delicious at room temperature. The zesty tomato salsa provides a lively contrast to the rich, creamy flavor of the avocado. A tropical fruit—mango, papaya, pineapple— can be substituted for the tomatoes.

AVOCADO SOUP WITH SHRIMP & SALSA

serves 6–8

3 large avocados, peeled, pitted, and coarsely chopped

3 cups (24 fl oz/750 ml) chicken broth

1 cup (8 fl oz/250 ml) heavy cream

2 Tbsp fresh lemon juice

Salt and freshly ground pepper

FOR THE SALSA

3 tomatoes (about 1 lb/500 g), finely chopped

1 small red onion, minced

2 or 3 jalapeño chiles, minced

2 cloves garlic, minced

3 Tbsp fresh lemon or lime juice

¼ cup (⅓ oz/10 g) chopped fresh cilantro

¼ cup (2 fl oz/60 ml) olive oil

Salt and freshly ground pepper

12–16 cooked shrimp, peeled and diced

Working in batches, purée the avocados, broth, and cream in a blender. Transfer to a bowl. Add the lemon juice and season with salt and pepper. Cover and refrigerate until cold but not overly chilled, about 1 hour.

Meanwhile, to make the salsa, stir together the tomatoes, onion, chiles, garlic, lemon juice, cilantro, and oil. Season with salt and pepper.

Serve the soup topped with the shrimp and garnished with the salsa.

8

Spicy grilled steak is tucked into warm corn tortillas and topped with a simple salsa for a healthy meal guaranteed to please many palates. The chipotle salsa adds a smoky flavor but only mild heat, while the avocado contributes a rich taste and creamy texture. If you like, add shredded red cabbage to the tacos for added flavor and fiber.

GRILLED STEAK TACOS WITH CHIPOTLE SALSA & AVOCADO

serves 4–6

½ cup (4 fl oz/125 ml) canola oil

1 yellow onion, thinly sliced

2 cloves garlic, chopped

1 jalapeño chile, seeded and minced

1 Tbsp chopped fresh oregano

1 tsp ground cumin

1 Tbsp ancho chile powder

2 Tbsp chopped fresh cilantro

1 Tbsp tequila

Salt

1 flank steak, 2½–3 lb (1–1.5 kg), trimmed of fat and silver skin

FOR THE CHIPOTLE SALSA

2 cloves garlic, unpeeled

2 ripe tomatoes, about 1 lb (500 g)

3 chipotle chiles in adobo

Salt

Oil, for grilling

12 corn tortillas

2 avocados, peeled, halved, and thinly sliced

In a small bowl, mix together the oil, onion, garlic, jalapeño, oregano, cumin, chile powder, cilantro, tequila, and 1½ tsp salt. Score the steak a few times across the grain. Put the steak in a baking dish and pour over the marinade. Cover and let marinate in the refrigerator, turning occasionally, for at least 6 hours or up to overnight. Remove from the refrigerator 30 minutes before grilling.

To make the salsa, preheat the broiler and line a small rimmed baking sheet with foil. Arrange the garlic and tomatoes on the baking sheet and place under the broiler. Broil until the vegetable skins are blackened on all sides, turning with tongs as they char, about 5 minutes for the garlic and 10–15 minutes for the tomatoes. Set aside to cool. Peel the garlic and add it to a blender along with the tomatoes (you do not need to peel the charred tomato skin) and chiles. Process briefly, until the mixture is thick but still chunky. Pour the salsa into a bowl, season with salt, cover, and let stand at room temperature for 20–30 minutes. ⤳

Prepare a grill for direct-heat cooking over high heat. Generously oil the grill rack. Preheat the oven to 200°F (95°C).

Remove the steak from the marinade, pat dry, and discard the marinade. Grill the steak directly over the heat, turning once, until well browned and medium-rare in the center, 9–10 minutes. (Move the steak to a cooler part of the grill if flare-ups occur.) The steak should not be cooked past medium-rare, as it will toughen. Transfer the meat to a platter, cover loosely with foil, and let rest for about 15 minutes.

Quickly grill the tortillas and then divide into two equal stacks. Wrap each stack tightly in foil. Place the tortillas in the oven and keep warm.

Slice the steak thinly against the grain.

To assemble the tacos, place the steak on one side of the tortilla, spoon a little salsa and avocado on top, fold, and serve.

9

CHICKEN TOSTADA SALAD

serves 4

FOR THE LIME VINAIGRETTE

Grated zest and juice of 2 limes

1 clove garlic, minced

Salt and freshly ground pepper

⅔ cup (5 fl oz/160 ml) olive oil

This is an updated version of the ubiquitous taco salad, with lean chicken and chopped vegetables piled high on a crispy tortilla. To save time, omit frying the tortillas and serve the chicken salad over large handfuls of good-quality corn tortilla chips.

1 can (15 oz/470 g) black beans, drained and rinsed

2 cups (12 oz/375 g) fresh corn kernels (from about 2 ears of corn, grilled if desired)

2 cups (12 oz/375 g) cherry tomatoes, halved

4 canned green chiles, chopped

1 cup (8 fl oz/250 ml) corn oil

4 corn tortillas, each 6 inches (15 cm) in diameter, halved

1 small head romaine lettuce, cut into bite-sized pieces

2 cups (¾ lb/375 g) shredded cooked chicken meat

1 avocado, peeled, pitted and sliced

Fresh cilantro leaves and sliced green onion for garnish (optional)

To make the vinaigrette, in a bowl, whisk together the lime zest and juice, garlic, ¼ tsp salt, and ⅛ tsp pepper. Add the oil in a thin stream, whisking constantly until the vinaigrette is smooth.

Transfer 3 Tbsp of the vinaigrette to a large bowl and add the beans, corn, tomatoes, and chiles; mix gently. Reserve the remaining vinaigrette. Let the salsa stand for at least 10 minutes to blend the flavors.

Meanwhile, in a frying pan, warm the corn oil over medium-high heat. When it is hot, slip 3 tortilla halves into the oil and cook until golden and almost crisp, 1–2 minutes. Using tongs, transfer to paper towels to drain. Repeat with the remaining tortilla halves.

Add the lettuce to the reserved vinaigrette and toss to coat. Place 2 fried tortilla halves on each of 4 plates and divide the lettuce among them. Spoon the salsa over the lettuce, top with the chicken and avocado, garnish with the cilantro and green onion, if desired, and serve.

10

LAMB BURGERS WITH SPINACH & SPICED YOGURT SAUCE

serves 4

¾ cup (3¾ oz/110 g) finely chopped red onion

½ cup (4 oz/125 g) plain whole-milk yogurt

½ tsp ground cumin

Pinch of cayenne pepper

Salt and freshly ground black pepper

1¼ lb (625 g) ground lamb

¾ tsp ground allspice

Olive oil, for brushing

4 whole-wheat buns

1 tomato, sliced

4 handfuls baby spinach leaves

Lean ground lamb is a novel alternative to beef in these robustly spiced burgers. Ditch the buns for a gluten-free option, and double the amount of spinach to serve the burgers on a bed of greens. Yogurt adds creaminess and protein to the slightly spicy sauce.

In a small bowl, mix ¼ cup (1 oz/30 g) of the onion with the yogurt, cumin, and cayenne. Season with salt and black pepper and set aside.

In a bowl, combine the lamb and allspice with the remaining onion, 1 tsp salt, and a generous amount of black pepper. Mix gently to blend. Form the lamb mixture into 4 patties, each ½ inch (12 mm) thick. Heat a large frying pan over medium-high heat and brush with oil. Add the lamb patties and cook to the desired doneness, about 5 minutes per side for medium.

Meanwhile, preheat the broiler. Brush the cut surface of the buns with oil, then broil, oiled side up, until beginning to brown, about 2 minutes. Divide the bun bottoms among 4 warmed plates. Top each with a patty.

Spoon some of the yogurt sauce over each patty, top with a couple slices of tomato and a handful of spinach leaves and top with the bun tops. Serve, passing additional sauce at the table.

11

Gremolata is an Italian herb condiment with vibrant flavor and color. This version includes some basil to add hints of licorice to parsley's herbal taste. Topped with this simple mixture, a garlic-infused zucchini soup gets a fresh, bold hit of summer.

GARLICKY ZUCCHINI SOUP WITH BASIL GREMOLATA

serves 6

3 leeks, about 1½ lb (750 g) total

2 lemons

3 Tbsp olive oil

3 zucchini, about 1½ lb (750 g) total, cut into ½-inch (12-mm) cubes

3 Tbsp minced garlic

Salt and freshly ground pepper

1 celery rib, finely chopped

8 cups (64 fl oz/2 l) chicken broth

1 russet potato, peeled and finely chopped

3 Tbsp minced fresh flat-leaf parsley

3 Tbsp minced fresh basil

Trim the dark green tops from the leeks. Cut the leeks lengthwise into quarters and then cut crosswise into ¼-inch (6-mm) pieces. Using a vegetable peeler, remove the zest in wide strips from 1 lemon.

In a large, heavy pot, heat 1½ Tbsp of the oil over high heat. Add two-thirds of the zucchini and spread in a single layer. Cook, without stirring, until beginning to brown, about 1½ minutes. Stir and then cook, stirring occasionally, until the zucchini is just tender, about 2 minutes. Stir in 1 Tbsp of the garlic and ¼ tsp salt and cook until fragrant, about 30 seconds. Transfer to a large plate.

Add the remaining 1½ Tbsp oil to the pot and heat over medium-high heat. Add the leeks, celery, 1 Tbsp of the garlic, and ¼ tsp salt and stir to mix well. Reduce the heat to low, cover, and cook, stirring occasionally, until the leeks soften, about 10 minutes. Add the broth, potato, lemon zest strips, and remaining zucchini, raise the heat to high, and bring to a boil. Reduce the heat to low, cover partially, and simmer, stirring occasionally, until the potato is tender, about 15 minutes.

Meanwhile, to make the gremolata, finely grate the zest from the remaining lemon. In a small bowl, stir together the grated zest, the remaining 1 Tbsp garlic, the parsley, and the basil. ⟶

Discard the lemon zest strips from the pot. Use a large spoon to mash the potato and zucchini against the sides of the pot and stir into the soup to thicken it slightly. Stir in the sautéed zucchini and 1 tsp salt, and season with pepper. Ladle the soup into bowls, garnish with the gremolata, and serve.

12

Rhubarb and strawberries continue to appear in markets as spring gives way to summer. When you don't have time to roll and shape a pie crust, just toss the fruits together in this easy-to-prepare crisp. Serve with vanilla ice cream, preferably flecked with vanilla bean.

STRAWBERRY-RHUBARB CRISP

serves 8

6 rhubarb stalks, cut into ½-inch (12-mm) pieces

1 pt (8 oz/250 g) strawberries, hulled and halved lengthwise

½ cup (4 oz/125 g) plus ⅓ cup (3 oz/90 g) granulated sugar

1 cup (5 oz/155 g) all-purpose flour

½ cup (1½ oz/45 g) rolled oats

⅓ cup (2½ oz/75 g) firmly packed light brown sugar

¼ tsp kosher salt

½ cup (4 oz/125 g) unsalted butter, melted

Preheat the oven to 350°F (180°C).

In a large bowl, stir together the rhubarb, strawberries, and ½ cup granulated sugar until well mixed. Pour into a 2½-qt (2.5-l) baking dish.

In another large bowl, stir together the flour, rolled oats, ⅓ cup (3 oz/90 g) granulated sugar, brown sugar, and salt until blended. Stir in the melted butter until evenly moistened crumbs form. Spoon the crumb mixture evenly over the filling.

Bake the crisp until the rhubarb is tender, the juices are bubbling, and the topping is golden brown, 35–40 minutes. Let cool on a wire rack for 10 minutes. Serve warm. The crisp can be cooled, covered with plastic wrap, and stored at room temperature for up to 2 days, then rewarmed in a preheated 250°F (120°C) oven for 15 minutes.

13

In Italian, sugo means "sauce" or "juice." Here, it is used for a rustic ragù of ground lamb, cubed zucchini, and tomatoes that is tossed with multigrain rotini. Other short pasta shapes, such as fusilli or penne, would also be good. For a more delicate, summery herb flavor, trade out the rosemary for 3 Tbsp chopped fresh basil, adding the basil along with the cheese.

PASTA WITH ROSEMARY-LAMB SUGO

serves 4

2 Tbsp olive oil

1 large onion, thinly sliced

1 Tbsp minced fresh rosemary

½ lb (500 g) ground lamb

Salt and freshly ground pepper

¼ cup (2 fl oz/60 ml) dry white wine

2 cans (14.5 oz/455 g each) diced tomatoes

2 large zucchini, cut into ½-inch (12-mm) cubes

12 oz (375 g) rotini pasta, preferably multigrain

¼ cup (1 oz/30 g) grated pecorino romano cheese, plus more for serving

In a large frying pan over medium-high heat, warm the oil. Add the onion and rosemary and sauté until the onion is tender, about 5 minutes. Add the lamb and sprinkle with salt and pepper. Sauté until the lamb is no longer pink, breaking up the meat with a wooden spoon, about 3 minutes. Add the wine and boil until absorbed, about 2 minutes. Add the tomatoes with their juices and bring to a boil. Stir in the zucchini. Reduce the heat to medium-low and boil until the sauce is thick, stirring occasionally, about 10 minutes.

Meanwhile, bring a large pot of salted water to a boil. Add the pasta, stir well, and cook until al dente, about 11 minutes, or according to package directions. Drain the pasta, then add to the sauce and toss to coat. Mix in the ¼ cup (1 oz/30 g) cheese.

Taste and adjust the seasoning. Transfer to warmed shallow bowls and serve, passing additional cheese at the table.

14

Tender zucchini and kernels of sweet corn star in this Tex-Mex classic. Wrapped in tortillas and smothered in a tangy green sauce and melted jack and Cheddar cheeses, this is a light but comforting vegetarian meal.

VEGETABLE ENCHILADAS

serves 4–6

12 corn tortillas, each 8 inches (20 cm) in diameter

2 Tbsp canola oil

Salt

1 cup (4 oz/125 g) shredded Monterey jack cheese

1 cup (4 oz/125 g) shredded white Cheddar cheese

2 cups (12 oz/375 g) fresh or thawed frozen corn kernels

2 zucchini, halved lengthwise and thinly sliced

1 large yellow onion, halved and thinly sliced

2 jars (12½ oz/390 g each) tomatillo salsa

¼ cup (2 oz/60 g) Mexican crema or sour cream

Preheat the oven to 300°F (150°C). Brush the tortillas with the oil, sprinkle with salt, and arrange on a baking sheet. Bake until warm and softened, about 1 minute. Remove from the oven and increase the oven temperature to 375°F (190°C).

In a small bowl, stir together half of the Monterey jack cheese, half of the Cheddar cheese, the corn, zucchini, and onion. Cover the bottom of a 9-by-13-inch (23-by-33-cm) baking dish with 1 jar of the salsa.

To assemble the enchiladas, place a tortilla on a work surface, add a few tablespoons of the vegetable filling down the center, and roll up the tortilla. Place it, seam side down, in the baking dish. Repeat with the remaining tortillas and filling. Spread the remaining jar of salsa over the top and sprinkle with the remaining cheese.

Cover the dish with foil and bake until the vegetables are tender and the cheese has melted, about 20 minutes. Uncover and continue to bake until the cheese is golden, 10–15 minutes. Let stand briefly before serving. Pass the crema at the table.

15

Picnics and barbecues call for crunchy, creamy coleslaw. Here, a homemade herb-flecked buttermilk dressing provides rich, tangy flavor, while a handful of golden raisins adds just enough natural sweetness. Mixing red and green cabbages results in a particularly pretty slaw.

BUTTERMILK COLESLAW WITH CARROTS & RAISINS

serves 4–6

FOR THE BUTTERMILK DRESSING

¾ cup (6 fl oz/180 ml) mayonnaise

½ cup (4 fl oz/125 ml) buttermilk

¼ cup (2 oz/60 g) sour cream

½ bunch fresh flat-leaf parsley, leaves and tender stems, finely chopped

½ bunch fresh chives, finely chopped

Salt and ground white pepper

½ cup (3 oz/90 g) golden raisins

1 large carrot, cut into thin matchsticks

½ red onion, thinly sliced

2 shallots, thinly sliced

3 Tbsp white vinegar

½ head green cabbage, cored and finely shredded

½ head red cabbage, cored and finely shredded

Salt and ground white pepper

Chopped fresh flat-leaf parsley leaves and chives for garnish

To make the dressing, in a bowl, stir together the mayonnaise, buttermilk, and sour cream. Stir in the parsley and chives. Season with salt and white pepper.

In a small bowl, soak the raisins in warm water to cover until plump, about 30 minutes. Drain the raisins. In another small bowl, combine the carrot, onion, shallots, and vinegar and toss to coat.

In a large bowl, toss together the green and red cabbage. Add the raisins, carrot-vinegar mixture, and buttermilk dressing and toss to coat. Season with salt and white pepper. Garnish with parsley and chives and serve.

16

The warm days of June put stone fruits and grilling on the menu. Cooking the fruits over an outdoor fire brings out their innate sweetness and adds appealing grill marks. Plums, peaches, and nectarines are all good choices for grilling, so choose the fruit in the market that looks and tastes the best.

BRINED PORK CHOPS WITH GRILLED STONE FRUIT

serves 6

FOR THE PORK BRINE

¼ cup (2 fl oz/60 ml) cider vinegar

¼ cup (2 oz/60 g) firmly packed brown sugar

1 tsp *each* dried thyme and juniper berries

⅛ tsp red pepper flakes

2 Tbsp salt

1 Tbsp freshly ground black pepper

6 bone-in pork chops, each at least 1 inch (2.5 cm) thick

Canola oil, for brushing

6 ripe but slightly firm plums, peaches, or nectarines, halved and pitted

To make the pork brine, in a large bowl, combine 6 cups (48 fl oz/1.5 l) water, the vinegar, brown sugar, thyme, juniper berries, red pepper flakes, salt, and black pepper and stir until the sugar dissolves.

Place the pork chops in a large locking plastic bag and pour in the brine. Seal the bag, massage the brine around the chops, and refrigerate overnight. Remove the chops from the refrigerator 30 minutes before you plan to begin grilling.

Discard the brine, rinse the chops briefly in cold water, and pat dry with paper towels. Prepare a grill for indirect cooking over medium heat; the temperature inside the grill should be 350°–375°F (180°–190°C). Brush and oil the grill grate.

Place the pork chops on the grill directly over the heat source and sear, turning once, until nicely grill-marked on both sides, 2–3 minutes per side. Move the chops to the area with no heat, cover the grill, and cook until the chops are somewhat firm to the touch, about 15 minutes for medium, or until an instant-read thermometer inserted horizontally into the center of a chop away from bone registers 145°F (63°C). Transfer the chops to a platter and let rest for 10 minutes.

Meanwhile, brush both sides of the fruit halves with oil and grill over direct heat until grill-marked, about 2 minutes per side. Serve the pork chops with the grilled fruit alongside.

17

A Greek specialty, gyro is lamb and beef roasted together on a vertical spit and served on pita with tomato, onion, and yogurt sauce. Greek spice blends typically pack a flavor punch, so you won't miss the meat in this all-vegetable spin on the traditional sandwich. If you don't have access to an outdoor grill, you can cook the vegetables on a stove-top grill pan.

GRILLED VEGETABLE GYROS WITH CUCUMBER-MINT SAUCE

serves 4–6

2 tsp salt

2 tsp chili powder

1 tsp *each* ground cumin, garlic powder, dried oregano, and dried thyme

½ tsp ground cinnamon

1 zucchini, halved lengthwise and thinly sliced

1 red pepper, seeds and ribs removed, and sliced

1 yellow pepper, seeds and ribs removed, and sliced

1 yellow onion, halved and thinly sliced

½ lb (250 g) mushrooms, halved

2 Tbsp olive oil

FOR THE CUCUMBER-MINT SAUCE

2 cups (16 oz/500 g) plain Greek yogurt

1 cucumber, peeled, seeded, and chopped

2 cloves garlic

2 Tbsp chopped fresh mint

2 Tbsp fresh lemon juice

Salt and freshly ground pepper

6 whole-wheat pitas, cut in half and split open to form pockets

Combine the salt, chili powder, cumin, garlic powder, oregano, thyme, and cinnamon in a large bowl. Add the zucchini, peppers, onion, mushrooms, and the oil and toss to combine. Set aside.

To make the sauce, in a food processor, combine the yogurt, cucumber, garlic, mint, and lemon juice and process until smooth. Season with salt and pepper and set aside.

Prepare a grill for direct-heat cooking over high heat. Place the reserved vegetables in a grill basket and place on the grill. Cook, stirring occasionally, until the vegetables are fork-tender and browned all over, about 12 minutes.

Divide the vegetables among the pita pockets and drizzle with a generous helping of the sauce. Serve, passing extra sauce at the table.

18

This hybrid potato-meets-bean salad makes a lovely, satisfying vegetarian lunch accompanied with only crusty whole-grain bread and perhaps a favorite cheese. The bold flavors of olives, capers, and fresh mint brighten the combination of green beans, potatoes, and chickpeas.

TWO-BEAN & POTATO SALAD

serves 4

Salt and freshly ground pepper

¼ lb (125 g) green beans, trimmed

1¼ (625 g) red-skinned potatoes, quartered

1 Tbsp whole-grain mustard

1 Tbsp red wine vinegar

1 Tbsp extra-virgin olive oil

1 cup (7 oz/220 g) cooked or canned chickpeas, drained and rinsed

1 small red onion, finely chopped

½ cup (¾ oz/20 g) coarsely chopped fresh flat-leaf parsley

½ cup (¾ oz/20 g) coarsely chopped fresh mint

4 Sicilian or other green olives, pitted and coarsely chopped

1 Tbsp capers, rinsed and chopped

Prepare a bowl of ice water. Bring a large pot of water to a boil, add 1 Tbsp salt and the green beans, and cook until bright green and tender-crisp, about 3 minutes. Using a slotted spoon, transfer to the bowl of ice water and let stand for 1–2 minutes. Drain the beans and place in a large bowl. Add the potatoes to the boiling water and cook until just tender, about 10 minutes. Drain and let cool.

In a small bowl, whisk together the mustard, vinegar, 1 tsp salt, and ⅛ tsp pepper. Gradually whisk in the oil until blended.

To the bowl with the green beans, add the chickpeas, onion, parsley, mint, olives, capers, and the cooled potatoes. Pour the dressing over the salad and toss to coat. Let the salad stand for about 15 minutes to blend the flavors, and serve.

19

ALBONDIGAS

serves 6

FOR THE MEATBALLS

¼ cup (1½ oz/45 g) masa harina, or ¼ cup (1 oz/30 g) fine dried bread crumbs

¼ cup (2 fl oz/60 ml) chicken broth

1 lb (500 g) lean ground pork

1 egg

1 yellow onion, finely chopped

2 cloves garlic, minced

1 Tbsp chopped fresh oregano

2 tsp ancho chile powder

½ tsp ground cumin

Salt and freshly ground pepper

2 Tbsp canola oil

1 yellow onion, chopped

2 cloves garlic, minced

1 tsp ground cumin

1½ tsp minced chipotle chiles in adobo

6 cups (48 fl oz/1.5 l) chicken broth

1 can (14½ oz/455 g) diced tomatoes

1 Tbsp fresh lime juice

Salt and freshly ground pepper

3 Tbsp chopped fresh cilantro

In this classic Mexican soup, pork meatballs are cooked in an aromatic broth flavored with garlic, cumin, and chipotle chiles. Ancho chile powder is smoky and mild. For a spicier flavor, add a big pinch of red pepper flakes with the chile powder. Warm corn tortillas or corn bread and a crisp salad are delicious on the side.

To make the meatballs, in a bowl, stir together the masa harina and chicken broth to make a paste. Add the pork, egg, onion, garlic, oregano, chile powder, cumin, 1 tsp salt, and ½ tsp pepper. Using your hands, gently but thoroughly blend the ingredients. Form the mixture into small meatballs about 1 inch (2.5 cm) in diameter. Set aside.

In a large saucepan over medium heat, warm the canola oil. Add the onion and sauté until softened and tinged with gold, about 5 minutes. Add the garlic and sauté for 30 seconds. Stir in the cumin and chipotles in adobo. Cook, stirring frequently for 30 seconds, then stir in the broth and tomatoes and bring to a simmer.

Drop the meatballs into the broth mixture and return to a simmer. Cover, reduce the heat to medium-low, and cook without stirring until the meatballs are firm, 15–20 minutes.

Uncover and stir in the lime juice. Season to taste with salt and pepper. Stir in the cilantro. Ladle into warmed shallow bowls and serve.

20

RISOTTO WITH SAUTÉED SCALLOPS

serves 6

7–8 cups (56–64 fl oz/1.75–2 l) shellfish broth or bottled clam juice

¼ cup (2 fl oz/60 ml) olive oil

½ cup (2½ oz/75 g) finely chopped yellow onion

Grated zest of 1 lemon

¾ lb (375 g) sea scallops, tough muscles removed

3 cups (21 oz/655 g) Arborio or Carnaroli rice

1 cup (8 fl oz/250 ml) dry white wine

1 tsp minced fresh tarragon, plus sprigs for garnish

2 Tbsp unsalted butter

Salt and freshly ground pepper

Although a lemony risotto is an apt partner for nearly any kind of seafood, it goes especially well with pan-seared sea scallops. Preheat your sauté pan well so the scallops crisp and brown at the edges but stay tender and soft at the center. Use a fine-rasp grater or zester to remove only the brightly colored zest from the lemon, leaving behind the bitter white pith.

In a saucepan, bring the broth to a gentle simmer over medium heat and maintain over low heat.

In a large, heavy saucepan, heat the oil over medium heat. Add the onion and sauté until softened, about 4 minutes. Add the lemon zest and cook until fragrant, about 1 minute. Add the scallops and cook until firm and opaque, 1–2 minutes. Using a slotted spoon, transfer the scallop mixture to a bowl.

Add the rice to the same pan and stir until well coated with oil and translucent, about 3 minutes. Add the wine and stir until completely absorbed. Add the minced tarragon to the simmering broth. Add the broth to the rice a ladleful at a time, stirring frequently after each addition. Wait until the broth is almost completely absorbed (but the rice is never dry on top) before adding the next ladleful. Reserve ¼ cup (2 fl oz/60 ml) broth to add at the end.

When the rice is tender to the bite and creamy, after about 20 minutes, gently stir in the scallops, butter, and reserved ¼ cup broth. Cook to heat through, about 1 minute. Season with salt and pepper and spoon into shallow bowls. Garnish with the tarragon sprigs and serve.

21

SPANISH PAELLA

serves 4–6

2 Tbsp olive oil

1 lb (500 g) cured Spanish-style chorizo or other spicy smoked sausage, cut into slices ½ inch (12 mm) thick

1 yellow onion, chopped

1 red bell pepper, seeded and chopped

3 cloves garlic, minced

Salt and freshly ground pepper

2 cups (14 oz/440 g) long-grain white rice, such as basmati

½ tsp saffron threads (optional)

4 cups (32 fl oz/1 l) chicken broth

1–2 lb (500 g–1 kg) small clams, such as littleneck or Manila, scrubbed

1 lb (500 g) large shrimp, peeled and deveined

1 cup (5 oz/155 g) thawed frozen baby peas

Paella is the national dish of Spain, where many distinctive regional variations exist. Here, the flavorful rice dish includes clams and shrimp, but you can add or substitute mussels, if you like. Be sure to scrub and debeard them before adding them to the pan. Pour a well-chilled white wine—Albariño, Sauvignon Blanc— or dry rosé at the table.

In a large frying pan or paella pan, heat the oil over medium-high heat. Add the sausage slices and cook, turning occasionally, until browned on both sides, about 3 minutes. Add the onion, bell pepper, and garlic and sauté until softened, 3–4 minutes. Season with salt and pepper. Add the rice, crumble in the saffron (if using), and cook, stirring, until the grains are well coated, about 2 minutes. Pour the broth into the pan and stir in 1½ tsp salt. Bring to a boil, reduce the heat to low, cover, and cook until the rice has absorbed nearly all of the liquid, about 20 minutes.

Press the clams, hinge side down, into the rice, discarding any that do not close to the touch. Spread the shrimp over the rice and top with the peas. Cover and cook until the shrimp are opaque and the clams have opened, about 5 minutes longer. Discard any unopened clams and serve.

22

MISO-GLAZED GRILLED ASIAN EGGPLANT

serves 4

¼-inch (6-mm) piece fresh ginger, peeled and coarsely chopped

1 clove garlic, coarsely chopped

¼ cup (2 oz/60 g) white miso

½ tsp Asian chile sauce such as Sriracha

2 Tbsp rice vinegar

2 tsp sugar

1 Tbsp mirin

4 Asian eggplants, halved lengthwise

Salt and freshly ground pepper

Canola oil for brushing

3 green onions, white and tender green parts, cut on the diagonal into slices ¼ inch (6 mm) thick

Slender Asian eggplants thrive in hot weather, just like their globe-shaped brothers, but their size and shape make them easier to split lengthwise and handle over the grill. The cut side offers a porous surface for basting with Asian flavors and allows the smoke to penetrate.

Prepare a charcoal or gas grill for direct-heat grilling over medium-high heat.

In a blender, combine the ginger, garlic, miso, chile sauce, vinegar, sugar, and mirin. Add 1 Tbsp water and process to form a smooth purée.

Sprinkle the eggplant halves lightly with salt and pepper. Lightly brush all over with the oil.

Arrange the eggplant halves, cut side down, on the grill rack, cover the grill, and cook until the flesh just starts to char and soften, 6–8 minutes. Turn the eggplants and grill, covered, until just tender, 3–4 minutes. Brush the cut sides of the eggplant with the miso mixture and cook, covered, until the eggplant is tender and the glaze has browned in spots, 3–4 minutes.

Transfer the eggplant halves to a platter, sprinkle with the green onions, and serve.

23

*Southern cooks
never pass up
an opportunity
to serve crusty,
tangy fried green
tomatoes. Make sure
to purchase hard,
unripened tomatoes,
not ripe green-
skinned heirloom
varieties. These
tomatoes are great
with baked ham
and make a tasty
breakfast topped
with crisp bacon,
especially if you
add the bacon fat to
the pan when you
fry the tomatoes.*

FRIED GREEN TOMATOES WITH RÉMOULADE

serves 6–8

FOR THE RÉMOULADE

1 cup (8 fl oz/250 ml) mayonnaise

1 Tbsp minced cornichons

1 Tbsp capers, rinsed

1 Tbsp minced fresh flat-leaf parsley

2 tsp minced fresh tarragon

1 tsp spicy brown mustard

½ tsp anchovy paste

1 small clove garlic, minced

¾ cup (4 oz/125 g) all-purpose flour

Salt and freshly ground black pepper

⅛ tsp cayenne pepper

1 cup (8 fl oz/250 ml) milk

2 eggs

1 cup (5 oz/155 g) yellow cornmeal, preferably stone-ground

3 unripened green tomatoes, about 7 oz (220 g) each, cut crosswise into slices about ¼ inch (6 mm) thick

1 cup (8 fl oz/250 ml) canola oil

To make the rémoulade, in a bowl, stir together the mayonnaise, cornichons, capers, parsley, tarragon, mustard, anchovy paste, and garlic until well blended. Cover and refrigerate for 1 hour before serving.

In a shallow dish, stir together the flour, 2 tsp salt, ½ tsp black pepper, and the cayenne. In a second shallow dish, whisk together the milk and eggs. Spread the cornmeal in a third shallow dish. Have ready a baking sheet.

One at a time, dip the tomato slices into the flour mixture to coat evenly, shaking off the excess. Dip into the egg mixture, letting the excess drip back into the bowl, and then place in the cornmeal, patting gently to help it adhere. Transfer to the baking sheet.

Preheat the oven to 200°F (95°C). Set a large wire rack on another baking sheet and place near the stove. In a large frying pan, heat the oil over medium-high heat until it shimmers. Working in batches, add the coated tomato slices to the hot oil and fry until golden ⇥

brown, about 2 minutes. Turn the slices and fry until browned on the second sides, about 2 minutes. Using a slotted spatula, transfer the slices to the rack and keep warm in the oven while you fry the remaining tomatoes. Serve hot, passing the rémoulade at the table.

24

*Fresh plums are
available from late
spring through
summer. These
juicy fruits come
in an assortment
of colors, from
yellow and green
to deep pink, purple,
and scarlet. For
baking pies, choose
a firm, fragrant
fruit with sweet,
tangy flesh. Check
out the varieties at
your local farmers'
market, such as
Simka, Santa Rosa,
Seneca, or Satsuma.*

DEEP-DISH PLUM PIE

serves 6–8

Flaky Pie Dough for single crust (see page 132)

1¼ cups (10 oz/315 g) sugar

2 Tbsp tapioca starch or arrowroot

¼ tsp ground cinnamon

Pinch of kosher salt

2½ lb (1.25 kg) plums, pitted and sliced ¼ inch (6 mm) thick

Vanilla ice cream for serving (optional)

Prepare the dough and chill as directed. On a lightly floured work surface, roll out the dough into a round about 12 inches (30 cm) in diameter and about ⅛ inch (3 mm) thick. Set in a cool place until ready to use.

In a small bowl, stir together the sugar, tapioca starch, cinnamon, and salt. Place the plums in a 10-inch (25-cm) ceramic or glass deep-dish pie dish, sprinkle with the sugar mixture, and toss to distribute evenly. Let stand for 5 minutes. Toss again.

Position the dough round over the plums. Trim the edge, leaving a 1-inch (2.5-cm) overhang. Fold the overhang under and press against the sides of the dish to seal. Using a small knife, cut 5 or 6 slits in the top. Refrigerate until the dough is firm, about 30 minutes.

Position a rack in the lower third of the oven and preheat to 375°F (190°C). Bake until the crust is golden and the filling is thick and bubbling, 50–60 minutes. Let cool completely on a wire rack. If you like, accompany each serving with ice cream.

25

STEAK PIPÉRADE

serves 4

1½ lb (750 g) skirt or flank steak

Salt and freshly ground pepper

2 Tbsp unsalted butter

2 Tbsp olive oil

1 red onion, chopped

3 red or yellow bell peppers, seeded and thinly sliced crosswise

3 cloves garlic, minced

1 Tbsp chopped fresh thyme

½ cup (4 fl oz/125 ml) dry white wine

1 can (14½ oz/455 g) diced tomatoes

Pipérade, a traditional Basque mixture of sweet peppers, tomatoes, and onions, is an excellent topping for quick-cooking steaks. Searing the steaks in a pan leaves some meaty flavor for the peppers, but you could also fire up the grill to make this easy dish.

Season the steak generously with salt and pepper. In a large frying pan, melt 1 Tbsp of the butter with 1 Tbsp of the oil over high heat. Add the steak and cook, turning once, for 4–6 minutes for medium-rare, or until done to your liking. Transfer the meat to a carving board and tent with foil.

Melt the remaining 1 Tbsp butter with the remaining 1 Tbsp oil in the same pan over medium heat. Add the onion, bell peppers, garlic, and thyme and sauté until the onion is barely softened, 3–4 minutes. Add the wine, bring to a boil, stir to scrape up any browned bits on the pan bottom, and cook for about 30 seconds. Stir in the tomatoes and their juice and simmer until the liquid is slightly reduced, about 5 minutes. Season with salt and pepper.

Cut the meat thinly across the grain on the diagonal. Arrange the slices on a warm platter, spoon the pepper sauce over the slices, and serve.

26

SPICY PORK KEBABS

serves 4–6

1 can (14 fl oz/430 ml) coconut milk

1 bunch fresh cilantro

2 cloves garlic, crushed

1 chipotle chile in adobo sauce

1 Tbsp ground coriander

Salt and freshly ground pepper

1 lime wedge

2 pork tenderloins, each 1½ lb (1.5 kg), cut into 1-inch (2.5-cm) cubes

2 sweet potatoes, peeled and cut into 1-inch (2.5-cm) cubes

Oil, for grilling

Creamy coconut milk and a handful of pungent spices are blended to make a delicious marinade for pork tenderloin. The spice-infused meat is then threaded onto skewers with sweet potato cubes. Serve this dish with your favorite yogurt-based dipping sauce and a green salad.

In a blender or food processor, combine the coconut milk, cilantro, garlic, chile, and coriander. Pulse to combine, and then process until the mixture is smooth. Add 1 tsp pepper and a squeeze of lime juice and process to mix. Taste and add salt and more lime juice, if needed.

Place the pork cubes in a large locking plastic bag and pour in the marinade. Seal the bag, massage the marinade around the meat, and refrigerate for at least 4 hours or up to overnight. At least 30 minutes before you plan to begin grilling, remove the pork from the refrigerator. Discard the marinade. If using wooden skewers, soak them in water for at least 30 minutes.

In a large pot, combine the sweet potato cubes with water to cover. Bring to a boil over high heat and cook for 5 minutes. Drain and let cool.

Prepare a grill for direct-heat cooking over high heat. Brush and oil the grill grate. Thread the pork and sweet potato cubes onto the skewers, leaving some space between the cubes. Grill the skewers until nicely grill-marked, about 5 minutes. Turn the skewers and cook for about 5 minutes longer. The pork should feel just firm to the touch (for medium), and the sweet potato cubes should be tender.

Transfer the skewers to a platter and let rest for 5 minutes. Slide the pork and sweet potato cubes off the skewers onto a platter and serve.

27

CHICKPEA & ROASTED RED PEPPER BURGERS WITH SMOKED PAPRIKA MAYONNAISE

serves 5

Even partisans of traditional burgers will be won over by these flavorful vegetarian patties, and slathering them with a smoky mayonnaise makes them even more appealing. Set out paper-thin red onion slices for those who might want them, and garnish each plate with pickle slices or wedges.

FOR THE SMOKED PAPRIKA MAYONNAISE

5 Tbsp (3 fl oz/80 ml) mayonnaise

1 tsp Spanish smoked paprika

2 tsp fresh lemon juice

Salt

1 small red potato

Salt and freshly ground pepper

1 Tbsp olive oil, plus more for frying

1 clove garlic, minced

1 tsp seeded and minced jalapeño chile

1 tsp ground cumin

¼ tsp chili powder

1 can (15 oz/470 g) chickpeas, drained and rinsed

¼ cup (2 oz/60 g) chopped roasted red bell pepper

2 eggs, lightly beaten

5 Tbsp (1 oz/60 g) panko

2 Tbsp minced fresh flat-leaf parsley

5 brioche buns, split

Lettuce leaves for serving (optional)

To make the paprika mayonnaise, in a small bowl, stir together the mayonnaise, smoked paprika, and lemon juice. Season with salt.

Put the potato in a small saucepan. Add water to cover by 1 inch (2.5 cm) and a generous pinch of salt. Bring to a boil over medium-high heat, reduce the heat to medium, and cook until the potato is fork-tender, about 15 minutes. Drain the potato and let cool, then cut into small dice.

In a small frying pan, warm the 1 Tbsp oil over medium heat. Add the garlic, jalapeño, cumin, and chili powder and cook, stirring, just until the garlic begins to soften and the spices are fragrant, about 1 minute.

In a food processor, pulse the chickpeas until finely chopped; do not purée. Transfer them to a large bowl and add the roasted pepper, eggs, panko, parsley, potato, and garlic mixture. Season with ½ tsp salt and ¼ tsp pepper. ⟫

Using your hands, mix until well combined and then form into 5 patties.

Pour enough oil into a large frying pan to coat the bottom, and heat over medium-high heat. Add the patties and cook, turning once, until golden brown and heated through, about 3 minutes per side. Place a lettuce leaf (if using) on the bottom half of each bun, top with a burger and a generous dollop of the mayonnaise, and serve.

28

ROASTED POTATO SALAD WITH GREEN ONION DRESSING

serves 10–12

Roasting adds unexpected texture to this salad, producing potatoes with crispy skin and a creamy interior. The rich, pale green dressing contrasts perfectly with the golden brown potatoes.

3 lb (1.5 kg) baby Yukon Gold potatoes, each about 1 inch (2.5 cm) in diameter

3 Tbsp olive oil

Salt

FOR THE GREEN ONION DRESSING

½ cup (½ oz/15 g) fresh cilantro leaves, plus sprigs for garnish

3 green onions, white and tender green parts, chopped

1 clove garlic, chopped

½ cup (4 oz/125 g) sour cream

¼ cup (2 fl oz/60 ml) mayonnaise

4 tsp red wine vinegar

4 tsp Dijon mustard

Salt and freshly ground pepper

Preheat the oven to 400°F (200°C). Put the potatoes on a rimmed baking sheet, drizzle with the oil, sprinkle with 1 Tbsp salt, and toss them to coat evenly. Roast, tossing every 15 minutes, until the skins are crisp and golden brown, about 45 minutes. Let cool.

To make the dressing, in a food processor or blender, combine the cilantro leaves, green onions, garlic, sour cream, mayonnaise, vinegar, and mustard, and process until smooth. Season with salt and pepper.

Transfer the cooled potatoes to a bowl, add the dressing, and toss to coat. Garnish with the cilantro sprigs and serve, or cover and refrigerate for up to 4 hours before serving.

29

For those who can't get enough of the tender sweetness of summer squash (or those faced with an overabundance in their garden), this simple preparation borrows from a classic, eggplant parmigiana, trading out the eggplant for yellow squash. On warm days, serve it at room temperature with crusty bread for mopping up the tomato sauce.

GRILLED SUMMER SQUASH PARMESAN

serves 4

4 Tbsp (2 fl oz/60 ml) extra-virgin olive oil

2 cloves garlic, crushed

1 can (28 oz/875 g) diced or crushed tomatoes

Salt and freshly ground pepper

10 fresh basil leaves, torn into small pieces

2 lb (1 kg) yellow summer squashes, cut lengthwise into slices ⅓ inch (9 mm) thick

¾ lb (340 g) fresh mozzarella cheese, thinly sliced

¼ cup (1 oz/30 g) grated Parmesan cheese

In a saucepan, warm 1 Tbsp of the oil over medium-low heat. Add the garlic and sauté until fragrant, about 2 minutes. Add the tomatoes and ½ tsp salt, raise the heat to medium-high, and simmer, stirring occasionally, until the sauce thickens, 25–30 minutes. Remove from the heat, discard the garlic, and stir in about half of the basil.

Prepare a charcoal or gas grill for direct-heat grilling over medium-high heat. Oil the grill rack. Preheat the oven to 375°F (190°C).

Place the squash slices on a baking sheet, drizzle with the remaining 3 Tbsp oil, season with salt and pepper, and toss to coat. Arrange the squash slices on the grill rack and cook, turning once, until lightly charred on both sides, 3–4 minutes per side. Transfer to a plate.

Lightly oil a large, shallow baking dish and spread about ¼ cup (2 fl oz/60 ml) of the tomato sauce on the bottom. Arrange one-fourth of the squash in the dish. Top with one-third of the mozzarella slices and a few pieces of basil. Cover with another ¼ cup sauce. Make 2 more layers of squash, mozzarella, basil, and sauce. Top with a final layer of squash and sauce and sprinkle with the Parmesan. Bake until the juices are bubbling and the top is lightly browned, about 35 minutes. Serve warm or at room temperature.

30

This is a great summer dessert, and it couldn't be simpler to make. A spoonful of the caramelized roasted fruit is like eating cobbler without the crust. Ricotta drizzled with honey adds a lush creaminess to the dish.

ROASTED SUMMER FRUITS WITH RICOTTA-VANILLA CREAM

serves 4

1 cup (8 oz/250 g) fresh whole-milk ricotta cheese

¼ cup (2 oz/60 g) crème fraîche

½ tsp pure vanilla extract

6 Tbsp (3 oz/90 g) sugar

2 peaches, halved and pitted

2 nectarines, halved and pitted

3 plums, halved and pitted

8 fresh figs

½ lb (250 g) cherries, pitted

1 Tbsp extra-virgin olive oil

Honey for serving

Preheat the oven to 475°F (245°C). In a bowl, combine the ricotta, crème fraîche, vanilla, and 2 Tbsp of the sugar and mix well. Cover and refrigerate until ready to use.

Cut the peach, nectarine, and plum halves in half again. Leave the figs and cherries whole. Combine all the fruits in a roasting pan large enough to hold them in a single layer. Drizzle with the olive oil and turn the fruits several times. Sprinkle with the remaining 4 Tbsp (2 oz/60 g) sugar and turn once or twice. Spread in an even layer. Roast until the fruits are slightly collapsed and golden or lightly charred, 15–20 minutes.

Divide the ricotta mixture among individual bowls and swirl a little honey into each. Spoon the fruits and their cooking juices into the bowls, over the ricotta mixture. Serve.

The searing heat of July invites firing up the outdoor grill for baby back ribs, for a salad of steak, onions, and peppers, or for that summertime classic, corn on the cob. Corn also appears in a new take on old-fashioned succotash, in avocado-corn salsa for scallops, and in a harmonious pairing with grilled chicken breasts. The season's sun-loving zucchini and yellow squashes are plentiful and versatile, especially when tossed with penne, cut into ribbons to mimic pasta, paired with shrimp on the grill, while a fruit dessert—peach cobbler, nectarine cheesecake, blueberry shortcake—is the favorite finish to nearly any meal.

1
PIZZA WITH PESTO, CHERRY TOMATOES & MOZZARELLA
page 156

2
CORNMEAL SHORTCAKES WITH BLUEBERRIES & CREAM
page 156

3
PENNE WITH GRILLED SUMMER VEGETABLES, HERBS & ALMONDS
page 158

8
BLACK BEAN, CORN & QUINOA SALAD
page 161

9
SMOKY SEA SCALLOPS WITH AVOCADO-CORN SALSA
page 162

10
QUINOA SALAD WITH GRILLED VEGETABLES & FETA
page 162

15
BABY BACK RIBS
page 167

16
PINEAPPLE SKEWERS WITH RUM & MOLASSES
page 167

17
FRIED RICOTTA-STUFFED ZUCCHINI BLOSSOMS
page 168

22
SPICY CHICKEN & BASIL STIR-FRY
page 173

23
SUMMER SQUASH NOODLES WITH MINT PESTO
page 173

24
MEDITERRANEAN-STYLE CHICKEN & VEGETABLE KEBABS
page 174

29
CHARRED EGGPLANT SOUP WITH CUMIN & GREEK YOGURT
page 177

30
HONEY-NECTARINE CHEESECAKE
page 179

31
SUMMER PANZANELLA SOUP WITH TINY PASTA
page 179

4
WHITE PEACH COBBLER WITH CRYSTALLIZED GINGER
page 158

5
TUNA KEBABS WITH SUMMER SUCCOTASH
page 159

6
MEXICAN LIME SOUP WITH CHICKEN
page 159

7
SUMMER CHICKEN BRAISE WITH WAX BEANS & TOMATOES
page 161

11
BEEF & BASIL STIR-FRY WITH SUMMER VEGETABLES
page 165

12
SPICY HALIBUT WITH RATATOUILLE
page 165

13
ONE-POT CLAMBAKE
page 166

14
MEXICAN-STYLE CORN ON THE COB
page 166

18
CHOCOLATE ICEBOX CAKE
page 168

19
GRILLED STEAK, PEPPER & ONION SALAD WITH ROMESCO DRESSING
page 170

20
EGGPLANT PARMESAN
page 171

21
SMOKY GRILLED CHICKEN & CORN
page 171

25
GRILLED LAMB CHOPS WITH FRESH PEACH SALSA
page 174

26
GRILLED LEMON SHRIMP & SUMMER SQUASH
page 176

27
CRISPY EGGPLANT, MISO BUTTER & CHARRED SUNGOLD TOMATO SALAD
page 176

28
BARBECUE-STYLE BRISKET
page 177

1

PIZZA WITH PESTO, CHERRY TOMATOES & MOZZARELLA

serves 2–4

1 lb (500 g) purchased whole-wheat pizza dough, at room temperature

Olive oil, for shaping and brushing

½ cup (4 fl oz/125 ml) prepared basil pesto

6 oz (185 g) cherry tomatoes, halved if large

¼ lb (125 g) fresh mozzarella cheese, sliced then torn into bite-sized pieces

Salt and freshly ground pepper

For this vegetarian pizza, store-bought pesto works fine in a pinch. But for a unique flavor, try a homemade arugula-mint pesto. In a blender, combine 5 cups (5 oz/155 g) packed arugula, ¾ cup (½ oz/15 g) packed fresh mint leaves, ½ cup (4 fl oz/125 ml) extra-virgin olive oil, ½ cup (2 oz/60 g) grated Parmesan cheese, the grated zest of 1 lemon, and 2 cloves garlic, minced. Season with salt and pepper and blend until smooth. Stir in 1 Tbsp fresh lemon juice and adjust the seasoning. Refrigerate until ready to serve.

Position a rack in the bottom of the oven. Place a baking stone on the rack. Preheat the oven to 550°F (290°C), or the highest setting, for at least 45 minutes.

Place a large sheet of parchment paper on a pizza peel or large rimless baking sheet and place the ball of dough in the center. Coat your fingers with oil and press the dough from the center outward into a 12-inch (30-cm) round with a slightly raised edge. Cover the dough round with a kitchen towel and let rise for 15 minutes.

Brush the raised edge of the dough with a light coating of oil. Spread the dough evenly with the pesto, leaving a ½-inch (12-mm) border. Scatter the tomatoes over the pesto, top with the mozzarella, and season generously with salt and pepper. Carefully slide the pizza-topped parchment paper onto the hot pizza stone. Bake until the crust is golden-brown and the cheese is bubbling, 9–12 minutes.

Using a pizza peel or a rimless baking sheet, remove the pizza from the oven and transfer it to a cutting board. Let stand for1 minute, then slice and serve.

2

CORNMEAL SHORTCAKES WITH BLUEBERRIES & CREAM

serves 8

6 pt (3 lb/1.5 kg) blueberries

½ cup (4 oz/125 g) sugar

1 Tbsp fresh lemon juice

2 cups (10 oz/315 g) all-purpose flour

⅓ cup (1½ oz/45 g) yellow cornmeal

2 tsp baking powder

½ tsp kosher salt

½ cup (4 oz/125 g) plus 2 Tbsp cold unsalted butter, cut into pieces

1 cup (8 fl oz/250 ml) heavy cream, plus more if needed

Whipped cream (see page 53)

Blueberries, which are at their best in June, July, and August, have a more assertive flavor than strawberries. To match that bolder taste, pair the berries with crunchy cornmeal biscuits for these seasonal shortcakes. Be sure to let the biscuits cool completely before splitting them, then generously top each split biscuit with the warm berry compote and a big spoonful of cream.

Preheat the oven to 400°F (200°C). Line a baking sheet with parchment paper.

Pour 4 pt (2 lb/1 kg) of the blueberries into a large bowl. In a saucepan, cook the remaining 2 pt (1 lb/500 kg) blueberries, the sugar, and the lemon juice over medium heat, stirring occasionally, until most of the berries have burst and are very juicy, 8–10 minutes. Pour over the blueberries in the bowl and stir gently to combine.

In another large bowl, whisk together the flour, cornmeal, baking powder, and salt. Add the butter and, using a pastry blender, work into the dry ingredients until the texture resembles coarse meal. Drizzle in the 1 cup cream and stir until evenly moistened. The dough should be moist and cohesive. If the dough feels dry, stir in more cream, 1 Tbsp at a time, until it comes together.

On a lightly floured work surface, pat the dough into a round ½ inch (12 mm) thick. Using a 3-inch (7.5-cm) round pastry cutter, cut out as many rounds as possible. Arrange on the prepared baking sheet. Gather the dough scraps together and repeat; you should have 8 rounds. Reduce the oven temperature to 375°F (190°C) and bake the shortcakes until golden brown, 16–18 minutes. Let cool completely on the baking sheet on a wire rack.

Halve the shortcakes horizontally. Place the bottom halves, cut side up, on plates. Top each with the blueberry mixture, dividing it evenly, then with whipped cream. Cover with the top halves and serve.

3

PENNE WITH GRILLED SUMMER VEGETABLES, HERBS & ALMONDS

serves 4

This light dish is a great way to showcase the season's colorful bell peppers and abundant fresh herbs. For the most complex flavor, use a combination of herbs, though using only one or two will still produce a delicious dish. Other short pasta shapes, such as cavatelli, gemelli, or trennette, can be substituted for the penne.

2 yellow crookneck squashes, cut lengthwise in thirds

1 red bell pepper, seeded and cut into quarters

1 yellow bell pepper, seeded and cut into quarters

1 large red onion, cut crosswise into slices about ½ inch (12 mm) thick

Olive oil, for brushing

Salt and freshly ground pepper

½ lb (250 g) penne, preferably multigrain

3 Tbsp extra-virgin olive oil

½ cup (¾ oz/20 g) mixed fresh herbs, such as mint, basil, and oregano, minced

¼ cup (1½ oz/45 g) pitted Kalamata olives, finely chopped

¼ cup (1 oz/30 g) almonds, finely chopped

1 small red chile, minced

½ cup (2½ oz/75 g) feta cheese, crumbled

Prepare a grill for direct-heat cooking over high heat. Arrange the squashes, bell peppers, and red onion in a single layer on a large rimmed baking sheet. Brush with the olive oil and sprinkle with salt and pepper on both sides. Transfer the vegetables to the grill and grill, covered, until tender and lightly browned, about 5 minutes per side. Remove from the grill and cut into 1-inch (2.5-cm) pieces.

Meanwhile, bring a large pot of salted water to a boil. Add the pasta, stir well, and cook until al dente, about 11 minutes.

Drain the pasta and transfer to a warmed shallow serving bowl. Add the grilled vegetables, extra-virgin olive oil, fresh herbs, olives, almonds, and chile to the pasta and toss to combine. Season to taste with salt and pepper, sprinkle with feta cheese, and serve.

4

WHITE PEACH COBBLER WITH CRYSTALLIZED GINGER

serves 8

Spicy, chewy bits of crystallized ginger are added to the biscuit topping of this old-fashioned cobbler, which features the season's prized white peaches. Grated fresh ginger and lemon zest and juice are added to the fruit to heighten its flavor. If you like, forgo tradition and serve the cobbler with dulce de leche ice cream in place of the vanilla.

10 white peaches, peeled, pitted, and sliced

1 lemon

1½-inch (4-cm) piece fresh ginger, peeled and grated

⅓ cup (3 oz/90 g) granulated sugar

2 Tbsp cornstarch

Kosher salt

2 cups (10 oz/315 g) all-purpose flour

2 tsp baking powder

½ cup (3 oz/90 g) crystallized ginger, coarsely chopped

4 Tbsp (2 oz/60 g) cold unsalted butter, cut into pieces

1¼ cups (10 fl oz/310 ml) heavy cream, plus cream for brushing

¼ cup (2 oz/60 g) turbinado sugar

Vanilla ice cream for serving

Preheat the oven to 375°F (190°C).

Put the peach slices in a bowl. Finely grate 2 tsp zest from the lemon, then squeeze 2 Tbsp juice. Add both to the peaches. Add the grated ginger, granulated sugar, cornstarch, and a pinch of salt and toss gently.

In a food processor, combine the flour, the baking powder, and ½ tsp salt. Add the crystallized ginger and pulse briefly to combine. Add the butter and pulse until the mixture resembles coarse meal. Transfer to a large bowl, add the 1¼ cups cream, and mix until the dough comes together. Turn the dough onto a lightly floured work surface and knead 2 or 3 times to bring it together into a ball. Shape the dough into a round about ½ inch (12 mm) thick, then cut the dough into 8 even wedges.

Transfer the peach mixture to a 9-by-13-inch (23-by-33-cm) baking dish and arrange the dough wedges on top in 2 rows of 4 wedges, alternating the points. Brush the wedges with cream and sprinkle with the turbinado sugar. Bake for 25 minutes. Loosely cover the dish with foil and continue baking until the topping is deep golden brown and the juices are bubbling, 10–20 minutes. Let cool, uncovered, for at least 20 minutes. Serve the cobbler with ice cream.

5

TUNA KEBABS WITH SUMMER SUCCOTASH

serves 4

A simple marinade is all that's needed for meaty ahi tuna. Tender cubes of grilled fish look appealing on top of a bed of summery pea-and-corn succotash. Be sure not to marinate the tuna for too long, or the acidity of the lemon will begin to cook the fish.

FOR THE TUNA KEBABS

2 Tbsp olive oil

Juice of 1 lemon

2 Tbsp chopped fresh basil

Salt and freshly ground pepper

1¼ lb (625 g) sushi-grade ahi tuna steaks, cut into 1-inch (2.5-cm) cubes

FOR THE SUCCOTASH

2 Tbsp olive oil

2 cloves garlic, minced

½ lb (250 g) sugar snap peas, cut on the diagonal into ¼-inch (6-mm) pieces

Kernels from 3 ears fresh corn

Juice of ½ lemon

2 Tbsp chopped fresh basil

Salt and freshly ground pepper

Canola oil for the grill

To make the tuna kebabs, in a small bowl, combine the olive oil, lemon juice, basil, ½ tsp salt, and ¼ tsp pepper. Add the tuna and toss to coat. Cover and refrigerate while you prepare the succotash. Soak 8 wooden skewers in water for at least 30 minutes.

Prepare a grill for direct-heat cooking over medium-high heat.

To make the succotash, warm the oil in a large frying pan over medium-high heat. Add the garlic and sauté just until it softens, about 1 minute. Add the snap peas and sauté, stirring often, until they begin to soften, about 3 minutes. Add the corn and stir to combine. Stir in the lemon juice and basil and sauté, stirring often, until most of the liquid is absorbed and the corn is tender, about 2 minutes. Season well with salt and pepper and turn off the heat. Keep warm.

Thread 4 or 5 pieces of tuna onto each wooden skewer. Oil the grill rack. Arrange the tuna kebabs on the grill, cover the grill, and cook until the tuna is grill-marked, turning occasionally, about 2 minutes per side for medium-rare.

Divide the succotash among 4 plates, top each with 2 tuna kebabs, and serve.

6

MEXICAN LIME SOUP WITH CHICKEN

serves 6

This Mexican-inspired version of chicken soup gets its distinctive flavor from the addition of lots of tart-sweet lime juice. The uniquely bright, bracing sharpness of the fresh limes is countered by fragrant garlic, herbal oregano, and spicy jalapeño.

8–10 small limes

2 skin-on, bone-in chicken breast halves (about 10 oz/315 g each)

Salt and freshly ground pepper

1 Tbsp olive oil

1 large white onion, chopped

5 cloves garlic, minced

1 jalapeño chile, seeded and minced

3 cups (24 fl oz/750 ml) chicken broth

1½ tsp dried oregano

1 avocado, pitted, peeled, and diced

2 oz (60 g) queso fresco or ricotta salata cheese, crumbled

Tortilla chips for serving

Cut 2 of the limes into wedges and reserve. Juice as many of the remaining limes as needed to measure out ¼ cup (2 fl oz/60 ml) juice.

Season the chicken breasts with 1 tsp salt and ½ tsp pepper. In a large, heavy pot, warm the oil over medium heat. Add the chicken, skin side down, and cook, turning once, until browned, about 5 minutes. Transfer to a plate. Add the onion and sauté until translucent, about 4 minutes. Stir in the garlic and jalapeño and sauté until fragrant, about 1 minute. Stir in the broth, 3 cups (24 fl oz/750 ml) water, the lime juice, and the oregano. Return the chicken to the pot. Raise the heat to high and bring the liquid to a boil, skimming off any foam on the surface. Reduce the heat to medium-low, cover partially, and simmer gently until the chicken is opaque throughout, about 40 minutes.

Keeping the soup at a simmer, remove the chicken. When it is cool enough to handle, remove and discard the skin and bones and shred the meat into bite-sized pieces. Stir the chicken into the soup. Serve, passing the avocado, cheese, tortilla chips, and lime wedges at the table.

7

SUMMER CHICKEN BRAISE WITH WAX BEANS & TOMATOES

serves 4

The colors of burnished chicken, yellow beans, red tomatoes, and green arugula make for a show-stopping presentation. Use a frying pan or Dutch oven that you can take straight to the table, and serve the chicken in shallow bowls to include the mustardy pan sauce. Offer plenty of warm crusty bread and encourage guests to soak up every last drop.

2 Tbsp olive oil

2 lb (1 kg) skin-on, bone-in chicken thighs and drumsticks

Salt and freshly ground pepper

1 yellow onion, chopped

1 carrot, chopped

6 cloves garlic, minced

1¼ cups (10 fl oz/310 ml) dry white wine

3 cups (24 fl oz/750 ml) chicken broth

3 sprigs fresh thyme

¼ cup (2 fl oz/60 ml) heavy cream

3 Tbsp Dijon mustard

1 cup (6 oz/185 g) cherry tomatoes

4 oz (125 g) small yellow wax beans

2 cups (3 oz/90 g) arugula leaves

Preheat the oven to 350°F (180°C).

In a large, heavy pot or a deep skillet, warm the oil over medium-high heat. Season the chicken with salt and pepper. Working in batches, sear the chicken, turning as needed, until browned, about 8 minutes. Transfer to a plate.

Add the onion, carrot, and garlic to the pot and season with salt and pepper. Sauté over medium-high heat until the vegetables soften, about 5 minutes. Add the wine, bring to a simmer, and cook until reduced by half, about 5 minutes. Add the broth and bring to a boil. Return the chicken to the pot, add the thyme, cover, and cook in the oven until the chicken is opaque throughout, about 55 minutes.

Transfer the chicken to a plate. Strain the braising liquid and return to the pot. Bring the liquid to a boil over high heat and cook until reduced by half, about 8 minutes. Reduce the heat to medium-high, stir in the cream and mustard, and cook until the sauce thickens, about 5 minutes. Season with salt and pepper. Arrange the chicken pieces in the pot, cover, and cook over low heat for 15 minutes to develop the flavors. Add the tomatoes and wax beans and cook, covered, until softened, about 5 minutes. Uncover, add the arugula, stir into the sauce, and cook just until wilted, about 1 minute. Serve directly from the pan.

8

BLACK BEAN, CORN & QUINOA SALAD

serves 4

A South American–inspired salad, this flavorful dish calls for protein-rich quinoa, tiny seeds harvested from a plant native to the Andean region. Ají amarillo paste, made from hot yellow South American chiles, can be found in Latin American stores. Serve the salad alongside grilled chicken or skirt steak.

½ cup (3 oz/90 g) quinoa, well rinsed

Salt and freshly ground pepper

2 Tbsp fresh lime juice

3 Tbsp white vinegar

2 Tbsp minced fresh cilantro

¼ tsp ají amarillo paste

¼ tsp dried oregano

½ cup (4 fl oz/125 ml) extra-virgin olive oil

1 cup (7 oz/220 g) drained and rinsed canned black beans

⅔ cup (4 oz/125 g) fresh corn kernels, cut from 2 ears of corn

1 tomato, halved, seeded, and finely chopped

1 small red bell pepper, seeded and finely diced

In a small saucepan, combine the quinoa, ¼ tsp salt, and 1½ cups (12 fl oz/375 ml) water. Cover and bring to a boil. Reduce the heat to low and simmer until the quinoa is tender and all the water has been absorbed, about 10 minutes. Transfer the quinoa to a colander and rinse under cold running water. Drain thoroughly and transfer to a large serving bowl.

Meanwhile, in a bowl, whisk together the lime juice, vinegar, cilantro, ají paste, and oregano. Season with ½ tsp salt and ½ tsp pepper. Whisking constantly, add the oil in a thin stream.

Add the beans, corn, tomato, and bell pepper to the quinoa. Pour in the vinaigrette, toss to coat all the ingredients well, and serve.

9

SMOKY SEA SCALLOPS WITH AVOCADO-CORN SALSA

serves 4

This colorful salsa, with its corn, avocado, tomato, and chile, is a celebration of the summer garden. The scallops take on an irresistible smoky flavor, first from the chipotle chiles in the marinade and then from their time on the grill. Look for dry-packed diver scallops for the best flavor and texture.

FOR THE AVOCADO-CORN SALSA

2 ears corn, grilled, shucked, and kernels cut from the cobs

2 ripe avocados, halved, pitted, peeled, and chopped

1 yellow onion, minced

1 tomato, seeded and coarsely chopped

1 jalapeño chile, seeded and chopped

2 cloves garlic, minced

⅓ cup (½ oz/15 g) chopped fresh cilantro

3 Tbsp fresh lime juice

Salt

2 canned chipotle chiles in adobo sauce, mashed

1 cup (1½ oz/45 g) chopped fresh cilantro

⅓ cup (3 fl oz/80 ml) fresh orange or lime juice

1 tsp ground cumin

Salt

2 lb (1 kg) sea scallops, side muscles removed

Vegetable oil, for brushing

To make the salsa, put the corn kernels in a bowl. Add the avocados, onion, tomato, jalapeño, garlic, and cilantro to the corn and toss to mix. Add the lime juice, mix well, and season to taste with salt. Cover and refrigerate until ready to serve.

In a bowl, stir together the chipotle chiles, cilantro, orange juice, and cumin. Season with salt.

Brush the scallops on both sides with the oil and then rub with the chipotle mixture. Cover and refrigerate for 30 minutes.

Prepare a grill for direct-heat cooking over medium-high heat. Oil the grill rack or a fish- or vegetable-grilling basket.

Arrange the scallops on the rack or in the basket over the hottest part of the fire. Cook, turning once, until the scallops are opaque throughout but still moist in the center when tested with a knife, 3–4 minutes per side.

Divide the scallops evenly among warmed individual plates, place a spoonful of the salsa alongside, and serve.

10

QUINOA SALAD WITH GRILLED VEGETABLES & FETA

serves 6–8

A perfect showcase for summer squashes, this healthy salad yields a good-size amount, making it ideal for entertaining. Prep is simple, too, with the vegetables cooked on a stove-top grill pan, eliminating the need to fire up the grill. To bring out the nutty flavor of the quinoa, it is lightly toasted in oil before it is simmered in liquid until tender.

¾ cup (6 fl oz/180 ml) olive oil

2 cups (12 oz/375 g) quinoa, well rinsed

3½ cups (28 fl oz/875 ml) water or vegetable stock

Salt and freshly ground pepper

1 red onion, cut into ¼-inch (6-mm) slices

2 zucchini, cut lengthwise into ¼-inch (6-mm) slices

2 summer squash, cut lengthwise into ¼-inch (6-mm) slices

2 cups (12 oz/375 g) grape tomatoes, halved

¼ cup (2 fl oz/60 ml) fresh lemon juice

⅓ cup (⅓ oz/10 g) fresh basil leaves, larger leaves torn

⅓ cup (⅓ oz/10 g) fresh mint leaves, larger leaves torn

¼ lb (125 g) feta cheese, crumbled

In a saucepan, warm 1 Tbsp of the oil over medium-high heat. Add the quinoa and cook, stirring, until lightly toasted, 2–3 minutes. Add the water, season with salt, and bring to a boil. Reduce the heat to medium-low, cover, and simmer until the grains are tender and the water is absorbed, about 15 minutes. Let the quinoa cool.

Prepare a charcoal or gas grill for direct-heat cooking over medium-high heat. Alternatively, preheat a stove-top grill pan over medium-high heat.

In a large bowl, combine the onion, zucchini, squash, and 3 Tbsp of the oil and toss gently to coat. Season with salt and pepper. Place the vegetables on the grill rack or in the grill pan and cook, turning once, until nicely grill-marked and tender, 3–4 minutes per side. Transfer to a cutting board and let cool slightly, then cut into rough ¼-inch (6-mm) dice. Add the vegetables and the tomatoes to the pot with the quinoa and stir gently to combine.

In a small bowl, whisk together the remaining ½ cup (4 fl oz/125 ml) oil and the lemon juice until blended. Season with salt and pepper. Drizzle the vinaigrette over the quinoa. Add the basil, mint, and half of the cheese and stir to combine. Top with the remaining cheese and serve.

11

BEEF & BASIL STIR-FRY WITH SUMMER VEGETABLES

serves 4

Thai basil, with its beautiful purple stems, adds an anise-like, mildly spicy flavor to this dish. If you cannot find Thai basil, sweet (common) basil can be substituted. This stir-fry is wonderful on its own or served over steamed rice or fresh Asian noodles.

¼ cup (2 fl oz/60 ml) soy sauce

3 Tbsp sherry

1 Tbsp honey

1 tsp cornstarch

2 Tbsp canola oil

1 lb (500 g) flank steak, thinly sliced, then cut into 1-inch (2.5-cm) pieces

Salt and freshly ground pepper

2 cloves garlic, minced

1-inch (2.5-cm) piece peeled fresh ginger, grated

1 yellow squash, cut into ½-inch (12-mm) matchsticks

2 carrots, cut into ½-inch (12-mm) matchsticks

4 oz (125 g) sugar snap peas, trimmed and halved

¼ cup (¼ oz/7 g) small fresh basil leaves, preferably Thai

In a small bowl, stir together the soy sauce, sherry, honey, and cornstarch.

In a wok or large frying pan, heat 1 Tbsp of the oil over high heat. Season the steak pieces with salt and pepper. Add to the pan and, tossing to sear on all sides, cook until browned but still rare inside, about 3 minutes. Transfer to a plate. Pour off any fat from the pan.

Return the pan to high heat and warm the remaining 1 Tbsp oil. Add the garlic and ginger and stir-fry until fragrant, about 1 minute, taking care not to let the garlic and ginger brown. Add the squash, carrots, and sugar snap peas and stir-fry for 4 minutes. Add the steak and the soy sauce mixture and stir to combine. Cook, stirring often, until the sauce thickens, about 3 minutes. Top with the basil leaves and serve.

12

SPICY HALIBUT WITH RATATOUILLE

serves 4

Traditional ratatouille is the rustic vegetable stew of France, featuring a bounty of summer vegetables: peppers, eggplants, zucchini, and tomatoes. Adding halibut fillets turns it into a robust meal. The fish stays moist thanks to a gentle simmer.

½ cup (4 fl oz/120 ml) olive oil

4 yellow onions, chopped

4 cloves garlic, minced

10 plum tomatoes, halved, seeded, and cut into chunks

6 zucchini, cut into chunks

2 eggplants, cut into chunks

3 large red bell peppers, seeded and cut into chunks

½ cup (4 fl oz/120 ml) vegetable broth

1 tsp minced fresh thyme

1 tsp minced fresh oregano

Salt and freshly ground pepper

4 halibut fillets, each about 6 oz (185 g)

¾ tsp hot paprika

In a large frying pan, warm ¼ cup (2 fl oz/ 60 ml) of the oil over medium heat. Add the onions and garlic and sauté until tender but not brown, about 10 minutes. Transfer to a slow cooker. Add the tomatoes, zucchini, eggplants, bell peppers, broth, thyme, and oregano. Season with 2 tsp each salt and pepper. Stir to combine. Cover and cook on the high setting for 4 hours or the low setting for 8 hours. Set aside 2 cups (12 oz/375 g) of ratatouille, and store the rest for another use.

Season the halibut fillets on both sides with the paprika and salt and pepper to taste. In a large frying pan, heat the remaining ¼ cup oil over medium-high heat. Add the fillets and cook, turning once, until golden brown, about 4 minutes per side.

Spoon the 2 cups ratatouille around the halibut fillets in the pan. Cover, reduce the heat to medium, and cook, stirring the ratatouille once or twice, until the ratatouille is heated through and the fillets are opaque throughout, about 4 minutes. Serve directly from the pan.

13

ONE-POT CLAMBAKE

serves 4

2 Tbsp olive oil

1 yellow onion, chopped

3 cloves garlic, minced

1 small fennel bulb, chopped, any fronds reserved for garnish

3 sprigs fresh thyme

Salt and freshly ground pepper

1½ cups (12 fl oz/375 ml) dry white wine

3 cups (24 fl oz/750 ml) chicken broth

1 lb (500 g) red-skinned potatoes, quartered

1 lb (500 g) kielbasa or other smoked sausage, thickly sliced

1 or 2 lobsters (1½ lb/750 g total weight)

2 ears of corn, each cut into 3 pieces

24 mussels, scrubbed and debearded

24 clams, scrubbed

12 large shrimp in the shell

1 lemon, cut into wedges

Leave the sand at the beach and serve this food-packed pot for a fun, casual gathering. Diners can pick out hunks of corn, potatoes, sausages, a clam here, and a lobster claw there. Provide them with plenty of napkins, a bowl for the discards, and a loaf of crusty bread.

In a large (16- to 20-qt/15- to 18-l) heavy-bottomed stockpot, heat the oil over medium-high heat. Add the onion, garlic, chopped fennel bulb, and thyme sprigs and season with salt and pepper. Sauté until the fennel is soft, about 8 minutes. Add the wine and cook until reduced by half, about 5 minutes. Add the broth and then layer the other ingredients on top in this order: the potatoes, the kielbasa, and the lobster(s). Cover the pot tightly and cook for 10 minutes. Remove the lid and nestle in the corn, mussels and clams (discarding any that do not close to the touch), and shrimp and cover tightly. Cook for another 10 minutes. Discard any unopened mussels or clams.

Using a slotted spoon, transfer the potatoes, corn, kielbasa, and seafood to a large platter. Season the broth in the stockpot to taste with salt and pepper and spoon it over the top of the seafood. Garnish with fennel fronds and lemon wedges, and serve.

14

MEXICAN-STYLE CORN ON THE COB

serves 6

½ cup (4 oz/125 g) unsalted butter, at room temperature, plus melted butter for brushing

2 Tbsp minced fresh cilantro

Finely grated zest from 1 lime

1 Tbsp fresh lime juice

6 ears corn, husks and silk removed

Ice water

Ancho chile powder or other pure chile powder for serving

Salt

Biting into hot corn on the cob slathered with butter is one of summer's greatest pleasures. Here, that classic is given a Latin accent with the addition of lime and cilantro to the butter and a sprinkle of ground chile at the table. Be careful not to overcook the corn; it tastes best when the kernels still carry some snap.

Using a rubber spatula, in a small bowl, mash together the ½ cup (4 oz/125 g) butter, the cilantro, and lime zest and juice, mixing well. Cover and set aside while you prepare the corn.

Prepare a charcoal or gas grill for direct-heat grilling over medium heat. Oil the grill rack.

Fill a large pot with cold water, add the corn, and let stand for 10 minutes.

Drain the corn and pat dry. Grill, turning often and basting with melted butter, until lightly charred on all sides and just tender, 15 to 20 minutes.

Serve the corn piping hot, with the cilantro-lime butter, chile powder, and salt on the side.

15

BABY BACK RIBS

serves 6–8

½ cup (¾ oz/60 g) paprika

¼ cup (¾ oz/20 g) granulated garlic

2 Tbsp firmly packed light brown sugar

1 Tbsp chili powder

1 Tbsp coarse salt

1 tsp freshly ground pepper

1 tsp each dry mustard and ground cumin

4 slabs baby back pork ribs
(about 5 lb/2.5 kg), trimmed

4–5 lb (2–2.5 kg) mesquite wood chunks
or chips, soaked for 30 minutes

2 cups (16 fl oz) barbecue sauce,
bottled or homemade

To save time, you can start the ribs in the oven and finish them on the grill. Preheat the oven to 350°F (180°C) and arrange the ribs in a shallow roasting pan. Roast the ribs, turning them occasionally, until they are cooked through, 2–2½ hours, then transfer them to the grill and cook, continuing to turn them occasionally, until they are charred in places and have taken on a smoky flavor.

To make a dry rub, in a small bowl, stir together the paprika, granulated garlic, brown sugar, chili powder, salt, pepper, mustard, and cumin.

Rinse the ribs under cold running water and pat dry with paper towels. Generously season all over with the rub, massaging it in. Cover and refrigerate overnight.

Prepare a charcoal or gas grill for indirect-heat grilling over medium-low heat. Brush and oil the grill rack.

If using a charcoal grill, rake the coals to the sides of the grill and place a drip pan in the fire bed. Sprinkle half the wood chips over the coals. Grill the ribs, covered, until fork-tender and well browned, 3–3½ hours, replenishing the coals and wood chips every hour to maintain temperature and smoke. If using a gas grill, raise the burner to high heat. Heat a smoker box half full of wood chips until smoking; reduce the heat to medium-low. Grill the ribs, covered, until fork-tender and browned, 3–3½ hours, replenishing the wood chips every hour.

Transfer the ribs to a cutting board and cut each slab into 3- or 4-rib portions. Brush generously with barbecue sauce on both sides; reserve about 1½ cups (12 fl oz) sauce for serving. Grill over direct heat until cooked through. Transfer the ribs to a cutting board. Cut the ribs between the bones and pile high on a platter. Serve hot, with the reserved barbecue sauce on the side.

16

PINEAPPLE SKEWERS WITH RUM & MOLASSES

serves 6–8

2 Tbsp dark molasses

2 Tbsp honey

2 Tbsp dark rum

1 pineapple

Grapeseed oil for brushing

3 Tbsp sugar

Firm pineapple flesh is fit for the grill. You can thread triangles onto skewers, as suggested here, or slice the fruit into thick rings and set them directly on the grate. Either way, the smokiness of the grill adds to the depth of flavor in the dark molasses.

Soak 12 bamboo skewers in water for about 30 minutes. In a small saucepan, whisk together the molasses, honey, and rum. Bring to a boil over medium heat and simmer until reduced slightly, 3–4 minutes.

Using a serrated knife, cut the pineapple in half lengthwise. Cut each half lengthwise into 6 wedges. Cut away and discard the core from each wedge. Place the wedges, skin side down, on a cutting board. Working with one wedge at a time, carefully run the knife between the skin and the flesh to separate the flesh. Cut the flesh crosswise into 6 equal chunks. Thread each row onto a skewer.

Prepare a charcoal or gas grill for direct grilling over high heat. Oil the grill rack.

Brush the fruit on all sides with oil and sprinkle with the sugar. Grill the skewers directly over high heat, turning once, until grill marks appear, about 4 minutes per side. Transfer the skewers to a serving platter. Drizzle with the rum-and-molasses syrup and serve.

17
JULY

In Italy, zucchini blossoms are often stuffed with mozzarella and anchovies, lightly coated with flour and egg, and fried until crisp. Here, herbed ricotta is tucked into the blossoms with delicious results. If the ricotta is very moist, spoon it into a cheesecloth-lined fine-mesh sieve set over a bowl and place in the refrigerator to drain overnight. Fresh squash blossoms are highly perishable, so use them as soon as possible.

FRIED RICOTTA-STUFFED ZUCCHINI BLOSSOMS
serves 4–6

1 cup (8 oz/250 g) ricotta cheese

1½ tsp chopped fresh flat-leaf parsley, plus more for garnish

1 Tbsp chopped fresh basil

Salt and freshly ground pepper

2 eggs

1 cup (5 oz/155 g) all-purpose flour

12 large zucchini blossoms

Olive or canola oil for frying

In a bowl, stir together the ricotta, 1½ tsp parsley, and the basil. Season with salt and pepper. Scrape the mixture into a pastry bag fitted with a large plain tip. In a small, shallow bowl, whisk the eggs until lightly beaten. Spread the flour on a plate.

Gently wipe the zucchini blossoms with damp paper towels, and carefully remove the stamens. Gently spread each flower open, insert the tip of the pastry bag, and pipe about 1 Tbsp of the ricotta mixture into the blossom. Do not overfill the blossoms, or the filling may seep out as they cook. Roll each blossom first in the flour, then in the eggs, and then again in the flour, gently shaking off the excess each time.

Preheat the oven to 200°F (95°C). Line a platter with paper towels. Pour oil to a depth of 1 inch (2.5 cm) into a heavy frying pan and heat to 375°F (190°C) on a deep-frying thermometer.

Add the blossoms, a few at a time, being careful not to crowd the pan. Fry the blossoms, turning once, until lightly golden, 3–4 minutes. Using a slotted spoon, transfer the blossoms to the paper towel–lined platter to drain and place in the oven to keep warm. Allow the oil to return to 375°F (190°C) between batches. Garnish with parsley and serve warm.

18
JULY

Icebox cake is molded and chilled, making it the perfect ending to a hot summer day. Use slices of homemade or high-quality purchased pound cake to line the loaf pan. The chocolate-cream filling will seep into the cake, softening it and infusing it with flavor.

CHOCOLATE ICEBOX CAKE
serves 8–10

1 pound cake, purchased, ends trimmed, cut into 10 slices, each about ¾ inch (2 cm) thick

2¼ cups (18 fl oz/560 ml) cold heavy cream

3 oz (90 g) unsweetened chocolate, finely chopped

2 oz (60 g) semisweet chocolate, finely chopped

½ cup (4 oz/125 g) unsalted butter, at cool room temperature

1¼ cups (5 oz/155 g) confectioners' sugar

½ tsp instant coffee powder, dissolved in 1 tsp water (optional)

1 tsp pure vanilla extract

Whipped cream (see page 53), for frosting

Lightly butter a 9-by-5-inch (23-by-13-cm) loaf pan. Line the bottom and sides with parchment paper, extending the paper up and over the edges on 2 sides. Line the bottom and sides of the pan with the cake slices, cutting to fit as necessary.

In the top pan of a double boiler, heat ½ cup (4 fl oz/125 ml) of the cream and the chocolates over (not touching) barely simmering water, stirring often until smooth. Remove from over the heat and stir in ¼ cup (2 fl oz/60 ml) of the cream. Refrigerate until cool, about 10 minutes.

In a large bowl, using an electric mixer, beat the butter, confectioners' sugar, dissolved coffee (if using), and vanilla on medium speed until smooth, about 1 minute. Mix in the chocolate mixture. In another large bowl, using the electric mixer, beat the remaining 1½ cups (12 fl oz/375 ml) cream on medium-high speed until firm peaks form. Using a rubber spatula, fold half of the cream into the chocolate mixture to lighten it and then fold in the remaining cream.

Spread the filling in the cake-lined pan, smoothing the top. Cover and refrigerate for at least 3 hours or up to overnight. Invert a plate on top of the pan and invert the plate and pan together. Holding the ends of the parchment firmly, lift off the pan. Frost the top and sides of the cake with the whipped cream and serve.

19

Spanish smoked paprika is rich with earthy nuances of chiles and cocoa. In this recipe, it lends a robust smokiness and gorgeous red color to a steak marinade and a romesco-style dressing. Uncork a full-bodied Spanish red to accompany the salad and serve a classic flan for dessert.

GRILLED STEAK, PEPPER & ONION SALAD WITH ROMESCO DRESSING

serves 6

½ cup (4 fl oz/125 ml) extra-virgin olive oil, plus 2 Tbsp

⅓ cup (3 fl oz/80 ml) sherry vinegar

2 Tbsp fresh orange juice

1 Tbsp Spanish sweet smoked paprika

5 cloves garlic, minced

1½ Tbsp fresh oregano leaves

2¾ lb (1.4 kg) flank steak

2 small red onions

3 bell peppers, in assorted colors

Salt and freshly ground pepper

FOR THE ROMESCO DRESSING

2 Tbsp extra-virgin olive oil

1 Tbsp fresh orange juice

2 Tbsp sherry vinegar

¼ tsp Spanish sweet smoked paprika

2 cloves garlic, minced

3 jarred piquillo peppers or roasted red peppers

1½ Tbsp chopped blanched almonds

Salt and freshly ground pepper

½ large head green-leaf lettuce, leaves torn into bite-sized pieces

2 Tbsp chopped fresh flat-leaf parsley

In a large baking dish, combine the ½ cup (4 fl oz/125 ml) oil, the vinegar, orange juice, paprika, garlic, and oregano. Lay the steak in the baking dish and turn a few times to coat it with the marinade. Cover and refrigerate for at least 2 hours or preferably overnight, turning once or twice.

About 1 hour before cooking, remove the flank steak from the refrigerator. Cut the onions crosswise into rounds ½ inch (12 mm) thick (do not separate the layers). Stem, seed, and derib the bell peppers, then cut into wide strips. Brush the vegetables with the 2 Tbsp oil and season lightly with salt and pepper. ⤳

Prepare a charcoal or gas grill for direct-heat cooking over medium-high heat.

Meanwhile, to make the dressing, in a food processor or blender, combine the oil, orange juice, vinegar, paprika, garlic, piquillo peppers, almonds, a scant ½ tsp salt, and a few grindings of pepper. Process until relatively smooth. Taste and adjust the seasonings. Set aside.

Grill the onions and peppers, turning once, until softened and lightly charred on both sides, 7–10 minutes for the onions and about 15 minutes for the peppers. Transfer to a plate. Remove the steak from the marinade and season both sides with salt and pepper. Grill, turning once, until the steak is browned on both sides and an instant-read thermometer inserted into the thickest part registers 130°F (54°C) for medium-rare, 10–15 minutes total, or until cooked to your liking. Transfer to a board and tent with foil. Cut the peppers into ½-inch (12-mm) strips and separate the onion slices into rings.

In a bowl, toss the lettuce with ⅛ tsp salt. Divide the lettuce among individual plates. Thinly slice the steak on the diagonal. Top each mound of lettuce with a portion of the steak, onions, and peppers. Spoon the dressing over each salad, sprinkle with a little parsley, and serve.

20

Eggplant breaded and then fried on the stove top is delicious, but the absorbent flesh does soak up oil. Oven-frying the eggplant is healthier, keeps the texture intact, and produces a custardy finish. Look for an eggplant that feels heavy in your hand and has a shiny, smooth skin.

EGGPLANT PARMESAN

serves 4–6

FOR THE TOMATO-BASIL SAUCE

3 Tbsp olive oil

5 large cloves garlic

3 lb (1.5 kg) plum tomatoes, cored and quartered

1 bay leaf

2 tsp sugar

Salt and freshly ground pepper

½ cup (1 oz/30 g) firmly packed torn fresh basil

¼ cup (2 fl oz/60 ml) olive oil

1 cup (5 oz/155 g) all-purpose flour

3 eggs, lightly beaten

1¾ cups (7 oz/220 g) dried bread crumbs

Salt and freshly ground pepper

½ cup (2 oz/60 g) grated Parmesan cheese

1 large eggplant, about 1½ lb (750 g), cut crosswise into 18 slices about ¼ inch (6 mm) thick

½ lb (250 g) fresh mozzarella cheese, cut into 18 pieces

To make the sauce, in a large saucepan, warm the oil over medium heat. Add the garlic and cook until golden on all sides, about 4 minutes. Remove from the heat. Working in batches, purée the tomatoes in a blender until smooth, and then strain through a coarse-mesh sieve into the pan with the oil and garlic. Add the bay leaf, the sugar, 1 tsp salt, and a few grinds of pepper. Bring to a boil over medium-high heat, reduce the heat to low, and simmer, uncovered, until thickened, about 45 minutes. Stir the basil into the sauce and simmer for 5 minutes. Season with salt and pepper.

Meanwhile, preheat the oven to 400°F (200°C). Pour the oil onto a rimmed baking sheet and swirl to cover the bottom.

Put the flour, eggs, and bread crumbs into 3 separate shallow bowls. Season each bowl with 1 tsp salt and a few grinds of pepper. Stir ¼ cup (1 oz/30 g) of the Parmesan into the bread crumbs. Dip each eggplant slice first in the flour, then in the eggs, and finally in the bread crumbs, gently tapping or shaking off the excess each time. Place on the prepared pan. »→

Bake for 15 minutes. Turn the slices and continue to bake until golden and tender, about 15 minutes. Let cool for 5–10 minutes.

Lightly oil a 9-by-13-inch (23-by-33-cm) baking dish. Overlap the eggplant slices in the prepared dish, alternating each slice with a piece of mozzarella. Spoon the sauce over the top and sprinkle with the remaining Parmesan. Bake until the cheese is melted and the sauce is bubbling, about 30 minutes. Let stand for 10 minutes before serving.

21

Grilling chicken that has been rubbed with a smoked paprika spice blend results in an extra-smoky finish. Serve this dish with grilled sliced vegetables, such as eggplant and zucchini.

SMOKY GRILLED CHICKEN & CORN

serves 4

1 Tbsp smoked paprika

1 Tbsp ground cumin

3 Tbsp olive oil

3 Tbsp fresh lime juice

1½ lb (750 g) chicken breast cutlets

4 ears fresh corn, husked

Salt and freshly ground pepper

1½ Tbsp grated lime zest

1½ Tbsp minced fresh thyme

In a small bowl, combine the paprika and cumin. Mix in the oil and lime juice. Place the chicken and corn on a large baking sheet. Brush the corn and chicken all over with the paprika mixture, and then sprinkle with salt and pepper.

Prepare a grill for direct-heat cooking over high heat. Add the corn to the grill, cover, and cook until the corn starts to brown in spots and is almost tender, turning frequently, about 10 minutes. Add the chicken to the grill, cover, and cook until the chicken is springy to the touch and cooked through, about 2½ minutes per side. Transfer the chicken and corn to a warmed platter. Sprinkle with lime zest and thyme, and serve right away.

22

*Sweet peppers
and chile peppers
join forces in this
chicken stir-fry. For
a more authentic
version of this dish,
seek out Thai basil,
which has smaller,
narrower leaves
than the common
Italian variety,
a reddish purple
cast, and a more
pronounced anise
flavor. Look for it
in Southeast Asian
stores or at farmers'
markets, or plant
seeds outdoors
in pots or beds for
easy harvests.*

SPICY CHICKEN & BASIL STIR-FRY

serves 4

6 Tbsp (3 fl oz/80 ml) chicken broth

2 Tbsp Asian fish sauce

2 tsp firmly packed light brown sugar

1 tsp cornstarch

2 Tbsp canola oil

1 large red bell pepper, seeded and thinly sliced

1 or 2 Thai or jalapeño chiles, cut crosswise into very thin rounds

2 cloves garlic, minced

4 skinless, boneless chicken breast halves, about 1 lb (500 g) total, cut across the grain into thin strips

¾ cup (1 oz/30 g) thinly sliced fresh basil, preferably Thai

3 green onions, white and tender green parts, cut into 3-inch (7.5-cm) lengths

Cooked short-grain or jasmine rice for serving

In a small bowl, whisk together the broth, fish sauce, and brown sugar. Add the cornstarch and whisk until the cornstarch and sugar are dissolved. Set aside.

In a wok or large frying pan, heat the oil over high heat. Add the bell pepper and stir-fry for 1 minute. Add the chile and the garlic and stir-fry until fragrant, about 20 seconds. Add the chicken strips and stir-fry until the chicken loses its pink color, about 3 minutes. Stir in the basil and green onions and stir-fry until the green onions are barely wilted, about 1 minute.

Whisk the sauce mixture and pour it into the pan. Cook just until the liquid comes to a boil. Serve the chicken and sauce spooned over the rice.

23

*This colorful
"pasta" is actually
long ribbons of
zucchini and yellow
squash tossed with
mint pesto and
Parmesan cheese.
For a prettier
presentation, the
squashes are left
unpeeled, so some
of the colored
skin is included
on many of the
ribbons. Be careful
not to overcook the
squashes. If they
remain on the heat
too long, they will
release too much
of their moisture.*

SUMMER SQUASH NOODLES WITH MINT PESTO

serves 4–6

FOR THE MINT PESTO

1 cup (1½ oz/45 g) firmly packed fresh mint leaves

⅓ cup (3 fl oz/80 ml) low-sodium vegetable broth

2 Tbsp grated Parmesan cheese

2 cloves garlic, chopped

2 tsp olive oil

3 *each* yellow summer squash and zucchini, about 1½ lb (750 g) total

Olive oil

¼ cup (1 oz/30 g) chopped shallots

1½ tsp dried thyme

Salt and freshly ground pepper

1 Tbsp grated Parmesan cheese, plus more for garnish

To make the pesto, in a blender or food processor, combine the mint, broth, Parmesan, garlic, and oil. Process until smooth.

Using a mandoline or a vegetable peeler, cut the yellow squashes and zucchini into long, narrow ribbons.

Pour enough oil into a large nonstick frying pan to film the bottom, and warm over medium heat. Add the shallots and sauté until softened, about 3 minutes. Add the squashes and thyme and season generously with salt and pepper. Sauté until the squashes are just tender, about 8 minutes longer. Stir in the mint pesto and heat for 1 minute. Remove from the heat and stir in the 1 Tbsp Parmesan.

Transfer to a warmed serving dish, sprinkle with additional cheese, and serve.

24

MEDITERRANEAN-STYLE CHICKEN & VEGETABLE KEBABS

serves 4–6

In this summery dish, boneless, skinless chicken breasts develop a delicious crust on the grill, while the zucchini soften and sweet cherry tomatoes turn even sweeter. Serve this dish with whole-wheat couscous to complete the meal.

1½ lb (750 g) boneless, skinless chicken breasts or thighs, cut into 2-inch (5-cm) chunks

½ cup (4 oz/125 g) plain yogurt

½ cup (1½ oz/45 g) chopped green onion, including tender green parts

1 large clove garlic, crushed

½ cup (¾ oz/20 g) chopped fresh cilantro

2 Tbsp extra-virgin olive oil

Salt and freshly ground pepper

1–2 medium zucchini, thickly sliced

1 cup (6 oz/185 g) cherry tomatoes

In a large nonreactive bowl, combine the chicken, yogurt, green onion, garlic, cilantro, and oil and mix well. Season with 1 tsp salt and a few grinds of pepper. Cover and refrigerate for at least 3 hours or up to overnight.

Soak 6 long wooden skewers in water to cover for at least 30 minutes. Prepare a grill for direct-heat cooking over medium-high heat. Oil the grill rack.

While the grill is warming, thread the chicken chunks, zucchini, and cherry tomatoes on the skewers, dividing evenly, and season lightly with salt and pepper. Place on the grill rack and grill, turning once, until the chicken is golden and opaque throughout but still juicy, about 8 minutes on each side. Serve.

25

GRILLED LAMB CHOPS WITH FRESH PEACH SALSA

serves 2

Lamb chops and a savory jam are a classic combination. Here, the "jam" is a bright-flavored peach salsa dressed with a little lime juice and chipotle chile. This same salsa would taste great alongside grilled chicken pieces or pork chops. If good peaches are not in the market, nectarines are an excellent substitute.

2 lamb shoulder round-bone chops, each 1 inch (2.5 cm) thick

½ tsp ground cumin

¼ tsp ground cinnamon

Salt and freshly ground pepper

Olive oil, for brushing

2 peaches, about 12 oz (375 g) total, peeled if desired, and chopped

3 Tbsp minced red onion

3 Tbsp roughly chopped fresh cilantro

1 tsp minced canned chipotle chiles in adobo sauce, or to taste

1 tsp fresh lime juice

Rub the lamb chops with the cumin and cinnamon. Season with salt and pepper, and then brush with oil.

In a small bowl, combine the peaches, red onion, cilantro, chile, and lime juice. Season to taste with salt and pepper.

Prepare a grill for direct-heat cooking over high heat. Place the lamb on the grill rack. Cover the grill and cook the lamb for about 3½ minutes on each side for medium-rare.

To serve, place 1 lamb chop on each plate. Spoon the salsa on top of the lamb.

26

GRILLED LEMON SHRIMP & SUMMER SQUASH

serves 4

2 tsp Dijon mustard

Grated zest of 1 lemon

2 Tbsp fresh lemon juice

⅓ cup (3 fl oz/80 ml) extra-virgin olive oil, plus more as needed

1 small serrano chile, seeded and minced

1 tsp minced fresh marjoram

1 Tbsp minced fresh basil

Salt and freshly ground pepper

1¼ lb (625 g) extra-large shrimp, peeled and deveined with tails intact

8 yellow summer squash, cut lengthwise into 3 pieces each

Grilled shrimp and squash are tossed in a lemony dressing for this healthy summer meal. Shrimp are a good source of lean protein, and summer squash are a savvy alternative to heavy carbohydrates like bread and pasta. Serve this dish alongside a salad of sliced cucumbers and tomatoes.

Prepare a grill for direct-heat cooking over medium-high heat. Soak bamboo skewers in water to cover for 30 minutes.

Add the mustard to a small bowl and stir in the lemon zest and juice. Gradually whisk in the olive oil. Mix in the chile and herbs. Season the sauce with salt and pepper.

Thread about 4 of the shrimp on each skewer, and then thread a second skewer through, parallel to the first, to prevent the shrimp from spinning around on the skewers. Place the squash slices and shrimp on a large baking sheet. Brush the shrimp and squash with oil, and sprinkle with salt and pepper.

Arrange the squash on the grill, cover, and cook until tender and lightly charred, about 5 minutes per side. Transfer to a plate. Place the shrimp on the grill and cook, uncovered, until just cooked through, about 3 minutes per side. Remove the shrimp from the skewers and cut the squash crosswise.

Transfer the shrimp and squash to a bowl and toss with the lemon-herb sauce. Season with salt and pepper and serve right away.

27

CRISPY EGGPLANT, MISO BUTTER & CHARRED SUNGOLD TOMATO SALAD

serves 4

4 Tbsp (2 oz/60 g) unsalted butter, at room temperature

2 Tbsp white miso

Salt

3–4 oz (90–125 g) Japanese noodles or thin spaghetti

2–3 Tbsp coconut oil

1 medium globe eggplant or 2 Asian eggplants, cut into ½-inch (12-mm) cubes

2 cups (12 oz/375 g) Sungold tomatoes

¼ cup (¼ oz/7 g) tightly packed fresh purple or green basil leaves, cut into thin strips

Eggplant can take on nearly any flavor profile, easily adapting to the cook's choice of seasonings and accompaniments. Miso, fermented soybean paste with an earthy, rich flavor and aroma, gives this quick noodle salad, finished with fresh basil, a light Japanese accent.

In a small bowl, mash together the butter and miso until well blended. Set aside.

Bring a pot of water to a boil over high heat. Add 1 tsp salt and the noodles, reduce the heat to medium-high, and cook until the noodles are tender to the bite, about 10 minutes. Drain well and transfer to a bowl. Add 1 Tbsp of the miso butter and toss to coat. Set aside.

In a large frying pan, warm 2 Tbsp of the coconut oil over medium heat. Add the eggplant cubes, sprinkle with ½ tsp salt, and cook, turning several times, until golden and crispy, about 7 minutes, adding more oil as needed. Set aside.

Prepare a charcoal or gas grill for direct-heat cooking over medium-high heat and preheat a grill basket. Alternatively, preheat a stove-top grill pan over medium-high heat.

Place the tomatoes in the grill basket or in the grill pan. Cook until charred, 1–2 minutes, turning once or twice.

Add the eggplant and 2 Tbsp of the miso butter to the bowl with the noodles and toss well. Transfer to a platter and add the tomatoes, tucking some into the noodles. Garnish with the basil and the remaining miso butter and serve.

28

BARBECUE-STYLE BRISKET

serves 6–8

¼ cup (2 oz/60 g) firmly packed dark brown sugar

¼ cup (2 fl oz/60 ml) cider vinegar

2 tomatoes, seeded and chopped

2 cups (16 fl oz/500 ml) beef broth

3 lb (1.5 kg) beef brisket

Salt and freshly ground pepper

2 Tbsp canola oil

2 yellow onions, thinly sliced

2 cloves garlic, minced

½ tsp ground allspice

2 Tbsp all-purpose flour

Brisket is one of the glories of the grilling season, but even if you own a smoker, it can be a labor of love. Slow cooking it in the oven renders equally tender results and is much easier. Beef brisket is sold without the bone and is divided into two sections, the flat cut and the point cut. At the meat counter, ask for the flat cut. It has less fat and slices more neatly.

In a small bowl, stir together the sugar, vinegar, tomatoes, and broth. Set aside.

Season the brisket generously with salt and pepper. In a large, heavy pot, heat the oil over medium-high heat. Add the brisket, fat side down, and cook, turning once, until browned on both sides, about 10 minutes. Transfer to a plate.

Pour off all but 2 Tbsp of the fat from the pot. Add the onions and sauté over medium-high heat until softened, about 3 minutes. Add the garlic and sauté for 1 minute. Stir in the allspice. Sprinkle the flour over the onion mixture, reduce the heat to medium, and cook, stirring frequently, until blended, about 3 minutes. Pour in the reserved broth mixture and stir to combine. Bring to a boil and season with salt and pepper.

Preheat the oven to 300°F (150°C). Return the brisket to the pot, cover, and cook in the oven until the brisket is very tender, 3–4 hours. Skim the fat from the surface of the cooking liquid.

Let the brisket cool in the cooking liquid then transfer the brisket to a cutting board and slice the brisket across the grain. Warm the cooking liquid over medium heat. Arrange the slices on a platter, top with the warm cooking liquid and onions, and serve.

29

CHARRED EGGPLANT SOUP WITH CUMIN & GREEK YOGURT

serves 6–8

2 large eggplants, about 2½ lb (1.25 kg) total, peeled and cut crosswise into slices 1 inch (2.5 cm) thick

3 ripe tomatoes, about 1¼ lb (625 g) total, halved and seeded

1 Tbsp extra-virgin olive oil, plus more for brushing

3 carrots, finely chopped

5 shallots, finely chopped

3 cloves garlic, minced

¾ tsp minced fresh thyme

¼ tsp ground cumin

1 cup (8 fl oz/250 ml) fruity white wine

5 cups (40 fl oz/1.25 l) chicken or vegetable broth

Salt and freshly ground pepper

½ cup (4 oz/125 g) plain Greek yogurt

The supple texture of cooked eggplant is transformed into a summertime soup that needs no cream to achieve its silken consistency. This easy-to-assemble recipe packs lots of flavor: eggplant asserts its smokiness, shallots and garlic add pungent sweetness, white wine brings brightness, and a touch of musky cumin imparts an exotic taste.

Prepare a charcoal or gas grill for direct-heat grilling over medium-high heat. Oil the grill rack. Brush the eggplant and tomato with oil and arrange on the grill rack. Cook, turning once, until softened and charred, about 8 minutes for the tomatoes and 10 minutes for the eggplant. Transfer to a cutting board and let cool. Remove and discard the skins from the tomatoes. Coarsely chop all but 1 of the eggplant slices. Finely chop the remaining eggplant slice and reserve for garnish.

In a large, heavy pot, heat the 1 Tbsp olive oil over medium-high heat. Add the carrots and sauté until just beginning to soften, about 4 minutes. Add the shallots, garlic, thyme, and cumin and cook, stirring occasionally, until fragrant, about 2 minutes. Add the tomatoes, coarsely chopped eggplant, wine, and broth and bring to a boil. Reduce the heat to low, cover partially, and simmer for 15 minutes to blend the flavors.

Working in batches, transfer the mixture to a blender and process to a coarse purée. Pour the purée back into the pot and season with salt and pepper. Cook gently over medium-low heat, stirring occasionally, until heated through, about 10 minutes. Adjust the seasoning if necessary. Ladle the soup into bowls. Garnish with dollops of yogurt and the finely diced eggplant and serve.

30

At the peak of summer, there's no more tantalizing smell than the floral aroma of a ripe nectarine. This surprisingly light no-bake cheesecake is sweetened with honey, a natural partner to stone fruit. Brushing the nectarine slices with a little melted jam gives them an attractive sheen, but feel free to skip this step if you want a more rustic look.

HONEY-NECTARINE CHEESECAKE

serves 8–10

FOR THE CRUST

1 cup (4 oz/125 g) sliced almonds, lightly toasted

1 cup (3 oz/90 g) graham cracker crumbs

¼ cup (2 oz/60 g) firmly packed light brown sugar

5 Tbsp (2½ oz/75 g) unsalted butter, melted

2 lb (1 kg) cream cheese

⅓ cup (4 oz/125 g) honey

¼ cup (2 oz/60 g) granulated sugar

1 cup (8 fl oz/250 ml) heavy cream

2 Tbsp fresh lemon juice

½ tsp almond extract

1 tsp unflavored gelatin

3 Tbsp apricot or peach jam

4 ripe nectarines, pitted and thinly sliced

Preheat the oven to 350°F (180°C). To make the crust, in a food processor, combine the almonds, graham cracker crumbs, and brown sugar. Process to grind finely. Add the melted butter and process until the crumbs begin to stick together. Press the crumbs firmly onto the bottom and 2 inches (5 cm) up the sides of a 9-inch (23-cm) springform pan. Bake the crust until set, about 10 minutes. Let cool completely.

In a large bowl, using an electric mixer, beat the cream cheese, honey, and granulated sugar on medium speed until smooth. Beat in ½ cup (4 fl oz/125 ml) of the cream, the lemon juice, and the almond extract.

Place 1 Tbsp water in a small saucepan. Sprinkle the gelatin over the surface and let soften for 5 minutes. Place over low heat and stir until the gelatin dissolves. Gradually whisk in the remaining ½ cup cream. Add the gelatin mixture to the cream cheese mixture and beat until fluffy, about 1 minute. Spoon the filling into the crust. Cover and refrigerate overnight or up to 2 days.

Remove the pan sides and, using a spatula, transfer the cake to a plate. In a small saucepan, stir the jam over medium heat until melted. Let cool slightly. Arrange the nectarine slices on the cheesecake. Using a pastry brush, brush the melted jam over the fruit. Cut the cake into wedges and serve.

31

Make this soup at the height of summer, when tomatoes are their most flavorful. Serve it with a simple endive salad topped with a light buttermilk dressing.

SUMMER PANZANELLA SOUP WITH TINY PASTA

serves 4–6

1 loaf crusty Italian bread

3 Tbsp olive oil

Salt and freshly ground pepper

8 oz (250 g) tiny pasta, such as conchigliette or ditalini

2 shallots, minced

3 cloves garlic, minced

2 lb (1 kg) ripe tomatoes, diced

2 cups (16 fl oz/500 ml) chicken broth

⅓ cup (⅓ oz/10 g) chopped basil

Grated Parmesan cheese for serving

Preheat the oven to 375°F (190°C). Cut enough of the bread up into cubes to measure out 2 cups (2 oz/60 g). Place the bread cubes on a baking sheet, toss with 1 Tbsp of the oil, and season with salt and pepper. Toast in the oven, stirring once, until browned, about 12 minutes. Set aside.

Bring a saucepan of salted water to a boil. Add the pasta and cook until al dente, about 8 minutes or according to the package directions. Drain and set aside.

In a large, heavy pot, warm the remaining 2 Tbsp oil over medium-high heat. Add the shallots and garlic and sauté until translucent, about 5 minutes. Add the tomatoes and sauté until they soften, about 5 minutes. Add the broth and bring to a boil. Reduce the heat to low and simmer for 15 minutes to blend the flavors. Remove from the heat and let cool slightly.

Purée half of the soup in a blender or food processor. Return to the pot and add the toasted bread. Continue to cook for 10 minutes. Stir in the pasta and basil and season with salt and pepper.

Serve, sprinkled with the Parmesan.

August, like July, is a month of hot days and warm, lazy evenings that keep the backyard grill in use—for calamari steaks, portobello burgers, chicken and vegetable kebabs—and the menus light and refreshing. Indoors, quick and easy stir-fries rule, such as chicken and lemongrass and tofu and Asian eggplant tossed in a salty-spicy sauce. Watermelon, an iconic fruit of summer, is matched with feta and mint in a refreshing salad, while citrusy ice pops, ice cream sandwiches, and berry pie are all signature desserts of high summer.

1
PULLED PORK WITH SPICY PEACH-MUSTARD SAUCE
page 183

2
PINK LEMONADE ICE POPS
page 183

3
GRILLED CALAMARI STEAKS WITH MEDITERRANEAN SALSA
page 184

8
CREAMY PASTA SALAD WITH LOBSTER
page 187

9
POBLANO CHILES STUFFED WITH BLACK BEANS & SUMMER VEGETABLES
page 189

10
INDIAN-SPICED CHAR WITH CUCUMBER & TOMATO SALAD
page 189

15
GRILLED PORK CHOPS WITH POTATO SALAD & ROMESCO
page 191

16
TOMATO, ZUCCHINI & GOAT CHEESE TART
page 192

17
SPANISH WHITE BEAN SOUP WITH CHORIZO & PIQUILLO PEPPERS
page 192

22
CRISPY OKRA, CORN & SHRIMP SALAD WITH HARISSA DRESSING
page 197

23
VIETNAMESE EGGPLANT CURRY
page 197

24
PAN-ROASTED PORK MEDALLIONS WITH SUMMER VEGETABLES
page 198

29
HALIBUT PROVENÇAL
page 201

30
GRILLED NAAN WITH SMOKY EGGPLANT PURÉE & GRILLED RED ONIONS
page 203

31
FRESH CORN SOUP WITH TURKEY & AVOCADO
page 203

4
GRILLED PORTOBELLO BURGERS
page 184

5
FRESH CORN, JALAPEÑO
& MONTEREY JACK TAMALES
page 186

6
WATERMELON, FETA & MINT SALAD
page 186

7
SPICY STIR-FRIED
EGGPLANT & TOFU
page 187

11
CAJUN SHRIMP BOIL
page 190

12
BLACKBERRY PURÉE
WITH WHIPPED CREAM
page 190

13
BLUEBERRY PIE
page 190

14
SPANISH SEAFOOD NOODLES
page 191

18
BREAD SALAD WITH CHARRED
TOMATOES, CUCUMBER & OLIVES
page 195

19
POMEGRANATE-GLAZED LAMB
& VEGETABLE SKEWERS
page 195

20
ICE CREAM SANDWICHES
page 196

21
STIR-FRIED LEMONGRASS CHICKEN
page 196

25
YELLOW GAZPACHO WITH
LEMON-BASIL RICOTTA
page 198

26
FRIED ZUCCHINI WITH CURRY DIP
page 200

27
BRAISED BEEF TIPS WITH CRANBERRY
BEANS, CHERRY TOMATOES & BASIL
page 200

28
CHOCOLATE–PEANUT BUTTER
ICE CREAM
page 201

august

AUGUST

2

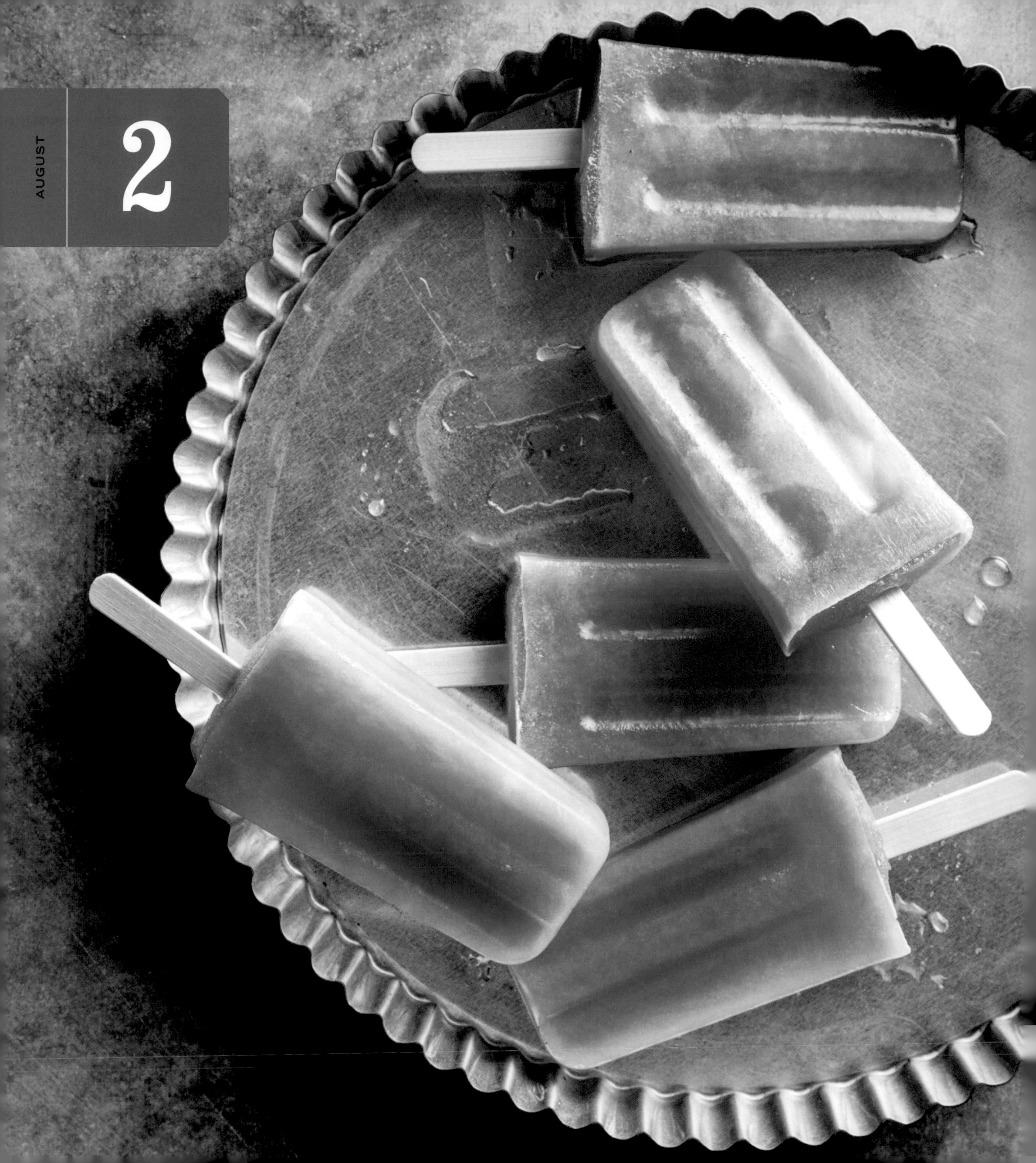

1

This pulled pork, doused in a sweet-and-sour soaking sauce with a generous helping of peach jam, is perfect picnic fare. Serve it on a platter alongside soft sandwich rolls, sliced dill pickles, and coleslaw and invite diners to assemble their own sandwiches.

PULLED PORK WITH SPICY PEACH-MUSTARD SAUCE

serves 12

Oil for brushing the pan

1 bone-in pork shoulder, about 6 lb (3 kg)

Salt and freshly ground pepper

1 Tbsp mustard seeds

2 cups (16 fl oz/500 ml) cider vinegar

4 yellow onions, sliced, plus 3 onions, chopped

½ cup (4 oz/125 g) unsalted butter

3 cloves garlic, minced

2 cups (16 fl oz/500 ml) canned crushed tomatoes

2 Tbsp tomato paste

1 cup (10 oz/315 g) peach jam

½ cup (4 oz/125 g) Dijon mustard

½ cup (4 fl oz/125 ml) aged Kentucky bourbon

½ cup (6 oz/185 g) honey

¼ cup (2 oz/60 g) firmly packed dark brown sugar

1 Tbsp hot-pepper sauce

12 soft sandwich rolls

Preheat the oven to 300°F (150°C). Lightly oil a large roasting pan.

Put the pork shoulder in the prepared pan and rub with 1 Tbsp salt, 1 Tbsp pepper, and the mustard seeds. Pour 1 cup (8 fl oz/250 ml) of the vinegar and 1 cup (8 fl oz/250 ml) water over and around the pork. Scatter the sliced onions over and around the meat. Cover with foil and roast for 4 hours.

Meanwhile, in a saucepan, melt the butter over medium heat. Add the chopped onions and the garlic and cook, stirring occasionally, until the onions are soft and beginning to brown, about 10 minutes. Add the tomatoes, tomato paste, jam, mustard, bourbon, honey, brown sugar, remaining 1 cup (8 fl oz/250 ml) vinegar, and hot-pepper sauce and stir to mix well. Season with salt and pepper. Bring to a boil, reduce the heat to very low, and simmer, uncovered, stirring occasionally, until the sauce is dark and thick, about 2 hours. Let cool for 15 minutes. »→

Remove the foil from the pork and continue to roast until an instant-read thermometer inserted into the thickest part of the pork away from the bone registers 180°F (82°C) and the juices run clear, about 1 hour. Remove the pork from the pan and let stand for 1 hour. Using 2 forks, shred the pork, discarding any fat. Put the pork in a bowl. Using a slotted spoon, lift the roasted onions from the pan and add to the pork. Mix well to combine.

Mix half of the sauce with the shredded pork. Mound the pork on a large platter and place the rolls on a plate. Serve, passing the remaining sauce at the table.

2

These ice pops are the perfect warm-weather treat. Blending just a couple of strawberries into the lemonade creates the signature pink hue and the essence of berries without compromising the bright lemon flavor.

PINK LEMONADE ICE POPS

makes 8–10 ice pops

1 tsp finely grated lemon zest

½ cup (4 fl oz/125 ml) fresh lemon juice

½ cup (3½ oz/105 g) plus 2 Tbsp superfine sugar

2 fresh or frozen strawberries, hulled

Pinch of kosher salt

In a blender or food processor, combine the lemon zest and juice and the sugar. Pour in 1¾ cups (14 fl oz/430 ml) water. Add the strawberries and salt and process until the mixture is smooth and pink.

Pour the pink lemonade mixture into a glass measuring cup with a spout. Divide the mixture evenly among ice pop molds. Insert the sticks. Freeze the ice pops for at least 8 hours or up to overnight. Run the molds under warm water for 30 seconds to release the pops.

The mixture can also be poured into small paper cups and frozen just until barely firm; add the sticks and freeze until solid. Peel away the cups and serve.

3

GRILLED CALAMARI STEAKS WITH MEDITERRANEAN SALSA

serves 4

Calamari steaks are broad, flat body pieces from large squid. They are a great lean protein option for anyone following a healthy diet, and they cook quickly, which every busy cook appreciates. Although fresh is always best, frozen steaks are often all you can find. Serve this dish with whole-grain Israeli couscous dressed with lemon olive oil.

FOR THE MEDITERRANEAN SALSA

1 cup (4 oz/125 g) Kalamata olives, pitted and chopped

⅔ cup (4 oz/125 g) cherry tomatoes, chopped

¼ cup (2 oz/60 g) capers, drained

2 cloves garlic, minced

1 Tbsp chopped fresh flat-leaf parsley

1 Tbsp olive oil

Grated zest of 1 lemon

1 Tbsp fresh lemon juice

¼ tsp freshly ground pepper

FOR THE CALAMARI STEAKS

4 calamari steaks, 4–6 oz (125–185 g) each

Juice of 1 lemon

1 Tbsp olive oil

1 Tbsp chopped fresh flat-leaf parsley

Salt and freshly ground pepper

Lemon wedges, for serving

To make the salsa, in a bowl, stir together the olives, tomatoes, capers, garlic, parsley, oil, lemon zest and juice, and pepper.

Place the calamari steaks in a nonreactive bowl and add half of the lemon juice, the olive oil, and the parsley. Season with salt and pepper and toss to combine.

Prepare a grill for direct-heat cooking over medium-high heat. Grill the steaks until opaque, about 2 minutes per side. Top the calamari with the salsa and a squeeze of lemon juice, and serve.

4

GRILLED PORTOBELLO BURGERS

serves 4

These garlic-brushed, cheese-topped grilled portobello burgers will satisfy vegetarians and carnivores alike. Serve them tucked into crusty rolls with pesto mayonnaise and thick, ripe tomato slices. Serve chips and pickles on the side.

2 Tbsp olive oil

1 Tbsp balsamic vinegar

1 clove garlic, minced

Salt and freshly ground pepper

4 large portobello mushrooms, stems removed

4 slices Monterey jack or smoked mozzarella cheese

4 round Italian rolls

2 Tbsp purchased pesto

½ cup (4 fl oz/125 ml) mayonnaise

1 or 2 tomatoes, sliced

Prepare a charcoal or gas grill for grilling over medium-high heat.

In a small bowl, stir together the oil, the vinegar, the garlic, ½ tsp salt, and ⅛ tsp pepper. Using a small spoon, remove the gills from the undersides of the mushrooms. Brush both sides of each mushroom with the oil mixture.

Place the mushrooms, stem side up, on the grill and cook until well marked, about 4 minutes. Turn and cook until tender, about 4 minutes. Place a slice of cheese on top of each mushroom about 2 minutes before you remove the mushrooms from the grill and cook until melted.

Cut the rolls in half horizontally. Place each half, cut side down, on the cooler part of the grill, and grill until lightly toasted, 2–3 minutes.

In a small bowl, mix together the pesto and mayonnaise and season with salt and pepper. Spread the pesto-mayonnaise on the toasted rolls. Place a grilled mushroom on the bottom of each roll and top with the tomato slices. Close with the top half of the roll, and serve.

5

FRESH CORN, JALAPEÑO & MONTEREY JACK TAMALES

serves 4–6

2 ears corn, husks intact

2 cups (8 oz/250 g) masa harina

½ cup (4 oz/125 g) unsalted butter, cut into pieces

½ tsp sugar

½ tsp baking powder

Salt and freshly ground pepper

½ cup (4 fl oz/125 ml) chicken or vegetable broth

2 tsp olive oil

1 small jalapeño chile, seeded and minced

¾ cup (3 oz/90 g) shredded Monterey jack cheese

Tamales are easy to make and are a fun dish to prepare with your kids, who will like stuffing and folding the corn husks. Look for masa harina, a traditional Mexican corn flour used to make tamales and tortillas, in well-stocked supermarkets and Latin markets. Accompany the tamales with a salad of tomatoes, avocados, and red onions.

Using a large knife, cut off the bottom ½ inch (12 mm) of each ear of corn so that the husks come free in whole pieces. Set the husks aside, and remove and discard the silk. Hold each ear of corn upright on a cutting board. Using a sharp knife, cut down along the ear, stripping off the kernels and rotating the ear a quarter turn after each cut.

In a food processor, pulse half of the kernels to chop roughly. Add the masa harina, the butter, the sugar, the baking powder, and 1 tsp salt. Process until completely combined. Add the broth and process just until smooth.

In a small frying pan, heat the oil over medium-high heat. Add the remaining corn kernels and the jalapeño, season with salt and pepper, and sauté just until the vegetables begin to soften, about 2 minutes. Let cool.

In a large pot with a steamer rack, add enough water to reach just below the rack. Cover the bottom of the rack with the small corn husks. Set the pot over medium heat.

Place 2–3 Tbsp of tamale dough on each of the largest corn husks. Top with 2 tsp of the corn and jalapeño mixture and 2 tsp of the cheese. Using your hands, slightly flatten 1 tsp of the dough, then place on the cheese. Wrap the tamale inside the corn husk, completely enclosing it, using 2 corn husks if necessary, and place in the steamer. Arrange any remaining corn ⟫

husks on top of the tamales, cover the pot, and steam until the dough pulls away from the husks, about 1 hour. Occasionally check the water level in the pot and add more if necessary.

Remove the tamales from the pot and serve in the husks.

6

WATERMELON, FETA & MINT SALAD

serves 6

¾ cup (¾ oz/20 g) fresh mint leaves

1 Tbsp sugar

1 serrano chile, seeded and chopped (optional)

2 Tbsp rice vinegar

1 Tbsp fresh lime juice

3 Tbsp extra-virgin olive oil

Salt and freshly ground pepper

1 small seedless watermelon, about 3 lb (1.5 kg), peeled and cut into wedges or cubes

6 oz (185 g) feta cheese, crumbled

Salty and tangy, feta cheese is a delicious match with sweet, crisp watermelon in this easy salad. The chile adds an interesting hit of heat, but you can leave it out with equally good results. A refreshing dressing with just enough acid from the vinegar and lime juice completes this ultimate summer side dish.

Process ½ cup (½ oz/15 g) of the mint leaves and the sugar in a food processor until well blended. Add the chile (if using), vinegar, and lime juice and process again. With the motor running, drizzle in the oil. Transfer the vinaigrette to a bowl and season with a pinch each of salt and pepper.

Arrange the watermelon and cheese on individual plates and drizzle with the vinaigrette. Garnish with the remaining mint and serve.

7

SPICY STIR-FRIED EGGPLANT & TOFU

serves 4

2 Tbsp sesame seeds

2 Tbsp low-sodium soy sauce

2 Tbsp dry white wine or dry sherry

1 tsp cornstarch

6 Tbsp (3 fl oz/90 ml) grapeseed oil

4 cloves garlic, minced

4 serrano chiles, seeded and minced

2 red Anaheim chiles, seeded and cut into 1-inch (2.5-cm) pieces

3 or 4 Asian eggplants, about 1 lb (500 g) total weight, cut into 1-inch (2.5-cm) cubes

1 lb (500 g) firm tofu, drained and cut into 1-inch (2.5-cm) cubes

¼ cup (⅓ oz/10 g) chopped fresh cilantro

Consider this recipe when you're looking for a quick, protein-packed vegetarian dish. The eggplant and chiles offer vitamins and phytochemicals, and the tofu lends low-fat protein and more beneficial micronutrients. Serve it over brown rice and offer chile sauce for dipping at the table.

In a small, dry frying pan over medium-low heat, toast the sesame seeds, stirring continuously, until lightly golden and fragrant, 2–3 minutes. Transfer to a small plate and set aside.

In a small bowl, stir together the soy sauce, wine, and cornstarch until the cornstarch dissolves. Set aside.

In a wok or large, deep frying pan over high heat, warm 2 Tbsp of the oil. When the oil is hot, add the garlic and serrano chiles and toss and stir until fragrant, about 30 seconds. Add another 2 Tbsp of the oil and, when it's hot, add the Anaheim chiles. Toss and stir for another 30 seconds. Add the remaining 2 Tbsp oil and again allow to heat. Add the eggplant and cook, turning often, until the eggplant has softened and browned a bit, 10–12 minutes. Quickly stir the soy sauce mixture and then add to the pan along with the tofu. Toss and stir to coat all the ingredients, then cover and cook until the eggplant is tender, the tofu is heated through, and the liquid has thickened slightly, 1–2 minutes longer.

Remove the stir-fry from the heat and stir in the cilantro. Transfer to a warmed serving dish, sprinkle with the toasted sesame seeds, and serve.

8

CREAMY PASTA SALAD WITH LOBSTER

serves 6

Salt and freshly ground black pepper

¾ lb (375 g) pasta shells

2 Tbsp extra-virgin olive oil

¾ lb (375 g) cooked lobster meat or 2–3 frozen lobster tails, thawed and halved lengthwise

½ cup (4 fl oz/125 ml) heavy cream

2 Tbsp tomato paste

3 Tbsp red wine vinegar

Cayenne pepper

8 cherry tomatoes, halved

Chopped fresh flat-leaf parsley for garnish

Chunks of lobster are coated with a rose-colored dressing in this elegant pasta salad fit for an upscale lunch. Pasta shells pool the sauce in their hollows—and nicely fit the crustacean theme. Fresh crab can replace the lobster, if desired. Serve with an aromatic white wine, such as a dry Riesling.

In a large pot over high heat, bring 5 qt (5 l) salted water to a boil. Add the pasta shells and cook until al dente, according to package directions. Drain the pasta and toss it immediately with 1 Tbsp of the oil. Cover and let cool completely in the refrigerator, at least 1 hour or overnight.

If using frozen lobster tails, bring a large pot three-fourths full of salted water to a boil over high heat. Add the lobster tails and boil them until the shells are bright red and the meat is almost opaque throughout, about 8 minutes.

Meanwhile, ready a large bowl full of ice. When the lobster tails are done, transfer them immediately to the bowl and cover with ice. Leave in the ice for 30 minutes. Remove the meat from the tails.

Whether using fresh or frozen, cut the cooked lobster meat into generous bite-sized pieces. Set aside.

In a large bowl, whisk the cream just until it begins to thicken, about 1 minute. Add the remaining 1 Tbsp oil, the tomato paste, vinegar, and cayenne to taste. Whisk until mixed thoroughly. Add the pasta shells, lobster, tomatoes, and salt and black pepper to taste. Toss to mix well.

Place in a serving bowl or divide among individual plates, garnish with the parsley, and serve.

9

Mild, heart-shaped poblano chiles flourish in the summer vegetable garden. Here, they are stuffed with a memorable filling of summer squashes and roasted chiles mixed with black beans and rice. Tangy crème fraîche binds the filling, and a garnish of Parmesan adds a salty accent.

POBLANO CHILES STUFFED WITH BLACK BEANS & SUMMER VEGETABLES

serves 4–6

8 poblano chiles

2 Tbsp olive oil

½ white onion, finely chopped

Salt and freshly ground black pepper

1 zucchini, chopped

2 yellow summer squash, chopped

1 ripe tomato, chopped

¼ tsp cayenne pepper

1 can (15 oz/470 g) black beans, drained and rinsed

Leaves from ¼ bunch fresh cilantro, coarsely chopped

1 cup (5 oz/155 g) cooked white rice

½ cup (4 oz/125 g) crème fraîche

Small piece of Parmesan cheese

Preheat the broiler. Line a baking sheet with foil. Place 2 of the chiles on the prepared sheet. Broil, turning occasionally, until charred on all sides, about 15 minutes. Transfer the chiles to a bowl, cover, and let steam for 5 minutes. Peel the charred skin from the chiles. Remove the stems and seeds, and chop the flesh. Preheat the oven to 400°F (200°C).

In each of the remaining chiles, cut a slit 2 inches (5 cm) long. With a paring knife, carefully scrape out the seeds from the insides of the chiles.

In a frying pan, warm the oil over medium heat. Add the onion and a pinch of salt and sauté until the onion is soft and translucent, 5–6 minutes. Add the zucchini and summer squash, cover, and cook until just tender, 5–6 minutes. Uncover, add the tomato, the cayenne, the chopped chiles, and a pinch each of salt and black pepper, and sauté for 2 minutes. Let the vegetables cool slightly.

Add the beans, cilantro, rice, and crème fraîche to the pan and mix well. Spoon the bean mixture into the chiles. Place the stuffed chiles, cut side up, in a baking dish, and add enough water to come ½ inch (12 mm) up the sides of the dish. Cover tightly with foil and bake until the stuffing is heated through and the water has evaporated, about 20 minutes. ⟫→

Remove the foil, grate some Parmesan over the tops of the chiles, and bake, uncovered, until the cheese melts, about 5 minutes. Remove from the oven and serve.

10

Arctic char is related to both salmon and lake trout. Its flesh can vary from light pink to dark red, and its flavor is mildly reminiscent of that of its kin. In this recipe, it is treated to an Indian-inspired yogurt marinade laced with heady spices. Serve the fish and salad with steamed basmati rice seasoned with fresh herbs.

INDIAN-SPICED CHAR WITH CUCUMBER & TOMATO SALAD

serves 4

⅓ cup (2½ oz /75 g) plain yogurt

4 Tbsp (2 fl oz/60 ml) lemon juice

1 Tbsp garam masala

2 cloves garlic, minced

1 Tbsp peeled and minced ginger

¼ tsp cayenne pepper

Salt and freshly ground black pepper

4 skin-on arctic char or salmon fillets, each about 6 oz (185 g)

2 cups (10 oz/315 g) peeled, halved, and thinly sliced cucumber

2 cups (12 oz/375 g) seeded and coarsely diced tomato

1 cup (3½ oz/105 g) thinly sliced red onion

1 Tbsp olive oil, plus more for drizzling

2 Tbsp finely chopped cilantro

In a large bowl, combine the yogurt, 2 Tbsp of the lemon juice, the garam masala, garlic, ginger, cayenne, ½ tsp salt, and a pinch of black pepper. Stir to blend, then add the fish fillets, coating them with the marinade. Cover and refrigerate for 2 hours.

While the fish marinates, in a bowl, combine the cucumber, tomato, and red onion and toss with the remaining 2 Tbsp lemon juice, ½ tsp salt, a pinch of black pepper, 1 Tbsp oil, and 1 Tbsp of the cilantro. Cover and refrigerate until serving time.

Preheat the broiler. Line the bottom of a broiler pan with foil and set the top rack in place. Remove the fish from the marinade and brush away the excess marinade. Drizzle the fillets with oil and season with salt and black pepper. Arrange the fish on the prepared pan and broil for about 4 minutes. Remove the fish from the oven and cover with foil. Let rest for 2 minutes. Serve with the vegetable salad and garnish with the remaining cilantro.

11

An old-fashioned shrimp boil is a great excuse for a casual gathering. Potatoes, corn, sausages, and shrimp all share the same pot. When it is time to eat, move outside where diners can munch corn off the cob and shell shrimp with abandon. Set out plenty of napkins, and don't forget to chill some beer.

CAJUN SHRIMP BOIL

serves 6

6 Tbsp Old Bay or other crab boil seasoning

2 large yellow onions, quartered

1 head garlic, unpeeled, halved crosswise

2 lemons, halved

2 lb (1 kg) small red-skinned potatoes

4 ears corn, each cut into 3 pieces

1½ lb (750 g) smoked pork or chicken sausages, cut into 1-inch (2.5-cm) slices

3 lb (1.5 kg) large shrimp, in the shell

Fill a large pot with water. Add the Old Bay seasoning, onions, garlic, and lemon halves and bring to a boil. Add the potatoes, reduce the heat to low, and simmer until the potatoes are tender, 15–20 minutes.

Add the corn and sausages to the pot and cook for 5 minutes. Remove from the heat, add the shrimp, cover, and let stand until the shrimp are opaque, about 4 minutes. Drain in a colander, transfer to a large shallow bowl, and serve.

12

Swirling dark blackberry juice into cream results in a stunning violet color and intense flavor. Make sure to whip the cream until it forms firm peaks, so it keeps its volume when you fold in the whole berries and purée.

BLACKBERRY PURÉE WITH WHIPPED CREAM

serves 8

2¼ cups (9 oz/280 g) blackberries

2 cups (16 fl oz/500 ml) cold heavy cream

¼ cup (1 oz/30 g) confectioners' sugar

1 Tbsp brandy, preferably blackberry (optional)

1 tsp pure vanilla extract

In a food processor, purée 1 cup (4 oz/125 g) of the blackberries. Using a rubber spatula, press the purée through a fine-mesh sieve into a small bowl. Discard the seeds.

In a large bowl, using an electric mixer, beat the cream, sugar, brandy (if using), and vanilla on medium-high speed until firm peaks form.

Using the rubber spatula, gently fold the blackberry purée and the remaining blackberries into the whipped cream. Spoon it into glass cups or bowls and serve.

13

Strawberries ripen early and reliably all summer long, but blueberries reach their peak in high summer. Bake the season's best berries into this flaky double-crusted pie. Tapioca starch leaves the juices from the berries thick and glossy without adding unwanted flavor.

BLUEBERRY PIE

serves 6–8

Flaky Pie Dough for double crust (see page 129)

5 cups (1¼ lb/600 g) blueberries

1 Tbsp fresh lemon juice, strained

¾ cup (6 oz/185 g) sugar

4 Tbsp tapioca starch

½ tsp finely grated lemon zest

¼ tsp kosher salt

1 Tbsp cold unsalted butter, cut into small pieces

Prepare the dough and chill as directed. Transfer the dough to a lightly floured work surface and cut in half. Roll each half into a round at least 12 inches (30 cm) in diameter and about ⅛ inch (3 mm) thick. Transfer one round to a 9-inch (23-cm) pie pan and ease into the pan. Trim the edge, leaving a ¾-inch (2-cm) overhang. Set the second dough round in a cool place until ready to use.

Place the berries in a large bowl, sprinkle with the lemon juice, and toss to coat evenly. In a small bowl, stir together the sugar, tapioca, lemon zest, and salt. Sprinkle the sugar mixture over the berries and toss to distribute evenly. Transfer to the dough-lined pan. Dot with the butter.

Position the reserved dough round over the filled pie. Trim the edge, leaving a 1-inch (2.5-cm) overhang. Fold the edge of the top round under the edge of the bottom round and crimp the edges to seal. Using a small, sharp knife, cut 5 or 6 slits in the dough. Refrigerate until the dough is firm, about 30 minutes.

Preheat the oven to 375°F (190°C). Bake the pie until the crust is golden and the filling is thick and bubbling, 50–60 minutes. Transfer to a wire rack and let cool completely to set before serving.

14

SPANISH SEAFOOD NOODLES

serves 4

¼ tsp saffron threads

3 Tbsp olive oil

1 yellow onion, finely chopped

½ cup (2½ oz/75 g) chopped green bell pepper

1 Tbsp minced garlic

3½–4 cups (28–32 fl oz/875 ml–1 l) fish broth or chicken broth

1 lb (500 g) fresh tomatoes, grated, or 1 cup (6 oz/185 g) canned crushed tomatoes

½ cup (4 fl oz/125 ml) dry white wine

1½ tsp Spanish smoked paprika

Salt and freshly ground pepper

12 oz (375 g) angel hair pasta, broken in half

¾ lb (375 g) halibut or other white fish fillets, cut into 1-inch (2.5-cm) chunks

½ lb (250 g) clams, scrubbed and soaked

½ lb (250 g) shrimp, peeled and deveined

3 Tbsp chopped fresh flat-leaf parsley

Similar to a seafood paella but made with noodles, this saffron-infused dish is a specialty of Valencia. It is made with fideos, short, thin noodles, though angel hair pasta, broken into pieces, can be used in their place. If you like, top each serving with a dollop of aioli.

In a large, deep frying pan, toast the saffron threads over medium heat, stirring constantly, until fragrant and a shade darker, about 1 minute. Pour the threads into a bowl and, when they cool, crumble.

In the frying pan, warm the oil over medium-high heat. Add the onion, bell pepper, and garlic and sauté until the vegetables are soft, 3–5 minutes. Add 3½ cups (28 fl oz/875 ml) of the broth and the tomatoes, wine, paprika, and saffron. Stir to combine and season with salt and pepper. Stir in the pasta. Bring to a boil over medium-high heat and cook, uncovered, for 8 minutes.

Adjust the heat to maintain a gentle simmer and add ½ cup (4 fl oz/125 ml) broth if the mixture looks dry. Add the halibut and the clams, discarding any clams that do not close to the touch. Push the fish down into the liquid. Cover and cook for 5 minutes. Add the shrimp, cover, and cook until the clams have opened (discard any unopened ones), the shrimp are pink, and most of the liquid is absorbed, 3–5 minutes longer.

Remove from the heat and let stand, covered, for 10 minutes. Sprinkle with the parsley and serve directly from the pan.

15

GRILLED PORK CHOPS WITH POTATO SALAD & ROMESCO

serves 4

FOR THE ROMESCO SAUCE

½ cup (3 oz/90 g) roasted red bell peppers

⅓ cup (2 oz/60 g) raw almonds

1 slice sourdough bread, crust removed

2 cloves garlic

2 Tbsp red wine vinegar

½ tsp red pepper flakes

¼ cup (2 fl oz/60 ml) extra-virgin olive oil

4 boneless, center-cut pork chops, each 1 inch (2.5 cm) thick

Salt and freshly ground black pepper

6 Tbsp (3 fl oz/90 ml) olive oil, plus more for grilling

1½ lb (750 g) Yukon Gold potatoes

1 Tbsp sherry vinegar

3 green onions, chopped

Pairing pork chops and potato salad makes for a filling, satisfying meal, perfect for serving at the end of a long, active day. Olive oil replaces the usual mayonnaise in the salad, for a lighter version of a summer favorite. A side of steamed green beans is all you will need to complete this seasonal supper.

To make the romesco, in a blender, combine the roasted red peppers, almonds, bread, garlic, red wine vinegar, and red pepper flakes and process until fairly smooth. With the blender running, slowly pour in the oil and process until smooth and thick.

Season the pork chops with salt. In a shallow glass or ceramic dish, whisk ¼ cup (2 fl oz/ 60 ml) of the romesco with 1 Tbsp of the oil. Add the chops, turn to coat, and let stand at room temperature for up to 1 hour.

Meanwhile, bring a saucepan of water to a boil over high heat. Add 1 Tbsp salt and the potatoes. Cook until the potatoes are tender, about 25 minutes. Drain, rinse under cold water, and let cool slightly. In a large bowl, whisk together the remaining oil and the sherry vinegar. Slice the potatoes and transfer to the bowl. Add the green onions, season with salt and black pepper, and toss to combine.

Prepare a grill for indirect-heat grilling over high heat and lightly oil the grill rack. Place the chops on the cooler area of the grill, cover, and cook for 5 minutes. Turn and cook until the chops feel firm when pressed, about 5 minutes. Serve with the potato salad and pass the romesco sauce alongside.

16

This savory tart features a simple combination of peak-of-summer vegetables and fresh goat cheese, all baked in a buttery cornmeal crust. Look for stone-ground cornmeal, which retains more nutrients and flavor. Serve thin slices of this tart for a striking appetizer, or accompany larger slices with a salad for a light lunch.

TOMATO, ZUCCHINI & GOAT CHEESE TART

serves 6–8

FOR THE CORNMEAL DOUGH

1 cup (5 oz/155 g) all-purpose flour

½ cup (2½ oz/75 g) fine-grind stone-ground cornmeal

Salt

6 Tbsp (3 oz/90 g) unsalted butter, cut into pieces

1 egg

1 Tbsp olive oil

½ lb (250 g) zucchini, cut crosswise into slices ⅛ inch (3 mm) thick

Salt and freshly ground pepper

5 oz (155 g) fresh goat cheese, crumbled

¾ lb (375 g) tomatoes, one size or a mixture of sizes, sliced or halved, depending on size

1 tsp coarsely chopped fresh thyme, plus more for garnish

To make the dough, in a food processor, combine the flour, cornmeal, and ½ tsp salt. Add the butter and pulse until the mixture resembles coarse crumbs. Add the egg and ¼ cup (2 fl oz/60 ml) cold water and pulse just until the dough begins to come together. Flatten the dough into a disk, wrap in plastic wrap, and refrigerate for at least 1 hour or up to 2 days.

In a large frying pan, warm the oil over medium-high heat. Add the zucchini and sprinkle lightly with salt and pepper. Reduce the heat to medium-low and cook, stirring frequently, until the zucchini is softened but not browned, about 5 minutes. Transfer the zucchini to paper towels to drain.

Position a rack in the lower third of the oven and preheat to 375°F (190°C). On a lightly floured work surface, roll out the dough into a 12-inch (30-cm) circle about ¼ inch (6 mm) thick. Carefully transfer the dough to a 9-inch (23-cm) fluted tart pan with removable sides. Press the dough into the bottom and sides of the pan. Fold the edges over and press into the sides of the pan, forming a double thickness around the pan rim. Trim off any excess dough overhanging the rim. ⇥

Sprinkle half of the cheese over the bottom of the crust. Arrange the tomatoes and zucchini in overlapping concentric circles or another attractive pattern on top of the cheese. Season lightly with salt and pepper. Top with the remaining cheese and the 1 tsp thyme.

Bake until the crust is golden brown and the juices are bubbling, 35–40 minutes. Let the tart cool for 10 minutes. Remove the pan sides, sprinkle with thyme, and serve warm.

17

Using chopped cured Spanish-style chorizo in this substantial soup creates little bursts of chewy flavor among the soft white beans and pepper strips. You can omit the chorizo for a vegetarian version, and the flavor will still be very good. Follow the soup with a green salad, crusty bread, and a selection of two or three cheeses.

SPANISH WHITE BEAN SOUP WITH CHORIZO & PIQUILLO PEPPERS

serves 6

1 lb (500 g) dried large white beans, such as Royal Corona, picked over and rinsed

1 bay leaf

¼ tsp dried winter savory

Salt and freshly ground pepper

¾ lb (375 g) smoked Spanish chorizo, cut into ¼-inch (6-mm) slices

2 jarred Spanish piquillo peppers, drained and cut into ¼-inch (6-mm) slices

Put the beans in a bowl with cold water to cover and soak overnight. Drain.

Transfer the beans to a large, heavy pot and add water to cover by 2½–3 inches (6–7.5 cm) (these are big beans and they will absorb a lot). Add the bay leaf. Place over medium-high heat and bring to a boil. Reduce the heat to low, cover, and simmer for 1 hour. Stir in the winter savory and 1 tsp salt. Cover and cook until the beans are almost tender, about 1 hour longer. Add 1 tsp salt, cover, and cook until the beans are completely tender and offer no resistance, up to 1 hour longer.

Add the chorizo, season with pepper, and simmer until the chorizo is warmed through, about 15 minutes. Taste and adjust the seasoning. Remove and discard the bay leaf. Stir in the piquillo peppers and serve.

AUGUST 18

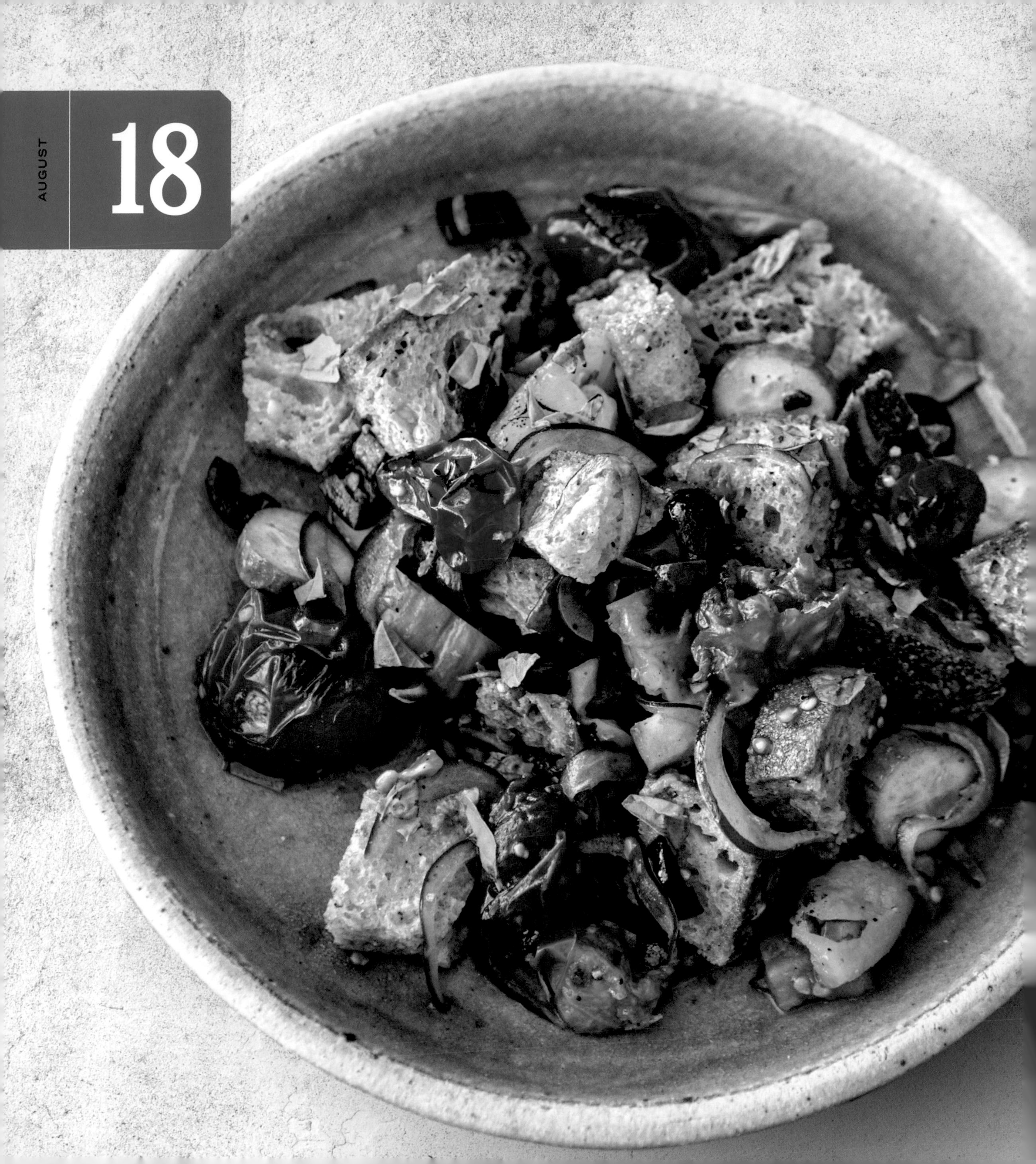

18

BREAD SALAD WITH CHARRED TOMATOES, CUCUMBER & OLIVES

serves 4

½ loaf coarse country Italian bread such as pugliese (about 8 oz/250 g)

3 or 4 large ripe tomatoes, about 2½ lb (1.25 kg) total, preferably a mixture of colors

1 small English cucumber

½ red onion, chopped or thinly sliced

¾ cup (4 oz/125 g) pitted and coarsely chopped Kalamata olives

⅓ cup (3 fl oz/80 ml) extra-virgin olive oil

2 Tbsp red wine vinegar

Salt and freshly ground pepper

Leaves from ½ bunch fresh basil, torn into small pieces

Layering pungent, bitter, and salty ingredients adds complexity to vegetable dishes. Kalamata olives offer all three qualities, which makes them a good match for the smoky-sweet charred tomatoes, crisp cucumber, and crusty bread cubes in this summer salad.

Preheat the oven to 375°F (190°C).

Cut the bread into ½-inch (12-mm) cubes and arrange in a single layer on a baking sheet. Lightly toast in the oven until the cubes are just dry and very light brown, 8–10 minutes. Remove the cubes from the baking sheet.

Preheat the broiler. Line the baking sheet with foil and place the tomatoes on the prepared sheet. Broil until the skins begin to char and blacken, 2–3 minutes. Turn the tomatoes and broil for another 2–3 minutes. Let cool.

Remove and discard any loose skin from the tomatoes (it's fine if a few charred bits remain), and then coarsely chop. Transfer the tomatoes to a large bowl. Cut the cucumber in half lengthwise and scrape out the seeds. Cut the halves crosswise into slices about ½ inch (12 mm) thick. (Alternatively, cut the whole cucumber crosswise into slices about ½ inch (12 mm) thick.) Add to the bowl with the tomatoes. Add the onion, olives, oil, and vinegar. Season with salt and pepper and stir well to mix. Let stand at room temperature for up to 1 hour to blend the flavors.

Add the toasted bread cubes to the salad and toss gently. Add the basil, toss gently to mix, and serve.

19

POMEGRANATE-GLAZED LAMB & VEGETABLE SKEWERS

serves 4

¼ cup (2 fl oz/60 ml) pomegranate molasses

1 shallot, minced

3 Tbsp olive oil

2 tsp cumin seeds, crushed

1¼ lb (625 g) boneless leg of lamb, well trimmed and cut into 1-inch (2.5-cm) cubes

2 zucchini, halved lengthwise and cut into 1-inch (2.5-cm) pieces

1 large red bell pepper, cut into 1-inch (2.5-cm) squares

1 red onion, cut into 1-inch (2.5-cm) squares

Salt and freshly ground pepper

Chopped fresh mint, for garnish

Pomegranate molasses, which is made by reducing pomegranate juice to a syrupy consistency, adds natural sweetness to marinades and sauces. Look for it in specialty foods stores or Middle Eastern markets. Accompany these lightly glazed skewers with whole-wheat couscous and sliced tomatoes. If you like, substitute chicken thigh meat for the lamb.

Soak 12 wooden skewers in water to cover for 30 minutes.

In a bowl, combine the pomegranate molasses, shallot, 1 Tbsp of the oil, and 1 tsp of the cumin; mix well. Add the lamb and stir to coat.

In a large bowl, combine the zucchini, bell pepper, onion, remaining 2 Tbsp oil, and remaining 1 tsp cumin. Sprinkle with salt and pepper and stir to coat.

Prepare a gas or charcoal grill for direct-heat grilling over high heat. Drain the skewers. Divide the lamb among 4 skewers; reserve the glaze remaining in the bowl. Sprinkle the lamb with salt and pepper. Divide the vegetables among 8 skewers, arranging them as you like. Brush the vegetables with the remaining glaze. Place the skewers on the grill. Cover the grill and cook the lamb as desired and the vegetables until they begin to brown and soften, about 5 minutes per side for medium-rare lamb and 6 minutes per side for the vegetables.

Sprinkle the skewers with mint and serve right away.

20

Ice cream sandwiches will make everyone smile—and get a little messy—at the end of an outdoor summertime dinner. Smash whatever kind of ice cream you like between the chocolate wafers: strawberry, vanilla, coffee, or mint chip. For an extra flourish, roll the edges in chopped toasted nuts, coconut, or mini chocolate chips before freezing.

ICE CREAM SANDWICHES

serves 6

1¼ cups (9 oz/280 g) firmly packed dark brown sugar

½ cup (4 oz/125 g) unsalted butter, plus more for greasing

3 oz (90 g) unsweetened chocolate, coarsely chopped

1 large egg

2 tsp pure vanilla extract

1¼ cups (6½ oz/200 g) all-purpose flour

¾ tsp baking soda

¼ tsp kosher salt

1½ cups (9 oz/280 g) semisweet chocolate chips

1½ pt (24 fl oz/750 ml) ice cream of choice, slightly softened

Preheat the oven to 350°F (180°C). Lightly butter 2 baking sheets.

In a heavy saucepan, cook the brown sugar, butter, and chopped chocolate over low heat, stirring frequently, until the chocolate melts. Transfer to a bowl and let cool to lukewarm.

Add the egg and vanilla to the chocolate mixture and whisk until smooth. In another bowl, whisk together the flour, baking soda, and salt. Add the dry ingredients to the chocolate mixture and stir until blended. Stir in the chocolate chips. Cover and refrigerate until firm, about 30 minutes.

Drop the dough by generous tablespoonfuls onto the prepared sheets, spacing the cookies at least 3 inches (7.5 cm) apart. You should have 12 cookies. With dampened fingers, smooth the cookies into slightly flattened rounds about 3 inches (7.5 cm) in diameter. Bake the cookies until the edges darken and the centers are still slightly soft, about 10 minutes. Transfer the cookies to wire racks to cool completely.

Lay half of the cookies, flat side up, on a work surface. Spread about ½ cup (4 fl oz/125 ml) of the ice cream on each cookie. Top each with one of the remaining cookies, flat side down. Smooth the sides and wrap each sandwich in plastic wrap. Lay on a clean, dry baking sheet and freeze until firm, at least 2 hours or up to 3 days.

21

Lemongrass is one of the main ingredients in the spice paste for this Vietnamese-inspired stir-fry. The distinctive lemon scent and flavor permeate the chicken while it marinates for at least 1 hour or preferably longer. Serve this bright-flavored stir-fry over steamed jasmine rice.

STIR-FRIED LEMONGRASS CHICKEN

serves 4–6

2 lemongrass stalks, center white part only, chopped

2 shallots, chopped

2 Tbsp peeled and chopped fresh ginger

3 cloves garlic, chopped

1 jalapeño chile, seeded and chopped

Salt and freshly ground pepper

5 Tbsp (3 fl oz/80 ml) canola oil

1½ lb (750 g) skinless, boneless chicken thighs, cut into 1-inch (2.5-cm) chunks

1 Tbsp soy sauce

1 Tbsp Asian fish sauce

1 tsp rice vinegar

½ tsp sugar

½ tsp cornstarch

1 small yellow onion, thinly sliced

2 Tbsp fresh basil leaves

Using a mini food processor or mortar and pestle, process or grind the lemongrass, shallots, ginger, garlic, chile, 1 tsp salt, and 1 Tbsp of the oil to form a smooth paste. Add 1–2 Tbsp water if needed to facilitate the grinding. Transfer the marinade to a large resealable plastic bag, add the chicken, and seal the bag. Turn the bag and gently massage the marinade into the chicken. Refrigerate for at least 1 hour or up to overnight.

In a small bowl, whisk together the soy sauce, fish sauce, vinegar, sugar, cornstarch, ⅛ tsp pepper, and 2 Tbsp water.

In a wok or large frying pan, warm 2 Tbsp of the oil over medium-high heat. Add the onion and stir-fry until tender and lightly browned, 7–8 minutes. Transfer to a bowl.

Remove the chicken from the marinade. Discard the marinade. In the same pan, heat the remaining 2 Tbsp oil over high heat. In batches, add the chicken and stir-fry until golden brown, 4–5 minutes. Return the onions to the pan. Pour in the soy sauce mixture and stir-fry until the sauce thickens and the chicken is opaque throughout, about 2 minutes. Transfer the stir-fry to a shallow serving bowl, garnish with basil, and serve.

22

CRISPY OKRA, CORN & SHRIMP SALAD WITH HARISSA DRESSING

serves 4

Here, grilled shrimp is treated to an imaginative triple-corn base of sweet fresh corn kernels, crunchy cornmeal-fried okra, and whimsical popped corn. Harissa, the spicy North African condiment, is toned down with a little creamy mayonnaise to dress the salad with just the right amount of heat.

2 Tbsp canola or grapeseed oil, plus more for frying

¼ cup (1½ oz/45 g) popcorn kernels

½ cup (4 fl oz/125 ml) mayonnaise

¼ cup (2 oz/60 g) harissa

2 Tbsp extra-virgin olive oil

Coarse sea salt and freshly ground pepper

12 medium shrimp, peeled and deveined

2 ears corn, husks and silk removed

2 large eggs

1 cup (5 oz/155 g) cornmeal

½ lb (250 g) okra, thinly sliced

Baby spinach for garnish (optional)

In a saucepan, warm the 2 Tbsp canola oil over medium-high heat. When it is hot, add the popcorn kernels, cover, and gently shake the pan over the heat. As the kernels begin to pop, continue shaking until there is only an occasional pop, about 3 minutes. Remove the pan from the heat and uncover it.

In a small bowl, stir together the mayonnaise, harissa, and olive oil until the dressing is well blended. Set aside.

Bring a pot of water to a boil over medium-high heat. Add 2 tsp salt and the shrimp and cook until just opaque and starting to curl, about 2 minutes. Using a slotted spoon, transfer the shrimp to a bowl and set aside.

Hold each ear of corn upright in a large bowl. Using a sharp knife, cut straight down between the kernels and the cob, rotating the ear about a quarter turn after each cut. Set aside.

Pour canola oil into a large frying pan to a depth of ¼ inch (6 mm) and heat over medium-high heat until it registers 375°F (190°C) on a deep-frying thermometer. Line a baking sheet with paper towels. In a shallow bowl, whisk the eggs until blended. In a second shallow bowl, stir together the cornmeal, 1 tsp salt, and 1 tsp pepper. Dip the okra slices into the eggs, allowing the excess to drip off, ⟩⟩

and then into the cornmeal, shaking off the excess. Add a few slices at a time to the hot oil. Do not crowd the pan. Fry, turning once, until lightly golden on both sides, about 1 minute per side. Using a slotted spoon, transfer to the paper towel–lined baking sheet. Repeat with the remaining okra.

Divide the popcorn and the corn kernels among individual plates. Top with the okra and place 3 shrimp alongside. Spoon 1 Tbsp of the dressing on each salad. Tuck spinach leaves along the edge of the salads, if desired, and serve with the remaining dressing on the side.

23

VIETNAMESE EGGPLANT CURRY

serves 4–6

Use either globe eggplants or smaller, more slender Asian eggplants for this recipe, both of which thrive in late summer. Leaving them unpeeled adds flavor and color to the dish and helps the eggplant pieces retain their shape when cooked. Serve with steamed jasmine rice.

3 Tbsp peanut or canola oil

1½ lb (750 g) Asian or globe eggplants, cut into 1-inch (2.5-cm) chunks

2 cloves garlic, minced

1 Tbsp Thai red curry paste

1 Tbsp Asian fish sauce (optional)

1 can (13½ fl oz/420 ml) unsweetened coconut milk

1 cup (8 fl oz/250 ml) vegetable or chicken broth

1 tsp grated lime zest

¾ lb (375 g) extra-firm tofu, rinsed, patted dry, and cut into ¾-inch (2-cm) chunks

3 green onions, white and tender green parts, thinly sliced

¼ cup (⅓ oz/10 g) chopped fresh cilantro

1 Tbsp fresh lime juice

Salt and freshly ground pepper

In a small, heavy pot, warm the oil over medium-high heat. Add the eggplant and sauté until just golden, 4–5 minutes. Stir in the garlic and sauté for 30 seconds. Stir in the curry paste and fish sauce (if using), and then the coconut milk, broth, and lime zest. Add the tofu, cover, reduce the heat to low, and simmer until the eggplant and tofu are soft but still hold their shape, 20–25 minutes.

Stir in the green onions, cilantro, and lime juice and season with salt and pepper. Serve.

24

AUGUST

PAN-ROASTED PORK MEDALLIONS WITH SUMMER VEGETABLES

serves 4

Mild in flavor, pork medallions have an affinity for tender summer vegetables. Pick out different colors of peppers and squashes for a particularly appealing dish. The herb oil, drizzled on just before serving, finishes the dish with the aroma of summertime.

FOR THE HERB OIL

¼ cup (¼ oz/7 g) loosely packed fresh basil leaves

¼ cup (¼ oz/7 g) loosely packed fresh tarragon leaves

⅔ cup (5 fl oz/160 ml) olive oil

1 pork tenderloin, about 1½ lb (750 g), silver skin removed, cut crosswise into 8 medallions

1 Tbsp olive oil, plus more for rubbing

Salt and freshly ground pepper

2 Tbsp unsalted butter

1 large shallot, minced

1 large red, orange, or yellow bell pepper, seeded and chopped

2 small zucchini, cut into very thin slices

1 yellow summer squash, cut into very thin slices

1 cup (6 oz/185 g) fresh corn kernels

To make the herb oil, bring a small saucepan of water to a boil. Add the basil and tarragon, stir once to immerse, and cook until bright green and wilted, about 45 seconds. Drain and rinse with cool water. Squeeze the herbs in a kitchen towel to extract as much water as possible. In a mini food processor, combine the herbs and oil. Pulse several times to blend thoroughly, scraping down the sides of the bowl as needed. Set aside.

Place the pork medallions between sheets of plastic wrap and, using the flat side of a meat mallet, pound to an even thickness of about 1¼ inches (3 cm). Rub both sides with a little oil. Let stand at room temperature for 15 minutes. Season both sides lightly with salt and pepper.

In a large frying pan, heat the 1 Tbsp oil over medium-high heat. Add the medallions and sear without moving them for 2 minutes. Turn and cook for 1 minute. Reduce the heat to very low and continue to cook, turning once, until the medallions are firm to the touch, about 1½ minutes per side. Transfer the medallions to a plate and tent with foil. »→

Pour off any oil from the pan. Place over medium-low heat and melt the butter. Add the shallot and bell pepper and sauté until the pepper is slightly softened, about 3 minutes. Add the zucchini, yellow squash, ½ tsp salt, and pepper to taste, and cook for about 3 minutes. Add the corn and cook, stirring occasionally, until the vegetables are tender but not mushy, about 2 minutes.

Arrange the medallions and vegetables on a platter. Drizzle generously with the herb oil and serve.

25

AUGUST

YELLOW GAZPACHO WITH LEMON-BASIL RICOTTA

serves 6–8

Adjust the spiciness of this ideal summertime soup as you like: add more hot sauce or even a fresh jalapeño. Serve the lemon-basil ricotta at room temperature so it incorporates easily. Any leftover ricotta makes a delicious spread for a vegetable sandwich wrap.

2 yellow bell peppers, seeded and chopped

1 English cucumber, peeled, seeded, and chopped

4 yellow tomatoes (about 2 lb/1 kg total), chopped, with all their juices

1 small yellow onion, chopped

2 cloves garlic, finely minced

2 Tbsp white wine vinegar

¼ cup (2 fl oz/60 ml) olive oil

Salt and freshly ground pepper

Tabasco sauce

FOR THE LEMON-BASIL RICOTTA

1 cup ricotta (8 oz/250 g), at room temperature

Grated zest of 1 lemon

¼ cup (⅓ oz/10 g) chopped basil

Salt

In a food processor, separately pulse the bell peppers, cucumber, tomatoes, and onion until finely chopped but not puréed. After processing each vegetable, transfer the contents to a large bowl. Add the garlic, white wine vinegar, and oil and stir to combine. Season to taste with salt, pepper, and Tabasco.

To make the lemon-basil ricotta, combine the ricotta, lemon zest, basil, and a pinch of salt in a bowl and stir to mix well.

Serve the gazpacho, topped with a dollop of lemon-basil ricotta.

26

FRIED ZUCCHINI WITH CURRY DIP

serves 4–6

Here, the zucchini is fried in a shallow layer of oil to ensure it stays crisp. For a pretty presentation, use a mix of green zucchini and yellow squashes. The dip, which can be made up to 3 days in advance, is also good served with steamed artichokes or roasted red potatoes.

FOR THE CURRY DIP

1 cup (8 fl oz/250 ml) mayonnaise

1 tsp curry powder

1 tsp fresh lemon juice

Salt

1 cup (4 oz/125 g) grated Parmesan cheese

¾ cup (2 oz/60 g) panko

2 Tbsp finely chopped fresh flat-leaf parsley

Salt and freshly ground pepper

2 eggs

3 zucchini, cut into pieces 3 inches (7.5 cm) long and 1 inch (2.5 cm) wide

Olive oil for frying

To make the dip, in a small bowl, stir together the mayonnaise, curry powder, and lemon juice. Season with ⅛ tsp salt and stir to combine.

Preheat the oven to 200°F (95°C). Line a large platter with paper towels. Pour oil to a depth of ½ inch (12 mm) into a deep, heavy frying pan and heat to 350°F (180°C) on a deep-frying thermometer or until a piece of zucchini slipped into the hot oil sizzles on contact.

Have ready a baking sheet. In a small bowl, stir together the Parmesan, panko, and parsley. Season with 1 tsp salt and ¼ tsp pepper and mix well. In another small bowl, beat the eggs just until blended. One at a time, dip each piece of zucchini into the eggs, allowing the excess to drip back into the bowl. Then dip it into the Parmesan mixture, coating evenly on all sides. Transfer to the baking sheet.

Working in batches of 5 or 6 pieces, fry the zucchini, turning as needed, until golden brown, about 2 minutes per side. Using a slotted spoon, transfer the zucchini to the paper towel–lined platter to drain and keep warm in the oven. Allow the oil to return to 350°F (180°C) between batches. Serve the zucchini hot, with the dip.

27

BRAISED BEEF TIPS WITH CRANBERRY BEANS, CHERRY TOMATOES & BASIL

serves 4

Shelling beans are harvested toward the end of summer and in early fall and can be eaten fresh or be left to dry. In this recipe, fresh cranberry beans, which have distinctive cream and red markings and a nutty flavor, are combined with beef, tomatoes, carrots, and other vegetables in an easy braise. Ask your butcher for sirloin tips for slow cooking, rather than for the more expensive filet mignon tips, which are best cooked quickly and eaten rare. Here, the beef becomes so tender you can cut it with a fork.

2 Tbsp olive oil

1½ lb (750 g) beef sirloin tips, cut into 1½-inch (4-cm) chunks

Salt and freshly ground pepper

1 large yellow onion, chopped

3 carrots, chopped

2 celery ribs, chopped

4 cloves garlic, minced

1½ cups (12 fl oz/375 ml) dry red wine

4 cups (32 fl oz/1 l) beef broth

2 Tbsp tomato paste

2 lb (1 kg) fresh cranberry beans, shelled

1 cup (6 oz/185 g) cherry tomatoes

⅓ cup (½ oz/15 g) chopped fresh basil

Preheat the oven to 350°F (180°C).

In a large, heavy ovenproofpot, heat the oil over medium-high heat. Season the beef with salt and pepper. Add to the pot and sear, turning as needed, until browned on all sides, 6–8 minutes. Transfer to a bowl.

Add the onion, carrots, celery, and garlic to the pot and sauté over medium-high heat until the vegetables are soft, about 8 minutes. Add the wine and stir to scrape up any browned bits on the pot bottom. Cook until the wine is reduced by half, 8–10 minutes. Add the broth and tomato paste and bring to a boil. Add the beef and any juices, cover, and cook in the oven until the meat is very tender, about 2½ hours.

Transfer the beef to a bowl. Strain the braising liquid, discarding the solids, then return the braising liquid and beef to the pot. Add the cranberry beans, tomatoes, and basil, stirring to combine. Cover and cook on the stove top over medium-high heat until the beans are tender, 15–20 minutes. Season with salt and pepper and serve directly from the pot.

28

This intensely flavored ice cream is for serious chocolate lovers. Natural peanut butter will pack the most nutty flavor. Be sure to stir it well before using to incorporate any oil that has settled on the top.

CHOCOLATE–PEANUT BUTTER ICE CREAM

makes about 1¾ qt (56 fl oz/1.75 l)

FOR THE CHOCOLATE ICE CREAM

2 cups (16 fl oz/500 ml) heavy cream

1½ cups (12 fl oz/375 ml) whole milk

7 large egg yolks

¾ cup (6 oz/185 g) granulated sugar

¼ cup (¾ oz/20 g) unsweetened natural cocoa powder, sifted

¼ tsp kosher salt

7 oz (220 g) bittersweet chocolate, finely chopped

2 tsp pure vanilla extract

6 Tbsp (3 oz/90 g) unsalted butter

¾ cup (3 oz/90 g) confectioners' sugar, sifted

¾ cup (7½ oz/235 g) crunchy natural peanut butter

3 Tbsp heavy cream

To make the chocolate ice cream, in a saucepan, warm the cream and milk over medium-high heat, stirring occasionally, until the mixture barely comes to a simmer, about 5 minutes. In a heatproof bowl, vigorously whisk the egg yolks, granulated sugar, cocoa, and salt until the mixture doubles in volume, about 2 minutes. Whisking constantly, slowly pour about 1 cup (8 fl oz/250 ml) of the warm cream mixture into the egg mixture and whisk until smooth. Pour into the saucepan, whisking constantly. Place over medium heat and add the chopped chocolate and vanilla. Stir until the chocolate melts and the mixture forms a custard thick enough to coat the back of a spoon, 1–2 minutes. Do not let it boil.

Pour the custard through a fine-mesh sieve into a bowl. Place in an ice bath and stir occasionally until the custard is cool. Cover the bowl and refrigerate until the custard is very cold, at least 4 hours or up to 3 days.

Just before churning the ice cream, in a bowl, using an electric mixer, beat the butter, confectioners' sugar, peanut butter, and cream on medium-high speed until light and fluffy, about 5 minutes.

Pour the cold chocolate custard into an ice cream maker and freeze according to the manufacturer's instructions. »→

Spoon half of the ice cream into a freezer-safe container. Top with dollops of the peanut butter mixture, using about half of it, and stir gently in a figure-eight motion to swirl the mixture into the ice cream. Repeat to swirl the remaining ice cream and peanut butter mixture. Place a piece of parchment paper directly on the surface. Cover and freeze until firm, at least 2 hours or up to 3 days, before serving.

29

Look for sustainably caught Pacific halibut and juicy tomatoes for this simple main course. Sprinkle the assembled dish with the garlic-herb mixture and the bread crumbs just before popping it into the oven. The crunchy topping that results adds a touch of elegance to the dish. Serve with white rice or fingerling potatoes.

HALIBUT PROVENÇAL

serves 4

3 Tbsp olive oil, plus more for greasing the baking dish

4 halibut fillets, 6–8 oz (185–250 g) each

Salt and freshly ground pepper

2 Tbsp dry white wine

1 lb (500 g) tomatoes, cut into slices ½ inch (12 mm) thick

1 clove garlic, minced

1 Tbsp chopped fresh tarragon

1 Tbsp chopped fresh flat-leaf parsley

¼ tsp fresh thyme leaves

2–3 Tbsp fine dried bread crumbs

Preheat the oven to 375°F (190°C). Lightly oil a baking dish just big enough to hold the fillets snugly in a single layer.

Place the fillets in the prepared dish. Sprinkle with salt and pepper and drizzle with the wine. Arrange the tomato slices in a single layer over the fish, overlapping them slightly if necessary.

In a small bowl, stir together 2 Tbsp of the oil and the garlic, tarragon, parsley, and thyme. Spoon the herb mixture evenly over the tomatoes, season with salt and pepper, and sprinkle with the bread crumbs. Drizzle with the remaining 1 Tbsp oil.

Transfer to the oven and cook until the bread crumbs are browned and the fish is opaque throughout but still moist in the center, 25–30 minutes. Arrange the fish and tomatoes on a platter and serve.

30

Chewy, flaky naan, India's best-known flatbread, is the perfect base for an herb-laced yogurt sauce and a smoky eggplant purée. Purchase whole-wheat naan for its greater nutrient content. If the cooked eggplant has big seed pockets, scoop them out and discard them before puréeing the flesh, as the seeds can be bitter. Garnish each serving with torn fresh mint leaves, if desired.

GRILLED NAAN WITH SMOKY EGGPLANT PURÉE & GRILLED RED ONIONS

serves 4–6

FOR THE HERBED YOGURT SAUCE

½ cup (4 oz/125 g) plain Greek yogurt

2 Tbsp finely chopped fresh flat-leaf parsley

1 Tbsp fresh lemon juice

1 clove garlic, minced

3 fresh mint leaves, finely chopped

Salt and freshly ground pepper

1 globe eggplant

2 cloves garlic, unpeeled

3 Tbsp tahini

2 Tbsp fresh lemon juice

2 Tbsp chopped fresh flat-leaf parsley

1½ tsp ground cumin

Salt and freshly ground pepper

1 red onion, halved and cut into ¾-inch (2-cm) slices

1½ Tbsp olive oil

½ tsp balsamic vinegar

4–6 pieces whole-wheat naan

To make the yogurt sauce, mix together the yogurt, parsley, lemon juice, garlic, and mint. Season with salt and pepper and set aside.

Preheat the broiler. Place the eggplant and garlic on a sheet pan and broil until blackened, turning as needed, about 15 minutes. Transfer to a bowl, cover with a kitchen towel, and let steam for 10 minutes. When cool enough to handle, peel the eggplant and garlic. Transfer the eggplant flesh and garlic to a food processor. Add the tahini, lemon juice, parsley, and cumin, and purée. Season with salt and pepper.

Warm a stove-top grill pan over high heat. In a bowl, toss the onion with ½ Tbsp oil and the vinegar and season with salt and pepper. Grill the onion, turning occasionally, until soft and caramelized, about 10 minutes. Transfer to a plate. Using the remaining oil, brush both sides of the naan and season with salt and pepper. Grill the naan until grill-marked, about 3 minutes per side.

Spread the sauce onto each naan, top with the eggplant purée and onions, and serve.

31

The annual corn season is winding down now, leaving you just enough time to make this easy Mexican-style soup. If you like, used home-roasted chicken thighs or store-bought rotisserie chicken in place of the turkey, and garnish each serving with finely diced red onion along with the avocado and cheese.

FRESH CORN SOUP WITH TURKEY & AVOCADO

serves 4–6

1 small bone-in, skin-on turkey breast, about 1¾ lb (875 g)

3 Tbsp olive oil, divided

Salt and freshly ground pepper

1 yellow onion, chopped

3 cloves garlic, chopped

½ jalapeño chile, seeded and minced

4 ears fresh corn, husks and silks removed, kernels cut from cobs

4 cups (32 fl oz/1 l) low-sodium chicken broth

¼ cup (⅓ oz/10 g) chopped fresh cilantro

2 avocados, pitted, peeled, and cubed

½ cup (2½ oz/75 g) crumbled queso fresco cheese (optional)

Preheat the oven to 400°F (200°C). Brush the turkey breast with 1 Tbsp of the oil and season well with salt and pepper. Roast until the turkey reads 165°F (74°C) when tested with a meat thermometer, 30–35 minutes. Remove and discard the skin and bones and cut the meat into ½-inch (12-mm) cubes. Set aside.

In a large, heavy saucepan, warm the remaining 2 Tbsp oil over medium-high heat. Add the onion, garlic, and jalapeño and sauté until the vegetables are soft, about 8 minutes. Stir in the corn kernels and season with salt and pepper. Sauté the corn just until it begins to soften, about 2 minutes. Add the broth and cubed turkey and bring to a boil. Reduce the heat to low and simmer for 10 minutes. Stir in the cilantro and adjust the seasoning with salt and pepper.

Ladle the soup into bowls, top each serving with avocado and queso fresco, if using, and serve.

As summer comes to a close, days begin to shorten and nights start to cool. Those changes bring on heartier appetites and more substantial fare, such as vegetable enchiladas, pork and quinoa casserole, and a chicken-packed potpie. Pumpkins and butternut, delicata, and other hard-skinned squashes begin to arrive in markets, ready for stirring into soups or stews or for filling pastas. And summer's stone fruits give way to flavorful figs, apples, and other fruits used in both savory mains and sweet finishes.

1
SALAD OF GRILLED PORK, PEARS & TOASTED PECANS
page 206

2
CHICKEN AGRODOLCE WITH DELICATA SQUASH
page 206

3
SOBA NOODLE SALAD WITH TOFU & MARINATED EGGPLANT
page 208

8
PLUM & LIME CRUMBLE
page 211

9
PUMPKIN-SAGE CANNELLONI
page 212

10
CHICKEN WITH CILANTRO & PUMPKIN SEED PESTO
page 212

15
CHORIZO & CHICKEN SOUP WITH AVOCADO CREMA
page 217

16
PORK TENDERLOIN WITH THYME & FIGS
page 217

17
WARM KALE & TUNA NIÇOISE
page 218

22
PORK, QUINOA & CHILE CASSEROLE
page 221

23
SPINACH-FETA QUICHE
page 223

24
LAMB & VEGETABLE KEBABS WITH INDIAN SPICES
page 223

29
CLASSIC BIRTHDAY CAKE
page 226

30
SPINACH, CORN & POTATO ENCHILADAS
page 226

4
**PASTINA & KALE SOUP
WITH ANDOUILLE**
page 208

5
**JERK CHICKEN WITH
PINEAPPLE SALSA**
page 209

6
**SWEET POTATO FRIES
WITH GARLIC & HERBS**
page 209

7
CHICKEN POTPIE
page 211

11
BEEF & PUMPKIN STEW
page 214

12
**GRILLED FIG & BACON KEBABS
WITH SHAVED PARMESAN**
page 214

13
**SPICED APPLE CAKE
WITH MAPLE FROSTING**
page 215

14
**PAN-ROASTED CLAMS
WITH POTATOES & FENNEL**
page 215

18
SPICY CAULIFLOWER GRATIN
page 218

19
**BRAISED DUCK LEGS WITH
PORT & FIGS**
page 220

20
**ZUCCHINI-PECORINO PURÉE
WITH ROASTED SALMON**
page 220

21
PUMPKIN TORTILLA SOUP
page 221

25
PROVENÇAL SEAFOOD STEW
page 224

26
CLASSIC CHOCOLATE CHIP COOKIES
page 224

27
**GREEN BEAN & POTATO SALAD
WITH HERBS & ANCHOVIES**
page 225

28
**FRESH SHELL BEANS WITH
BUTTERNUT SQUASH, BACON & SAGE**
page 225

september

1

SALAD OF GRILLED PORK, PEARS & TOASTED PECANS

serves 6

Ideal for a quick weeknight supper, this main-course salad matches grilled pork with the first pears of the season. If the weather is too chilly to fire up the grill, you can slip the tenderloins under the broiler.

½ cup (2 oz/60 g) pecans

1 Tbsp peanut oil

Salt and freshly ground pepper

Pinch of sugar

2 pork tenderloins, about ¾ lb (375 g) each, trimmed

1 Tbsp olive oil

FOR THE HAZELNUT VINAIGRETTE

6 Tbsp (3 fl oz/90 ml) olive oil

2½ Tbsp sherry vinegar

1 Tbsp hazelnut oil

2 firm but ripe pears, preferably Bosc

6 handfuls (about 6 oz/185 g) mixed salad greens

Preheat the oven to 350°F (180°C). In a bowl, combine the pecans, peanut oil, salt and pepper to taste, and sugar and toss well to coat the nuts. Spread the pecans evenly on a baking sheet and bake until lightly golden, 5–7 minutes. Let cool.

Prepare a charcoal or gas grill for direct-heat cooking over high heat, or preheat the broiler.

Brush the pork tenderloins with the 1 Tbsp olive oil and season with salt and pepper. Place on the grill rack or on a broiler pan 4 inches (10 cm) from the heat source and cook, turning occasionally to brown evenly, until an instant-read thermometer inserted into the thickest part registers 150°F (66°C) or the pork is pale pink when cut in the thickest portion, about 12 minutes. Transfer to a cutting board, cover loosely with foil, and let rest for 2–3 minutes before carving. Cut crosswise into slices ¼ inch (6 mm) thick.

To make the vinaigrette, in a small bowl, whisk together the 6 Tbsp olive oil, vinegar, and salt and pepper to taste. Add the hazelnut oil in a thin stream, whisking constantly until the dressing is smooth.

Halve, core, and cut the pears lengthwise into very thin slices. In a large bowl, combine the greens, pecans, and vinaigrette and toss to mix well. Arrange the dressed greens on a platter or individual plates, top with the pork and pear slices, and serve.

2

CHICKEN AGRODOLCE WITH DELICATA SQUASH

serves 4

Agrodolce, literally "sour-sweet," is a traditional sauce style popular in Italy, especially in the south. Here, the sweetness comes from honey and orange juice, while lemon juice and balsamic vinegar provide the sour element. As the dish cooks, the flavors deepen and the sauce thickens and caramelizes. Pour a Pinot Noir or other medium-bodied red wine.

½ cup (2½ oz/75 g) all-purpose flour

Salt and freshly ground black pepper

4 chicken drumsticks

4 skin-on, bone-in chicken thighs

4 Tbsp (2 fl oz/60 ml) olive oil

3 bay leaves

10 allspice berries

3 cloves garlic, sliced

1 small delicata squash, peeled and cut into 1-inch (2.5-cm) pieces

1 large red onion, cut into 1-inch (2.5-cm) pieces

¼ cup (3 oz/90 g) honey

¼ cup (2 fl oz/60 ml) balsamic vinegar

½ cup (4 fl oz/125 ml) dry white wine

½ cup (4 fl oz/125 ml) fresh orange juice

¼ cup (2 fl oz/60 ml) fresh lemon juice

¼ tsp cayenne pepper

3 Tbsp pine nuts, toasted

Spread the flour on a plate and season with salt and black pepper. Dredge each of the chicken pieces in the flour.

In a large, heavy pot, warm 3 Tbsp of the oil over medium-high heat. Add the bay leaves, allspice, and chicken pieces and cook, turning the chicken once, until browned, about 7 minutes. Transfer the chicken to a plate.

Add the remaining 1 Tbsp oil to the pot and heat over medium-high heat. Add the garlic, squash, and red onion, and sauté until the vegetables begin to caramelize, about 8 minutes. Add the honey, vinegar, and wine, and cook until the liquid is reduced by half, about 6 minutes. Add the orange juice, the lemon juice, 1 tsp salt, ½ tsp black pepper, and the cayenne, and stir to combine. Nestle the chicken in the liquid and bring to a boil. Reduce the heat to low, cover, and simmer for 15 minutes. Uncover, turn the chicken, and continue cooking until the sauce is thickened and the chicken is opaque throughout, about 15 minutes. Add the pine nuts and cook just until the nuts begin to soften, 2–3 minutes. Remove from the heat and serve.

3

Asian eggplants remain in markets in late summer and early fall. Here, they are cubed, marinated in a mixture of sesame oil and soy, cooked until tender, and then tossed with golden cubes of stir-fried tofu. If you cannot find Japanese soba noodles at the store, thin whole-wheat spaghetti makes a good substitute.

SOBA NOODLE SALAD WITH TOFU & MARINATED EGGPLANT

serves 4

FOR THE MARINADE

1 Tbsp toasted sesame oil

2 Tbsp sherry vinegar

2 Tbsp soy sauce

½ tsp sugar

1 clove garlic, chopped

FOR THE DRESSING

½ tsp toasted sesame oil

1 Tbsp sherry vinegar

1 tsp soy sauce

2 tsp peanut oil

1 Tbsp grated fresh ginger

3 Japanese eggplants, trimmed

Salt

8 oz (250 g) soba noodles

½ tsp peanut oil, plus 2 Tbsp, or as needed

12 oz (375 g) firm tofu, cut into ½-inch (12-mm) cubes

5 green onions, including tender green parts, thinly sliced

To make the marinade, in a large bowl, combine the sesame oil, vinegar, soy sauce, sugar, and garlic and stir well. Set aside.

To make the dressing, in a large bowl, combine the sesame oil, vinegar, soy sauce, peanut oil, and ginger and stir to mix well. Set aside.

Halve the eggplants lengthwise and cut into ½-inch (12-mm) pieces. Add to the bowl with the marinade, toss, and let stand for at least 1 hour.

In a large saucepan over medium-high heat, bring 4 cups (32 fl oz/1 l) water to a boil. Reduce the heat to medium, add 1 tsp salt and the soba noodles, and cook until tender but not mushy, about 6 minutes. Drain and rinse with cold water until cool. Drain again, transfer to a bowl, and toss with the ½ tsp peanut oil. Set aside.

In a wok over medium-high heat, warm the 2 Tbsp peanut oil, tilting the wok to coat the pan. »→

When the oil is hot, add the eggplant cubes and cook, turning until they are golden and tender, 3–5 minutes. Remove with a slotted spoon and set aside. Put the tofu cubes in the wok, adding more oil if needed, and cook until they are just golden, 3–4 minutes. Remove and set aside along with the eggplant.

Put the soba noodles in the bowl with the dressing and turn to coat. Add the eggplant and tofu and mix and coat. Sprinkle with the green onions and serve.

4

This soup is flavor packed, thanks to the spicy andouille, and nutrition rich, thanks to the kale. Serve with bruschetta rubbed with garlic and topped with chopped ripe tomatoes and fresh basil.

PASTINA & KALE SOUP WITH ANDOUILLE

serves 4

1 cup (7 oz/200 g) small soup pasta, such as stelline, orzo, or ditalini

3 links andouille sausage (10 oz/315 g)

1 Tbsp olive oil

1 yellow onion, chopped

2 cloves garlic, minced

1 bunch kale, ribs removed, leaves chopped

4 cups (32 fl oz/1 l) chicken broth

1 Tbsp tomato paste

Salt and freshly ground pepper

Grated Parmesan cheese

Bring a pot of salted water to a boil over high heat. Add the pasta and cook until al dente, according to package directions. Drain and set aside.

In a large, heavy pot, cook the sausage over medium heat until no longer pink in the center, about 15 minutes. Remove from the pot and cut into slices ¼ inch (6 mm) thick.

Add the oil to the pot and warm over medium-high heat. Add the onion and garlic and sauté until translucent, about 5 minutes. Add the kale, stir to coat, and sauté for 3–4 minutes. Add the broth and bring to a boil. Reduce the heat to low. Add the pasta, sausage, and tomato paste and stir well to combine. Simmer, stirring often, for 5 minutes. Season with salt and pepper and serve, topped with the Parmesan.

5

Here, a tangy, mildly spiced pineapple salsa is paired with fiery Jamaican-style grilled chicken. Serve this dish with a salad of your favorite greens tossed with cucumbers, bell peppers, and a light vinaigrette. Leftover pineapple can be cubed and used in smoothies or sliced and sautéed in a little butter and brown sugar for a simple dessert.

JERK CHICKEN WITH PINEAPPLE SALSA

serves 6

FOR THE JERK PASTE

3 *each* green onions and garlic cloves, chopped

1–3 habanero chiles, seeded and chopped

¼ cup (2 fl oz/60 ml) *each* fresh lime juice and extra-virgin olive oil

2 Tbsp low-sodium soy sauce

1 Tbsp *each* firmly packed light brown sugar and chopped fresh thyme

2 tsp ground allspice

1 tsp freshly grated nutmeg

½ tsp ground cinnamon

Salt and freshly ground pepper

6 whole chicken legs

FOR THE PINEAPPLE SALSA

4 thick slices peeled, cored fresh pineapple

1 red onion, thickly sliced

Olive oil, for drizzling

1 jalapeño chile

½ avocado, peeled and diced

1 Tbsp finely chopped fresh mint

Juice of 1 lime

Salt

To make the jerk paste, in a blender, combine the green onions, garlic, chiles, lime juice, oil, soy sauce, sugar, thyme, allspice, nutmeg, cinnamon, and 2 tsp each of salt and pepper. Process until smooth.

Coat the chicken evenly on all sides with the jerk paste. Cover and refrigerate for at least 8 hours or up to overnight. Remove from the refrigerator 30 minutes before grilling.

Prepare a grill for direct-heat cooking over high heat. Oil the grill grate. To make the salsa, drizzle the pineapple and onion slices with oil, then place on the grill. Cook, turning once, until each piece is grill marked and heated through, about 8 minutes total. Cook the chile, turning, until charred on all sides. Chop the pineapple and onion into chunks and place in a bowl. When the chile is cool enough to handle, peel, stem, seed, and dice it, then add it to the bowl. Stir in the avocado and mint. Add the lime juice, stir again, and season with salt. ⟫

Let the grill cool to medium heat. If using charcoal, bank the coals on either side of the grill, leaving a strip in the center without heat. If using gas, turn off 1 burner to create a cooler zone. Brush and oil the grill grate.

Place the chicken on the grill over the direct-heat area and sear, turning once, until nicely browned on both sides, about 2 minutes on each side. Move the chicken to the indirect-heat area and cook until firm to the touch and an instant-read thermometer inserted into the thickest part of the thigh away from bone registers 170°F (77°C), about 30 minutes. Transfer the chicken to a platter and let rest for 10 minutes. Serve, passing the salsa at the table.

6

Anyone who likes classic French fries is guaranteed to like these cheese-and-herb-dusted sweet potato fries. They are roasted rather than deep-fried, which cuts calories dramatically without sacrificing flavor. Leaving the peel on adds more taste and texture to the dish and more nutrients to your diet. If your pocketbook allows, splurge on either Maldon sea salt or fleur de sel.

SWEET POTATO FRIES WITH GARLIC & HERBS

serves 4

2 lb (1 kg) orange-fleshed sweet potatoes

2 Tbsp olive oil

Coarse sea salt

3 Tbsp grated Parmesan cheese

2 Tbsp chopped fresh flat-leaf parsley

1 clove garlic, minced

Preheat the oven to 450°F (230°C).

Rinse and dry the sweet potatoes. Cut the unpeeled potatoes lengthwise into slices ½ inch (12 mm) thick, and then cut each slice into batons about ¼ inch (6 mm) wide and 3 inches (7.5 cm) long.

Place the potatoes on a baking sheet. Drizzle with the oil, sprinkle with ¼ tsp salt, and toss to coat. Spread the potatoes out evenly. Roast, stirring with a spatula midway through, until the potatoes are tender and browned on the edges, 20–25 minutes.

In a large bowl, stir together the Parmesan, parsley, and garlic. Add the warm fries and mix gently to coat. Season with salt and serve.

CHICKEN POTPIE

serves 4–6

As the weather cools and the days begin to shorten, hunker down with comfort foods. Kids and adults alike are unable to resist the charms of chicken in a creamy sauce studded with peas and carrots and topped with flaky pastry.

FOR THE PIE DOUGH

1½ cups (7½ oz/235 g) all-purpose flour

Salt

6 Tbsp (3 oz/90 g) cold vegetable shortening

2 Tbsp cold unsalted butter

About ⅓ cup (3 fl oz/80 ml) cold water

Salt and freshly ground pepper

1 cup (4 oz/125 g) sliced carrots (¼-inch/6-mm slices)

1 cup (5 oz/155 g) fresh or frozen peas

1 cup (6 oz/185 g) corn kernels (from 2–3 ears)

2 Tbsp unsalted butter

4 skinless, boneless chicken thighs, about 1¼ lb (625 g) total, cut into bite-sized chunks

2 Tbsp chopped shallot

¼ cup (1½ oz/45 g) all-purpose flour

1½ cups (12 fl oz/375 ml) chicken broth

½ cup (4 fl oz/125 ml) dry white wine

½ cup (4 fl oz/125 ml) half-and-half

1 Tbsp chopped fresh flat-leaf parsley

1 egg yolk beaten with 1 tsp water

To make the dough, stir together the flour and 1 tsp salt. Using a pastry blender, cut in the shortening and butter until a coarse meal forms. Toss with a fork while adding enough of the water for the dough to clump together. Form into a disk, wrap in plastic wrap, and refrigerate for 30 minutes.

Meanwhile, preheat the oven to 400°F (200°C). Bring a saucepan of salted water to a boil. Add the carrots and peas and cook until tender-crisp, 3–5 minutes. Using a slotted spoon, transfer to a colander and drain, then transfer to a bowl. Repeat with the corn, cooking it for 1 minute.

In a large frying pan, melt the butter over medium-high heat. Add the chicken and cook, stirring occasionally, until browned on all sides, about 8 minutes. Add the shallot and cook, stirring, until softened, about 2 minutes. Sprinkle in the flour and stir well. Stir in the broth, wine, half-and-half, and parsley and bring to a simmer. Cover, reduce the heat to low, and simmer for 10 minutes. Stir in the carrots, peas, and corn. Season with salt and pepper. Transfer to a 9-inch (23-cm) pie dish. →→

On a floured work surface, roll out the dough into a round about ⅛ inch (3 mm) thick and large enough to fit over the pie dish. Brush some of the egg yolk mixture in a 1-inch (2.5-cm) border around the edge of the round. Place the round, egg side down, over the filling, and press the dough to the rim of the dish. Crimp or trim off any overhanging dough and brush the surface lightly with the remaining egg yolk mixture. Cut a few slits in the center of the top.

Place the pie dish on a baking sheet. Bake until the crust is golden brown, about 30 minutes. Remove from the oven and serve.

PLUM & LIME CRUMBLE

serves 6–8

The flavor of red-fleshed plums pairs well with citrusy lime zest in this sweet-tart crumble. If you like, use an assortment of red plum varieties— Satsuma, Elephant Heart, Black Splendor—or mix plums with Pluots or Apriums. You can also bake this crumble in eight ½-cup (4-oz/125-g) individual ramekins for 30 minutes.

FOR THE CRUMBLE TOPPING

1½ cups (7½ oz/235 g) all-purpose flour

¾ cup (6 oz/185 g) sugar

1 tsp kosher salt

1 cup (8 oz/250 g) cold unsalted butter, cut into pieces

1 cup (3 oz/90 g) rolled oats

3½ lb (1.75 kg) red plums, pitted and sliced

Finely grated zest from 2 limes

¾ cup (6 oz/185 g) sugar

¼ cup (1½ oz/45 g) all-purpose flour

Vanilla ice cream for serving (optional)

Preheat the oven to 375°F (190°C). In a food processor, pulse the flour, sugar, and salt until combined. Add the butter and pulse until the mixture resembles coarse crumbs. Add the oats and pulse to combine. Transfer to a bowl.

In a bowl, stir together the plums, lime zest, sugar, and flour. Spread the fruit in a 9-by-13-inch (23-by-33-cm) baking dish. Using your fingers, press the topping into large clumps and scatter over the fruit.

Bake until the fruit is bubbling and the topping is golden and crisp, about 1 hour. Serve warm or at room temperature with ice cream, if you like.

9

Fresh pumpkin and sage create a flavorful and aromatic filling for pasta shells. You can substitute butternut squash for the pumpkin, but don't use canned pumpkin, which "has a high water content that may affect the texture." Serve the cannelloni with garlicky sautéed greens, such as spinach or kale, on the side.

PUMPKIN-SAGE CANNELLONI

serves 6

3 lb (1.5 kg) baking pumpkin

3 Tbsp olive oil

Salt and freshly ground pepper

8 oz (250 g) cannelloni pasta shells

5 Tbsp (2½ oz/75 g) unsalted butter

1 yellow onion, chopped

3 cloves garlic, minced

¼ cup (⅓ oz/10 g) fresh sage leaves, chopped

¾ cup (6 oz/185 g) ricotta cheese

1 cup (4 oz/125 g) plus 3 Tbsp grated Parmesan cheese

1 egg, lightly beaten

3 Tbsp flour

3 cups (24 fl oz/750 ml) whole milk

Preheat the oven to 450°F (230°C). Halve the pumpkin and scoop out the seeds, then cut into wedges and trim away the peel. Cut the flesh into ½-inch (12 mm) chunks. Toss the pumpkin with 2 Tbsp of the oil, season with salt and pepper, and lay it in a single layer on a baking sheet lined with parchment paper. Roast in the oven until the pumpkin is caramelized, about 30 minutes. Set aside.

Reduce the oven to 375°F (190°C) and position a rack in the upper third of the oven. Bring a large pot of salted water to a boil over medium-high heat. Add the cannelloni shells and cook for 7 minutes. Drain the pasta and lay the shells on a baking sheet so they don't stick together. Set aside.

In a frying pan, melt 2 Tbsp of the butter over medium-high heat. Add the onion and the garlic and sauté until very soft, about 5 minutes. Add the sage, season with salt and pepper, and continue to cook for 2 minutes. Stir in the pumpkin and, using a potato masher or a fork, smash the pumpkin, leaving some small chunks. Cook for another 3 minutes and transfer to a large bowl. Add the ricotta, ⅓ cup (1½ oz/45 g) of the Parmesan cheese, and the egg and stir to combine. Set aside.

In a small saucepan, melt the remaining 3 Tbsp butter over medium-high heat. Add the flour and cook, stirring, for 2 minutes. ⟫→

Add the milk and bring to a boil. Add ⅔ cup (2½ oz/80 g) of the Parmesan and stir until it is melted. Season to taste with salt and pepper.

Cover the bottom of a 9-by-13-inch (23-by-33-cm) baking dish with a thin layer of the sauce. Fill each cannelloni shell with the pumpkin mixture and place in the baking dish in a single layer. Top with the remaining sauce and the remaining 3 Tbsp Parmesan cheese. Cover tightly with foil and bake on the top rack for 30 minutes. Remove the foil and continue to bake until warmed through and the top is lightly browned, about 15 minutes. Serve directly from the dish.

10

Pumpkin seeds add protein and an earthy nuttiness to pesto. They're also chock-full of nutrients. If you like, toast extra pumpkin seeds to munch on while you're cooking the chicken.

CHICKEN WITH CILANTRO & PUMPKIN SEED PESTO

serves 4

½ cup (2 oz/60 g) hulled pumpkin seeds

2 cups (2 oz/60 g) packed cilantro leaves

5 Tbsp (3 fl oz/80 ml) olive oil, plus more for greasing

3 Tbsp fresh lime juice

1 clove garlic

½ serrano chile, seeded

Salt and freshly ground pepper

4 boneless, skinless chicken breast halves, about 6 oz (185 g) each

Preheat the oven to 350°F (180°C). Spread the pumpkin seeds on a baking sheet and toast until fragrant and just golden, 8–10 minutes.

In a food processor, purée the toasted pumpkin seeds, cilantro, 4 Tbsp (2 fl oz/60 ml) of the oil, the lime juice, garlic, chile, ¼ tsp salt, and ¼ cup (2 fl oz/60 ml) water until smooth, scraping down the sides of the bowl with a rubber spatula as needed.

Prepare a grill for direct-heat cooking over medium-high heat, and oil the rack. Brush the chicken on both sides with the remaining 1 Tbsp oil and season with salt and pepper. Grill, turning once, until cooked through, 12–13 minutes.

Transfer the chicken to warmed plates, spoon the pesto on top, and serve.

11

BEEF & PUMPKIN STEW

serves 6

3 lb (1.5 kg) beef bottom round, cut into 1¼-inch (3-cm) chunks

Salt and freshly ground pepper

2 Tbsp olive oil

1 yellow onion, finely chopped

2 sprigs fresh thyme

3 bay leaves

4 cloves garlic, minced

1 cinnamon stick

⅓ cup (3 fl oz/80 ml) dry red wine

2 Tbsp plus 1 tsp red wine vinegar

2 carrots, cut into ¾-inch (2-cm) chunks

1 can (14½ oz/455 g) diced tomatoes, drained

⅓ cup (3 fl oz/80 ml) beef or chicken broth

1 lb (500 g) baking pumpkin or butternut squash, peeled, seeded, and cut into ¾-inch (2-cm) chunks

2 green onions, thinly sliced

1 Tbsp chopped fresh mint

In this late-summer, early-autumn healthful take on a traditional dish, the addition of a light vinaigrette laced with green onions and peppery mint just before serving infuses the stew with bright, fresh flavors. If you like, serve this hearty stew over steamed couscous.

Season the beef well with salt and pepper. In a large, heavy frying pan, warm 1 Tbsp of the oil over medium-high heat. Working in batches, add the beef and sauté until golden brown on all sides, about 8 minutes. Using a slotted spoon, transfer to a plate.

Pour off most of the fat from the pan and return to medium-high heat. Add the onion, thyme sprigs, and bay leaves and sauté until the onion begins to brown, about 6 minutes. Add the garlic and cinnamon and cook for 1 minute. Pour in the wine and the 2 Tbsp vinegar and stir to scrape up any browned bits on the pan bottom. Transfer the contents of the pan to a slow cooker and stir in the carrots, tomatoes, and broth. Add the beef, cover, and cook on the low setting for 5 hours.

Scatter the pumpkin over the top of the beef, re-cover, and continue to cook for 3 hours. The beef and pumpkin should be very tender. Remove and discard the cinnamon stick, thyme sprigs, and bay leaves. Let the stew stand 5 minutes, then skim the fat from the cooking liquid.

In a bowl, whisk together the remaining 1 Tbsp olive oil and the 1 tsp vinegar, ¼ tsp salt, and several grindings of pepper. Stir in the green onions and mint. Spoon over the stew, and serve.

12

GRILLED FIG & BACON KEBABS WITH SHAVED PARMESAN

serves 6–8

2-oz (60-g) piece Parmesan cheese

16 figs (any variety)

5 Tbsp (3 fl oz/80 ml) extra-virgin olive oil

⅓–½ lb (155–250 g) thick bacon slices, cut into pieces 1½ inches (4 cm) long

3 tsp sherry vinegar

Salt and freshly ground pepper

5 cups (5 oz/155 g) baby arugula

Fig leaves for serving (optional)

The salty-sweet combination of figs and bacon is always popular, and serving these skewers on peppery arugula heightens the flavors. Figs arrive in the market in shades of crimson, green, brown, purple, yellow, and cream. Select those that are fully ripe, indicated by softness and a bent neck, or stem. If a fig is firm to the touch, pass it up, as its sugars have not developed, and it will not ripen off the tree.

If using wooden skewers, soak 16 skewers in water for 30 minutes, then drain.

Using a vegetable peeler, shave the cheese into thin pieces. Set aside.

Place the figs in a single layer in a shallow baking dish. Drizzle with 2 Tbsp of the oil and turn gently to coat them.

Thread one piece of bacon onto a skewer, pushing it toward the top, then thread on a fig and push it toward the top. Add another piece of bacon, leaving a long length of skewer empty to use as a handle. Repeat with the remaining skewers, bacon, and figs. Set aside.

In a bowl, whisk together the remaining 3 Tbsp oil, the vinegar, ¼ tsp salt, and ¼ tsp pepper until the vinaigrette is well blended. Set aside.

Prepare a charcoal or gas grill for direct-heat cooking over medium-high heat. Alternatively, preheat a stove-top grill pan over medium-high heat. Place the skewers on the grill rack or in the grill pan and cook, turning once or twice, until the fig skins start to glisten and lightly char and the bacon browns on the outside, 3–5 minutes.

Add the arugula to the bowl with the vinaigrette and toss to coat well.

Line a platter with fig leaves, if desired. Mound the salad on top, scatter with the cheese, and place the kebabs on the platter. Serve hot or warm.

13

This versatile cake can be dressed up or simplified depending on the occasion. Bake it in a rectangular pan and cut it into squares for a school lunch box, or spread it with a rich maple frosting and take it to a party. Use a soft, tart apple, such as Gravenstein or McIntosh. Pippin or Granny Smith apples work well, too.

SPICED APPLE CAKE WITH MAPLE FROSTING

serves 10–12

2 cups (10 oz/315 g) all-purpose flour

1 tsp baking powder

1 tsp baking soda

1 tsp ground cinnamon

½ tsp freshly grated nutmeg

½ tsp kosher salt

¾ cup (6 oz/185 g) unsalted butter, at cool room temperature

1½ cups (12 oz/375 g) granulated sugar

3 large eggs

½ cup (4 fl oz/125 ml) buttermilk

2 cups (8 oz/250 g) peeled, cored, and diced apples

FOR THE MAPLE FROSTING

1 cup (11 oz/345 g) pure maple syrup

¼ cup (2 oz/60 g) unsalted butter

½ cup (4 fl oz/125 ml) heavy cream

1 tsp pure vanilla extract

2 cups (8 oz/250 g) confectioners' sugar

Preheat the oven to 350°F (180°C). Butter the bottom and sides of a 9-by-13-inch (23-by-33-cm) baking pan.

Sift the flour, baking powder, baking soda, cinnamon, nutmeg, and salt together onto a sheet of parchment paper.

In a large bowl, using an electric mixer, beat the butter and granulated sugar on medium-high speed until light and fluffy, 3–5 minutes. Beat in the eggs one at a time, beating well after each addition. Using a rubber spatula, gently fold in one-third of the dry ingredients until almost fully incorporated. Fold in one-half of the buttermilk, then fold in another third of the flour mixture, followed by the remaining buttermilk. Add the remaining flour mixture and the apples, and fold in just until the batter is smooth and the flour is incorporated. Do not fold too vigorously, or the cake will be tough.

Spread the batter in the prepared pan. Bake the cake until the top is brown and a toothpick inserted into the center comes out clean, 35–40 minutes. Watch the time closely at the end so that the cake does not overbake. »→

Let cool completely in the pan on a wire rack while you make the frosting.

To make the maple frosting, in a saucepan, simmer the maple syrup over medium-high heat until it reduces by half, about 15 minutes. Stir in the butter. Remove from the heat and stir in the cream and vanilla. Sift the confectioners' sugar into a bowl. Pour the warm maple mixture over the sugar and beat with a whisk until smooth and creamy. Let cool completely before using it to frost the cake.

14

Nothing could be easier and tastier than this one-pan meal of tender red potatoes, aromatic fennel, pale gold garlic, and briny littleneck clams. Red pepper flakes and dry white wine finish the dish, mixing with the clams' juices to create a sauce with just a hint of heat.

PAN-ROASTED CLAMS WITH POTATOES & FENNEL

serves 4

2 lb (1 kg) baby red potatoes, quartered

1 fennel bulb, cut into slices ¼ inch (6 mm) thick, any fronds reserved for garnish

5 cloves garlic, roughly chopped

¼ cup (2 fl oz/60 ml) olive oil

Salt and freshly ground black pepper

4 lb (2 kg) littleneck clams, scrubbed and soaked

½ tsp red pepper flakes

¼ cup (2 fl oz/60 ml) dry white wine

Preheat the oven to 475°F (245°C).

Heat a large roasting pan over medium-high heat. Add the potatoes, fennel slices, garlic, and oil. Season with 1 tsp salt and ¼ tsp black pepper. Cook, stirring, for about 5 minutes. Transfer the pan to the oven and roast until the potatoes have browned, about 20 minutes.

Add the clams, discarding any that do not close to the touch, and the red pepper flakes. Cover the pan and roast, stirring the clams once, until most of the clams have opened, about 15 minutes. Remove the pan from the oven, pour in the wine, cover, and let stand for 1 minute. Discard any unopened clams. Garnish with fennel fronds and serve.

CHORIZO & CHICKEN SOUP WITH AVOCADO CREMA

serves 4–6

1 skinless, boneless chicken breast half

½ lb (250 g) Mexican chorizo, cut into slices ½ inch (12 mm) thick

2 Tbsp olive oil

1 yellow onion, chopped

2 cloves garlic, minced

1 red bell pepper, seeded and chopped

4 cups (32 fl oz/1 l) chicken broth

1 Tbsp minced fresh thyme

Salt and freshly ground pepper

FOR THE AVOCADO CREMA

1 avocado, pitted and peeled

¼ cup (2 oz/60 g) sour cream

1 Tbsp fresh lime juice

Salt

For the avocado crema, lime juice and sour cream are added to mashed avocados for a smooth, tangy version of guacamole. It melts into this soup, adding a creamy element and also helping to tame the spiciness of the chorizo.

In a small saucepan, combine the chicken breast with cold water to cover by 1 inch (2.5 cm) and bring to a boil over high heat. Reduce the heat to low and simmer until the chicken is cooked through, 15–18 minutes, skimming off any foam on the surface. Remove the chicken from the pan. When it is cool enough to handle, shred the meat.

Warm a large, heavy pot over medium-high heat. Add the chorizo and cook, stirring often, until browned on both sides, about 8 minutes. Transfer to a bowl. Add the oil and warm over medium-high heat. Add the onion and garlic and sauté until translucent, about 5 minutes. Add the bell pepper, stir to coat, and cook for 3 minutes. Add the shredded chicken, chorizo, broth, and thyme and simmer, uncovered, for about 15 minutes to blend the flavors. Season with salt and pepper.

To make the avocado crema, put the avocado in a small bowl and mash with a fork until creamy and smooth. Add the sour cream, the lime juice, and 2 large pinches of salt and stir to combine.

Serve the soup, accompanied by the avocado crema.

PORK TENDERLOIN WITH THYME & FIGS

serves 4

8 Mission figs, quartered

¾ cup (6 fl oz/180 ml) dry red wine

1 pork tenderloin, about 1¼ lb (625 g)

Salt and freshly ground pepper

1 Tbsp olive oil

3 fresh thyme sprigs

1 Tbsp fig jam

1 tsp grated lemon zest

Figs have an unbeatable sweet taste and rich texture and are irresistible when roasted in pork drippings. Despite their luscious character, they are a good source of many vitamins and minerals and are a relatively low-calorie fruit. Wilted kale dressed in a garlic vinaigrette would be an ideal side dish.

Place the figs and wine in a small saucepan over medium-high heat. Bring to a boil, reduce the heat to low, and simmer for 5 minutes. Remove from the heat, let stand for 15 minutes, and drain the figs, reserving the wine.

Preheat the oven to 400°F (200°C). Pat the pork dry. Trim any excess fat and silvery membrane. Sprinkle with salt and pepper.

Heat the oil in an ovenproof frying pan over high heat. Add the tenderloin and turn to brown on all sides, about 4 minutes total. Arrange the figs and thyme sprigs around the pork. Transfer the pan to the oven and bake until a thermometer inserted into thickest part of the meat reaches 140°F (60°C), 18–25 minutes.

Transfer the tenderloin and figs to a platter. Cover with foil and let rest for 10 minutes. Meanwhile, add the reserved wine, jam, and lemon zest to the frying pan. Bring to a boil over high heat, stirring to scrape up any browned bits from the bottom of the pan, until the mixture is reduced to ½ cup (4 fl oz/125 ml), 4–5 minutes. Remove and discard the thyme.

Slice the pork tenderloin diagonally across the grain into pieces ½ inch (12 mm) thick. Arrange the figs around the pork on a platter, spoon the sauce over both, and serve.

17

WARM KALE & TUNA NIÇOISE

serves 4

6 small yellow potatoes

Salt and freshly ground pepper

¾ lb (375 g) green beans

3 Tbsp olive oil

½ cup (2½ oz/75 g) pitted Kalamata olives, halved lengthwise

2 anchovies packed in oil, chopped

2 cloves garlic, chopped

2 bunches kale, stemmed and chopped

1 lemon, halved

1 lb (500 g) sushi-grade ahi tuna

4 hard-boiled eggs, quartered

½ cup (3 oz/90 g) cherry tomatoes, halved

Extra-virgin olive oil, for drizzling

Niçoise-style salads are typically composed salads, meaning the ingredients are plated in a decorative manner rather than tossed together. This version is a hybrid of the two salad styles. Deep green, curly-leaved kale adds a strong nutritional punch here and is especially flavorful sautéed with anchovies, capers, and olives. Although seared ahi tuna makes a beautiful presentation, it can be replaced with canned tuna packed in oil, the tuna traditionally used in niçoise salads in France.

Place the potatoes in a saucepan with 1 tsp of salt and cover with cold water by 2 inches (5 cm). Bring to a boil then reduce the heat to low and cook until the potatoes are fork-tender, 20–25 minutes. Drain, then cut into quarters when cool enough to handle. Set aside.

Refill the saucepan with water and bring to a boil over high heat. Add a big pinch of salt and the green beans and cook until just tender, about 3 minutes. Drain and rinse under cold running water. Set aside.

Warm 2 Tbsp of the olive oil in a frying pan over medium-high heat. Add the olives, anchovies, and garlic and sauté until the garlic is soft, about 3 minutes. Add the kale and cook, stirring often, until wilted, about 5 minutes. Squeeze half the lemon on the kale and season with salt and pepper. Transfer the kale to 4 plates, dividing evenly.

Warm the remaining 1 Tbsp olive oil in the frying pan over high heat. Season both sides of the tuna with salt and pepper. Sear the tuna until browned on the outside but still pink in the middle, about 1½ minutes per side. Transfer to a cutting board and slice. Divide the tuna among the 4 plates on top of the kale.

Garnish the plate with the potatoes, green beans, hard-boiled eggs, and tomatoes and drizzle with extra-virgin olive oil and the juice from the remaining half lemon. Top with freshly ground pepper and serve.

18

SPICY CAULIFLOWER GRATIN

serves 4

1 medium head cauliflower

1½ Tbsp butter

3½ Tbsp all-purpose flour

1½ cups (12 fl oz/375 ml) whole milk

Salt and freshly ground black pepper

⅓ cup (⅔ oz/20 g) fresh bread crumbs

1 Tbsp capers, drained

1 tsp red pepper flakes

A bubbling béchamel sauce highlights the best qualities of cruciferous vegetables, especially mildly cabbagey, highly nutritious cauliflower florets. Here, the classic sauce is updated with a sprinkling of capers and red pepper flakes, with the latter packing a pleasant hint of heat.

Preheat the oven to 400°F (200°C). Butter a baking dish.

In a large saucepan fitted with a steamer basket, bring 1–2 inches (5–7.5 cm) of water to a boil. Add the cauliflower, cover, and cook until nearly fork-tender, 15–20 minutes. Transfer to a cutting board and let cool. Cut the cauliflower lengthwise into 8 spearlike wedges and arrange in the prepared dish.

In a saucepan, melt 1 Tbsp of the butter over medium heat. Remove from the heat and whisk in the flour. Return to medium heat and slowly add the milk, whisking constantly. Reduce the heat to low, add 1 tsp salt and ½ tsp black pepper, and cook, whisking occasionally, until the sauce is thickened and smooth, about 15 minutes.

In a small frying pan, melt the remaining ½ Tbsp butter over medium heat. Add the bread crumbs and cook, stirring often, until golden, 3–4 minutes.

Stir the capers and red pepper flakes into the sauce and pour over the cauliflower. Sprinkle evenly with the toasted bread crumbs. Bake until the sauce is bubbling and the edges are golden, about 30 minutes. Remove from the oven and serve.

19

BRAISED DUCK LEGS WITH PORT & FIGS

serves 6

1½ tsp ground coriander

½ tsp ground allspice

Salt and freshly ground pepper

6 duck legs

¼ cup (2 fl oz/60 ml) olive oil

1½ cups (12 fl oz/375 ml) ruby port

1 cup (8 fl oz/250 ml) chicken broth

1 yellow onion, quartered and each quarter stuck with 1 clove

2 bay leaves

2 cloves garlic, crushed

6 juniper berries, slightly crushed

3 strips orange zest, each about 4 inches (10 cm) long

2 tsp fresh rosemary leaves

2 tsp fresh thyme leaves

18 dried figs, halved

2 Tbsp honey

2 Tbsp chopped fresh chives

Dried figs pair exceptionally well with port and duck. Trim away any visible fat from the duck during prep and skim off the fat after cooking. The duck can be prepared a day in advance and stored in the braising liquid. Before serving, remove the solidified fat and reheat the duck in a Dutch oven, adding the figs and honey and continuing with the final step of reducing the sauce before serving.

In a small bowl, stir together the coriander, allspice, 1½ tsp salt, and ¾ tsp pepper. Rub the spice mixture all over the duck legs. In a large, heavy pot, heat the oil over high heat. Working in batches, sear the duck legs, skin side down, until brown, about 5 minutes per side. Transfer to a plate.

Pour off most of the fat from the pot. Add the port, taking care to avoid splattering, and stir to scrape up any browned bits on the pot bottom. Bring to a boil and cook until reduced by about half, about 10 minutes. Stir in the broth and bring to a boil.

Preheat the oven to 325°F (165°C). Return the duck legs to the pot. Spoon the port mixture over the duck. Add the onion quarters, bay leaves, garlic, juniper berries, orange zest, rosemary, and thyme. Reduce the heat to low, cover, and cook for 1½ hours. Uncover and skim as much of the fat as possible from the surface. Immerse the figs in the cooking liquid around the duck legs and drizzle with the honey. Cover and cook until the duck is tender, about 30 minutes.

Transfer the duck and figs to a serving platter and cover loosely with foil. ↠

Simmer the cooking liquid briskly over medium-high heat until reduced to a light syrupy consistency, 10–12 minutes. Spoon the sauce over the duck legs, garnish with the chives, and serve.

20

ZUCCHINI-PECORINO SOUP WITH ROASTED SALMON

serves 4

4 Tbsp (2 fl oz/60 ml) olive oil

2 shallots, chopped

2 lb (1 kg) zucchini, chopped

Salt and freshly ground pepper

2 cups (16 fl oz/500 ml) vegetable or chicken broth

¼ cup (1 oz/30 g) grated pecorino romano cheese

Grated zest and juice of 1 lemon

1 lb (500 g) center-cut salmon, preferably wild, cut into 4 equal pieces, skin and pin bones removed

Although this recipe includes two components, the puréed soup and the roasted salmon, it comes together quickly. Have the fish ready to slip into the hot oven just before the soup is ready. The pecorino romano cheese pairs well with zucchini, but a different Italian grating cheese, such as Parmesan, Asiago, or grana padano, can be substituted.

In a large, heavy pot, warm 2 Tbsp of the oil over medium-high heat. Add the shallots and cook, stirring occasionally, until soft, about 4 minutes. Add the zucchini, season with salt and pepper, and cook, stirring occasionally, until the zucchini begins to soften, about 4 minutes. Add the broth and bring to a boil. Reduce the heat to low and cook until the zucchini is tender, about 15 minutes. Let cool slightly.

Working in batches, purée the soup in a food processor or blender. Return it to the pot and place over medium heat. Add the cheese and stir until it melts, about 4 minutes. Stir in the lemon juice and season with salt and pepper. Keep warm over low heat.

Preheat the oven to 400°F (200°C). Line a baking sheet with aluminum foil. Brush the salmon with the remaining 2 Tbsp oil and season with salt and pepper. Place on the prepared baking sheet and roast until opaque throughout, about 8 minutes.

Serve the soup, topped with a piece of salmon and a sprinkling of the lemon zest.

21

PUMPKIN TORTILLA SOUP

serves 4–6

3 corn tortillas

3 Tbsp canola or vegetable oil

Salt and freshly ground pepper

½ white onion, chopped

2 cloves garlic, chopped

1 small jalapeño chile, seeded, deribbed, and chopped

2 tsp ground cumin

½ tsp dried Mexican oregano

1 can (14½ oz/455 g) fire-roasted diced tomatoes with juices

1 can (15 oz/470 g) black beans, drained

3 cups (24 fl oz/750 ml) vegetable or chicken broth

3 cups (20 oz/625 g) cubed peeled pumpkin (1-inch/2.5-cm cubes)

1 avocado, pitted, peeled, and cubed

½ cup (2 oz/60 g) shredded Monterey jack cheese (optional)

3 green onions, white and tender green parts, chopped

2 radishes, stemmed, halved, and thinly sliced

This vegetarian version of the popular tortilla soup is equally satisfying. You can trade out the cool-weather pumpkin used here for fresh corn in the summer and for mushrooms in the spring. Serve with cheese quesadillas and with a salad of sliced oranges and sweet onions dressed with a toasted-cumin vinaigrette.

Preheat the oven to 450°F (230°C). Stack the tortillas and cut them in half, then into ½-inch (12-mm) strips. In a bowl, toss together the tortilla strips and 1 Tbsp of the oil. Place in a single layer on a baking sheet and season generously with salt. Bake until golden brown and crispy, about 5 minutes. Set aside.

In a large, heavy pot, warm the remaining 2 Tbsp oil over medium-high heat. Add the white onion and cook, stirring occasionally, until soft, about 6 minutes. Add the garlic and jalapeño and cook, stirring occasionally, until soft, about 2 minutes. Stir in the cumin and oregano, and season with salt and pepper. Cook, stirring, to toast the spices, about 1 minute. Add the tomatoes with their juices, the beans, and broth and bring to a boil. Add the pumpkin, reduce the heat to low, and simmer until the pumpkin is fork-tender, 15–18 minutes. Season with salt and pepper.

Serve, topped with the tortilla strips, avocado, cheese (if using), green onions, and radishes.

22

PORK, QUINOA & CHILE CASSEROLE

serves 4

2 tsp canola or grapeseed oil

½ cup (3 oz/90 g) quinoa, rinsed

Salt and freshly ground pepper

1 Tbsp olive oil

1 lb (500 g) boneless pork loin, cut into 1-inch (2.5-cm) chunks

2–5 serrano chiles, seeded and chopped

¼ cup (1 oz/30 g) chopped onion

2 cloves garlic, minced

½–1 tsp chili powder

½ tsp ground cumin

½ cup (4 fl oz/125 ml) chicken broth

¼ cup (1 oz/30 g) shredded Monterey jack or manchego cheese

12 pitted oil-cured black olives

Quinoa cooks in just minutes, making it a good choice for a busy weeknight. Here, it is mixed with pork, chiles, and pungent spices and then topped with olives and cheese and baked, in a contemporary take on Tex-Mex cuisine.

Preheat the oven to 375°F (190°C).

In a saucepan, heat the canola oil over medium-high heat. Add the quinoa and sauté until the grains separate and are opaque, 3–4 minutes. Add 1 cup (8 fl oz/ 250 ml) water and ½ tsp salt and bring to a boil. Reduce the heat to low, cover, and simmer until the quinoa is tender, about 12 minutes. Drain in a fine-mesh sieve.

In a large, heavy pot, heat the olive oil over medium-high heat. Add the pork and cook, turning as needed, until lightly browned on all sides, 4–5 minutes. Stir in the chiles, onion, and garlic, and sprinkle with the chili powder, cumin, and ½ tsp salt. Cook until the onion is soft, about 2 minutes.

Add the broth and stir to scrape up any browned bits on the pan bottom. Remove from the heat, add the quinoa, and toss and stir until the ingredients are evenly distributed. Sprinkle with the cheese and dot with the olives. Bake, uncovered, until the cheese is melted and the pork is opaque throughout, about 15 minutes. Serve.

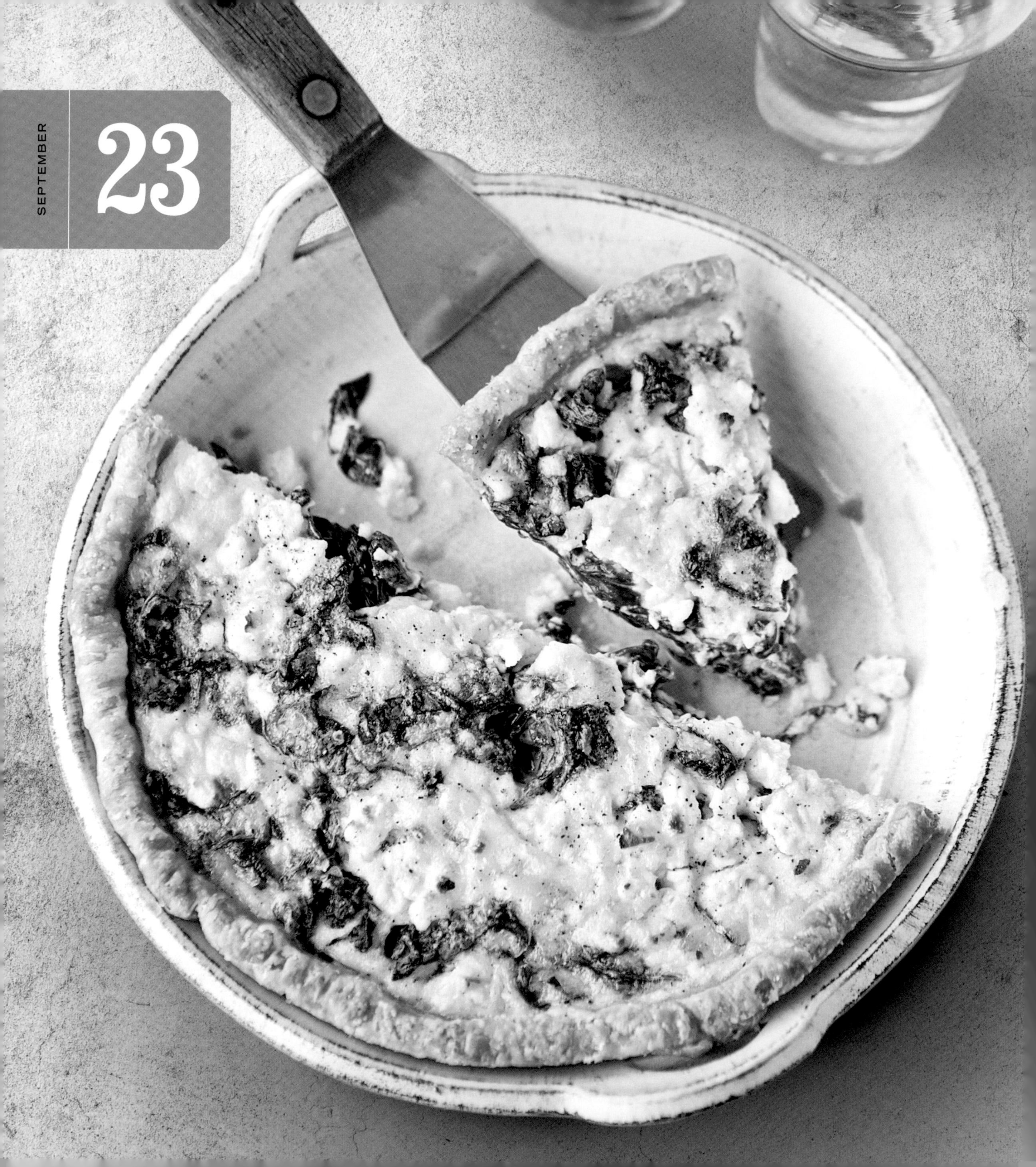

23

*Quiche was
traditionally offered
as a first course,
but now it is more
commonly served
as a main course at
brunch or lunchtime.
You can move it to
the dinner menu
with a filling of
early-autumn
greens and briny,
sharp cheese. Here,
spinach is used, but
Swiss chard or kale,
minus the stems,
can be substituted.*

SPINACH-FETA QUICHE

serves 8

FOR THE TART DOUGH

1⅓ cups (7 oz/220 g) all-purpose flour

1 Tbsp sugar

Salt

½ cup (4 oz/125 g) cold unsalted butter,
cut into small pieces

4 Tbsp (2 fl oz/60 ml) ice water,
or more as needed

1 cup (1 oz/30 g) steamed fresh spinach
or thawed frozen spinach, drained
and squeezed completely dry

3 eggs

Salt and freshly ground pepper

Pinch of grated nutmeg

¾ cup (6 fl oz/180 ml) heavy cream

¾ cup (6 fl oz/180 ml) whole milk

1 cup (5 oz/155 g) crumbled feta cheese

1 Tbsp unsalted butter, cut into
¼-inch (6-mm) pieces

To make the tart dough, in a food processor,
combine the flour, sugar, and ¼ tsp salt. Pulse
to mix. Add the butter and pulse 8 times.
Add the 4 Tbsp ice water and pulse about
10 times. If the dough crumbles, add more ice
water, 1 Tbsp at a time, and pulse just until
the dough holds together. Transfer the dough
to a floured work surface, shape into a 6-inch
(15-cm) disk, wrap in plastic wrap, and
refrigerate for at least 1 hour or up to overnight.

Preheat the oven to 400°F (200°C). On a
floured work surface, roll out the dough
into a round about 10½ inches (26.5 cm) in
diameter and ¼ inch (6 mm) thick. Carefully
transfer it to a 9-inch (23-cm) quiche pan
or other straight-sided pan with 1-inch
(2.5-cm) sides. Press the dough into the
bottom and sides of the pan. Pinch the dough
around the rim to form a fluted edge.

Line the dough with foil and fill with pie
weights or dried beans. Bake until the
crust is dry, about 15 minutes. Remove from
the oven and lift out the weights and foil.
Transfer to a wire rack. Reduce the oven
temperature to 350°F (180°C) and set a rack
in the bottom third of the oven.

Arrange the spinach evenly in the prebaked
crust. In a large bowl, whisk together ⟶

the eggs, ½ tsp salt, ⅛ tsp pepper, and
nutmeg. Add the cream and milk and whisk
until well blended. Slowly pour the egg
mixture over the spinach in the crust. Dot
the top with the cheese and the butter.

Bake on the bottom oven rack until the top
is lightly browned and the filling is just
barely set, 40–45 minutes. Transfer to the
wire rack and let stand for 5 minutes.
Cut into wedges and serve.

24

*Grilling lamb
chunks on skewers
is a healthy
alternative to
panfrying and
roasting because
the fat
drips away from
the meat. Serve
these kebabs with
a sauce of plain
Greek yogurt
flavored with
coarsely grated
cucumber, crushed
garlic, olive oil,
lemon juice,
and mint.*

LAMB & VEGETABLE KEBABS WITH INDIAN SPICES

serves 6

2 lb (1 kg) boneless leg of lamb, trimmed of
excess fat and cut into 1-inch (2.5-cm) chunks

2 Tbsp garam masala

Olive oil, for brushing

2 green bell peppers, seeded and
cut into thick slices

2 Asian eggplants, cut crosswise into
thick slices

6 green onions, trimmed and
cut into 3-inch (7.5-cm) pieces

6 cherry tomatoes

Season the lamb with the garam masala.
Cover and refrigerate for at least 6 hours
or up to overnight.

At least 1 hour before you are ready to
begin grilling, remove the lamb from the
refrigerator. If using wooden skewers, soak
6–12 of them in water for at least 30 minutes.
Prepare a grill for direct-heat cooking over
high heat. Brush and oil the grill grate.
Thread the lamb chunks, bell pepper,
eggplant, green onions, and cherry tomatoes
onto the skewers, dividing them evenly, and
beginning and ending with a lamb chunk.
Grill the skewers directly over the heat,
turning frequently, until the vegetables
are tender and the lamb is nicely browned,
12–15 minutes for medium-rare to medium.
Transfer the skewers to a platter and let
rest for 5 minutes.

Slide the lamb and the vegetables off the
skewers onto a platter and serve.

25

Based on Provençal bouillabaisse, this stew is much simpler to make but still has the flavors of the classic. The traditional oil- or mayonnaise-based rouille has been replaced with a puréed mixture of sautéed red bell peppers, garlic, and shallots, for a lighter, lower-calorie garnish. You can replace part of the scallops or squid with shrimp for a more varied seafood mix. At the table, pour a white or rosé wine from Provence, a rich white Burgundy, or a Sauvignon Blanc.

PROVENÇAL SEAFOOD STEW

serves 4

FOR THE ROUILLE

1 Tbsp olive oil

2 Tbsp minced shallots

3 cloves garlic, chopped

¼ tsp red pepper flakes

Salt

2 red bell peppers, roasted, peeled, seeded, and chopped

½ lb (250 g) small yellow potatoes, cut into ¼-inch (6-mm) cubes

3 Tbsp olive oil

1 lb (500 g) scallops, tough muscles removed

Salt and freshly ground black pepper

¾ lb (375 g) cleaned squid, bodies cut into ½-inch (12-mm) rings and tentacles coarsely chopped

1 fennel bulb, stalks and fronds discarded, quartered, cored, and sliced

4 cloves garlic, chopped

3 Tbsp shallots, chopped

2 tomatoes, chopped

½ cup (4 fl oz/125 ml) dry white wine

2 cups (16 fl oz/500 ml) fish stock or bottled clam juice

2 Tbsp chopped fresh flat-leaf parsley

To make the rouille, in a small saucepan over medium heat, warm the oil. Add the shallots and garlic and sauté until softened, about 2 minutes. Add the red pepper flakes, season with salt, and sauté for 30 seconds more. Add the bell peppers, stir to combine, and cook until they begin to break down, about 4 minutes. Allow to cool slightly, then purée in a blender and season to taste with salt.

Boil the potatoes in salted water until tender, about 20 minutes. Drain and set aside.

In a large saucepan over medium-high heat, warm 1 Tbsp of the oil. Pat the scallops dry with a paper towel and season with salt and black pepper. Sear until golden and medium-rare, about 3 minutes per side. Transfer to a plate. Warm another 1 Tbsp oil in the saucepan. Season the squid with salt and pepper, add it to the pan, and sauté until opaque, about 3 minutes. Transfer the squid to the plate.

Add the remaining 1 Tbsp oil to the saucepan and warm over medium heat. ⟫

Add the fennel, garlic, and shallots and sauté until soft, about 5 minutes. Add the tomatoes and season with salt and black pepper. Sauté until the tomatoes begin to soften and release their juices, about 4 minutes. Add the wine and cook until the liquid is reduced by half, 2–3 minutes. Add the stock and potatoes and bring to a boil. Turn off the heat and add the scallops and the squid with all the juices on the plate. Season with salt and black pepper and ladle into shallow bowls. Top with a dollop of rouille, garnish with parsley, and serve.

26

These cookies are crisp on the outside, chewy on the inside, and are studded with just the right amount of meltingly rich semisweet chocolate. Switch up the flavor by using 2 cups (12 oz/375 g) mixed chocolate chips, such as semisweet, white, and milk.

CLASSIC CHOCOLATE CHIP COOKIES

makes about 30 cookies

1¼ cups (6½ oz/200 g) all-purpose flour

1 tsp baking soda

½ tsp kosher salt

½ cup (4 oz/125 g) unsalted butter, at cool room temperature

½ cup (3½ oz/105 g) firmly packed light brown sugar

⅓ cup (3 oz/90 g) granulated sugar

1 large egg

1 tsp pure vanilla extract

2 cups (12 oz/375 g) semisweet chocolate chips

Preheat the oven to 350°F (180°C). Line 2 baking sheets with parchment paper.

Sift the flour, baking soda, and salt together into a bowl. In a large bowl, using an electric mixer, beat the butter and sugars on medium speed until smooth. Add the egg and vanilla and beat on low speed until well blended. Slowly add the dry ingredients and beat on low speed until just incorporated. Mix in the chocolate chips.

Drop the dough by heaping tablespoonfuls onto the prepared sheets, spacing them about 2 inches (5 cm) apart. Bake the cookies, 1 sheet at a time, until the bottoms and edges are lightly browned and the tops feel firm when lightly touched, 10–13 minutes. Let the cookies cool on the pans for 5 minutes, then transfer them to wire racks to cool completely.

27

Look for anchovies packed in oil in small jars, which typically offer better flavor and texture than the canned options. This pungent Italian-inspired dressing would also complement sliced tomatoes, grilled squash or eggplant, or a pasta salad with cherry tomatoes.

GREEN BEAN & POTATO SALAD WITH HERBS & ANCHOVIES

serves 6–8

1 lb (500 g) green beans

3 lb (1.5 kg) small potatoes, preferably Yukon Gold

6 olive oil–packed anchovy fillets

2 small shallots

1 large clove garlic

½ tsp sugar

1 tsp Dijon mustard

½ cup (½ oz/15 oz) fresh basil leaves

½ cup (½ oz/15 oz) fresh tarragon leaves

½ cup (½ oz/15 oz) fresh flat-leaf parsley leaves

6 Tbsp (3 fl oz/90 ml) white wine vinegar

¾ cup (6 fl oz/180 ml) olive oil

Salt and freshly ground pepper

Bring a saucepan of salted water to a boil. Add the green beans and cook until bright green and just tender-crisp, about 4 minutes. Drain the beans in a colander, rinse under cold running water, and drain again.

In the same saucepan, combine the potatoes and water to cover by 1 inch (2.5 cm) and bring to a boil. Reduce the heat to medium, cover partially, and simmer until the potatoes are just tender when pierced with a knife, 8–10 minutes. Drain and let cool. Cut the potatoes into thick slices or small chunks. Transfer to a large bowl.

In a food processor, combine the anchovies, shallots, and garlic and pulse until minced. Add the sugar, mustard, basil, tarragon, parsley, vinegar, and oil and process until a relatively smooth dressing forms, about 10 seconds.

Add about three-fourths of the dressing to the warm potatoes and toss well to coat. Add the green beans, the remaining dressing, 1¼ tsp salt, and ¼ tsp pepper. Toss well and serve.

28

Woodsy sage pairs nicely with a variety of early-autumn vegetables, like creamy cubes of sweet butternut squash and earthy shelling beans. Toasted pecans and salty bacon provide contrasting tastes and textures.

FRESH SHELL BEANS WITH BUTTERNUT SQUASH, BACON & SAGE

serves 4

1 lb (500 g) fresh shelling beans such as cranberry beans, shelled

1 small butternut squash, about 1½ lb (750 g)

2 thick slices bacon

1½ Tbsp minced fresh sage

Olive oil for drizzling

Sea salt and freshly ground pepper

¼ cup (1 oz/30 g) pecan halves, toasted

Bring a large saucepan of water to a boil. Add the beans, reduce the heat to medium, and simmer until the beans are tender but not falling apart, 25–30 minutes. Drain the beans.

Halve the squash lengthwise and scoop out and discard the seeds. Cut the skin away from the flesh, and cut the flesh into ½-inch (12-mm) cubes.

Heat a frying pan over medium heat. Add the bacon and cook, turning once, until browned and crisp, 7–9 minutes. Transfer to paper towels to drain. Pour off all but 1 Tbsp of the bacon fat from the pan. When the bacon has cooled, crumble it into pieces.

Warm the bacon fat over medium-high heat. Add the squash and cook, stirring frequently, until lightly browned and just tender when pierced with a knife, 8–10 minutes. Add the sage and beans, drizzle with oil, and season lightly with salt and pepper. Cook, stirring frequently, until the beans are heated through and the flavors are blended, about 1 minute. Stir in the bacon and pecans. Transfer to a platter and serve.

29

CLASSIC BIRTHDAY CAKE

serves 10–12

2¾ cups (11 oz/345 g) cake flour

3 tsp baking powder

½ tsp kosher salt

1 cup (8 oz/250 g) unsalted butter,
at room temperature

1¾ cups (14 oz/440 g) sugar

4 large whole eggs and 2 large egg yolks

2 tsp pure vanilla extract

1 cup (8 oz/250 g) sour cream

Dark Chocolate Frosting (see page 86)

A moist yellow layer cake bound by rich chocolate frosting is a time-tested favorite. A few crumbs may come away as you start to frost, but that's a promising sign of a tender cake. Just seal them in as best you can and keep smoothing the frosting over the top.

Preheat the oven to 350°F (180°C). Butter the bottoms of three 9-inch (23-cm) round cake pans. Line with parchment paper. Lightly butter the parchment and sides of the pans and lightly dust with flour.

Sift the flour, baking powder, and salt together into a bowl. In the bowl of a stand mixer fitted with the paddle attachment, beat the butter and sugar on medium-high speed until fluffy. Add the whole eggs and yolks one at a time, beating well after each addition. Beat in the vanilla. Beating on low speed, add half of the dry ingredients and beat until combined. Beat in the sour cream and then the remaining dry ingredients, beating until combined.

Divide the batter among the prepared pans. Bake until a toothpick inserted into the center of the cakes comes out clean, about 15 minutes. Let the cakes cool in the pans on wire racks for 15 minutes, then invert onto the racks, peel off the parchment, and let cool completely before frosting.

Brush away any loose crumbs from the cake layers. Place one layer, top side down, on a flat plate. With an icing spatula, spread a layer of frosting evenly on top. Place the second cake layer, top side down, on the first layer, press gently, and spread a layer of frosting on top. Place the third cake layer, top side down, on the second layer, and press gently. Spread frosting all over the entire cake. Keep covered at room temperature until ready to serve.

30

SPINACH, CORN & POTATO ENCHILADAS

serves 6

2 large baking potatoes

1 Tbsp olive oil

1 large red bell pepper, seeded and diced

1 yellow onion, coarsely chopped

½ cup (3 oz/90 g) fresh or frozen corn kernels

10 oz (315 g) spinach leaves, thinly sliced

1 can (28 fl oz/875 ml) enchilada sauce

Salt and freshly ground pepper

12 corn tortillas

¼ lb (125 g) Cheddar cheese, shredded

Many enchilada recipes call for frying the tortillas, but in this healthier version, they are dipped into the sauce without frying them first. Don't leave the tortillas in the sauce too long, however, or they'll fall apart. Serve these vegetarian enchiladas with a green salad and your favorite Mexican beer.

Preheat the oven to 375°F (190°C). Place the potatoes on a baking sheet and bake until tender when pierced with the tip of a knife, 40–45 minutes. Let cool completely, then dice and set aside. Reduce the oven temperature to 350°F (180°C).

In a saucepan over medium-high heat, warm the oil. Add the bell pepper and onion and sauté until softened, about 5 minutes. Add the potatoes, corn, and spinach. Add 1 cup (8 fl oz/250 ml) of the enchilada sauce and mix well. Place over medium heat, cover tightly, and cook until the spinach is wilted, 5–6 minutes. Remove from the heat, season with salt and pepper, and set aside.

Pour ½ cup (4 fl oz/125 ml) of the remaining enchilada sauce into a 9-by-13-inch (23-by-33-cm) baking dish and spread to cover the bottom of the dish.

In a wide frying pan over medium heat, warm the remaining enchilada sauce. One at a time, dip each tortilla into the warm sauce, allowing it to warm just enough to become pliable. Place it in the prepared baking dish, and spoon about one-twelfth of the potato mixture along its center. Roll it up and arrange it in the dish, seam side down. Repeat with remaining tortillas and filling. The dish should be tightly packed.

Pour any sauce remaining in the pan over the enchiladas. Sprinkle with the cheese. Bake until the enchiladas are heated through and the cheese is melted, 20–25 minutes. Serve directly from the dish.

The signs of fall deepen in October, when the juicy fruits, colorful vegetables, and delicate greens of summer begin to disappear, to be replaced by roots and tubers, sturdier greens, and a growing cast of winter squashes. Tacos are a favorite menu item this month, folded around seasonal root vegetables or wrapped around spicy shrimp and red cabbage slaw. Big soups show up, too, with chickpeas and meatballs and with split peas and kabocha squash. Fall fruit continues to shine in both mains, such as pork chops with Asian pears, and desserts, including a pear crisp and an apple tart.

1
ROOT VEGETABLE TACOS WITH LIME-CILANTRO CREAM
page 230

2
CHICKPEA & SWEET POTATO CURRY
page 230

3
APPLE FRANGIPANE TART
page 233

8
BAKED GNOCCHI WITH TALEGGIO, PANCETTA & SAGE
page 235

9
POLENTA CROSTINI WITH CHANTERELLES
page 236

10
LAMB SHOULDER WITH SALSA VERDE
page 236

15
ROASTED CAULIFLOWER & PARMESAN SOUP
page 241

16
BIBIMBOP WITH BROWN RICE & BULGOGI
page 241

17
GLAZED CRANBERRY-LEMON CAKE
page 242

22
GRILLED PORK CHOPS WITH ASIAN PEARS & TORPEDO ONIONS
page 244

23
THREE-BEAN SALAD WITH CORIANDER VINAIGRETTE
page 246

24
SPICY SHRIMP TACOS WITH RED CABBAGE SLAW
page 246

29
SESAME NOODLES WITH GRILLED CHICKEN, CARROTS & EDAMAME
page 249

30
CHICKPEA & TURKEY MEATBALL SOUP WITH MUSTARD GREENS
page 250

31
OATMEAL PEAR CRISP
page 250

4
SPICED BUTTERNUT SQUASH TAGINE
page 233

5
CURRIED YELLOW SPLIT PEA SOUP WITH KABOCHA SQUASH
page 234

6
BRAISED CHICKEN WITH PEPPERS, OLIVES & CAPERS
page 234

7
ACORN SQUASH & CHORIZO TART
page 235

11
BROCCOLI & CAULIFLOWER WITH PICKLED ONIONS & BACON
page 238

12
ROASTED SNAPPER & BELGIAN ENDIVE
page 238

13
MISSISSIPPI MUD PIE
page 239

14
CHEDDAR & HARD CIDER SOUP WITH FRIED SHALLOTS
page 239

18
CHILE VERDE
page 242

19
ARUGULA & FENNEL SALAD WITH BLACK PEPPER–CRUSTED TUNA
page 243

20
PUMPKIN PURÉE WITH TOASTED PUMPKIN SEEDS
page 243

21
FISH TAGINE WITH CARROTS & OLIVES
page 244

25
RICOTTA WITH HONEY & FIGS
page 247

26
BUTTERNUT SQUASH PIZZA
page 247

27
SPANISH CHICKEN STEW
page 247

28
ALE-BRAISED SHORT RIBS
page 249

october

1

ROOT VEGETABLE TACOS WITH LIME-CILANTRO CREAM

serves 4–6

Root vegetables make this vegetarian main dish filling and original. Adjust the amount of chili powder based on how much heat you want. In the summer months, substitute grilled seasonal vegetables that have marinated in the spice mixture for the root vegetables. Serve with pinto or black beans on the side and ice-cold Mexican beer.

2 sweet potatoes, peeled and chopped

4 parsnips, peeled and cut into ¼-inch (6-mm) dice

2 Tbsp canola oil

1 Tbsp ground cumin

1 tsp ground coriander

½ tsp chili powder

Salt

FOR THE LIME-CILANTRO CREAM

½ cup (4 oz/125 g) sour cream

¼ cup (⅓ oz/10 g) finely chopped fresh cilantro, plus more for garnish

Juice of 1 lime

Salt and freshly ground pepper

FOR THE TOMATILLO SALSA

6 tomatillos, husked and halved

1 jalapeño chile, halved lengthwise and seeded

¼ cup (⅓ oz/10 g) fresh cilantro leaves

¼ white onion, roughly chopped

1 clove garlic

Salt and freshly ground pepper

10–12 small corn tortillas, warmed

Preheat the oven to 450°F (230°C). Line a baking sheet with parchment paper. Put the sweet potatoes and parsnips in a bowl. Add the oil, cumin, coriander, chili powder, and ½ tsp salt. Transfer the vegetables to the prepared sheet and spread in a single layer. Roast, stirring once, until the vegetables are caramelized, about 20 minutes.

Meanwhile, to make the lime-cilantro cream, in a small bowl, stir together the sour cream, cilantro, and lime juice. Season with salt and pepper.

To make the tomatillo salsa, preheat the broiler. Arrange the tomatillos and the jalapeño cut side down on a baking sheet. Broil until charred, about 7 minutes. Let cool briefly. Place the tomatillos, jalapeño, cilantro, onion, and garlic in a blender and purée. Season with salt and pepper. Transfer to a small bowl. ⤳

Top the lime-cilantro cream with cilantro. Place 3 Tbsp of the root vegetables on each tortilla, top with the salsa, and serve, passing the lime-cilantro cream at the table.

2

CHICKPEA & SWEET POTATO CURRY

serves 4

This South Asian–inspired curry is satisfying on its own or can be served alongside chicken marinated in yogurt, lemon juice, and spices and broiled or baked. The flavors will deepen if the curry is prepared a day ahead and then reheated. Add a little water or broth to thin it when reheating.

2 Tbsp canola oil

1 small yellow onion, chopped

2 cloves garlic, finely chopped

1 Tbsp peeled and chopped fresh ginger

1 Thai or jalapeño chile, seeded and finely chopped

1 Tbsp Madras curry powder

Salt and freshly ground pepper

1 large sweet potato, peeled and cut into ½-inch (12-mm) cubes

1 can (15 oz/470 g) chickpeas, drained and rinsed

1 can (14 fl oz/430 ml) coconut milk

½ cup (2½ oz/75 g) frozen peas

½ cup (3 oz/90 g) canned diced tomatoes, drained

Steamed basmati rice for serving (optional)

In a large saucepan, warm the oil over medium-low heat. Add the onion, garlic, ginger, and chile and cook, stirring occasionally, until the onion is translucent, about 4 minutes. Stir in the curry powder and cook, stirring constantly, until fragrant, about 30 seconds. Season to taste with salt and pepper.

Add the sweet potato, chickpeas, coconut milk, and 1 cup (8 fl oz/250 ml) water to the pan. Raise the heat to medium-high, bring just to a boil, reduce the heat to low, and simmer, uncovered, until the sweet potato is tender, about 10 minutes. Add the peas and tomatoes and cook until heated through, about 5 minutes.

Serve the curry in bowls over steamed rice, if desired.

3

APPLE FRANGIPANE TART

serves 8

1 sheet frozen puff pastry
(about 1 lb/500 g), thawed

1½ cups (6 oz/185 g) sliced almonds,
lightly toasted

⅔ cup (5 oz/155 g) sugar

¼ tsp kosher salt

2 large eggs, lightly beaten

1 tsp pure vanilla extract

1 tsp almond extract

2 Tbsp unsalted butter, melted

2 large baking apples, such as
Pink Lady or Gravenstein, quartered,
cored, and cut into very thin slices

½ lemon

¼ cup (2½ oz/75 g) apricot jam
for glazing (optional)

With its elegant layers of airy pastry, nutty-sweet almond frangipane, and thinly sliced apples, this tart is a guaranteed showstopper. Look for all-butter puff pastry for the best flavor. For a more decadent version, top each serving with lightly whipped crème fraîche.

Position a rack in the upper third of the oven and preheat to 425°F (220°C). Line a baking sheet with parchment paper.

On a lightly floured work surface, roll out the puff pastry into a 16-by-12-inch (40-by-30-cm) rectangle (it should just fit onto the baking sheet). Transfer to the prepared pan, fold over the edges to form a rim, and pinch together. Refrigerate while you make the frangipane.

In a food processor, combine the almonds, sugar, and salt and process until the almonds are finely ground. Add the eggs, vanilla and almond extracts, and melted butter and process until the mixture comes together. In a bowl, toss the apple slices with a squeeze of lemon juice.

Prick the chilled puff pastry all over with a fork. Bake until it looks dried out and very lightly browned, about 8 minutes. Remove from the oven and reduce the oven temperature to 350°F (180°C). Smear a thin, even layer of the frangipane on the pastry and then top evenly with the sliced apples. Bake until the tart is golden and the apples are tender-crisp, about 30 minutes. Transfer to a wire rack.

If you want to glaze the tart, heat the jam in a saucepan over low heat until it liquefies. Pour through a fine-mesh sieve set over a small bowl. Gently brush the top of the tart with a thin coating of jam, cut, and serve.

4

SPICED BUTTERNUT SQUASH TAGINE

serves 6

6–8 saffron threads

2 Tbsp olive oil

1 large yellow onion, finely chopped

1 tsp ground ginger

½ tsp ground cinnamon

½ tsp ground turmeric

1 butternut squash, about ¼ lb (625 g),
halved, seeded, peeled, and cut into
1-inch (2.5-cm) cubes

1 large carrot, peeled and cut on the
diagonal into slices ½ inch (12 mm) thick

2 plum tomatoes, halved, seeded,
and chopped

3 Tbsp dried currants

1 Tbsp honey

Salt and freshly ground pepper

1 large sweet potato, about ½ lb (250 g),
peeled, halved lengthwise, and then
each half cut crosswise into slices
¾ inch (2 cm) thick

This fragrant Moroccan stew combines winter squash, sweet potato, onion, and carrot with an aromatic blend of spices and the sweetness of dried currants and honey. It is traditionally cooked in a conical earthenware pot known as a tagine, but a Dutch oven or other heavy pot can be substituted. Butternut squash is the ideal winter squash for this dish, as it contains less water than many other varieties.

In a small bowl, combine the saffron with 1 Tbsp warm water and let soak for 10 minutes.

In a large, heavy pot, heat the oil over medium-high heat. Add the onion and cook, stirring frequently, until softened, about 5 minutes. Stir in the ginger, cinnamon, and turmeric and cook, stirring, until the spices are fragrant, about 30 seconds. Add the squash, carrot, tomatoes, currants, honey, and saffron with its soaking liquid. Pour in ¾ cup (6 fl oz/180 ml) water. Season with salt and pepper. Bring to a boil, reduce the heat to medium, cover, and simmer for 10 minutes.

Add the sweet potato to the pot and cook, covered, until the vegetables are tender but still hold their shape, about 25 minutes. Ladle into bowls and serve hot.

5

CURRIED YELLOW SPLIT PEA SOUP WITH KABOCHA SQUASH

serves 4–6

High in protein and rich in nutrients, split peas come in yellow and green, and either can be used in this recipe. Curry powder varies from country to country and from region to region. If you have a favorite curry powder, use it here. If not, a Madras-style powder is a good middle-of-the-road choice. Top slices of crusty bread with shredded Monterey jack cheese, run them under the broiler to melt the cheese, and serve alongside the soup.

1 kabocha squash (about 2¼ lb/1.15 kg), peeled, seeded, and cut into 1-inch (2.5-cm) pieces

4 Tbsp (2 fl oz/60 ml) olive oil

Salt and freshly ground pepper

1 yellow onion, chopped

2 cloves garlic, chopped

1 Tbsp curry powder

1½ cups (10½ oz/330 g) yellow split peas, picked over and rinsed

5 cups (40 fl oz/1.25 l) chicken or vegetable broth

½ cup (2 oz/60 g) roasted and salted sunflower seeds

½ cup (4 oz/125 g) sour cream (optional)

Preheat the oven to 400°F (200°C). Line a baking sheet with parchment paper. Pile the squash on the prepared baking sheet and toss with 2 Tbsp of the oil. Spread in a single layer and season with salt and pepper. Roast, stirring once, until golden, about 30 minutes. Set aside.

In a large, heavy pot, warm the remaining 2 Tbsp oil over medium-high heat. Add the onion and cook, stirring occasionally, until soft, about 6 minutes. Add the garlic, season with salt and pepper, and cook, stirring occasionally, until soft, about 2 minutes. Stir in the curry powder and split peas and allow them to toast, about 2 minutes. Add the broth and bring to a boil. Reduce the heat to low, cover, and simmer, stirring a couple of times to prevent sticking, until the split peas are soft, 25–35 minutes. Let cool slightly.

Purée half of the soup in a food processor or blender. Return to the pot and stir to combine. Stir in the squash and season with salt and pepper.

Serve, garnished with the sunflower seeds and a dollop of sour cream, if using.

6

BRAISED CHICKEN WITH PEPPERS, OLIVES & CAPERS

serves 4

Fresh rosemary, a touch of peppery pancetta, briny olives, and tart capers turn a simple stew into a popular weeknight meal. If possible, use a mixture of red and yellow peppers for color. Spoon the stew over bulgur wheat or rice and accompany with wilted greens or steamed green beans.

1 chicken, about 3½ lb (1.75 kg), cut into 10 pieces

Salt and freshly ground black pepper

1 Tbsp olive oil

2 Tbsp fresh rosemary, minced

2 large red or yellow bell peppers, seeded and sliced

1 large onion, halved, then sliced

1½ oz (45 g) pancetta, chopped

½ tsp red pepper flakes

1 can (14½ oz/455 g) diced tomatoes

1 cup (8 fl oz/250 ml) dry white wine

⅓ cup (2 oz/60 g) pitted Kalamata olives

2 Tbsp capers, rinsed

Pat the chicken dry. Season on both sides with salt and black pepper. In a large, heavy pot over medium-high heat, warm the oil. Add the rosemary, then the chicken pieces, in batches if necessary. Cook until the chicken is browned, about 5 minutes on each side. Transfer to a plate.

Add the bell peppers, onion, pancetta, and red pepper flakes to the pot. Season with salt and black pepper, and sauté until the vegetables begin to soften, about 5 minutes. Add the tomatoes with their juices, wine, olives, and capers. Bring to a boil. Return the chicken to the pot. Reduce the heat to low, cover, and simmer until the breasts are just cooked, about 20 minutes. Transfer the breasts to a plate. Cover and cook the dark meat 10 minutes longer. Uncover and simmer until the dark meat is tender and the sauce has thickened slightly, about 15 minutes longer. Return the chicken breasts to the sauce and simmer to heat through.

Divide the chicken and sauce among 4 warmed plates and serve.

7

Sweet autumn squash deepens in flavor when roasted in the oven. It pairs particularly well with spicy, salty flavors, such as the Spanish chorizo used here. Encased in a buttery crust, this savory tart is comfort food at its best.

ACORN SQUASH & CHORIZO TART

serves 6

FOR THE PASTRY DOUGH

1¾ cups (9 oz/280 g) all-purpose flour

1 tsp sugar

½ tsp coarse salt

½ cup (4 oz/125 g) cold unsalted butter, cut into small pieces

3 Tbsp cold vegetable shortening

4–5 Tbsp ice water

½ lb (250 g) acorn squash, peeled, seeded, and cut into ½-inch (12-mm) chunks

2 Tbsp olive oil

Salt

¼ lb (125 g) cured Spanish-style chorizo, diced

1 yellow onion, finely chopped

1 clove garlic, minced

½ cup (2 oz/60 g) shredded Monterey jack cheese

1 egg yolk

In a food processor, pulse the flour, sugar, and salt to combine. Sprinkle in the butter pieces and add the shortening. Pulse the mixture just until combined and with a few pea-sized pieces of butter. Sprinkle in 3 Tbsp of the ice water and pulse again until the dough just comes together when squeezed in your hand. If the dough is still dry, add a bit more water as needed. Turn the dough out onto a large sheet of plastic wrap and press it into a disk. Cover with another sheet of plastic and, using a rolling pin, roll into a rough circle about 13 inches (33 cm) in diameter. Put the dough round on a baking sheet lined with parchment paper and refrigerate until firm, about 20 minutes.

Meanwhile, position a rack in the lower third of the oven and preheat to 400°F (200°C). Put the squash on a baking sheet, drizzle with 1 Tbsp of the oil, and toss to coat. Spread in an even layer, season with salt, and roast until almost tender, about 10 minutes. Let cool.

In a frying pan over medium-high heat, warm the remaining 1 Tbsp oil. ⇥

Add the chorizo and sauté until lightly browned, about 2 minutes. Transfer to paper towels. Pour off all but 1½ Tbsp of the fat and return the pan to medium-high heat. Add the onion and sauté until tender, about 5 minutes. Season with salt, add the garlic, and cook for 1 minute. Let cool.

Remove the chilled dough round from the refrigerator. Spread evenly with the onion mixture, leaving a 1½-inch (4-cm) border. Evenly distribute the squash and chorizo and sprinkle with the cheese. Fold the edge up and over the filling, forming loose pleats. Lightly beat the egg yolk with 1 tsp water and brush on the border.

Bake until the crust is browned and the cheese is melted, about 30 minutes. Cut into wedges and serve.

8

Pick up packages of fresh gnocchi, the little potato dumplings, to create easy—but filling— dinners in a pinch. They are lovely boiled until tender and simply sauced, but they are also easily dressed up with pancetta and cheeses in a gratin. You can make this recipe using 1 lb (500 g) penne or rigatoni instead of gnocchi.

BAKED GNOCCHI WITH TALEGGIO, PANCETTA & SAGE

serves 4

2 packages (13 oz/410 g each) prepared gnocchi

¼ lb (125 g) pancetta, cut into ½-inch (12-mm) pieces

2 Tbsp chopped fresh sage

1½ cups (12 fl oz/375 ml) half-and-half

½ lb (250 g) Taleggio cheese, rind removed, cut into ¼-inch (6-mm) cubes

¼ cup (1 oz/30 g) bread crumbs, toasted

Freshly ground pepper

Preheat the oven to 375°F (190°C). Butter four 7-inch (18-cm) shallow oval baking dishes.

Cook the gnocchi according to the package directions. Drain and set aside.

In a large frying pan, sauté the pancetta over medium heat until it starts to brown, about 4 minutes. Remove from the heat and stir in the sage, half-and-half, Taleggio, and gnocchi.

Divide the gnocchi mixture among the prepared dishes. Sprinkle with the bread crumbs and season with pepper.

Bake the gnocchi until golden brown, about 15 minutes. Remove from the oven and serve.

9

POLENTA CROSTINI WITH CHANTERELLES

serves 8–10

The subtle quality of polenta makes it the perfect bed for sautéed vegetables, such as the chanterelle mushrooms that top these lightly fried polenta crostini. Aficionados describe these trumpet-shaped golden mushrooms as having a fruity aroma that recalls apricots. Be sure to add the polenta to the water slowly and to stir constantly to avoid lumps. Uncork a Merlot or Cabernet Sauvignon to accompany these elegant crostini.

FOR THE POLENTA

1 bay leaf

Salt and freshly ground pepper

2 Tbsp olive oil

1 cup (5 oz/155 g) polenta

1 Tbsp unsalted butter

FOR THE MUSHROOMS

4 Tbsp (2 oz/60 g) unsalted butter

3 shallots, minced

½ lb (250 g) chanterelle mushrooms, roughly chopped

Salt and freshly ground pepper

½ cup (4 oz/125 g) mascarpone cheese

2 Tbsp minced fresh flat-leaf parsley

Wedge of Parmesan cheese

To make the polenta, in a saucepan, bring 4 cups (32 fl oz/1 l) water to boil. Add the bay leaf, 1 Tbsp salt, and 1 Tbsp of the oil. Slowly add the polenta, stirring constantly. Reduce the heat to low and cook, stirring often, until the polenta pulls away from the sides of the pan, about 30 minutes. Remove and discard the bay leaf.

Rinse an 8-by-10-inch (20-by-25-cm) baking dish but do not dry. Immediately pour the polenta into the dish. It should be about ½ inch (12 mm) thick. Set aside to cool until firm, about 30 minutes.

Just before serving, prepare the mushrooms. In a large sauté pan, melt the 4 Tbsp butter over medium heat. Add the shallots and sauté until slightly wilted, about 2 minutes. Add the chanterelles, season with salt and pepper, and sauté until golden brown and tender, about 4 minutes. Remove from the heat and set aside.

Cut the cooled polenta into pieces about 1 by 2 inches (2.5 by 5 cm). In a large frying pan, melt the 1 Tbsp butter with the remaining 1 Tbsp oil over medium-high heat. Working in batches, fry the polenta pieces, turning once, until barely golden on both sides and heated through, about 3 minutes per side. ⇥

Arrange the polenta on a platter. Place a small dollop of mascarpone on each piece. Spoon the mushrooms over the mascarpone, dividing them evenly, and garnish with the parsley. Using a vegetable peeler or a cheese plane, shave a little Parmesan over each piece. Serve warm.

10

LAMB SHOULDER WITH SALSA VERDE

serves 6

To make the salsa verde: In a food processor, combine 2 cloves garlic, chopped; 2½ cups (2½ oz/75 g) fresh flat-leaf parsley leaves; ½ cup (½ oz/15 g) fresh mint leaves; 2 Tbsp capers, rinsed and drained; 1 Tbsp Dijon mustard; and 1 Tbsp red wine vinegar. Pulse until finely chopped. With the processor running, drizzle in ⅔ cup (5 fl oz/160 ml) extra-virgin olive oil in a steady stream and process until smooth. Cover and refrigerate for 1 hour to marry the flavors before using.

3-lb (1.5-kg) piece boneless lamb shoulder, cut into 1¼-inch (3-cm) chunks

Salt and freshly ground pepper

2 Tbsp olive oil

1 large yellow onion, finely chopped

2 sprigs fresh thyme

4 cloves garlic, minced

1 tsp dried oregano

⅔ cup (5 fl oz/160 ml) dry white wine

1 Tbsp balsamic vinegar

⅔ cup (5 fl oz/160 ml) beef or chicken broth

Salsa verde for serving *(left)*

Season the lamb generously all over with salt and pepper. In a large frying pan, heat the oil over medium-high heat. Working in batches, sear the lamb, turning as needed, until well browned on all sides, 6–7 minutes. Transfer to a slow cooker.

Pour off most of the fat from the pan and return it to medium-high heat. Add the onion and thyme sprigs and sauté until the onion is golden brown, about 5 minutes. Add the garlic and oregano and cook for 1 minute. Pour in the wine and vinegar and stir to scrape up any browned bits on the pan bottom. Add the broth and bring to a simmer. Transfer the contents of the pan to a slow cooker, cover, and cook on the low setting for 8 hours. The lamb should be very tender.

Transfer the lamb to a warm platter and moisten it with some of the braising liquid. Drizzle the salsa verde generously over the lamb and serve.

11

The cooler temperatures of fall fill produce bins with broccoli and cauliflower. Although the most common cauliflower is snowy white or ivory, you can occasionally find heads with green, orange, or purple florets. In every case, look for evenly colored, tightly packed, firm florets. The leftover pickled onions can be slipped into sandwiches or tossed into a salad of mixed lettuces and feta cheese.

BROCCOLI & CAULIFLOWER WITH PICKLED ONIONS & BACON

serves 6–8

2 cups (16 fl oz/500 ml) cider vinegar

3 Tbsp sugar

16 peppercorns

10 whole cloves

Salt and freshly ground pepper

1 large red onion, thinly sliced

5 slices bacon

Ice water

1 head cauliflower, cut into 1-inch (2.5-cm) florets (about 4 cups/12 oz/375 g)

1 large head broccoli, cut into 1-inch (2.5-cm) florets (about 6 cups/12 oz/375 g)

¼ cup (2 fl oz/60 ml) extra-virgin olive oil

In a small, nonreactive saucepan, combine the vinegar, sugar, peppercorns, and cloves. Season with ¼ tsp salt and bring to a boil. Reduce the heat to medium-low and simmer for 10 minutes to infuse the flavors. Pour the mixture into a heatproof nonreactive bowl, add the onion, and let stand at room temperature for 1 hour.

Meanwhile, in a large frying pan, cook the bacon over medium heat, turning once, until crisp and browned, about 7 minutes. Transfer to paper towels to drain. Let cool to room temperature and then coarsely chop.

In a large pot fitted with a steamer basket, bring 1–2 inches (5–7.5 cm) water to a boil. Have ready a large bowl of ice water. Stir 1 Tbsp salt into the ice water. Place the cauliflower florets in a single layer in the steamer basket, cover, reduce the heat to medium, and cook until tender-crisp, about 8 minutes. Transfer the cauliflower to the ice water. Let stand until cool. Using a slotted spoon, transfer the cauliflower to a large bowl. Steam the broccoli florets in the same manner until tender-crisp, about 4 minutes, then transfer to the ice water until cool. Drain well and add to the bowl with the cauliflower.

Drizzle the oil over the cauliflower and broccoli, season with salt and pepper, and toss well. Top with some of the pickled onion slices (reserve the remaining slices for another use). Sprinkle with the bacon and serve.

12

As the frost sets in, bitter greens such as endive develop a pleasingly crisp texture. Their slight bitterness, which softens during cooking, complements mild snapper. Many species of saltwater fish are sold as snapper, but true red snapper has a rosy pink skin and red eyes. Rockfish, also known as Pacific snapper, is a good substitute in this recipe, as is sea bass or halibut.

ROASTED SNAPPER & BELGIAN ENDIVE

serves 4

6–8 heads white or red Belgian endives, or a combination, 12–14 oz (375–440 g) total

2 Tbsp unsalted butter, melted

Salt and freshly ground pepper

¼ cup (2 fl oz/60 ml) chicken broth

1 Tbsp sherry vinegar

½ tsp sugar

2 skinless red snapper fillets, 10–12 oz (315–375 g) each, or 4 small fillets, 5–6 oz (155–185 g) each

Olive oil for brushing

Sweet paprika

Preheat the oven to 450°F (230°C).

Cut the endives in half lengthwise, then cut out the hard core and discard. Cut the halves lengthwise into strips about ½ inch (12 mm) wide. Pour the melted butter into a shallow baking dish just large enough to hold the fish in a single layer. Add the endive strips and toss to coat with the butter. Sprinkle with salt and pepper.

Place the dish in the oven and roast the endives for 10 minutes. Remove from the oven and turn the endive strips with a spatula. Add the broth, vinegar, and sugar. Continue to roast for another 10 minutes.

Meanwhile, lightly brush both sides of the fillets with olive oil, then season both sides with salt and pepper. Lightly sprinkle one side with paprika.

Remove the dish from the oven and place the fillets, paprika side up, on top of the endive strips. Roast the fish until opaque throughout, 8–10 minutes. Serve directly from the dish.

13

Cookies, candy, ice cream, and fudge all come together in this guilty pleasure. Look for packaged toffee bits in the baking section of well-stocked markets, or chop up a toffee candy bar. Kids will love the sugary crunch, but you can leave out the toffee bits if you like and double the amount of toasted almonds.

MISSISSIPPI MUD PIE
serves 8–10

FOR THE CRUMB CRUST

1¼ cups (4 oz/125 g) chocolate wafer crumbs

5 Tbsp (2½ oz/75 g) unsalted butter, melted

3 Tbsp granulated sugar

1 cup (6 oz/185 g) semisweet chocolate chips

¼ cup (2 oz/60 g) unsalted butter

¼ cup (2 fl oz/60 ml) heavy cream

2 Tbsp light corn syrup

1 cup (4 oz/125 g) confectioners' sugar, sifted

1 tsp pure vanilla extract

½ cup (2½ oz/75 g) toffee bits

1 qt (32 fl oz/1 l) coffee ice cream, softened

½ cup (2½ oz/75 g) chopped whole almonds, toasted

To make the crust, preheat the oven to 350°F (180°C). In a bowl, stir together the crumbs, melted butter, and sugar until the crumbs are evenly moistened. Pat the mixture firmly and evenly into the bottom and up the sides of a 9-inch (23-cm) pie pan or dish. Bake until the crust is firm, 5–10 minutes.

Place the chocolate chips, butter, cream, and corn syrup in the top of a double boiler set over (not touching) barely simmering water, and heat, stirring occasionally, until the chocolate is melted. Add the confectioners' sugar and vanilla and mix well. Reserve ½ cup (4 fl oz/125 ml) of the chocolate mixture for the top of the pie. Spread the remaining mixture evenly in the bottom of the cookie crust. Sprinkle with half of the toffee bits. Refrigerate until well chilled, about 1 hour.

In a large bowl, using an electric mixer, beat the ice cream on medium speed until it is spreadable but not runny. Immediately mound into the pie shell and spread evenly. Freeze until the ice cream is firm, at least 2 hours or up to overnight.

Reheat the reserved chocolate mixture in the top of the double boiler over barely simmering water until it is spreadable but not hot. Spread it over the ice cream. Sprinkle with the remaining toffee bits and the almonds. Freeze the pie until completely firm, 3–4 hours, before serving.

14

Cheddar cheese and apple, a classic sharp and tart pairing—does it get any better? Yes it does when crispy, crunchy fried shallot rings are added to the mix. Serve a lightly dressed green salad and whole-grain wheat or rye bread on the side.

CHEDDAR & HARD CIDER SOUP WITH FRIED SHALLOTS
serves 6–8

4 Tbsp (2 oz/60 g) unsalted butter

2 yellow onions, chopped

1 celery rib, chopped

1 Yukon Gold potato, peeled and chopped

2 cloves garlic, minced

2 Tbsp all-purpose flour

2½ cups (20 fl oz/625 ml) chicken broth

2½ cups (20 fl oz/625 ml) hard apple cider

1 cup (8 fl oz/250 ml) half-and-half

2 bay leaves

2 thyme sprigs

2 Tbsp applejack or Calvados brandy

¾ lb (375 g) English Cheddar cheese, shredded

Salt and freshly ground pepper

Fried shallots (see page 88)

In a large, heavy pot, melt 3 Tbsp of the butter over medium-high heat. Add the onions, celery, potato, and garlic and stir. Reduce the heat to low, cover, and cook, stirring occasionally, until the vegetables are softened, about 12 minutes. Sprinkle the flour over the vegetables and cook, stirring constantly, until the flour is incorporated. While stirring constantly, gradually add the broth, cider, and half-and-half. Raise the heat to medium-high, add the bay leaves and thyme sprigs, and bring to a boil. Reduce the heat to low and simmer to blend the flavors, about 10 minutes.

Remove the bay leaves and thyme sprigs from the soup and discard. Remove the soup from the heat and let cool slightly.

Working in batches, purée the soup in a blender. Pour into a clean pot. Stir in the applejack. Off the heat, while whisking constantly, gradually add the cheese one handful at a time. Continue whisking until all the cheese is melted. Place over medium-low heat, stir in 1 tsp salt and pepper to taste, and cook gently, stirring often, until heated through, about 10 minutes.

Taste and adjust the seasoning. Serve, garnished with the fried shallots.

OCTOBER

16

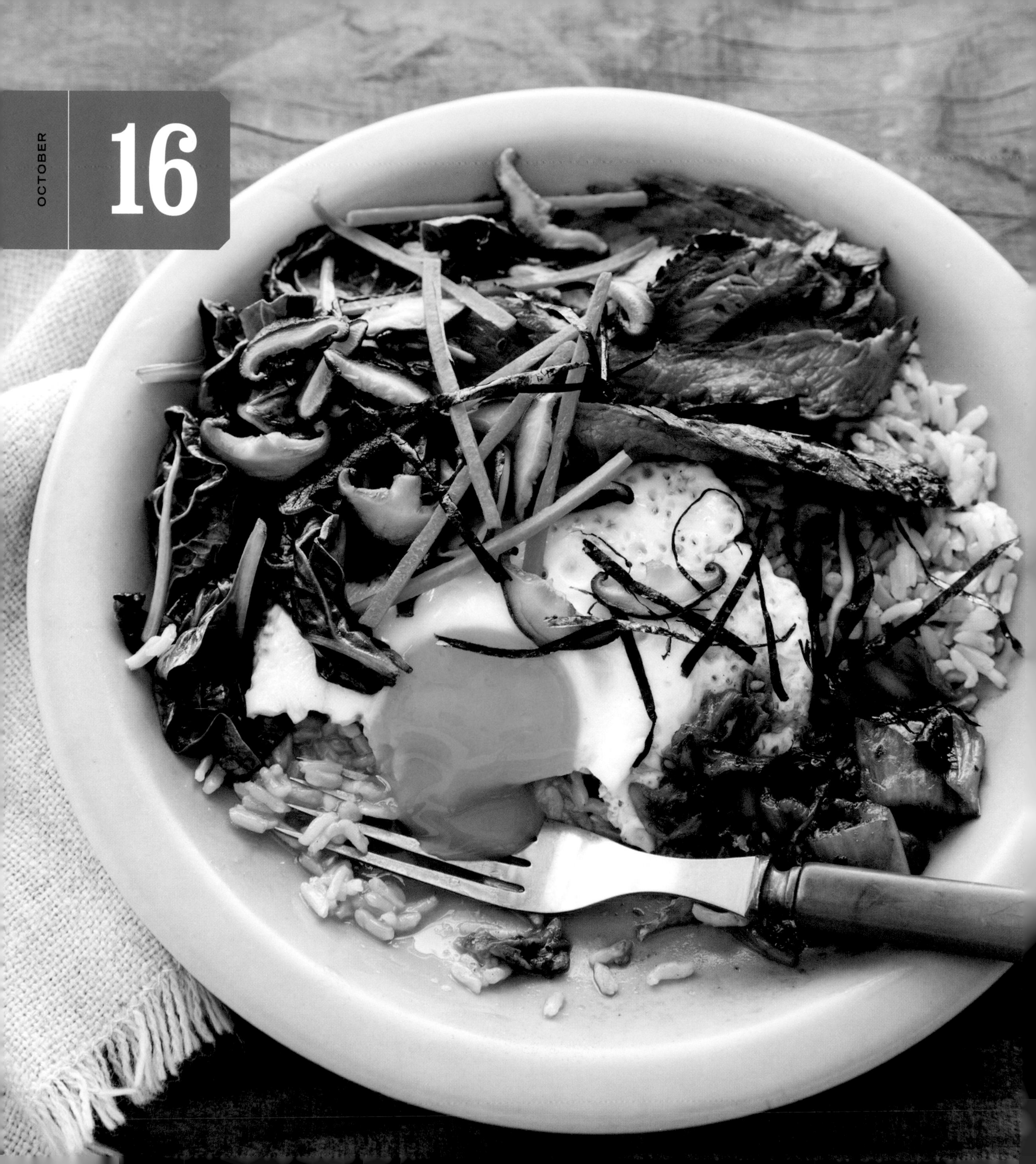

15

This soup might be your answer to getting more vegetables on the family table. Roasted cauliflower turns sweet, and Parmesan adds a salty-nutty complement. Use a good-quality Parmesan and serve with garlic bread and a green salad.

ROASTED CAULIFLOWER & PARMESAN SOUP

serves 4–6

1 head cauliflower (about 2 lb/1 kg), stemmed and cut into florets

2 Tbsp olive oil

Salt and freshly ground pepper

2 Tbsp unsalted butter

1 yellow onion, chopped

3 cloves garlic, minced

3 cups (24 fl oz/750 ml) chicken broth, plus more as needed

½ cup (2 oz/60 g) grated Parmesan cheese

Preheat the oven to 400°F (200°C) and line a rimmed baking sheet with parchment paper. Toss the cauliflower with the oil and season with salt and pepper. Spread on the prepared baking sheet and roast in the oven until very tender, 30–35 minutes.

In a large, heavy pot, melt the butter over medium-high heat. Add the onion and garlic and sauté until translucent, about 5 minutes. Add the cauliflower and 3 cups (24 fl oz/750 ml) broth and bring to a boil. Reduce the heat to low and simmer for 15 minutes to blend the flavors. Remove from the heat and let cool slightly.

Working in batches, purée the soup in a blender or food processor. Return to the pot over low heat. If needed, add more broth, ¼ cup (2 fl oz/60 ml) at a time, until you achieve the desired consistency. Add the Parmesan and stir until melted. Season to taste with salt and pepper and serve.

16

Bibimbop, literally "mixed rice," is a popular Korean dish of hot rice topped with freshly cooked vegetables and meat and a fried or raw egg. Bulgogi, marinated and grilled beef slices, is a common meat choice, though here the beef is cooked on the stove top instead of on the grill. This recipe calls for brown rice rather than the traditional white rice, though the latter can be used in its place.

BIBIMBOP WITH BROWN RICE & BULGOGI

serves 4

FOR THE BULGOGI

3 Tbsp low-sodium soy sauce

1 Tbsp sesame seeds

1 clove garlic, minced

2 tsp sugar

1 tsp toasted sesame oil

¾ lb (375 g) flank steak, thinly sliced against the grain

2 Tbsp toasted sesame oil

1 Tbsp canola oil

10 shiitake mushrooms, stemmed and thinly sliced

6 cups (6 oz/185 g) spinach leaves

4 large eggs

4 cups (20 oz/625 g) hot cooked brown rice

2 carrots, peeled, shredded, and tossed with a few drops of sesame oil

2 green onions, thinly sliced (optional)

1 sheet of nori, cut into strips (optional)

Prepared kimchi (optional)

To make the bulgogi, in a bowl, stir together the soy sauce, sesame seeds, garlic, sugar, and sesame oil. Add the flank steak and toss to combine. Cover and refrigerate for 1 hour.

Combine the 2 Tbsp sesame oil and 1 Tbsp canola oil in a small bowl. Warm half of the oil in a frying pan over medium-high heat and sauté the mushrooms, stirring often, until softened and golden-brown, about 4 minutes. Transfer to a plate. Add the remaining oil to the pan and sauté the spinach, cooking just until wilted, about 2 minutes. Transfer to the plate. Fry the eggs until they are set but still runny, 5–6 minutes. Remove from the pan and keep warm.

Warm the frying pan over high heat. Add the bulgogi strips and cook until medium-rare, about 3 minutes on each side. Remove from the heat and keep warm in the frying pan.

Divide the rice among 4 bowls and top each with the bulgogi, mushrooms, spinach, eggs, carrots, green onions, and nori, if using. Serve with kimchi on the side, if using.

17

Fresh cranberries and lemon zest and juice add bright flavors to this butter-rich cake. As the cake bakes, the cranberries are transformed into a sweet-tart compote-like topping. A simple lemon glaze gives the cake a pretty finish.

GLAZED CRANBERRY-LEMON CAKE

serves 10–12

⅓ cup (2½ oz/75 g) firmly packed light brown sugar

3 cups (12 oz/375 g) cranberries

2½ cups (12½ oz/390 g) all-purpose flour

2½ tsp baking powder

½ tsp baking soda

1 tsp kosher salt

1½ cups (12 oz/375 g) granulated sugar

2 lemons

¾ cup (6 fl oz/180 ml) buttermilk

1½ tsp pure vanilla extract

¾ cup (6 oz/185 g) unsalted butter

3 large eggs

1 cup (4 oz/125 g) confectioners' sugar, plus more as needed

Preheat the oven to 350°F (180°C). Generously butter a 3-qt (3-l) Bundt pan. Sprinkle the brown sugar in the bottom of the pan, then distribute the cranberries over the sugar.

Sift the flour, baking powder, baking soda, and salt together into a bowl. Place the granulated sugar in the bowl of a stand mixer. Finely grate the zest from the lemons over the sugar and mix briefly. Juice the lemons and strain the juice into a small bowl. In a liquid measuring cup, combine 2 Tbsp of the lemon juice, the buttermilk, and the vanilla; reserve the remaining lemon juice.

Add the butter to the bowl with the sugar and beat on medium-high speed until light and fluffy, 1–2 minutes. Beat in the eggs one at a time. Reduce the speed to low and add the dry ingredients in 3 batches, alternating with the lemon-buttermilk mixture in 2 batches. Increase the speed to medium-high and beat for 2 minutes.

Scrape the batter into the pan and spread it evenly over the cranberries. Bake until the cake is golden and a toothpick inserted into the center comes out clean, 35–40 minutes. Let cool in the pan for 5 minutes, then invert the cake onto a plate and let cool completely. ⟩⟩

In a bowl, whisk together the 1 cup confectioners' sugar and 1½ Tbsp of the reserved lemon juice until thick and smooth. Test the consistency by drizzling a bit of glaze over the cake. If it runs off the cake, whisk in a little more confectioners' sugar; if it sits on the cake without moving, whisk in a little more lemon juice. Drizzle the glaze over the cake and let set for at least 15 minutes before serving.

18

A favorite dish of Mexico and the American Southwest, this colorful stew, which combines bite-size pieces of pork with mild green chiles and tomatillos, could not be simpler to make. Many home cooks add ripe red tomatoes, which flavor the dish without interfering with its signature green color. Serve warm corn tortillas alongside for wrapping around spoonfuls of the stew.

CHILE VERDE

serves 8–10

4 lb (2 kg) boneless pork shoulder, cut into 1-inch (2.5-cm) chunks

Salt and freshly ground pepper

4 cans (7 oz/220 g each) diced fire-roasted green chiles

2 cans (12 oz/375 g each) whole tomatillos, drained and broken up by hand

1 large yellow onion, finely chopped

4 cloves garlic, minced

1 large jalapeño chile, seeded and minced

2 cups (16 fl oz/500 ml) chicken broth

¾ lb (375 g) ripe tomatoes, seeded and finely chopped

1 Tbsp dried oregano

2 tsp ground cumin

Warmed corn tortillas for serving

Sour cream for garnish

Chopped fresh cilantro for garnish

Put the pork in a large, heavy pot and season with 2 tsp salt and 1 tsp pepper. Add the green chiles, tomatillos, onion, garlic, jalapeño, broth, tomatoes, oregano, and cumin and stir briefly to combine. Bring to a boil over high heat, reduce the heat to very low, partially cover, and cook until the pork is very tender and a thick sauce has formed, 2–3 hours.

Ladle the chile verde into a large shallow serving bowl. Pass the tortillas, sour cream, and cilantro at the table.

19

Coating one side of each tuna steak with coarsely cracked peppercorns adds just enough peppery heat to his company-worthy salad. Although fennel season is just getting under way in October, sweet, ovoid yellow Vidalia onions are beginning to disappear from the market, so put this easy salad on your calendar while they are still available.

ARUGULA & FENNEL SALAD WITH BLACK PEPPER–CRUSTED TUNA

serves 6

¼ cup (2 fl oz/60 ml) balsamic vinegar

1 large shallot, minced

2 tsp Dijon mustard

½ tsp sugar

Salt

10 Tbsp (5 fl oz/160 ml) extra-virgin olive oil

2 small, sweet onions such as Vidalia, thinly sliced

2 Tbsp black peppercorns

6 tuna steaks (2 lb/1 kg total weight), each about 1 inch (2.5 cm) thick

8 cups (8 oz/250 g) arugula leaves, stemmed

1 large fennel bulb, trimmed and thinly sliced

In a small bowl, whisk together the vinegar, shallot, mustard, sugar, and ¼ tsp salt until the sugar dissolves. Add 7 Tbsp (3½ fl oz/ 105 ml) of the oil in a thin stream, whisking constantly until the vinaigrette is smooth and thick. Taste and adjust the seasonings and set aside.

In a large nonstick frying pan over medium heat, warm 2 Tbsp of the oil. Add the sliced onions and 1 tsp salt and sauté until the onions are softened and browned, 10–12 minutes. Transfer to a plate and set aside. Wipe the pan clean.

Place the peppercorns in a resealable plastic bag and seal. Using a mallet or the bottom of a small, heavy pan, coarsely crack the peppercorns. Season each tuna steak on both sides with a little salt. Then, dividing them evenly, press the cracked peppercorns into one side of each tuna steak.

Return the frying pan to medium-high heat and add the remaining 1 Tbsp oil. When the oil is hot but not smoking, add the tuna steaks, peppered side down. Sear, turning once, until lightly golden on the outside and still dark pink and rare in the center, about 2 minutes per side, or until cooked to your liking. Transfer to a platter, tent with foil, and let rest for 5 minutes. ↠

In a large bowl, toss together the arugula, fennel, and ¼ tsp salt. Whisk the vinaigrette to recombine, then drizzle about half of it over the arugula mixture and toss well. Taste and adjust the seasonings. Divide the dressed arugula mixture among individual plates. Spoon the sautéed onions over the top. Thinly slice each tuna steak and arrange on top of the onions. Drizzle each salad with some of the remaining vinaigrette and serve.

20

Don't try to use a carving pumpkin here. "Cooking" pumpkins have denser flesh and a sweeter flavor and are not as fibrous. If you cannot find a Sugar Pie pumpkin, Sugar Baby, Autumn Gold, and Long Island Cheese pumpkins are also good choices for baking.

PUMPKIN PURÉE WITH TOASTED PUMPKIN SEEDS

serves 4

½ cup (2½ oz/75 g) pepitas (pumpkin seeds)

1 Sugar Pie pumpkin, about 2 lb (1 kg)

1 tsp ground cinnamon

½ tsp ground cloves

½ tsp ground nutmeg

Salt

Preheat the oven to 350°F (180°C). In a small, dry frying pan, toast the pepitas over medium heat, stirring occasionally, until they begin to darken. Transfer to a plate to cool.

Place the pumpkin on a baking sheet and bake until tender, about 1 hour. Remove from the oven, let cool until it can be handled, then cut in half, discard the seeds, and scoop the flesh into a food processor. Process until smooth, then stir in the spices and salt to taste. Spoon into bowls, sprinkle with the pepitas, and serve.

21

The warming, homey flavors of cumin, cinnamon, and honey infuse this North African fish dish. To accompany the tagine, stir wilted spinach and chopped toasted almonds into whole-wheat couscous and serve the fish and vegetables spooned over the top.

FISH TAGINE WITH CARROTS & OLIVES

serves 4

6 Tbsp (3 fl oz/90 ml) olive oil

¼ cup (⅓ oz/10 g) chopped fresh cilantro, plus more for garnish

2 Tbsp fresh lemon juice

3 cloves garlic, chopped

Salt and freshly ground pepper

4 halibut or rock cod fillets, each about 6 oz (185 g)

1 Tbsp honey

1 tsp ground cumin

½ tsp ground cinnamon

½ tsp ground ginger

¼ tsp ground turmeric

1 lb (500 g) carrots, peeled and thinly sliced

1 large onion, thinly sliced

1 lemon, thinly sliced

24 Kalamata olives

In a bowl, mix 4 Tbsp (2 fl oz/60 ml) of the oil with the ¼ cup (⅓ oz/10 g) cilantro, the lemon juice, garlic, ½ tsp salt, and ⅛ tsp pepper. Add the fish and turn to coat. Refrigerate for 30 minutes, turning once.

In another bowl, combine the honey, cumin, cinnamon, ginger, and turmeric with the remaining 2 Tbsp oil, ½ tsp salt, and ⅛ tsp pepper. Whisk to combine. Add the carrots and toss to coat.

Preheat the oven to 375°F (190°C). Arrange the carrot slices over the bottom of a 9-by-13-inch (23-by-33-cm) glass baking dish. Layer half the onion and lemon slices on top of the carrots.

Drain the fish and reserve the marinade. Arrange the fish atop the lemon slices and top with the remaining onion and lemon slices. Season with salt and pepper, and sprinkle the olives on top. Pour the reserved marinade on top and cover the dish with foil. Bake for about 1 hour, or until the fish flakes easily and the vegetables are tender.

Garnish with chopped cilantro and serve directly from the dish.

22

Purplish red torpedo onions, which are shaped like footballs, are slightly sweeter than most common round red onions. Here, they are grilled along with Asian pears for a sweet, smoky vegetable-and-fruit topping that complements the pork chops. Round out the menu with a side of roasted squash or sweet potatoes.

GRILLED PORK CHOPS WITH ASIAN PEARS & TORPEDO ONIONS

serves 4

4 rib pork chops, each about 4 oz (125 g) and ¾ inch (2 cm) thick

4 Tbsp (¼ oz/7 g) fresh sage leaves

1 tsp salt

1 tsp freshly ground pepper

3 Asian pears, peeled, halved, cored, and cut into wedges about ½ inch (12 mm) thick

2 red torpedo onions, cut into wedges about ½ inch (12 mm) thick

2 Tbsp grapeseed oil

Prepare a grill for direct-heat cooking over medium-high heat. Sprinkle the pork chops with 2 Tbsp of the sage leaves and ½ tsp each of the salt and pepper. Set aside.

In a bowl, mix together the pears and onions and drizzle with the oil. Toss to coat. Add the remaining ½ tsp each salt and pepper and 2 Tbsp of the sage. Stir to mix well. The onions will fall apart.

When the grill is medium-hot, place an oiled grilling basket on the grill rack to preheat it. When it is hot, place the onions and pears in it, close the basket, and grill until golden on the underside, 4–5 minutes. Turn the basket and continue to cook until golden on the second side and tender when pierced, 4–5 minutes longer. Remove the onions and pears from the basket, transfer to a warmed platter, and keep warm.

Place the pork chops on the grill rack and grill, turning once, until browned and the juices run clear when a chop is cut into with a knife, 3–4 minutes on each side.

Arrange the chops on the platter or warmed individual plates, spoon the pears and onions on top or alongside, and serve.

23

The three-bean salad has long been a favorite of picnics, potlucks, and buffets. Here is an updated version that calls for fresh shelling beans, slender French green beans, and pale wax beans. You can substitute Blue Lake or other green beans for the haricots verts. The flavor intensifies if the salad is allowed to marinate for at least 1 hour.

THREE-BEAN SALAD WITH CORIANDER VINAIGRETTE

serves 6–8

Salt and freshly ground pepper

½ lb (250 g) fresh flageolet beans or other fresh shelling beans, shelled

1 lb (500 g) yellow wax beans, stem ends trimmed and beans cut into 2-inch (5-cm) lengths

1 lb (500 g) haricots verts, stem ends trimmed

FOR THE CORIANDER VINAIGRETTE

1 tsp ground coriander

¼ cup (2 fl oz/60 ml) fresh lemon juice

2 Tbsp white wine vinegar

2 shallots, minced

¾ cup (6 fl oz/180 ml) safflower oil

1 tsp grated lemon zest

Bring a large saucepan three-fourths full of salted water to a boil. Add the shelling beans and boil just until tender, 10–15 minutes. Have ready a bowl of ice water. Scoop out the beans and immediately immerse in ice water to stop the cooking. Scoop the beans out of the ice water and set aside to drain. Repeat with the yellow wax beans and haricots verts, cooking the wax beans for 7–8 minutes and the haricots verts for 3–4 minutes.

To make the vinaigrette, in a small, dry frying pan, toast the coriander over medium heat, shaking the pan occasionally, until aromatic, 2–3 minutes. Pour onto a plate to cool and set aside. In a small bowl, combine the lemon juice, vinegar, and shallots. Add the safflower oil in a thin stream, whisking constantly until the dressing is smooth. Stir in the lemon zest and coriander and season with salt and pepper.

Combine all the beans in a large mixing bowl. Add the vinaigrette and toss to mix well. Let stand for at least 1 hour, or refrigerate for up to 3 hours. Serve at room temperature or chilled.

24

Shrimp cooks quickly and is rich in omega-3 fatty acids, making this recipe a good option for a healthy weeknight meal. If you cannot find red cabbage, which makes a particularly colorful slaw, green cabbage can be substituted. To make an easy pico de gallo, in a bowl, stir together 5 plum tomatoes, diced; 1 jalapeño chile, seeded and minced; ½ white onion, diced; ¼ cup (⅓ oz/10 g) chopped fresh cilantro; 2 cloves garlic, minced; and the juice of 1 lime and season with salt.

SPICY SHRIMP TACOS WITH RED CABBAGE SLAW

serves 4–6

1 Tbsp plus 2 tsp chili powder

1 Tbsp plus 1 tsp ground cumin

3 cloves garlic, minced

1 bay leaf, torn in half

3 Tbsp canola oil

2 lb (1 kg) medium shrimp, peeled and deveined

FOR THE RED CABBAGE SLAW

¼ cup (2 fl oz/60 ml) rice vinegar

2 Tbsp canola oil

2 tsp sugar

3 cups (9 oz/270 g) shredded red cabbage

¼ cup (⅓ oz/10 g) chopped fresh cilantro

Salt and freshly ground pepper

Nonstick cooking spray

Pico de gallo (*left*)

10–12 small corn tortillas, warmed

2 avocados, peeled, pitted and sliced, for garnish (optional)

Combine the chili powder, cumin, garlic, bay leaf, and oil in a bowl. Add the shrimp and stir to coat. Cover and refrigerate for 1 hour.

Meanwhile, to make the slaw, stir together the vinegar, oil, and sugar in a large bowl until the sugar dissolves. Add the cabbage and cilantro, toss to combine, and season with salt and pepper.

Remove the shrimp from the refrigerator and discard the bay leaf. Heat a stove-top grill pan over high heat. Using nonstick cooking spray, coat the grill. Grill the shrimp until opaque, about 2 minutes per side.

To serve, place the shrimp, slaw, pico de gallo, tortillas, and avocado, if using, on platters and allow guests to make their own tacos.

25

This simple and seasonal dessert features fresh figs with a rich sheep's milk cheese and a drizzle of honey. For a more rustic presentation, cut or tear the figs gently into halves.

RICOTTA WITH HONEY & FIGS

serves 4

1 lb (500 g) whole-milk ricotta cheese

8 ripe, fresh figs

¼ cup (6 oz/185 g) light, aromatic
honey such as orange blossom

Line a fine-mesh sieve with a double layer of cheesecloth and set the sieve over a bowl. Spoon the ricotta into the cheesecloth. Gather the corners of the cheesecloth and tie into a bundle. Set aside at room temperature to drain for 1 hour. Divide the cheese into 4 pieces and place on plates.

Using a small, sharp knife, remove the woody stems from the figs. Cut each fig into quarters lengthwise and arrange them, flesh side up, next to the cheese on each plate.

Drizzle the honey over the cheese and figs, and serve.

26

Butternut squash and whole-wheat dough make up this filling pizza, full of good-for-you carbs that metabolize slowly to keep you feeling fuller longer. If you like, top slices with extra arugula instead of making a side salad.

BUTTERNUT SQUASH PIZZA

makes two 12-inch (30-cm) pizzas; serves 4

1½ lb (750 g) butternut squash

4 Tbsp (2 fl oz/60 ml) olive oil

Salt and freshly ground pepper

1 tsp minced fresh thyme

2 lb (500 g) purchased whole-wheat
pizza dough

3–4 oz (90–125 g) soft goat cheese

¼ cup (1 oz/30 g) grated Parmesan cheese

½ cup (½ oz/15 g) baby arugula leaves

Preheat the oven to 350°F (180°C). Halve and seed the squash, then cut into slices 2 inches (5 cm) thick. Put the squash in a bowl and add 2 Tbsp of the oil, 1 tsp salt, 1 tsp pepper, and the thyme. Turn to coat well. Pour the squash on a baking sheet and bake until fork-tender, about 1¼ hours. Let cool to the touch, then cut away the skin and cut the squash flesh into bite-size pieces. Raise the oven temperature to 500°F (260°C).

Flatten each dough ball and roll out each into a disk about 12 inches (30 cm) in diameter. Sprinkle 2 baking sheets with cornmeal and lay a dough disk on each one. ⟩⟩

Drizzle each dough disk with 2 tsp of the oil. Dot the oiled dough with pieces of squash and goat cheese. Sprinkle with Parmesan. Bake until the crust is browned and the goat cheese is slightly melted, 12–15 minutes. Remove the pizzas from the oven and drizzle with the remaining oil. Top with arugula, cut into wedges, and serve.

27

Olives and almonds are staples of Spanish cuisine. Here, they are combined with chicken, peppers, tomatoes, and garlic for a full-flavored one-pot stew. Serve it with small red, yellow, or white potatoes, and pour a medium-bodied Rioja or other Spanish wine.

SPANISH CHICKEN STEW

serves 4–6

3–4 lb (1.5–2 kg) assorted chicken pieces,
skin on and bone in

Salt and freshly ground pepper

2 Tbsp unsalted butter

2 Tbsp canola oil

2 red or yellow bell peppers,
seeded and finely chopped

1 yellow onion, thinly sliced

1 clove garlic, minced

2 tomatoes, seeded and chopped

2 tsp smoked paprika

1 can (15 oz/470 g) chickpeas,
rinsed and drained

¾ cup (5 oz/155 g) pitted green olives

½ cup (2 oz/60 g) sliced almonds,
toasted, plus more for garnish

Season the chicken with salt and pepper. In a large, heavy pot, melt the butter with the oil over medium-high heat. Working in batches, sear the chicken, turning as needed, until browned, about 10 minutes. Transfer to a plate.

Pour off all but 1 Tbsp fat from the pot. Add the bell peppers and onion and sauté until softened, about 5 minutes. Add the garlic and cook for 1 minute. Stir in the tomatoes and paprika. Return the chicken to the pot. Cover and cook over medium-low heat until the chicken is tender and opaque throughout, about 40 minutes. Uncover and add the chickpeas, olives, and the ½ cup (2 oz/60 g) almonds. Cover and cook until the chickpeas are warmed through, about 10 minutes.

Garnish with the toasted almonds and serve directly from the pot.

OCTOBER 28

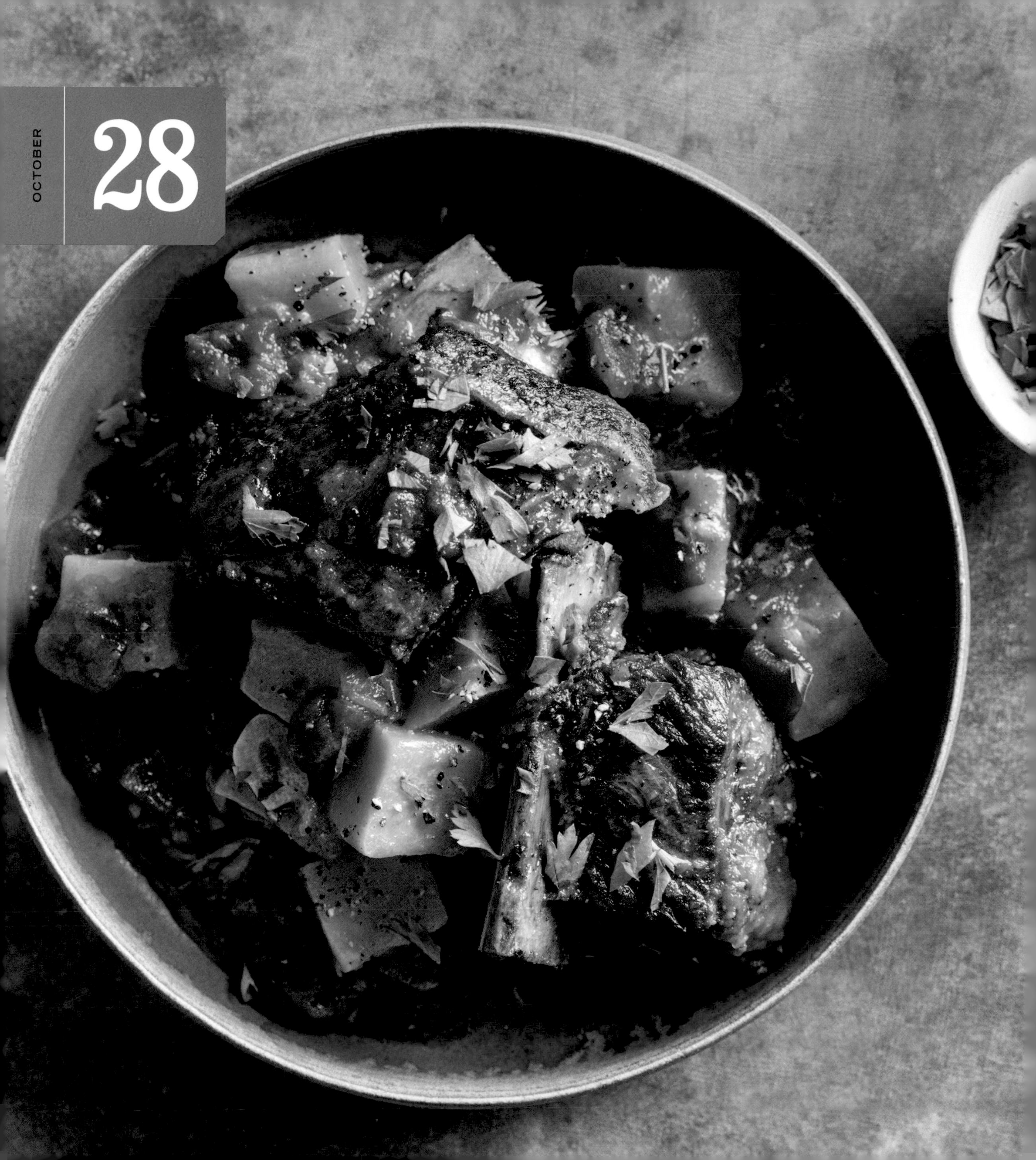

28

OCTOBER

*Adding a bottle
of beer to a beef
braise produces a
full-flavored dish
ideal for an autumn
meal. The bones in
the short ribs work
their magic in
the slow cooker,
contributing their
collagen to an
especially rich
sauce. Chunks of
winter squash cook
along with the
beef, sweetening
the braise. Serve
with a green salad
and pour a Cabernet
Sauvignon or
Pinot Noir.*

ALE-BRAISED SHORT RIBS

serves 6

4–5 lb (2–2.5 kg) bone-in beef short ribs,
cut into 3-inch (7.5-cm) pieces

Salt and freshly ground pepper

2 yellow onions, thinly sliced

3 cloves garlic, sliced

1 butternut squash, about 2 lb (1 kg),
peeled and cut into chunks

1 can (14½ oz/455 g) diced tomatoes

1 bottle (12 fl oz/375 ml) ale or dark beer

3 Tbsp all-purpose flour

Chopped fresh flat-leaf parsley leaves
for garnish

Preheat the broiler. Generously season the
ribs on all sides with salt and pepper. Working
in batches, arrange the ribs on a broiler pan
and broil, turning once, until well browned,
about 3 minutes on each side. Transfer the
ribs to a slow cooker.

Scatter the onions and garlic over the ribs.
Add the squash. Pour in the tomatoes with
their juices and the ale. Cover and cook
on the high setting for 5–6 hours or on the
low setting for 7–8 hours. The meat should
be falling off the bones, and the squash
should be tender.

Using a slotted spoon, transfer the ribs and
squash to a platter and tent with foil. Skim
the fat from the surface of the sauce. Put the
slow cooker on the high setting. In a small
bowl, whisk together the flour and ¼ cup
(2 fl oz/60 ml) water. Whisk the flour mixture
into the sauce and cook uncovered, stirring
occasionally, until the sauce is slightly
thickened, about 15 minutes. Season with
salt and pepper. Spoon the sauce over the
ribs and squash and serve with the parsley.

29

OCTOBER

*If you cannot find
fresh Chinese egg
noodles, use dried
egg noodles in
their place. Just
follow the package
instructions for
cooking. The
dressing, with its
heady mix of spicy,
sour, and salty
tastes, infuses the
boiled edamame
and grilled chicken
strips with Asian
flavors. If you are
craving more
vegetables, cut
bok choy into
narrow strips,
blanch briefly in
boiling water, and
add to the bowl with
the noodles and
other ingredients.*

SESAME NOODLES WITH GRILLED CHICKEN, CARROTS & EDAMAME

serves 6

¼ cup (2 fl oz/60 ml) canola or vegetable oil

¼ cup (2 fl oz/60 ml) rice wine vinegar

¼ cup (2 fl oz/60 ml) soy sauce

3 Tbsp fresh orange juice

2 Tbsp brown sugar

1½ Tbsp toasted sesame oil

1 Tbsp garlic, minced

1 tsp Sriracha sauce, or to taste

¾ lb (375 g) boneless, skinless
chicken breasts

Salt and freshly ground pepper

1 cup (5 oz/155 g) shelled edamame

1 lb (500 g) fresh Chinese egg noodles

2 carrots, grated

¼ cup (¼ oz/40 g) thinly sliced green onions

2 Tbsp toasted sesame seeds

In a bowl, combine the canola oil, vinegar,
soy sauce, orange juice, brown sugar, sesame
oil, garlic, and Sriracha sauce to make a
dressing. Reserve 2 Tbsp of the dressing for
the chicken and set the rest aside.

Warm a stove-top grill pan over medium-
high heat. Season the chicken with salt and
pepper and brush it with the 2 Tbsp reserved
dressing. Grill the chicken until cooked
through, 3–4 minutes on each side. Set the
chicken aside and, when it's cool enough to
handle, cut it into strips about 2 inches (5 cm)
long and ½ inch (12 mm) wide.

Bring a large pot of generously salted water
to a boil over high heat. Add the edamame
and cook until just tender and heated through,
2–3 minutes. Remove the edamame with a
slotted spoon, drain well, and bring the water
back to a boil. Add the noodles and cook until
al dente, 3–4 minutes, or according to package
directions. Drain the noodles well.

In a large bowl, toss together the noodles,
chicken, remaining dressing, edamame
carrots, green onions, and sesame seeds.
Serve warm, or refrigerate up to 6 hours
and serve at room temperature.

30

Do yourself a favor and make a double recipe of these homemade meatballs, then cook and freeze the extra batch for up to a couple of months. You are then halfway to a great soup supper on a busy weeknight. A different meat—chicken, beef, pork, lamb—can be used in place of the turkey, and Swiss chard or kale can be substituted for the mustard greens.

CHICKPEA & TURKEY MEATBALL SOUP WITH MUSTARD GREENS
serves 4–6

FOR THE TURKEY MEATBALLS

¾ lb (375 g) ground turkey

1 clove garlic, minced

3 Tbsp panko bread crumbs

2 Tbsp grated Parmesan cheese

1 egg, lightly beaten

1 Tbsp tomato paste

2 Tbsp chopped oregano

Salt and freshly ground pepper

2 Tbsp olive oil

1 small yellow onion, chopped

2 cloves garlic, chopped

2 Tbsp tomato paste

2 cans (15 oz/470 g each) chickpeas, drained

Salt and freshly ground pepper

4 cups (32 fl oz/1 l) chicken broth

1 bunch mustard greens, thick stems and ribs removed, leaves cut into 2-inch (5-cm) pieces

Preheat the oven to 375°F (190°C). Line a baking sheet with aluminum foil and spray with nonstick cooking spray.

To make the meatballs, in a bowl, combine the ground turkey, garlic, panko, cheese, egg, tomato paste, and oregano. Season with salt and pepper and stir just until combined. Using a heaping teaspoonful of the mixture, form each mini meatball and place about ½ inch (12 mm) apart on the prepared baking sheet. Roast until the meatballs are cooked through, 15–18 minutes. Set aside.

In a large, heavy pot, warm the oil over medium-high heat. Add the onion and cook, stirring occasionally, until soft, about 6 minutes. Add the garlic and cook, stirring occasionally, until soft, about 2 minutes. Stir in the tomato paste and chickpeas, and season with salt and pepper. Add the broth and bring to a boil. Reduce the heat to low and simmer for 15 minutes. Let cool slightly. ⟫

Purée half of the soup in a food processor or blender. Return to the pot and stir to combine. Season with salt and pepper. Place over medium-low heat and add the meatballs and the mustard greens. Cook until the meatballs are warmed through and the mustard greens wilt, about 4 minutes, then serve.

31

Many crisps and crumbles rely on the texture of oats, but this version emphasizes the flavor of the grain by including oat bran, as well. Spicy, resinous, sweet cardamom also adds a unique depth of flavor to the topping. Enjoy this dessert warm, with lightly sweetened whipped cream or tangy crème fraîche.

OATMEAL PEAR CRISP
serves 6

5 firm, just-ripe pears, peeled, cored, and sliced

3 Tbsp granulated sugar

2 Tbsp lemon juice

½ cup (3½ oz/105 g) firmly packed light brown sugar

1 cup (3 oz/90 g) rolled oats

¼ cup (½ oz/15 g) oat bran

⅔ cup (3½ oz/105 g) all-purpose flour

1 tsp baking powder

½ tsp ground cardamom

6 Tbsp (3 oz/90 g) unsalted butter, cut into small pieces

Whipped cream (see page 53)

Preheat the oven to 350°F (180°C). Place the pear slices in a bowl. Sprinkle with the granulated sugar and toss gently. Spread the slices in an even layer in a shallow baking dish 12 inches (30 cm) in diameter. Sprinkle with the lemon juice.

In a bowl, stir together the brown sugar, oats, oat bran, flour, baking powder, and cardamom. Add the butter and rub into the oat mixture with your fingertips until the mixture is crumbly. Sprinkle evenly over the fruit. Bake until golden and crisp, about 40 minutes. Serve hot or warm, topped with a big dollop of whipped cream.

With the arrival of cooler weather and longer nights, cooks begin to put more comfort food on the menu. That might translate into a bread-thickened vegetable soup, a cheese-crowned winter squash lasagna, or slow-cooked osso buco. Pumpkins fill seasonally tuned kitchens, where they are added to chicken curry, baked with white beans and caramelized onions in a vegetarian main, and turned into the perfect pie for Thanksgiving dinner. This is the height of cranberry time, too, when the fruit joins horseradish and spices in a burger relish, wild rice and pecans in a pilaf, and wheat berries, parsnips, and squash in a healthful main or side.

1
UDON NOODLE SOUP WITH
PORK BELLY & SOFT EGGS
page 254

2
OSSO BUCO WITH GREMOLATA
page 256

3
BUTTERNUT SQUASH RISOTTO
WITH SAGE
page 256

8
TURKEY TETRAZZINI
page 260

9
MUSSELS IN THAI COCONUT BROTH
page 260

10
BUTTERNUT SQUASH LASAGNA
page 262

15
PUMPKIN WITH
WHITE BEANS, CARAMELIZED
ONIONS & ROASTED GARLIC
page 265

16
SHREDDED KALE SALAD WITH
PANCETTA & HARD-COOKED EGG
page 266

17
SPICY COCONUT-MANDARIN SOUP
WITH MUSHROOMS
page 266

22
TURKEY MOLE ENCHILADAS
page 271

23
ROASTED SQUASH WITH
CRANBERRIES & THYME
page 271

24
TURKEY BURGERS WITH
CRANBERRY RELISH
page 272

29
BROCCOLI RABE, PESTO & SMOKED
MOZZARELLA STRATA
page 275

30
TIRAMISÙ
page 277

4
HONEY-GLAZED SWEET POTATO & CURRIED PECAN SALAD
page 257

5
MAPLE ALMOND SQUARES
page 257

6
ITALIAN-STYLE RIBOLLITA
page 259

7
PULLED CHICKEN SLIDERS WITH APPLE-JICAMA RELISH
page 259

11
TURKEY & JASMINE RICE SOUP WITH LEMONGRASS
page 262

12
CUBAN-STYLE STUFFED FLANK STEAK
page 263

13
BULGUR WITH PERSIMMONS, PISTACHIOS & POMEGRANATE
page 263

14
PORTER-BRAISED CHICKEN WITH ROOT VEGETABLES
page 265

18
SOBA WITH SHIITAKES & MUSTARD GREENS
page 269

19
ASIAN-STYLE CABBAGE ROLLS
page 269

20
THAI PUMPKIN & CHICKEN CURRY
page 270

21
OLD-FASHIONED APPLE PIE
page 270

25
WHEAT BERRIES WITH ROASTED PARSNIPS, BUTTERNUT SQUASH & DRIED CRANBERRIES
page 272

26
BROWN SUGAR PUMPKIN PIE
page 274

27
WILD RICE PILAF WITH DRIED CRANBERRIES & PECANS
page 274

28
MOLASSES-GLAZED ROAST PORK & SWEET POTATOES
page 275

november

1

It may be difficult to find fresh udon for this homey Asian-inspired soup, but 1 lb (500 g) dried udon, cooked according to the package instructions, can be substituted. You can also use fresh Chinese egg noodles in place of the udon. If you don't have time to roast the pork belly and you live near a Chinese delicatessen, purchase a piece of crispy skin pork, a Cantonese specialty, and ask the clerk to slice it for you.

UDON NOODLE SOUP WITH PORK BELLY & SOFT EGGS

serves 4–6

8 cups (2 qt/2 l) chicken broth

1 pork belly (2¼–2½ lb/1.1–1.25 kg)

2 Tbsp olive oil

Salt and freshly ground pepper

7 cloves garlic

4 star anise

2 cinnamon sticks

2 Tbsp unsalted butter

1 Tbsp light sesame oil

2-inch (5-cm) piece fresh ginger, peeled and grated

1 jalapeño chile, seeded, deribbed, and sliced

5 Tbsp (3 fl oz/80 ml) low-sodium soy sauce

1½ oz (45 g) dried shiitake mushrooms

3 packages (7 oz/220 g each) fresh udon noodles (flavor packets discarded if included)

4 eggs

3 green onions, white and tender green parts, thinly sliced

Preheat the oven to 500°F (260°C). In a roasting pan, combine 2 cups (16 fl oz/500 ml) of the broth and 1 cup (8 fl oz/250 ml) water. Place the pork belly, fat side up, in the pan. Brush with the olive oil and season with salt and pepper. Cut 4 of the garlic cloves in half lengthwise and scatter into the broth along with the star anise and cinnamon sticks. Roast until the top is golden and beginning to bubble, about 15 minutes. Reduce the oven temperature to 325°F (165°C) and continue to roast until an instant-read thermometer inserted into the thickest part of the pork belly registers 145°F (63°C), about 1 hour longer. Remove from the oven, tent the pan with aluminum foil, and keep the pork warm in the braising juices.

Mince the remaining 3 garlic cloves. In a large, heavy pot, melt the butter with the sesame oil over medium-high heat. Add the garlic, ginger, and jalapeño and cook, stirring occasionally, until soft, about 2 minutes. ⇢

Add the remaining 6 cups (48 fl oz/1.5 l) broth and the soy sauce and bring to a boil. Reduce the heat to low, stir in the dried mushrooms, and simmer until very soft, about 15 minutes.

Raise the heat to high and return the broth to a boil. Add the udon noodles and cook until al dente, about 4 minutes or according to the package directions.

Meanwhile, bring a saucepan of water to a boil over medium-high heat. Gently lower the eggs into the pan and cook for exactly 8 minutes. Drain, rinse the eggs under cold water, and peel. Cut the eggs in half lengthwise.

Transfer the pork belly to a cutting board and cut crosswise into ¾-inch (2-cm) slices.

Using tongs, fill bowls with the udon noodles. Ladle the broth over the noodles and top each with a few slices of pork and 2 egg halves. Garnish with the green onions and serve.

OSSO BUCO WITH GREMOLATA

serves 6–8

¾ cup (4 oz/125 g) all-purpose flour

Salt and freshly ground pepper

6 bone-in veal shanks, about 6 lb (3 kg) total, each cut into slices about 1 inch (2.5 cm) thick

½ cup (4 fl oz/120 ml) olive oil

1 yellow onion, chopped

1 carrot, chopped

1 celery rib, chopped

2 cloves garlic, minced

1½ cups (12 fl oz/375 ml) dry red wine

1 cup (6 oz/185 g) canned diced tomatoes

5 cups (40 fl oz/1.25 l) beef broth

FOR THE GREMOLATA

½ cup (¾ oz/20 g) minced fresh flat-leaf parsley

Grated zest of 1 lemon

2 cloves garlic, minced

Kick off dinner-party season with this signature northern Italian dish in which veal shanks are slowly braised until the meat nearly falls from the bone. The traditional accompaniments are gremolata, a parsley and lemon zest garnish that provides a welcome counterpoint to the richness of the meat, and risotto perfumed with saffron.

Put the flour on a plate and season with salt and pepper. Dust the veal shanks with the seasoned flour, shaking off the excess. In a large, heavy sauté pan with a lid, warm the oil over medium-high heat. Working in batches, sear the shanks, turning once, until well browned on both sides, about 8 minutes. Transfer to a plate.

Return the pan to medium heat, add the onion, carrot, celery, and garlic, and sauté until softened, 3–4 minutes. Add the wine and stir to scrape up any browned bits on the pan bottom. Raise the heat to high and cook until the liquid has thickened and is reduced by half, 3–4 minutes. Add the tomatoes and broth and bring to a boil. Reduce the heat to low, return the veal shanks to the pan, cover, and simmer, turning occasionally, for 1 hour. Uncover and cook until the veal is tender, about 30 minutes.

Meanwhile, to make the gremolata, in a small bowl, stir together the parsley, lemon zest, and garlic.

Divide the veal shanks among plates. Top with the pan sauce, sprinkle with the gremolata, and serve.

BUTTERNUT SQUASH RISOTTO WITH SAGE

serves 4

2–3 cloves garlic, chopped

Salt and freshly ground pepper

1 small butternut squash, about 1 lb (500 g)

4 cups (32 fl oz/1 l) vegetable or chicken broth

4 Tbsp (2 oz/60 g) unsalted butter

2 Tbsp olive oil

1 yellow onion, chopped

1½ cups (10½ oz/330 g) Arborio or Carnaroli rice

5 fresh sage leaves, finely shredded

1½ cups (12 fl oz/375 ml) dry white wine

Pinch of grated nutmeg

1 cup (4 oz/125 g) grated Parmesan cheese

Sweet butternut squash has an affinity for sage, whether in soups, pasta dishes, or roasted. This basic Parmesan risotto is the perfect way to highlight the flavors of shredded squash and sage leaves, which are stirred directly into the creamy rice.

In a small bowl, using a fork, crush the garlic with a pinch of salt. Halve the squash and scoop out the seeds and fibers. Peel the halves. Cut one half into ½-inch (12-mm) cubes and coarsely shred the remaining half.

In a saucepan, bring the broth to a gentle simmer over medium heat and maintain over low heat. In a large, heavy saucepan, melt 2 Tbsp of the butter with the oil over medium heat. Add the cubed squash and the onion and sauté until softened, 5–7 minutes. Raise the heat to medium-high, add the rice, and cook, stirring, until well coated with the butter and oil and translucent, 3–5 minutes.

Add the sage and pour in half of the wine. Cook, stirring, until the wine is absorbed. Stir in the remaining wine and cook and stir until absorbed. Add the simmering broth a ladleful at a time, stirring until almost all the broth is absorbed (but the rice is never dry on top) before adding more. When the rice is almost tender, after about 15 minutes, stir in the shredded squash. Continue to cook, adding more broth and stirring constantly, until the rice is firm but tender, 20–25 minutes total. Stir in the garlic and the nutmeg, and season with salt and pepper. Add additional hot broth if needed.

Stir in some of the Parmesan. Spoon the risotto onto plates. Divide the remaining 2 Tbsp butter into 4 pieces and top each serving with a piece of butter. Serve with the remaining Parmesan.

HONEY-GLAZED SWEET POTATO & CURRIED PECAN SALAD

serves 4

The warm flavors of spices, honey, and brown sugar dominate this salad. Curry powder, a blend that typically includes cumin, chile, coriander, and other spices, flavors the pecans. The dressing is seasoned with cumin and chile as well and calls for honey, which turns the sweet potato cubes a lush golden brown. The pecans can be addictive, so you may want to double or triple the recipe to have extra on hand.

FOR THE DRESSING

¼ cup (2 fl oz/60 ml) extra-virgin olive oil

2 Tbsp sherry vinegar

2 tsp honey

¼ tsp chili powder

¼ tsp ground cumin

Salt

FOR THE CURRIED PECANS

1 tsp curry powder

½ tsp light brown sugar

Salt

½ cup (3 oz/90 g) pecan halves

1 Tbsp unsalted butter, melted

FOR THE SWEET POTATO

1 large sweet potato, cut into ½-inch (12-mm) cubes, peeled

2 tsp extra-virgin olive oil

Salt and freshly ground pepper

1 Tbsp honey

2 cups (2 oz/60 g) baby spinach

2 cups (2 oz/60 g) baby arugula

6 oz (185 g) fresh goat cheese, crumbled

Preheat the oven to 350°F (180°C). Line a baking sheet with aluminum foil or parchment paper.

To make the dressing, in a large bowl, whisk together the oil, vinegar, honey, chili powder, cumin, and ¼ tsp salt until the dressing is well blended. Set aside.

To make the curried pecans, in a small bowl, stir together the curry powder, brown sugar, and ⅛ tsp salt. Put the pecans in a separate small bowl and pour the melted butter over them. Add the curry mixture and stir to coat well. Place the pecans in a single layer on the prepared baking sheet. Roast, stirring once or twice, until the pecans are fragrant and a slight crust has formed on them, about 15 minutes. Let cool. Leave the oven on. The pecans can be stored in an airtight container at room temperature for up to 7 days.

To make the sweet potato, put the sweet potato cubes in a single layer in an ⇥

oven-safe frying pan. Drizzle with the oil, sprinkle with ½ tsp salt and ¼ tsp pepper, and stir to coat well. Roast in the oven, turning them once or twice, until tender when pierced with a knife, about 15 minutes. Using an oven mitt, transfer the pan to the stove top and place over medium-high heat. Drizzle the potato cubes with the honey and cook until golden brown underneath, about 4 minutes. Turn them and brown the other side, about 2 minutes. Remove from the heat and keep warm.

Add the spinach and arugula to the bowl with the dressing and toss to coat. Divide the greens among individual plates. Top with the sweet potato cubes and the pecans. Dot with the goat cheese and serve.

MAPLE ALMOND SQUARES

makes about 24 squares

This is quite possibly one of the easiest cookie recipes you can make. Oats and nuts are bound together with maple syrup and two other ingredients. The squares are compact and don't crumble easily, which makes them ideal for packed lunches.

½ cup (4 oz/125 g) unsalted butter, plus more for greasing

¼ cup (2 oz/60 g) firmly packed dark brown sugar

⅓ cup (3½ oz/105 g) maple syrup

2 cups (6 oz/185 g) rolled oats

1 cup (5 oz/155 g) whole almonds, coarsely chopped

Preheat the oven to 350°F (180°C). Lightly butter a 9-inch (23-cm) square baking pan. Line the bottom and 2 sides with parchment paper, extending the paper up and over the sides. Butter the parchment.

In a large saucepan, heat the ½ cup (4 oz/125 g) butter, the brown sugar, and maple syrup over low heat, stirring frequently, until the butter melts and the sugar dissolves. Remove from the heat and stir in the oats and almonds until well blended. Pour the mixture into the prepared pan and press firmly into an even layer with the back of a spoon.

Bake until golden brown, about 30 minutes. Let cool in the pan on a wire rack. Using the parchment, lift the sheet from the pan and place on a work surface. Peel back the parchment from the sides and cut into squares. Serve.

6

ITALIAN-STYLE RIBOLLITA

serves 6

½ cup (4 fl oz/125 ml) extra-virgin olive oil, plus more for drizzling

1 yellow onion, chopped

2 carrots, peeled and chopped

1 celery rib, chopped

1 cup (3 oz/90 g) coarsely chopped cauliflower

4 lacinato kale leaves, chopped

1 cup (2 oz/60 g) chopped chard leaves

2 zucchini, trimmed and diced

1 large boiling potato, peeled and diced

2 cups (14 oz/440 g) drained cooked cannellini beans

¼ cup (⅓ oz/10 g) minced mixed fresh flat-leaf parsley, rosemary, and sage

2½ qt (2.5 l) low-sodium chicken or vegetable broth

Salt and freshly ground pepper

12 thin slices day-old coarse country whole-wheat bread

½ cup (2 oz/60 g) freshly grated Parmesan cheese

When Tuscan cooks make this soup, they often serve it over two days. On the first day, it is a hearty vegetable soup. On the second day, the leftover soup is layered with stale bread, drizzled with olive oil, cooked again, and declared ribollita, or "reboiled." This version is packed with lacinato kale, a popular green in fall markets.

In a large soup pot over medium-high heat, warm the ½ cup (4 fl oz/125 ml) oil. Add the onion, carrots, and celery and sauté until the onion is golden, 3–4 minutes. Add the cauliflower and sauté until tender-crisp, about 5 minutes. Add the remaining vegetables and cook, stirring, for 5 minutes.

Add the beans and herbs to the pot, stir well, and pour in the broth. Bring to a boil over medium-high heat, and cook, uncovered, until the vegetables are tender, about 30 minutes. Season with salt and pepper. Remove from the heat.

Position a rack in the middle of the oven and preheat to 425°F (220°C). Ladle enough soup into a 9-by-13-inch (23-by-33-cm) baking dish to cover the bottom. Top with one-third of the bread slices, trimming them to fit if necessary. Add another layer of soup. Sprinkle evenly with one-third of the cheese. Top with half of the remaining bread slices, then the soup, and finally the cheese. Repeat for a third layer, using all the ingredients. Bake until heated through, about 20 minutes. Remove from the oven and drizzle with oil. Spoon the soup into warmed soup bowls, and serve.

7

PULLED CHICKEN SLIDERS WITH APPLE-JICAMA RELISH

serves 4–6

1 whole chicken, about 3½ lb (1.75 kg)

½ lemon

2 dried bay leaves

Salt and freshly ground pepper

1 cup (8 fl oz/250 ml) tomato purée

1 cup (8 oz/250 g) Dijon mustard

¾ cup (6 fl oz/375 ml) apple cider vinegar

3 Tbsp firmly packed light brown sugar

2 cloves garlic, minced

Hot-pepper sauce

FOR THE APPLE-JICAMA RELISH

1 Granny Smith apple, finely diced

¾ cup (4 oz/125 g) finely diced jicama

¼ cup (1 oz/30 g) finely diced red onion

2 Tbsp minced fresh cilantro

1 Tbsp extra-virgin olive oil

1 tsp apple cider vinegar

Salt and freshly ground pepper

12 small soft rolls

Jicama, a root vegetable in season from fall into spring, has a mild taste and crisp texture similar to that of water chestnuts. Here, it is combined with apples and red onions in a crunchy slaw-like relish for dressing up chicken sliders. When shopping for slider buns, look for small, spongy rolls, either plain or whole wheat.

Place the chicken in a large saucepan with the lemon, bay leaves, 1 tsp salt, and ½ tsp pepper. Fill the saucepan with water to cover the chicken and bring to a boil over high heat. Reduce the heat to medium-low and simmer until the chicken is cooked through, about 1 hour. Carefully remove the chicken from the water and, when it's cool enough to handle, remove the meat, discarding the skin and bones. Using your hands, shred the chicken into a large bowl.

In a saucepan, combine the tomato purée, mustard, vinegar, brown sugar, garlic, 3 shakes of hot sauce, 1 tsp salt, and ½ tsp pepper. Set over high heat and bring to a boil. Reduce the heat to low and simmer until the flavors come together and the color deepens, about 25 minutes. Season with salt and pepper. Cool slightly, then pour over the shredded chicken. Stir to mix.

To make the relish, in a bowl, mix the apple, jicama, onion, cilantro, oil, and vinegar. Season with salt and pepper.

Spoon the chicken onto the rolls, top with about 1 Tbsp of the relish, and serve.

8

TURKEY TETRAZZINI

serves 6–8

Olive oil for greasing

7 Tbsp (3½ oz/105 g) unsalted butter

2 shallots, minced

½ lb (250 g) button mushrooms, sliced

⅓ cup (2 oz/60 g) all-purpose flour

3 cups (24 fl oz/750 ml) chicken broth

Salt and ground white pepper

3 cups (18 oz/560 g) shredded cooked turkey

½ lb (250 g) egg noodles, cooked according to package directions

¾ cup (3 oz/90 g) grated Parmesan cheese

2 green onions, white and tender green parts, chopped

1 cup (2 oz/60 g) fresh bread crumbs

This retro casserole uses up leftover turkey in a tangle of egg noodles, button mushrooms, and cheese with delicious results. Whether baked in one large pan, or divided among individual ramekins, it is sure to become an annual post-holiday tradition. Use both white and dark turkey meat, as the dark meat will add moisture.

Preheat the oven to 450°F (230°C). Oil a 9-by-13-inch (23-by-33-cm) baking dish or 6 individual ramekins or baking dishes.

In a large frying pan, melt 2 Tbsp of the butter over medium-high heat. Add the shallots and mushrooms and sauté until the mushrooms begin to brown, about 5 minutes. Transfer to a large bowl.

Add 4 Tbsp of the butter to the pan and melt over medium-high heat. Add the flour and cook, stirring constantly, for 2 minutes. Add the broth and bring to a boil. Cook, stirring frequently, until the sauce thickens, about 4 minutes. Season with 1 tsp salt and ½ tsp pepper. Pour the sauce into the bowl with the mushrooms and add the turkey, the cooked noodles, ½ cup (2 oz/60g) of the Parmesan, and the green onions and stir to combine.

In a small bowl, mix the bread crumbs with the remaining ¼ cup (1 oz/30 g) Parmesan.

Transfer the turkey mixture to the prepared dish(es). Sprinkle evenly with the bread crumb mixture. Using your fingers, break the remaining 1 Tbsp butter into small pieces and sprinkle over the top.

Bake until the tetrazzini is bubbly around the edges and the bread crumbs are golden brown, about 15 minutes. Serve.

9

MUSSELS IN THAI COCONUT BROTH

serves 4

2 lb (1 kg) mussels, well scrubbed and debearded

½ cup (4 fl oz/125 ml) dry white wine

1 Tbsp canola oil

2 heads baby bok choy, trimmed and cut into 1-inch (2.5-cm) pieces

1 red bell pepper, seeded and finely julienned

2 shallots, thinly sliced

2 tsp light brown sugar

1 tsp curry powder

Large pinch of cayenne pepper

1 can (13 fl oz/430 ml) unsweetened coconut milk, well shaken

¼ cup (¼ oz/7 g) fresh cilantro leaves

4 lime wedges

Store mussels for no more than a day after purchase, covered with a damp kitchen towel in your refrigerator, then scrub and debeard them just before cooking. Serve this dish with crusty whole-wheat bread for sopping up the spice-laden broth.

Place the mussels in a large saucepan, discarding any that fail to close to the touch. Add the wine and bring to a boil over high heat. Cover and cook, shaking the pan occasionally, until the mussels open, about 5 minutes. Using a slotted spoon, transfer the mussels to a bowl, discarding any that failed to open; cover and keep warm. Strain the liquid in the pan through a fine-mesh sieve lined with cheesecloth into a bowl.

Wipe out the pan, add the oil, and place over medium-high heat. Add the bok choy, bell pepper, and shallots and cook, stirring, until the vegetables are soft, about 5 minutes. Stir in the brown sugar, curry powder, and cayenne. Pour in the coconut milk and the reserved mussel cooking liquid and bring to a boil over high heat.

Divide the mussels among warmed bowls and ladle the broth over the top, dividing evenly. Sprinkle with the cilantro and serve with lime wedges for squeezing.

10

*Lasagna is both
a quintessential
comfort food and
a great party food:
it can be assembled
ahead and then baked
just before serving.
This vegetarian
version relies on
butternut squash,
tomatoes, and a trio
of cheeses for its rich,
satisfying flavor.
Serve it with a green
salad and coarse
country bread and
pour a Pinot Noir
or a Merlot.*

BUTTERNUT SQUASH LASAGNA

serves 6

1 butternut squash, about 2½ lb (1.25 kg),
halved, seeded, peeled, and cut into
½-inch (12-mm) cubes

3 Tbsp olive oil

Salt and freshly ground pepper

1 Tbsp unsalted butter

2 cloves garlic, minced

1 yellow onion, chopped

1 Tbsp chopped fresh rosemary

2 cups (1 lb/500 g) ricotta cheese

1 egg, beaten

½ cup (4 fl oz/125 ml) heavy cream

½ lb (250 g) mozzarella cheese, shredded

¼ cup (1 oz/30 g) grated Parmesan cheese,
plus 2 Tbsp

Pinch of freshly grated nutmeg

1 can (14½ oz/455 g) diced tomatoes

6 oz (186 g) lasagna noodles, cooked
according to package directions

Preheat the oven to 450°F (230°C). Oil
a 9-by-13-inch (23-by-33-cm) baking dish.

Line a baking sheet with parchment paper.
Place the squash on the prepared baking sheet,
drizzle with 2 Tbsp of the oil, season with
salt and pepper, and toss to coat. Spread the
squash out evenly. Roast, stirring once, until
the squash is tender and caramelized, about
25 minutes. Remove from the oven and reduce
the oven temperature to 375°F (190°C).

In a large frying pan, melt the butter with
the remaining 1 Tbsp oil over medium-high
heat. Add the garlic, onion, and rosemary and
cook, stirring, until the onion is translucent,
about 6 minutes. Turn off the heat, add the
squash, and stir to combine, then gently
mash about half of the squash.

In a bowl, combine the ricotta, egg, cream,
mozzarella, and ¼ cup (1 oz/30 g) Parmesan.
Season with the nutmeg and with salt and
pepper, and stir to combine.

Spread one-third of the ricotta mixture
on the bottom of the prepared baking dish.
Top with half of the squash and half of the
tomatoes and their juice, and cover with a
single layer of lasagna noodles. Spread half
of the remaining ricotta mixture on top ⇥

of the noodles and cover with the remaining
squash and the remaining tomatoes and
their juice. Top with a single layer of the
lasagna noodles. Finish with the remaining
ricotta mixture and sprinkle with the
2 Tbsp Parmesan.

Bake until the cheese turns golden brown
and the lasagna is bubbling around the edges,
25–30 minutes. Let cool slightly before serving.

11

*Lemongrass is
citrusy and lightly
herbal in taste, with
a crisp, refreshing
aroma. The fragrant
herb shines new
light on a familiar
turkey soup that
also receives a
flavor boost from
ginger, garlic,
and hot chiles.
The addition of
jasmine rice adds
both body and a
floral fragrance
to the soup.*

TURKEY & JASMINE RICE SOUP WITH LEMONGRASS

serves 6–8

1-inch (2.5-cm) piece fresh ginger

3 serrano chiles

2 tsp canola oil

1 yellow onion, finely chopped

3 cloves garlic, minced

4 lemongrass stalks, center white part only,
smashed and minced

3 carrots, peeled and thinly sliced

8 cups (2 qt/2 l) chicken or turkey broth

1 cup (8 fl oz/250 ml) dry white wine

¾ cup (5 oz/155 g) jasmine rice or other
long-grain white rice

Leftover shredded cooked turkey meat

Salt and freshly ground pepper

Peel the ginger, cut it into 4 equal slices,
and crush each piece with the flat side of a
chef's knife. Seed and mince 2 of the serrano
chiles; cut the remaining chile crosswise
into very thin rings and set aside.

In a large, heavy pot, warm the oil over
medium heat. Add the onion and sauté until
softened, about 5 minutes. Stir in the garlic,
minced chiles, and lemongrass and cook
until fragrant, about 45 seconds. Raise the
heat to high, add the ginger, carrots, broth,
and wine and bring to a boil. Stir in the
rice, turkey, 2 tsp salt, and pepper to taste.
Reduce the heat to low and simmer until
the rice is tender, about 15 minutes. Remove
and discard the ginger pieces.

Season the soup with salt and pepper
and serve, garnished with the reserved
chile slices.

12

Flank steak, an inexpensive cut of beef, is transformed into something quite spectacular when stuffed with spicy sausage, garlic, cheese, and herbs. Pop it into the slow cooker in the morning and prepare to be amazed come dinnertime.

CUBAN-STYLE STUFFED FLANK STEAK

serves 4–6

1½ lb (750 g) flank steak

¼ lb (125 g) smoked sausage such as andouille, finely chopped

½ cup (1 oz/30 g) fresh bread crumbs

1 large clove garlic, minced

2 Tbsp grated Parmesan cheese

2 Tbsp chopped fresh mint

½ tsp grated nutmeg

Salt and freshly ground pepper

1 egg, lightly beaten

2 Tbsp olive oil

1 large yellow onion, finely chopped

2 carrots, peeled and finely chopped

1 tsp dried oregano

2 Tbsp tomato paste

½ cup (4 fl oz/125 ml) medium-dry sherry

1 can (14½ oz/455 g) diced tomatoes, drained

3 bay leaves

Place the flank steak between 2 sheets of plastic wrap. Using a meat pounder or heavy pan, pound it into a large rectangle about ¼ inch (6 mm) thick (or ask your butcher to do this).

In a bowl, stir together the sausage, bread crumbs, garlic, Parmesan, mint, and nutmeg. Season with salt and pepper. Add the egg and mix well. Spread the sausage mixture evenly over the flank steak, leaving a ¼-inch (6-mm) border uncovered all around. Starting at a short end, roll up the steak and tie securely with kitchen twine at evenly spaced intervals.

In a large, heavy frying pan, warm the oil over medium-high heat. Add the rolled steak and cook, turning as needed, until well browned on all sides, about 10 minutes total. Transfer to a slow cooker. Add the onion, carrots, and oregano to the pan and sauté over medium-high heat until softened and beginning to brown, about 6 minutes. Stir in the tomato paste and cook for 1 minute. Pour in the sherry and stir to scrape up any browned bits on the pan bottom. Stir in the tomatoes and bay leaves, and then transfer the contents of the pan to the slow cooker. »→

Cover and cook on the low setting for about 5 hours. The steak should be very tender.

Transfer the rolled steak to a cutting board, tent with foil, and let rest for 15 minutes. Discard the bay leaves, and reserve the braising vegetables and liquid. Snip the strings from the rolled steak and cut crosswise into slices about ¾ inch (2 cm) thick. Arrange on a platter, spoon some of the braising liquid and vegetables over the slices, and serve.

13

Whole grains like nutty-tasting bulgur take well to a wide range of seasonings, fruits, and nuts. This recipe showcases the Middle Eastern flavors of pistachio and pomegranate. For a heartier version, top the finished salad with thinly sliced grilled lamb.

BULGUR WITH PERSIMMONS, PISTACHIOS & POMEGRANATE

serves 4

1 cup (6 oz/185 g) bulgur wheat

1 cup (8 fl oz/250 ml) boiling water

Salt

¼ cup (2 fl oz/60 ml) fresh lemon juice

¼ cup (2 fl oz/60 ml) extra-virgin olive oil

1 cup (1½ oz/45 g) chopped fresh flat-leaf parsley, plus extra for garnish

⅓ cup (½ oz/15 g) minced fresh mint, plus extra for garnish

½ cup (1½ oz/45 g) chopped green onion, including tender green parts

½ cup (2 oz/60 g) shelled pistachios

3 Fuyu persimmons, finely chopped

¼ cup (1 oz/30 g) pomegranate seeds

In a heatproof bowl, combine the bulgur, boiling water, and 1½ tsp salt. Cover and let stand until the bulgur is soft and the water has been absorbed, 15–20 minutes. Add the lemon juice, oil, parsley, mint, and green onion and stir to combine. Let stand at room temperature for at least 15 minutes or up to 2 hours.

In a small frying pan, toast the pistachios over medium-high heat, shaking the pan occasionally, until the nuts are fragrant, 3–4 minutes. Roughly chop the pistachios. Transfer to a small bowl.

Just before serving, add the persimmon and all but 1 Tbsp each of the pistachios and pomegranate seeds to the bulgur and stir gently to mix well. Transfer the salad to a serving bowl. Sprinkle with the remaining pistachios and pomegranate seeds and serve.

NOVEMBER

14

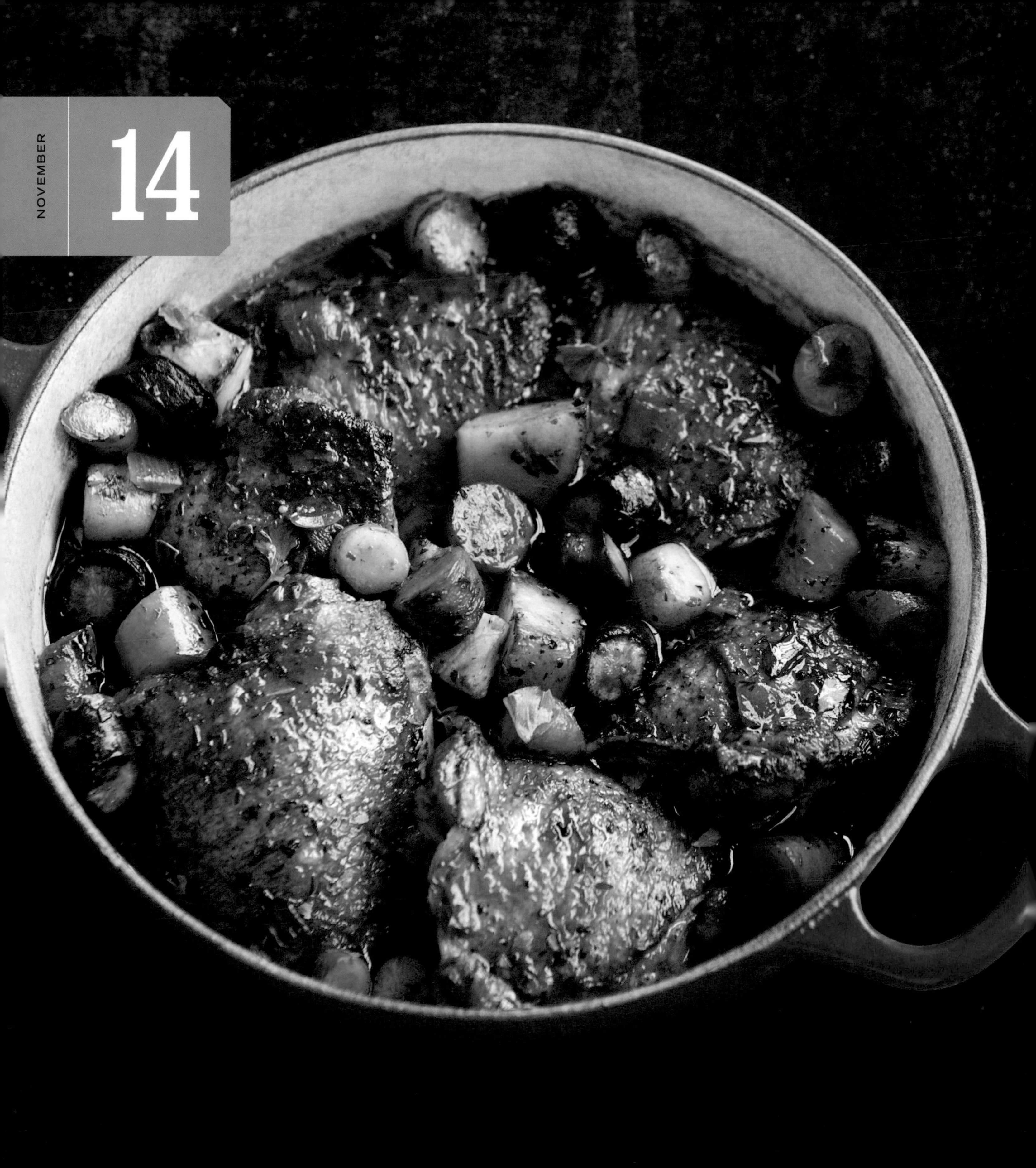

14

PORTER-BRAISED CHICKEN WITH ROOT VEGETABLES

serves 4

Slightly bitter and with a deep coffee-like flavor, porter, a very dark ale, makes this braise rustic and hearty. Porter's toastiness, plus the sweetness of cool-weather root vegetables and the spiciness of Dijon mustard, creates a stew full of contrasting yet harmonious flavors.

8 skin-on, bone-in chicken thighs, about 3½ lb (1.75 kg) total

Salt and freshly ground pepper

2 Tbsp canola oil

2 Tbsp unsalted butter, plus 5 Tbsp (2½ oz/75 g), at room temperature

1 large yellow onion, chopped

2 carrots, peeled and cut into 1-inch (2.5-cm) chunks

2 red potatoes, cut into 1-inch (2.5-cm) chunks

1 celery root, about 14 oz (440 g), peeled, trimmed, halved, and cut into 1-inch (2.5-cm) chunks

2 bottles (12 fl oz/375 ml each) porter

2 cups (16 fl oz/500 ml) chicken broth

2 Tbsp firmly packed light brown sugar

2 Tbsp Dijon mustard

2 tsp tomato paste

1 tsp dried thyme

⅓ cup (2 oz/60 g) all-purpose flour

Season the chicken thighs with salt and pepper. In a large, heavy pot, heat the oil over medium-high heat. Working in batches, sear the chicken thighs, turning once or twice, until lightly browned on both sides, about 5 minutes. Transfer to a plate. Pour off the fat in the pot.

Reduce the heat to medium and melt the 2 Tbsp butter. Add the onion and sauté until golden, about 6 minutes. Add the carrots, potatoes, and celery root, and stir in the porter, broth, sugar, mustard, tomato paste, and thyme. Return the chicken thighs to the pot, submerging them in the liquid, and bring to a simmer. Cover, reduce the heat to medium-low, and simmer, stirring occasionally, for 30 minutes.

In a heatproof bowl, mash together the 5 Tbsp butter and the flour to form a thick paste. Gradually whisk about 2 cups (16 fl oz/500 ml) of the hot cooking liquid into the flour-butter mixture, and then stir this mixture into the pot. Cover and simmer, stirring occasionally, until the chicken is opaque throughout, about 10 minutes. Adjust the seasoning and serve.

15

PUMPKIN WITH WHITE BEANS, CARAMELIZED ONIONS & ROASTED GARLIC

serves 6–8

Pumpkin cubes, white beans, roasted garlic, and savory onions bake under a crisp topping of Parmesan-flavored bread crumbs in this vegetarian main dish. You can roast the garlic, caramelize the onions, and even assemble the dish the day before you plan to serve it. Feel free to substitute kabocha, butternut, or other orange-fleshed squash for the pumpkin.

2 heads garlic, halved crosswise

3 Tbsp olive oil

2 yellow onions, halved and thinly sliced

4 cans (15 oz/470 g each) cannellini beans, drained and rinsed

1 Sugar Pie pumpkin, about 2 lb (1 kg), peeled, seeded, and cut into ½-inch (12-mm) cubes

1 cup (8 fl oz/250 ml) vegetable broth

½ tsp dried thyme

Salt and freshly ground pepper

1 cup (2 oz/60 g) fresh bread crumbs

¼ cup (1 oz/30 g) grated Parmesan cheese

Preheat the oven to 375°F (190°C). Wrap the garlic halves together in foil. Bake until the cloves are soft, about 45 minutes. Let cool, and then squeeze the cloves from the cut halves into a bowl, discarding the papery skins.

In a large, heavy ovenproof sauté pan, heat 2 Tbsp of the oil over medium-high heat. Add the onions and sauté until softened. Reduce the heat to medium-low and continue to cook, stirring frequently, until the onions are very soft and browned, 25–30 minutes. Reduce the heat to low and stir in 1 Tbsp water if necessary to keep the onions from sticking. Stir in the beans, pumpkin, broth, thyme, and reserved garlic. Season with ¼ tsp salt and ⅛ tsp pepper.

Cover and bake until the pumpkin is tender, about 1 hour. In a small bowl, stir together the bread crumbs, Parmesan, and the remaining 1 Tbsp oil. Uncover the pot and sprinkle the crumb mixture over the top. Continue to bake, uncovered, until the crumbs are browned, 10–15 minutes. Remove from the oven and serve.

16

SHREDDED KALE SALAD WITH PANCETTA & HARD-COOKED EGG

serves 4–5

Shredding and briefly blanching kale for a salad softens its sturdy texture but keeps it crunchy enough to support hearty, heavier ingredients, like hard-cooked eggs and pancetta. The kale can be left raw, too, for a crunchier effect.

5 large eggs

2 bunches kale

Salt and freshly ground black pepper

¼ lb (125 g) thick-cut pancetta or bacon, coarsely chopped

3 Tbsp extra-virgin olive oil

1 clove garlic, minced

4 Tbsp (2 fl oz/60 ml) balsamic vinegar

2 Tbsp red wine vinegar

4 Tbsp (⅓ oz/10 g) fresh flat-leaf parsley

½ tsp cayenne pepper

To hard-cook the eggs, place them in a saucepan just large enough to hold them. Add cold water to cover by 1 inch (2.5 cm) and bring just to a boil over high heat. Remove the pan from the heat and cover. Let stand for 15 minutes. Have ready a bowl of ice water. Drain the eggs, then transfer to the ice water and let cool before peeling. Mince the eggs and set aside.

With a knife, strip the ribs from the kale, then roll the leaves up and slice them thinly crosswise. Bring a large saucepan three-fourths full of water to a boil over medium-high heat. Add 1 tsp salt and the kale and cook until the greens are just tender, about 5 minutes. Using a slotted spoon, lift out the kale and drain it well. Rinse under cold running water until cool. Drain again and gently squeeze out the excess liquid from the kale with your hands, then coarsely chop it. Gently squeeze out the liquid with your hands again. Set aside.

In a frying pan, cook the pancetta or bacon over medium heat, turning occasionally, until nearly golden, about 5 minutes. (If using bacon, pour off the rendered fat at this point.) Add 1 Tbsp of the oil and the garlic and cook just until the garlic is golden, about 1 minute. Using a slotted spoon, transfer the pancetta or bacon and garlic to paper towels to drain.

Add 2 Tbsp of the balsamic vinegar to the frying pan and cook over medium heat, stirring to scrape up any browned bits on the pan bottom. Pour into a bowl and whisk in the remaining 2 Tbsp balsamic vinegar, the ⇥

red wine vinegar, and the remaining 2 Tbsp oil. Add the kale, the pancetta and garlic, 3 Tbsp of the parsley, and ½ tsp black pepper. Mix well. Add the minced eggs and gently fold them in.

Garnish the mixture with the remaining 1 Tbsp parsley and the cayenne and serve.

17

SPICY COCONUT-MANDARIN SOUP WITH MUSHROOMS

serves 6

The combination of citrus and coconut milk is common in Southeast Asian dishes, especially in curries and soups. Mandarins, whose peak season runs from early winter through early spring, are typically a little sweeter than oranges, though oranges could be used here, as well. This soup is served over rice for a main dish, but it would also make a satisfying appetizer without the rice.

1 cup (7 oz/220 g) long-grain white or brown rice

1 cup (8 fl oz/250 ml) chicken broth

1 can (14 fl oz/430 ml) coconut milk

1 Tbsp grated mandarin orange zest

½ cup (4 fl oz/125 ml) mandarin orange juice, strained (from about 3 oranges)

1 Tbsp Asian fish sauce

1 tsp Thai chile paste

1 serrano chile, seeded and minced

2 cups (6 oz/185 g) enoki mushrooms or quartered button mushrooms

½ cup (1½ oz/45 g) chopped oyster mushrooms

½ cup (¾ oz/20 g) chopped fresh basil

Salt and freshly ground pepper

In a saucepan, bring 2 cups (16 fl oz/500 ml) water to a boil over medium-high heat. Add the rice, reduce the heat to low, cover, and cook until the rice is tender and the water has been absorbed, about 20 minutes for white rice and about 40 minutes for brown rice. Remove from the heat and keep covered.

In a large, heavy pot, combine the broth, coconut milk, mandarin orange zest and juice, fish sauce, chile paste, and serrano chile. Place over medium-high heat and bring to a boil. Reduce the heat to medium and simmer for about 5 minutes. The soup will be slightly foamy and will have turned a golden-orange color. Add the mushrooms and cook until tender, about 5 minutes. Remove from the heat and stir in the basil, ½ tsp salt, and ¼ tsp pepper.

Spoon the rice into bowls, ladle the soup over the rice, and serve.

18

SOBA WITH SHIITAKES & MUSTARD GREENS

serves 2

4-inch (10-cm) square dried kombu

²/₃ cup (⅓ oz/10 g) dried bonito flakes

¼ lb (125 g) young, tender mustard greens, ribs removed

½ lb (250 g) dried soba noodles

7 oz (220 g) Japanese-style firm tofu

3 Tbsp mirin

2 Tbsp low-sodium soy sauce

1 cup (3 oz/90 g) sliced fresh shiitake mushroom caps

2 green onions, thinly sliced (optional)

Kombu, a variety of edible kelp, and bonito flakes, thin shavings of dried smoked skipjack tuna, flavor the broth for this simple noodle dish. The mustard greens add a distinctive peppery flavor, but another dark, leafy green can be substituted. Serve a side dish of thinly sliced cucumbers tossed with sesame oil and soy sauce.

In a saucepan, combine the kombu and 4 cups (32 fl oz/1 l) water. Bring to a simmer, add the bonito flakes, and let stand for 1–2 minutes. Strain the broth through a fine-mesh sieve into a large bowl.

Bring a large saucepan three-fourths full of salted water to a boil. Add the mustard greens and boil just until tender, about 1 minute. Lift them out with a wire skimmer and place under running cold water. Gently squeeze to remove excess water. Add the soba to the boiling water and cook until al dente, 8–10 minutes, or according to package directions. Drain through a sieve and rinse with warm water; set aside in the sieve.

Fill the saucepan three-fourths full of water and bring to a boil over high heat. Cut the tofu into ½-inch (12-mm) cubes. Place the broth in another clean saucepan and add the tofu, mirin, soy sauce, and mushrooms. Bring to a simmer and simmer gently until the mushrooms are tender, about 3 minutes. Dip the sieve containing the soba into the boiling water. Lift the sieve, let the water drain, then divide the hot soba between 2 bowls. Top with the mustard greens. Ladle the hot broth with the mushrooms and tofu over all. Garnish with the green onions, if using, and serve.

19

ASIAN-STYLE CABBAGE ROLLS

serves 4–6

2 Tbsp canola oil

1 tsp toasted sesame oil

2-inch (5-cm) piece fresh ginger, peeled and minced

3 cloves garlic, minced

4 oz (125 g) shiitake mushrooms, stems removed and caps thinly sliced

1 lb (500 g) ground pork

¾ cup (4 oz/125 g) cooked brown rice

1 carrot, peeled and shredded

2 green onions, white and tender green parts, sliced

¼ cup (⅓ oz/10 g) fresh cilantro leaves, minced

½ tsp red pepper flakes

1 Tbsp soy sauce

3 tsp rice vinegar

1 head napa cabbage, cored and leaves separated

¼ cup (2 fl oz/60 ml) hoisin sauce

These cabbage rolls are packed with Asian flavors, like fresh ginger, cilantro, and shiitake mushrooms, and are brushed with a hoisin and rice vinegar glaze, which keeps them moist as they bake. You can adjust the spiciness by adding more or fewer red pepper flakes. Accompany these vegetarian rolls with a simple noodle salad.

In a frying pan, heat the canola and sesame oils over medium-high heat. Add the ginger, garlic, and mushrooms and sauté until the mushrooms begin to caramelize, about 5 minutes. Let cool slightly and transfer to a bowl.

Add the pork, rice, carrot, green onions, cilantro, pepper flakes, and soy sauce to the bowl. Sprinkle with 1 tsp of the vinegar. Using your hands, mix until well combined.

Lay a cabbage leaf on a work surface with the stem end closest to you. Put a heaping ¼ cup (2 oz/60 g) of the pork mixture near the stem end, fold the stem end over the filling, fold both sides toward the middle, and roll up the leaf tightly around the filling. Place the roll, seam side down, in a 9-by-9-inch (22-by-22-cm) baking dish. Repeat rolling cabbage leaves until all the filling is used (reserve any extra leaves for another use).

In a small bowl, stir together the hoisin sauce and the remaining 2 tsp vinegar. Brush the sauce over the rolls. Bake until the pork is cooked through, about 30 minutes. To test for doneness, carefully unwrap a bundle and check that the pork is cooked through. Remove from the oven and serve.

20

Orange-fleshed winter squash teams up with tender chunks of meaty chicken thighs in this fragrant Thai curry. The warming red chile paste is tempered with sweet coconut milk. Serve over steamed jasmine rice.

THAI PUMPKIN & CHICKEN CURRY

serves 4

1 small baking pumpkin or butternut squash, about 1½ lb (750 g), halved, seeded, peeled, and cut into bite-sized chunks

2 shallots, chopped

3 cloves garlic, coarsely chopped

1 Tbsp Thai red curry paste

1 can (13½ fl oz/420 ml) unsweetened coconut milk

2 Tbsp Asian fish sauce

Juice of 1 lime

2 tsp firmly packed light brown sugar

3 Tbsp corn or peanut oil

1 lb (500 g) skinless, boneless chicken thighs, cut into bite-sized chunks

2 Tbsp sliced fresh basil, preferably Thai

Cooked jasmine rice for serving

Bring a large pot of water to a boil. Add the pumpkin and boil just until barely tender, about 7 minutes. Drain well.

In a blender, combine the shallots, garlic, and curry paste with 2 Tbsp water and process until smooth. In a small bowl, combine the coconut milk, fish sauce, lime juice, and sugar and stir to dissolve the sugar.

In a wok or large frying pan, warm 2 Tbsp of the oil over medium heat. Add the chicken and sear until light brown on all sides, 5–7 minutes. Using a slotted spoon, transfer to a bowl. Return the pan to medium heat and add the remaining 1 Tbsp oil. Add the curry paste mixture and cook, stirring, until fragrant, about 10 seconds. Stir in the coconut milk mixture and bring to a boil. Add the chicken and pumpkin, reduce the heat to low, and simmer until the pumpkin is tender and the chicken is opaque throughout, about 5 minutes.

Transfer to a serving bowl, garnish with the basil, and serve with rice.

21

Apple-picking season brings cravings for classics such as this old-fashioned pie. Load up on tart baking apples, toss them with lemon juice and cinnamon sugar, then tuck them inside a buttery double crust. Set the pie on the table after a big roast dinner— though it's equally tempting to sneak a slice with coffee the next morning.

OLD-FASHIONED APPLE PIE

serves 6–8

Flaky Pie Dough for double crust (see page 129)

½ cup (4 oz/125 g) sugar

½ tsp ground cinnamon

⅛ tsp kosher salt

1 Tbsp cornstarch

7 large, tart, firm apples, peeled, cored, and sliced ½ inch (12 mm) thick

2 Tbsp cold unsalted butter, cut into small pieces

Vanilla ice cream for serving (optional)

Prepare the dough and chill as directed. Transfer the dough to a lightly floured work surface and cut in half. Roll each half into a round at least 12 inches (30 cm) in diameter and about ⅛ inch (3 mm) thick. Transfer one round to a 9-inch (23-cm) pie pan and ease into the pan. Trim the edge, leaving a ¾-inch (2-cm) overhang. Set the second dough round in a cool place until ready to use.

Position a rack in the lower third of the oven and preheat to 350°F (180°C).

In a large bowl, stir together the sugar, cinnamon, salt, and cornstarch. Add the sliced apples and toss to distribute evenly. Pour the apples into the dough-lined pan. Dot with the butter.

Position the reserved dough round over the filled pie. Trim the edge, leaving a 1-inch (2.5-cm) overhang. Fold under the edge of the bottom round and crimp to seal. Using a small knife, cut 5 or 6 slits in the top.

Bake the pie until the crust is golden and the apples are tender, 60–70 minutes. Let cool in the pan on a wire rack until just slightly warm, about 45 minutes. If you like, accompany each serving with ice cream.

22

*Take advantage
of leftover turkey
with a pan of
cheese-topped
enchiladas. The
bittersweet chocolate
in the mole sauce is
an apt match for the
bold flavor of the
poultry. For an easy
variation, make soft
tacos by warming
the corn tortillas
as described in the
recipe and reheating
the mole mixture
separately in a
saucepan over
medium heat.
Spoon the hot
turkey mole into
each tortilla,
passing the cheese,
sour cream, and
avocado slices
at the table.*

TURKEY MOLE ENCHILADAS

serves 4

2 Tbsp olive oil, plus more for greasing

1 yellow onion, chopped

¼ cup (1 oz/30 g) slivered almonds

1½ tsp chili powder

½ tsp ground cumin

¼ tsp ground cinnamon

1 cup (7 oz/220 g) canned diced tomatoes, drained

2 Tbsp chopped bittersweet chocolate

½ tsp dried oregano

Salt and freshly ground pepper

1½ cups (12 fl oz/375 ml) chicken broth

3½ cups (21 oz/655 g) shredded cooked turkey, both white and dark meat

8 corn tortillas

2 cups (8 oz/250 g) shredded Monterey jack cheese

6 Tbsp (3 oz/90 g) sour cream

1 avocado, halved, pitted, peeled, and sliced

In a large frying pan, heat the oil over high heat. Add the onion and almonds and sauté until just golden, 8–10 minutes. Stir in the chili powder, cumin, and cinnamon and sauté until fragrant, about 30 seconds. Add the tomatoes, chocolate, oregano, 2 tsp salt, 1 tsp pepper, and ½ cup (4 fl oz/125 ml) of the broth and stir until the chocolate has melted, about 1 minute. Let cool slightly.

Working in batches, purée the mixture in a food processor or blender. Return the purée to the pan over medium-high heat. Add the remaining 1 cup (8 fl oz/250 ml) broth, bring to a simmer, and cook until the sauce thickens and darkens in color, about 15 minutes.

Set aside about 1½ cups (12 fl oz/375 ml) of the mole sauce to use for topping the enchiladas. Add the shredded turkey to the pan and stir to combine with the remaining sauce. Allow to cool, then stir in half the cheese.

Preheat the oven to 375°F (190°C). Lightly oil a baking dish large enough to hold 8 enchiladas side by side. Spread ½ cup (4 fl oz/125 ml) of the reserved mole sauce into the bottom of the baking dish.

Warm a heavy frying pan over medium heat. One at a time, soften the tortillas by ⤖

placing them in the pan for about 15 seconds on each side, taking care not to burn them. Spread ½ cup (4 fl oz/125 ml) of the turkey mole down the center of each tortilla, roll up the tortilla, and place it seam side down in the baking dish. Spread the remaining reserved sauce over the top of the enchiladas and sprinkle with the remaining cheese.

Bake the enchiladas until the filling is bubbling and the cheese is melted and golden, about 20 minutes. Serve garnished with the sour cream and avocado slices.

23

*Here, the maple
syrup both
complements the
natural sweetness
of the squash and
lends a smoky
accent. For a lighter
glaze, substitute
honey for the maple
syrup, or use only
butter. You can also
use lemon zest in
place of the orange
zest and fresh
rosemary or sage
as a substitute
for the thyme.*

ROASTED SQUASH WITH CRANBERRIES & THYME

serves 6–8

2–3 small squashes, such as delicata or acorn, about 1 lb (500g) each

Salt and freshly ground pepper

2 Tbsp unsalted butter

2 Tbsp pure maple syrup

1 Tbsp chopped fresh thyme, plus sprigs for garnish

2 tsp grated orange zest

3 Tbsp fresh cranberries, whole or coarsely chopped

Preheat the oven to 400°F (200°C).

Oil a baking sheet. Trim the ends from each squash and cut into slices or quarters. Scrape out the seeds, reserving some for roasting. Season the slices generously with salt and pepper and arrange on the prepared pan. Roast the squash slices for 10 minutes.

Meanwhile, in a small saucepan, melt the butter. Stir in the maple syrup, chopped thyme, and orange zest and remove from the heat.

When the squash slices have roasted for 10 minutes, remove the pan from the oven and brush the slices with the butter mixture. Sprinkle with the cranberries and reserved seeds. Continue to roast the squash slices until glazed, browned, and tender when pierced with a fork, 10–15 minutes.

Transfer the squash slices to a platter. Garnish with thyme sprigs and serve.

24

TURKEY BURGERS WITH CRANBERRY RELISH

serves 6

This dish comes together quickly with the help of premade and leftover items. Cubed corn bread makes a moist and hearty binder for the burgers. When shopping for the cranberry sauce, select a low-sugar brand. Load these sandwiches with romaine lettuce leaves and thin red onion slices to bump up the nutrients.

FOR THE CRANBERRY RELISH

1 cup (10 oz/315 g) whole cranberry sauce

2 Tbsp prepared horseradish

2 tsp fresh lemon juice

Pinch *each* of ground cinnamon and cloves

Salt and freshly ground pepper

1 Tbsp olive oil

½ cup (2½ oz/75 g) *each* finely chopped celery and yellow onion

1½ lb (750 g) ground turkey

1 cup (4 oz/125 g) day-old corn bread cubes

2 Tbsp chopped fresh flat-leaf parsley

1 Tbsp *each* chopped fresh sage and thyme

1 tsp poultry seasoning

Salt and freshly ground pepper

1 large egg

6 whole-wheat sandwich rolls, split

To make the relish, in a bowl, stir together the cranberry sauce, horseradish, lemon juice, cinnamon, and cloves. Season with salt and pepper and let stand for at least 15 minutes to blend the flavors.

In a small frying pan over medium heat, warm the oil. Add the celery and onion and sauté until softened, about 4 minutes. Let cool completely. In a large bowl, combine the turkey, corn bread, parsley, sage, thyme, poultry seasoning, 1 tsp salt, ½ tsp pepper, the egg, and the onion mixture. Using your hands, mix the ingredients until evenly distributed. Divide the mixture into loose patties, each about 4 inches (10 cm) in diameter and about ¾ inch (2 cm) thick. Take care not to handle the meat more than necessary.

Warm a stove-top grill pan over medium-high heat. Oil the pan. Cook the patties, turning once, until opaque throughout, about 8 minutes per side. About 1 minute before the patties are done, place the rolls, cut sides down, along the edges of the grill pan until lightly toasted.

Serve the patties in the rolls with the cranberry relish.

25

WHEAT BERRIES WITH ROASTED PARSNIPS, BUTTERNUT SQUASH & DRIED CRANBERRIES

serves 4–6

Just about everyone knows that eating whole grains is a healthful choice, and this appealing recipe, which marries wheat berries—whole wheat kernels— and roasted root vegetables makes that choice easy.

1 cup (6 oz/185 g) wheat berries, rinsed

Salt and freshly ground pepper

3 parsnips, cut into ½-inch (12-mm) pieces

1 small butternut squash, halved, seeded, peeled, and cut into ½-inch (12-mm) pieces

1 large red onion, cut into ½-inch (12-mm) pieces

5 cloves garlic, unpeeled

¼ cup (2 fl oz/60 ml) olive oil, plus more as needed

2 Tbsp balsamic vinegar

½ cup (¾ oz/20 g) chopped fresh flat-leaf parsley

½ cup (2 oz/60 g) dried cranberries

2 green onions, light green parts only, chopped

In a pot, combine 3½ cups (28 fl oz/875 ml) water, the wheat berries, and ½ tsp salt and bring to a boil. Reduce the heat to low, cover, and cook until tender, about 1 hour. Drain and place in a large bowl.

Meanwhile, preheat the oven to 450°F (220°C). Line a baking sheet with parchment paper. Put the parsnips, squash, red onion, and garlic on the prepared sheet. Drizzle with the ¼ cup (2 fl oz/60 ml) oil and the vinegar and season generously with salt and pepper. Roast, stirring once, until the vegetables are caramelized and fork-tender, about 25 minutes. Peel the roasted garlic and break into small pieces.

Add the roasted vegetables and garlic to the bowl with the wheat berries and stir to combine. Add the parsley, cranberries, and green onions and mix well. Drizzle with additional oil if the mixture needs more moisture. Season with salt and pepper and serve.

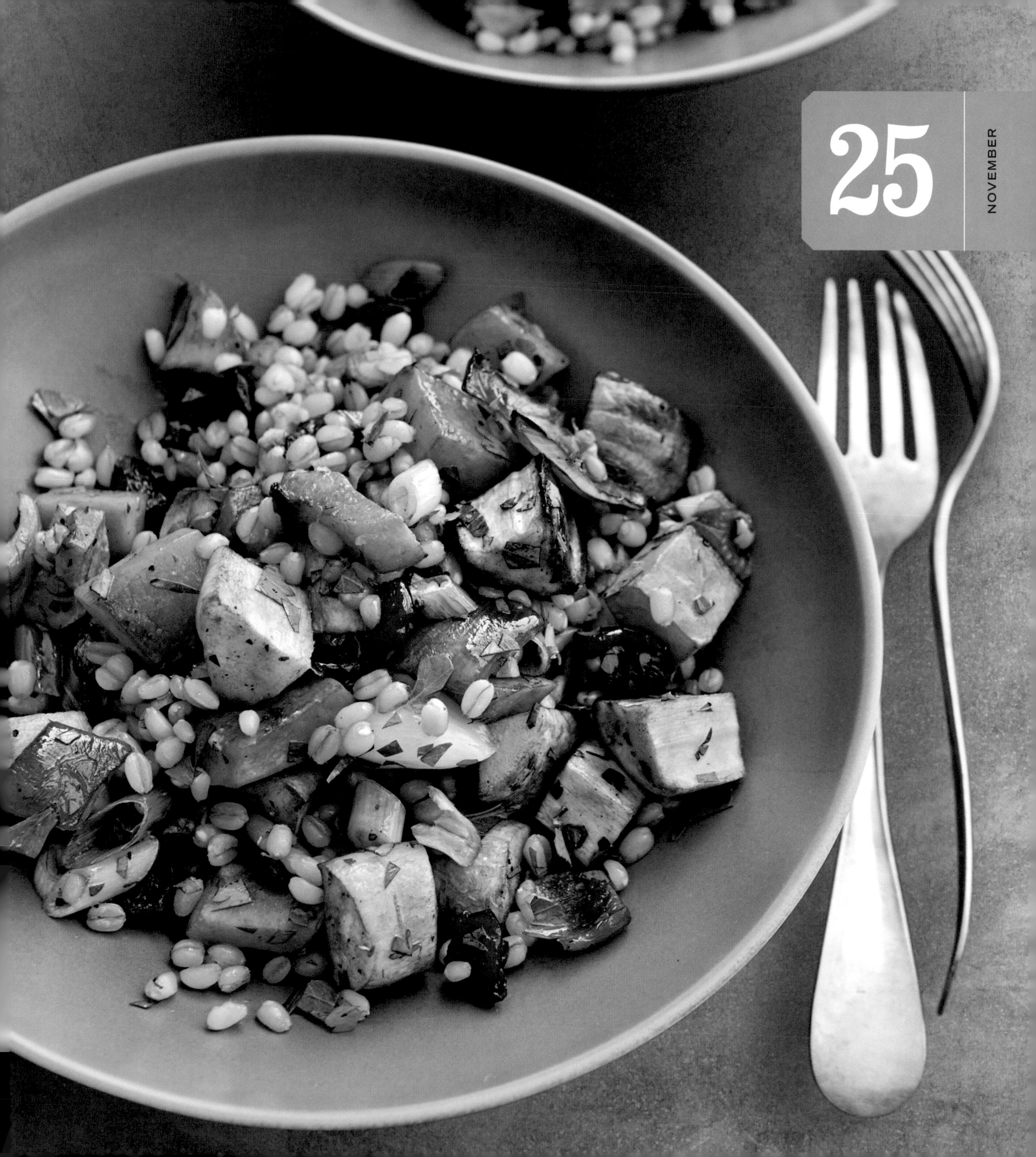
25
NOVEMBER

26

A Thanksgiving feast just isn't complete without a big slice of homemade pumpkin pie topped with an equally big dollop of whipped cream. This flavorful version is sure to become your favorite. The creamy pumpkin custard is spiced with cinnamon, nutmeg, and ginger and sweetened with brown sugar and maple syrup. Top each serving with a scattering of chopped toasted pecans for a seasonal garnish.

BROWN SUGAR PUMPKIN PIE

serves 6–8

Flaky Pie Dough for single crust (see page 132)

1 can (15 oz/470 g) pumpkin purée (about 1½ cups)

⅔ cup (5 oz/155 g) firmly packed light brown sugar

⅓ cup (3½ oz/105 g) maple syrup

⅔ cup (5 fl oz/160 ml) whole milk

½ cup (4 fl oz/125 ml) heavy cream

2 large eggs, lightly beaten

2 Tbsp all-purpose flour

1 tsp ground cinnamon

¼ tsp ground ginger

⅛ tsp freshly grated nutmeg

½ tsp kosher salt

Whipped cream (see page 53)

Prepare the dough and chill as directed. On a lightly floured work surface, roll out the dough into a round about 13 inches (33 cm) in diameter and ⅛ inch (3 mm) thick. Line a deep 9-inch (23-cm) pie pan with the dough. Trim the edge, leaving a ½-inch (12-mm) overhang. Tuck the dough under itself, and pinch to form a decorative edge. Chill in the freezer for about 20 minutes.

Preheat the oven to 400°F (200°C). Line the pie shell with foil and fill with pie weights or dried beans. Bake until the crust starts to look dry, about 15 minutes. Remove the foil and weights and bake until the crust is just barely golden, about 5 minutes. Remove from the oven and reduce the oven temperature to 350°F (180°C).

In a large bowl, whisk together the pumpkin, brown sugar, and maple syrup. Add the milk, cream, and eggs and whisk until smooth. Sift the flour, cinnamon, ginger, nutmeg, and salt over the pumpkin mixture and whisk to combine.

Place the pie pan on a baking sheet. Pour the filling into the shell. Bake until the filling is just set and still jiggles very slightly in the center when the pan is gently moved, 60–70 minutes. Let cool on a wire rack for at least 1 hour. Serve wedges of the pie with whipped cream.

27

With its nutty flavor and chewy texture, wild rice is a welcome addition to the holiday table. Here, it is mixed with pecans, cranberries, shallots, and herbs for a particularly festive and flavorful dish. For lunch or a light dinner, serve the pilaf with a butter lettuce salad.

WILD RICE PILAF WITH DRIED CRANBERRIES & PECANS

serves 8–10

4 cups (32 fl oz/1 l) chicken or vegetable broth

2 Tbsp unsalted butter

1 Tbsp canola or grapeseed oil

3 large shallots, minced

2 cups (12 oz/375 g) wild rice, or 2 cups (14 oz/440 g) short-grain brown rice, or a mixture

½ cup (2 oz/60 g) dried cranberries

1 bay leaf

2 sprigs fresh thyme, or ¼ tsp dried thyme, crumbled

Salt and ground white pepper

½ cup (2 oz/60 g) pecans, toasted and coarsely chopped

¼ cup (⅓ oz/10 g) minced fresh flat-leaf parsley

Preheat the oven to 375°F (190°C). In a saucepan, bring the broth to a gentle simmer over medium heat.

In a large, heavy pot, melt the butter with the oil over medium heat. Add the shallots and sauté until translucent, 2–3 minutes. Add the rice and stir until well coated with the butter and oil, about 3 minutes. Stir in the simmering broth, dried cranberries, bay leaf, and thyme. Season with ½ tsp salt and ⅛ tsp white pepper. Bring to a simmer, stir, and cover. Transfer to the oven and bake until all the liquid has been absorbed and the rice is tender, 40–45 minutes.

Remove the pilaf from the oven. Discard the bay leaf and the thyme sprigs. Adjust the seasoning. Stir in the pecans and parsley, and serve.

28

An easy glaze made from molasses, mustard, and fresh rosemary coats both the pork and sweet potatoes in this homey supper dish. Serve with a side dish of sautéed greens or steamed broccoli.

MOLASSES-GLAZED ROAST PORK & SWEET POTATOES

serves 4

¼ cup (2½ oz/75 g) light molasses

¼ cup (2 oz/60 g) Dijon mustard

1 Tbsp fresh rosemary, minced

1 tsp red pepper flakes

1½ lb (750 g) orange-fleshed sweet potatoes, unpeeled, cut into ½-inch (12-mm) slices

2½ Tbsp olive oil, plus more for brushing

Salt and freshly ground black pepper

2 pork tenderloins, each about 12 oz (375 g)

1 shallot, minced

½ cup (4 fl oz/125 ml) low-sodium chicken broth

Preheat the oven to 400°F (200°C). In a bowl, combine the molasses, mustard, rosemary, and ½ tsp red pepper flakes; stir to combine. In a large bowl, combine the sweet potatoes with 1½ Tbsp oil and the remaining ½ tsp red pepper flakes. Sprinkle with salt and black pepper and toss to coat the sweet potatoes evenly. Brush a large rimmed baking sheet with oil. Arrange the potatoes on the pan in a single layer, leaving a space in the center of the pan. Place the pan in the oven and roast the sweet potatoes for 15 minutes.

Meanwhile, season the pork lightly with salt and pepper. Warm the remaining 1 Tbsp oil in a large frying pan over medium-high heat. Add the pork and brown on all sides, about 6 minutes. Remove the baking sheet from the oven and place the pork in the center. Brush the pork and potatoes with some of the molasses mixture. Return to the oven and roast until the potatoes are tender and a thermometer inserted into the pork registers 145°F (63°C), about 15 minutes. Transfer to a warmed platter.

Pour off all but 1 Tbsp fat from the pan, and set over medium-high heat. Add the shallot and sauté, scraping up the browned bits on the pan bottom, until it begins to soften, about 3 minutes. Add the remaining molasses mixture and the broth. Bring to a boil, stirring frequently. Simmer until the sauce thickens slightly, about 3 minutes.

Slice the pork, drizzle with sauce, and serve.

29

Broccoli rabe—also known as broccoli raab, rapini, and Italian broccoli— has slender stalks with dark green leaves and small florets. It has a slightly bitter taste with overtones of sweet mustard. Layer it with egg-soaked sourdough, pesto, and Italian cheese in this delicious winter strata.

BROCCOLI RABE, PESTO & SMOKED MOZZARELLA STRATA

serves 4–6

Salt and freshly ground pepper

¾ lb (375 g) broccoli rabe, thick stems removed

Oil for baking dish

5–7 slices sourdough bread, each about ½ inch (12 mm) thick, crusts removed

¼ cup (2 fl oz/60 ml) prepared pesto

1½ cups (6 oz/185 g) shredded smoked mozzarella or fontina cheese

1 cup (8 fl oz/250 ml) whole milk

¾ cup (6 fl oz/180 ml) heavy cream

4 eggs

2 tsp Dijon mustard

Bring a large saucepan of lightly salted water to a boil. Add the broccoli rabe and cook until almost tender, about 5 minutes. Drain and rinse with cold water, and then squeeze out as much water as possible. Coarsely chop the broccoli rabe.

Generously oil a 7-by-11-inch (18-by-28-cm) baking dish. Place a few slices of the bread in the bottom of the prepared dish, cutting them as necessary to make an even layer. Spread the broccoli rabe evenly over the bread. Dollop the pesto over the broccoli rabe, spacing it evenly. Scatter with half of the smoked mozzarella and top with the remaining bread, again cutting to fit.

In a large bowl, combine the milk, cream, eggs, and mustard. Season with ½ tsp salt and a generous grinding of pepper. Whisk vigorously until smooth. Pour over the bread and use the back of a large spoon to press the bread down into the egg mixture. Cover the dish with plastic wrap and let stand at room temperature for about 30 minutes.

Meanwhile, preheat the oven to 350°F (180°C). Press the bread down into the egg mixture after about 15 minutes and again just before placing in the oven.

Sprinkle the top with the remaining cheese. Bake until puffed, golden, and crisp, about 45 minutes. Let stand for 5 minutes before serving.

NOVEMBER

30

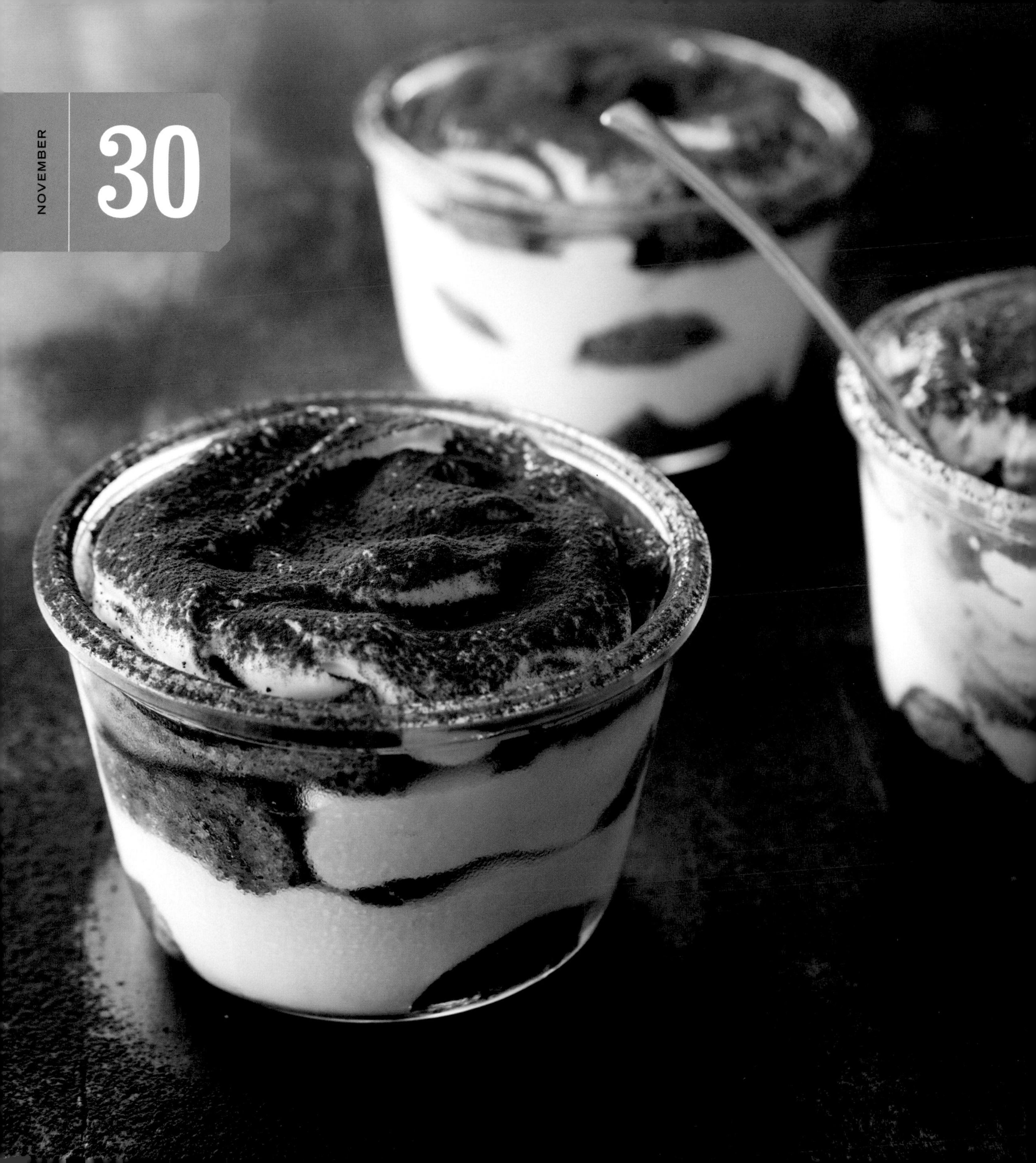

Delicate ladyfingers soaked in espresso and rum, layered with mascarpone custard, and dusted with cocoa make up this favorite Italian dessert. To make individual portions, layer the soaked ladyfingers and custard in individual cups or bowls, cutting the ladyfingers as needed to fit the cups. Depending on the size of the cups, you may not need as many ladyfingers.

TIRAMISÙ
serves 8–10

½ cup (4 oz/125 g) sugar

1½ cups (12 fl oz/375 ml) **freshly brewed espresso**

⅓ cup (3 fl oz/80 ml) **dark rum**

FOR THE FILLING

⅓ cup (3 oz/90 g) sugar

6 large egg yolks

½ cup (4 fl oz/125 ml) **heavy cream**

1½ cups (12 oz/375 g) **mascarpone cheese**

1½ tsp **pure vanilla extract**

45 **ladyfingers or savoiardi**

Unsweetened cocoa powder for dusting

In a small saucepan, bring the sugar and ⅓ cup (3 fl oz/80 ml) water to a simmer over medium heat and cook, stirring, until the sugar is dissolved, about 3 minutes. Remove from the heat, stir in the espresso, and let cool to room temperature. Stir in the rum. Pour the espresso mixture into a wide, shallow bowl and set aside.

To make the filling, select a heatproof bowl that fits snugly in the rim of a saucepan. Pour water to a depth of about 2 inches (5 cm) into the saucepan and bring to a gentle simmer. In the bowl, whisk together the sugar and egg yolks until the sugar has dissolved and the mixture is pale yellow and creamy, about 2 minutes. Place the bowl over (not touching) the simmering water in the pan. Using an electric mixer, beat the yolk mixture on medium speed until thick and tripled in volume, about 6 minutes. Remove the bowl from over the heat and set the yolk mixture aside to cool completely, stirring often as it cools.

In another bowl, beat the cream on medium-high speed until stiff peaks form.

Add the mascarpone and vanilla to the cooled yolk mixture. Beat with the mixer on medium speed just until smooth and well blended. Using a large rubber spatula, fold in the whipped cream just until combined. ⟩⟩→

Working in batches, immerse 15 ladyfingers in the espresso mixture, then arrange the ladyfingers in a single layer in the bottom of a 9-inch (23-cm) square cake pan. Using the rubber spatula, evenly spread one-third of the filling over the ladyfingers. Soak another 15 ladyfingers in the espresso mixture and place them over the filling, and evenly spread with half of the remaining filling. Soak the remaining ladyfingers, place them in the pan, and top with the remaining filling, again spreading evenly. Gently tap the pan against the counter to settle the ingredients. Cover with plastic wrap and refrigerate for at least 6 hours or up to overnight.

Run a small knife around the inside edge of the pan to loosen the sides. Dust the top with cocoa powder and serve.

Markets everywhere are now fully stocked with the winter harvests: hearty root vegetables; cabbage, kale, and other sturdy greens; and a colorful array of citrus fruits. One-pot suppers, such as shellfish stew, chicken tikka masala, or braised lamb shanks, are welcome this time of year. So, too, are such dishes as red cabbage salad with dried fruits, lentil burgers with a yogurt sauce, and braised kale with white beans, all of which draw on the best of the season's produce. At dessert time, new-crop pecans go into a traditional holiday pie, while individual warm chocolate cakes are guaranteed to brighten any winter day.

1
CITRUS-BRAISED LAMB SHANKS
page 280

2
NAPA CABBAGE & KUMQUAT SALAD WITH SEARED SCALLOPS
page 280

3
SOUTHERN PECAN PIE
page 283

8
KALE, TURKEY SAUSAGE & BARLEY STEW
page 285

9
STIR-FRIED BEEF & BOK CHOY WITH GINGER
page 286

10
FENNEL-ROASTED CHICKEN WITH CELERY ROOT PURÉE
page 286

15
BRAISED BLACK COD WITH SHIITAKE MUSHROOMS
page 291

16
WARM MOLTEN CHOCOLATE CAKES
page 292

17
VIETNAMESE BEEF NOODLE SOUP
page 292

22
BRAISED DINOSAUR KALE WITH WHITE BEANS & SMOKED HAM
page 296

23
SWEET POTATO SOUP WITH CHEDDAR & CAVIAR CROUTONS
page 297

24
BEEF TENDERLOIN WITH SHALLOT & RED WINE REDUCTION
page 297

29
BEEF BOURGUIGNON
page 301

30
RICOTTA WITH BLOOD ORANGE, PISTACHIOS & HONEY
page 302

31
SHIITAKE BROTH WITH BUTTER-POACHED LOBSTER & CHIVE
page 302

4
**BRAISED WINTER VEGETABLES
WITH COCONUT & RED CURRY**
page 283

5
CHICKEN TIKKA MASALA
page 284

6
**SEARED SCALLOPS WITH WARM
SHREDDED BRUSSELS SPROUTS
& PROSCIUTTO**
page 284

7
TRUFFLED MAC & CHEESE
page 285

11
**VIETNAMESE-STYLE RICE NOODLES
WITH CRAB & BLACK PEPPER**
page 288

12
**RED LENTIL BURGERS WITH
LEMON-HERB YOGURT SAUCE**
page 288

13
WINTER SQUASH & PECORINO TART
page 289

14
**CHICKEN MEATBALLS WITH
SPICY TOMATO SAUCE**
page 291

18
**CRISPY CHICKEN & CABBAGE SALAD
WITH PEANUT DRESSING**
page 293

19
CIOPPINO
page 294

20
**BRAISED CHICKEN WITH TANGERINE
& STAR ANISE**
page 294

21
**BITTERSWEET CHOCOLATE
& DARK CARAMEL TARTLETS**
page 296

25
**DUCK BREAST SALAD WITH
WALNUTS & ORANGES**
page 299

26
**WINTER SALAD OF RED CABBAGE
& DRIED FRUITS**
page 299

27
SPICY DARK GINGERBREAD
page 300

28
**BREAD PUDDING WITH CHARD,
SUN-DRIED TOMATOES & FONTINA**
page 300

december

1

CITRUS-BRAISED LAMB SHANKS

serves 4

2 Tbsp olive oil

4 lamb shanks, about 1 lb (500 g) each

Salt and freshly ground pepper

1 carrot, finely chopped

1 yellow onion, finely chopped

2 celery ribs, finely chopped

3 small sprigs fresh thyme

1 bay leaf

3 cloves garlic, minced

1½ Tbsp tomato paste

2 cups (16 fl oz/500 ml) dry white wine

1 cup (8 fl oz/250 ml) chicken broth

Grated zest and juice of 1 lemon

Grated zest and juice of 1 lime

Grated zest and juice of 1 orange

Lamb shanks meet a bright trio of winter citrus—lemon, lime, and orange—in this hearty dish. The rich braising liquid that results from the slow cooking almost surpasses the lamb shanks themselves. If you want to stretch the recipe to serve six, shred the meat from the bones, divide it among shallow bowls, and serve over rice, orzo, or polenta, with the reduced juices drizzled over each serving.

In a large, heavy pot, heat 1 Tbsp of the oil over medium-high heat. Season the shanks with salt and pepper. Working in batches, sear the shanks, turning as needed, until browned on all sides, 6–8 minutes. Transfer to a platter and pour off the fat from the pot.

Preheat the oven to 250°F (120°C). Add the remaining 1 Tbsp oil to the pot and place over medium-low heat. Add the carrot, onion, and celery and sauté until softened, about 5 minutes. Add the thyme, bay leaf, garlic, and tomato paste. Stir in ½ tsp salt, season with pepper, and stir for 1 minute. Add the wine, broth, and lemon and lime zests and juices.

Return the shanks to the pot and bring the liquid to a gentle simmer. Cover and cook in the oven, turning the shanks every hour, until the meat is completely tender, about 2½ hours. Transfer the shanks to a platter and keep warm in the oven.

Pour the juices from the pot into a large, heatproof measuring pitcher and let stand for 1 minute. The fat will rise to the top. Use a bulb baster to transfer the juices underneath the fat to a small saucepan. Simmer to reduce slightly. Stir in the orange zest and juice.

Drizzle the reduced juices over the lamb shanks and serve.

2

NAPA CABBAGE & KUMQUAT SALAD WITH SEARED SCALLOPS

serves 4

12 large sea scallops, tough muscles removed

1 tsp sesame seeds

2 tsp light soy sauce

1 Tbsp fresh lemon juice

½ tsp sugar

1 head napa cabbage, shredded

12–15 kumquats, cut crosswise into paper-thin slices and seeded

Salt and freshly ground pepper

2 tsp unsalted butter

2 tsp extra-virgin olive oil

Pale green, mild Chinese cabbage marries well with the sweet-sharp tang of kumquats and the saltiness of fermented black beans. Look for the beans in Asian markets, where they are typically sold in plastic bags. Don't stray from the stove while the scallops cook, as they cook quickly.

Rinse the scallops and pat dry.

In a small frying pan, toast the sesame seeds over medium heat, stirring every 2–3 minutes, until lightly golden, about 2 minutes total. Transfer to a small bowl and set aside.

In a large bowl, whisk together the soy sauce, lemon juice, and sugar until the dressing is well blended. Add the cabbage and half of the kumquats and stir well.

Season the scallops with 1 tsp salt and ½ tsp pepper. In a large frying pan, melt the butter with the oil over medium-high heat and sear the scallops, turning once, until a golden crust has formed and the scallops are still translucent in the center, 1–2 minutes per side. Do not overcook.

Divide the cabbage mixture among individual plates and top each with 3 scallops. Garnish with the remaining kumquats and the sesame seeds and serve.

3

In the American South, pecans are harvested in late fall. If you see new-crop pecans in the market, buy a big bag and store it for up to a month in the refrigerator or up to a year in the freezer. Here, pecans are mixed into the filling, but during baking they float to the surface, covering the pie with a wonderfully crunchy topping. This is the perfect pie for the holidays.

SOUTHERN PECAN PIE
serves 6–8

Flaky Pie Dough for single crust (see page 132)

3 large eggs

½ cup (4 oz/125 g) sugar

1 cup (10 oz/315 g) dark corn syrup

1 tsp pure vanilla extract

¼ cup (2 oz/60 g) unsalted butter, melted

1½ cups (6 oz/185 g) large pecan pieces, cut into halves and quarters

Whipped cream (see page 53)

Prepare the dough and chill as directed. On a lightly floured work surface, roll out the dough into a round about 12 inches (30 cm) in diameter and about ⅛ inch (3 mm) thick. Line a 9-inch (23-cm) pie pan with the dough round. Trim the edge, leaving a ¾-inch (2-cm) overhang. Fold the overhang under itself and use a fork to create a decorative edge. Refrigerate or freeze the dough until firm, about 30 minutes.

Preheat the oven to 400°F (200°C). Line the pie shell with foil and fill with pie weights. Bake until the crust starts to look dry, about 15 minutes. Remove the foil and weights, and continue baking until lightly golden, about 5 minutes longer. Let cool completely.

To make the filling, in a large bowl, whisk together the eggs, sugar, corn syrup, and vanilla until blended, then whisk in the melted butter. Stir in the pecans. Pour the filling into the prebaked crust.

Bake the pie until the filling is set but the center still jiggles slightly when the pan is gently shaken, 45–50 minutes. Let cool on a wire rack. Serve warm or at room temperature, topped with whipped cream.

4

Coconut milk lends richness and an exotic flavor to this seasonal mixture of sweet potato, celery root, and winter squash. At the same time, it helps to offset the spiciness of the red curry paste and pungency of the fish sauce that spike the broth. Accompany the curry with steamed white or brown rice and serve fresh fruit for dessert

BRAISED WINTER VEGETABLES WITH COCONUT & RED CURRY
serves 4

2 tsp canola oil

1 clove garlic, minced

¼-inch (6-mm) slice fresh ginger, peeled and grated

2 tsp Thai red curry paste

1 tsp Thai fish sauce

1 sweet potato, about ½ lb (250 g), peeled and cut into ½-inch (12-mm) chunks

1 celery root, about ½ lb (250 g), peeled and cut into ½-inch (12-mm) chunks

3 cups (24 fl oz/750 ml) coconut milk

1 delicata squash, about ½ lb (250 g), sliced and seeded

2 limes

8 fresh cilantro sprigs

In a large saucepan, warm the oil over medium heat. Add the garlic and ginger and sauté until fragrant but not browned, about 1 minute. Add the curry paste and cook, stirring, for 1 minute. Add the fish sauce, sweet potato, and celery root and stir to combine. Reduce the heat to medium-low, pour in the coconut milk, and cook, stirring occasionally, for 10 minutes. Add the squash and cook until the vegetables are just tender when pierced with a knife but are not falling apart, 12–15 minutes.

Meanwhile, finely grate the zest from 1 of the limes and reserve the fruit for another use. Stir the lime zest into the vegetables.

Spoon the vegetables and braising liquid into bowls. Garnish each serving with the cilantro. Cut the second lime into wedges and serve the lime wedges on the side of the curry for squeezing.

5

One of the most popular Anglo-Indian dishes—a uniquely British invention—is chicken tikka masala, succulent cubes of chicken breast bathed in a sweet, spicy sauce. Plenty of ginger and spice makes it a warming dish for a cold night. Packaged naan is now easy to find at many supermarkets. Stack buttered and toasted pieces alongside the curry.

CHICKEN TIKKA MASALA

serves 4

¼ cup (2 oz/60 g) Greek yogurt or other plain yogurt

Juice of 1½ limes

3 tsp peeled and grated fresh ginger

1 tsp ground cumin

1¼ tsp garam masala

2 tsp sweet paprika

4 skinless, boneless chicken breast halves, about 1 lb (500 g), cut into 1-inch (2.5-cm) chunks

Salt

5 Tbsp (3 fl oz/80 ml) sunflower oil

1 small yellow onion, finely chopped

1 clove garlic, minced

5 green cardamom pods

1 tsp ground cumin

1 tsp ground coriander

½ tsp ground turmeric

½ tsp ground chile

1 can (14½ oz/455 g) diced tomatoes

1 jalapeño chile, thinly sliced

½ cup (4 fl oz/125 ml) heavy cream

Juice of ½ lemon

Warmed naan or pita breads

In a nonreactive bowl, stir together the yogurt, lime juice, 2 tsp of the ginger, the cumin, 1 tsp of the garam masala, and the paprika. Add the chicken to the marinade, stir, cover, and refrigerate for at least 1 hour or up to 7 hours.

Preheat the broiler. Remove the chicken from the marinade, shaking off the excess, and place on a plate. Season with salt, drizzle with 2 Tbsp of the oil, and toss to coat. Arrange the chicken in a single layer on a foil-lined pan and broil, turning once, until browned, 3 minutes on each side.

In a saucepan, warm the remaining 3 Tbsp oil over medium heat. Add the onion, remaining 1 tsp ginger, and garlic and cook, stirring frequently, until the onion is soft, 4–5 minutes. Add the cardamom, cumin, coriander, turmeric, and ground chile and cook, stirring constantly, for about 2 minutes. »→

Add the tomatoes and cook, stirring frequently, until the oil separates from the tomato mixture, 5–8 minutes. Add the jalapeño, cream, and ½ cup (4 fl oz/125 ml) water, bring to a boil, reduce the heat to low, and simmer until the mixture forms a creamy sauce, 8–10 minutes.

Stir in the cooked chicken and the remaining ¼ tsp garam masala, season with salt, and simmer until the chicken is heated through, 8–10 minutes. Stir in the lemon juice. Serve with the naan.

6

You can shred the brussels sprouts for this seasonal dish in one of three ways: with a sharp knife, on the shredding blade of a mandoline, or with the shredding disk on a food processor. The prosciutto adds a welcome salty contrast to the mild scallops.

SEARED SCALLOPS WITH WARM SHREDDED BRUSSELS SPROUTS & PROSCIUTTO

serves 4

3 Tbsp olive oil

3 cloves garlic, minced

2 thin slices prosciutto, chopped

¾ lb (375 g) brussels sprouts, shredded

Salt and freshly ground pepper

Juice of 1 lemon

1 lb (500 g) sea scallops, side muscles removed

In a large nonstick frying pan over medium-high heat, warm 2 Tbsp of the oil. Add the garlic and the prosciutto and sauté until the garlic softens and the prosciutto begins to crisp, about 3 minutes. Add the brussels sprouts and season well with salt and pepper. Cook, stirring often, until the brussels sprouts begin to soften and brown slightly on their edges, about 4 minutes. Stir in the lemon juice and cook for another 2 minutes. Season with salt and pepper and transfer to a platter.

Using a paper towel, wipe out the frying pan and return it to high heat. Warm the remaining 1 Tbsp oil. Pat the scallops dry with a paper towel and season with salt and pepper. Sear the scallops until medium-rare, about 3 minutes per side.

Arrange the scallops on top of the brussels sprouts, and serve.

7

*This is the time
of the year to
break out the
special-occasion
ingredients. Old-
fashioned macaroni
and cheese rises to a
new sophistication
with a drizzle of
fragrant truffle
oil. You can also
bake this dish in
individual portions
in buttered mini
muffin pans and
pass a tray of
mini macs at
your next party.*

TRUFFLED MAC & CHEESE

serves 6

Salt and freshly ground pepper

1 lb (500 g) elbow macaroni

2 tsp truffle oil

4 Tbsp (2 oz/60 g) butter, plus more
for greasing

¼ cup (1½ oz/45 g) all-purpose flour

½ tsp sweet paprika

½ tsp Dijon mustard

2 cups (16 fl oz/500 ml) whole milk

1 cup (8 fl oz/250 ml) half-and-half

1½ cups (6 oz/185 g) shredded Gruyère cheese

1½ cups (6 oz/185 g) shredded white
Cheddar cheese

2 Tbsp minced chives

Preheat the oven to 375°F (190°C). Butter
a 9-by-13-inch (23-by-33-cm) baking dish.

Bring a large saucepan of salted water to
a boil. Add the macaroni and cook, stirring
occasionally, until not quite al dente, about
2 minutes less than the package directions.
Drain and transfer to a large bowl. While
the pasta is still warm, drizzle with the
truffle oil and stir well.

Add the butter to the saucepan and melt
it over medium-high heat. Add the flour,
paprika, and mustard and cook, stirring well,
until no visible flour remains, 1–3 minutes.
Whisk in the milk, half-and-half, and a
generous pinch of salt and bring to a boil.
Simmer, whisking frequently to smooth out
any lumps, for 4–5 minutes. Remove from
the heat. Add a pinch of pepper and 1 cup
(4 oz/125 g) each of the Gruyère and
Cheddar. Stir until smooth.

Pour the cheese sauce onto the macaroni,
add the chives, and mix well. Transfer to the
prepared dish and top with the remaining
cheeses. Bake until the top is lightly browned
and the sauce is bubbly, 25–30 minutes. Let
stand for 5 minutes before serving.

8

*Here is a dish
made for a cold
winter evening.
Kale, a nutritional
powerhouse, pairs
perfectly with the
barley, but Swiss
chard or spinach
can be substituted.
You can also opt
for spicy turkey
sausage for a bigger
flavor. This is a
great dish to take
to a holiday potluck.*

KALE, TURKEY SAUSAGE & BARLEY STEW

serves 4–6

1 cup (7 oz/220 g) quick-cooking barley

Salt and freshly ground pepper

2 Tbsp olive oil

1 lb (500 g) turkey sausage links

1 yellow onion, chopped

4 cloves garlic, chopped

1 can (14.5 oz/455 g) diced tomatoes

6 cups (48 fl oz/1.5 l) low-sodium
chicken broth

4 cups (4 oz/125 g) kale, stemmed and
chopped

In a saucepan over medium-high heat,
bring 2 cups (16 fl oz/500 ml) water to
a boil. Add the barley and a big pinch
of salt, cover, and reduce the heat to low.
Cook until tender, 10–12 minutes. Drain
and set aside.

In a large saucepan over medium-high heat,
warm 1 Tbsp of the oil. Add the sausage and
brown on all sides, about 7 minutes.
Transfer to a plate lined with paper towels.

Add the remaining 1 Tbsp oil, the onion,
and the garlic to the saucepan and sauté until
the onion is translucent, about 4 minutes.
Cut the sausage links into 1-inch (2.5-cm)
slices and return to the saucepan. Cook,
stirring often, until the sausage is cooked
through, about 5 minutes. Add the tomatoes
with their juices and the chicken broth.
Bring to a boil, reduce the heat to low, and
simmer for 10 minutes. Add the barley and
the kale and cook just until the kale softens,
about 5 minutes. Season with salt and
pepper, and serve.

9

STIR-FRIED BEEF &
BOK CHOY WITH GINGER

serves 4

2 Tbsp dry sherry

1 Tbsp soy sauce

½ tsp Asian chile paste

1 lb (500 g) baby bok choy

2 tsp peanut oil

2 cloves garlic, minced

1 Tbsp peeled and grated fresh ginger

1 lb (500 g) flank steak, thinly sliced
across the grain

*Winter produces
the crispest,
crunchiest brassicas
of the year, and bok
choy is no exception.
Pair it with thinly
sliced flank steak
and a few simple
but bold seasonings.
Serve this quick
and hearty stir-fry
with wide rice
noodles or steamed
brown rice.*

In a small bowl, stir together the sherry,
soy sauce, and chile paste. Cut the bok
choy lengthwise into halves or quarters,
depending on size.

In a wok or a large frying pan, heat 1½ tsp of
the oil over high heat. Add the bok choy and
stir-fry just until tender-crisp, 3–4 minutes.
Transfer to a bowl.

Add the remaining ½ tsp oil to the pan. Add
the garlic and ginger and stir-fry until fragrant
but not browned, 15–30 seconds. Add the
beef and cook, stirring, just until no longer
pink, about 2 minutes.

Return the bok choy to the pan, add the
sherry mixture, and cook for 1 minute
until heated through. Serve.

10

FENNEL-ROASTED CHICKEN
WITH CELERY ROOT PURÉE

serves 4

4 small (1½ lb/750 g total) bone-in,
skin-on chicken breast halves

1 Tbsp olive oil

2 tsp fennel seed

Salt and freshly ground pepper

4 small celery roots (2 lb/1 kg), peeled
and cut into 1-inch (2.5-cm) cubes

1 small potato, peeled and cut into
1-inch (2.5-cm) cubes

2½ cups (20 fl oz/625 ml) low-fat milk

*Celery root purée
looks like mashed
potatoes but is
much lighter and
more healthful.
The addition of
the potato helps
thicken the purée,
while low-fat milk is
used in place of the
usual high-fat cream
and butter. Fennel
seeds add a pleasant
anise-like flavor to
the roasted chicken
breasts served
atop the purée.
Accompany the
dish with a side
of your favorite
winter greens.*

Preheat the oven to 375°F (190°C). Put the
chicken breasts in a medium baking dish
and brush them with the oil and season with
the fennel seed, salt, and pepper. Bake until
the chicken is cooked through and golden-
brown, about 35 minutes.

Meanwhile, put the celery root, potato,
milk, and 2 cups (16 fl oz/500 ml) water
into a saucepan over medium-high heat and
bring to a boil. Reduce the heat to low and
simmer until the vegetables are fork-tender,
about 30 minutes. Drain, reserving 1 cup
(8 fl oz/125 ml) of the cooking liquid.

Transfer the vegetables to a food processor
and purée with ½ cup (4 fl oz/125 ml) of
the reserved cooking liquid. If needed,
add 1 Tbsp more liquid at a time until
you achieve the desired consistency.
Season to taste with salt and pepper.

Divide the celery root purée among
4 warmed plates, top each with a chicken
breast, and serve.

VIETNAMESE-STYLE RICE NOODLES WITH CRAB & BLACK PEPPER

serves 6

Dungeness crab, which is prized for its sweet, briny flavor, comes to market in winter. Purists prefer it boiled, cooled, cracked, and served with lemon wedges. Here, in a fancier presentation, Dungeness crabmeat is tossed with rice vermicelli, fragrant herbs, and an Asian-style sauce.

6 oz (185 g) rice vermicelli

½ cup (4 fl oz/125 ml) low-sodium chicken broth

1 large egg

3 Tbsp Asian fish sauce

1 Tbsp fresh lime juice

1 tsp sugar

1 tsp Sriracha sauce

1 tsp minced garlic

1 tsp freshly ground pepper

¼ cup (⅓ oz/10 g) coarsely chopped fresh cilantro

¼ cup (⅓ oz/10 g) chopped fresh mint

2 Tbsp grapeseed oil

1 cup (3½ oz/105 g) thinly sliced green onion

1 lb (500 g) Dungeness crabmeat, picked over for shell fragments

2 Tbsp roasted peanuts

1 jalapeño chile, thinly sliced, seeded if desired

Place the vermicelli in a heatproof bowl and cover with very hot tap water. Let the noodles soak until tender and opaque, about 10 minutes. Drain well.

In a small bowl, combine the chicken broth, egg, fish sauce, lime juice, sugar, Sriracha, garlic, and ½ tsp pepper. Mix well to combine. Add 2 Tbsp cilantro and 2 Tbsp mint, stir to combine, and set aside.

Warm a wok over medium-high heat. Add the oil and, when it's hot, add the onion and stir-fry until just tender, 2–3 minutes. Add the sauce and the crab and cook, stirring to combine. Stir in the noodles and cook just until they are heated through, 1–2 minutes.

Transfer the mixture to a warm serving dish and top with the peanuts, sliced jalapeño, and the remaining ½ tsp pepper, cilantro, and mint. Serve warm or at room temperature.

RED LENTIL BURGERS WITH LEMON-HERB YOGURT SAUCE

serves 4

Red lentils are appreciated for their relatively quick cooking time, their high nutritional value, and their versatility. This is a great dish if you are watching calories, as the burgers are served on greens rather than in buns and the creamy yogurt sauce adds richness with only modest fat.

FOR THE RED LENTIL BURGERS

1 cup (7 oz/220 g) red lentils, picked over and rinsed

Salt and freshly ground pepper

2 tsp olive oil

1 carrot, shredded

¼ small yellow onion, finely chopped

2 cloves garlic, finely chopped

2 tsp ground cumin

1 large egg, slightly beaten

½ cup (¾ oz/20 g) whole-wheat panko bread crumbs

¼ cup (⅓ oz/10 g) minced fresh cilantro

FOR THE LEMON-HERB YOGURT SAUCE

¾ cup (6 oz/185 g) plain Greek yogurt

¼ cup (⅓ oz/10 g) minced fresh cilantro

Grated zest and juice of 1 lemon

Salt and freshly ground pepper

Nonstick cooking spray

6 cups (6 oz/185 g) mixed salad greens

To make the burgers, put the lentils and a big pinch of salt in a saucepan and cover with water by 1 inch (2.5 cm). Bring to a boil over medium-high heat. Reduce the heat to low and simmer until tender, about 20 minutes. Drain well and transfer to a bowl. In a small frying pan over medium-high heat, warm the oil. Add the carrot, onion, and garlic and sauté until soft, about 3 minutes. Add the cumin, season with salt and pepper, and cook for 2 minutes. Add this mixture to the bowl with the lentils along with the egg, panko, and cilantro and season with salt and pepper. Mix well and form into 8 small patties. Refrigerate the patties for 30 minutes.

Meanwhile, to make the sauce, combine the yogurt, cilantro, and lemon zest and juice in a small bowl. Season with salt and pepper.

Warm a nonstick frying pan over medium-high heat and coat lightly with nonstick cooking spray. Cook the patties until golden-brown, about 4 minutes per side.

Divide the greens among plates, top with the burgers, drizzle with the sauce, and serve.

So many winter squash varieties are available nowadays that you do not have to be limited to the two suggested here. Others, such as Banana, Buttercup, Golden Nugget, or Table Queen, would be equally good in this savory tart. Most pecorinos you see are aged, but a quality cheese counter will carry a pecorino fresco, or "young pecorino."

WINTER SQUASH & PECORINO TART

serves 6–8

FOR THE PASTRY

1⅓ cups (7 oz/220 g) all-purpose flour

¼ tsp sugar

Salt

½ cup (4 oz/125 g) cold unsalted butter, cut into ½-inch (12-mm) pieces

¼ cup (2 fl oz/60 ml) ice water

1 butternut or kabocha squash, about 2 lb (1 kg)

4 Tbsp (2 fl oz/60 ml) olive oil

1 red onion, finely chopped

1 tsp minced fresh thyme

2 eggs

1 cup (8 fl oz/250 ml) heavy cream

Salt and freshly ground pepper

½ cup (2 oz/60 g) grated pecorino fresco or other mild, semifirm sheep's milk cheese

½ cup (2 oz/60 g) grated Parmesan cheese

To make the dough, in a food processor, combine the flour, sugar, and ¼ tsp salt and pulse to blend. Add the butter and pulse until the mixture resembles coarse crumbs. With the motor running, drizzle in the ice water and process just until a ball of dough begins to form. Turn the dough out onto a lightly floured work surface and pat it into a disk. Wrap in plastic wrap and refrigerate for at least 1 hour or up to overnight. Remove the dough from the refrigerator about 20 minutes before rolling it out.

Preheat the oven to 425°F (220°C).

Cut the squash in half lengthwise and remove the seeds and strings. Rub 1 Tbsp of the oil over the flesh and place the halves, cut side down, on a baking sheet. Bake until the skin is browned and the flesh is soft, about 40 minutes. Let cool for 15 minutes. Scoop the flesh into a bowl and mash with a fork until smooth.

In a frying pan, heat the remaining 3 Tbsp oil over medium-low heat. Add the onion and thyme and sauté until the onion is softened, 7–8 minutes. Reduce the heat to low and cook, stirring occasionally, until the onion is very soft, about 30 minutes. »→

In a large bowl, whisk together the eggs, cream, ¾ tsp salt, and a grind of pepper. Add the mashed squash and stir until smooth.

On a lightly floured work surface, roll out the dough into an 11-inch (28-cm) circle. Transfer the dough to a 9-inch (23-cm) tart pan with a removable bottom. Trim the overhanging dough flush with the top of the pan sides. Place the pan on a baking sheet. Spoon the onion into the dough-lined pan and sprinkle with the cheeses. Pour the squash mixture over the cheese. Bake for 10 minutes. Reduce the oven temperature to 400°F (200°C) and bake until the filling is puffed up and set, about 20 minutes.

Transfer the tart to a wire rack and let cool for 10 minutes. Remove from the pan and transfer to a plate. Serve warm or at room temperature.

DECEMBER 14

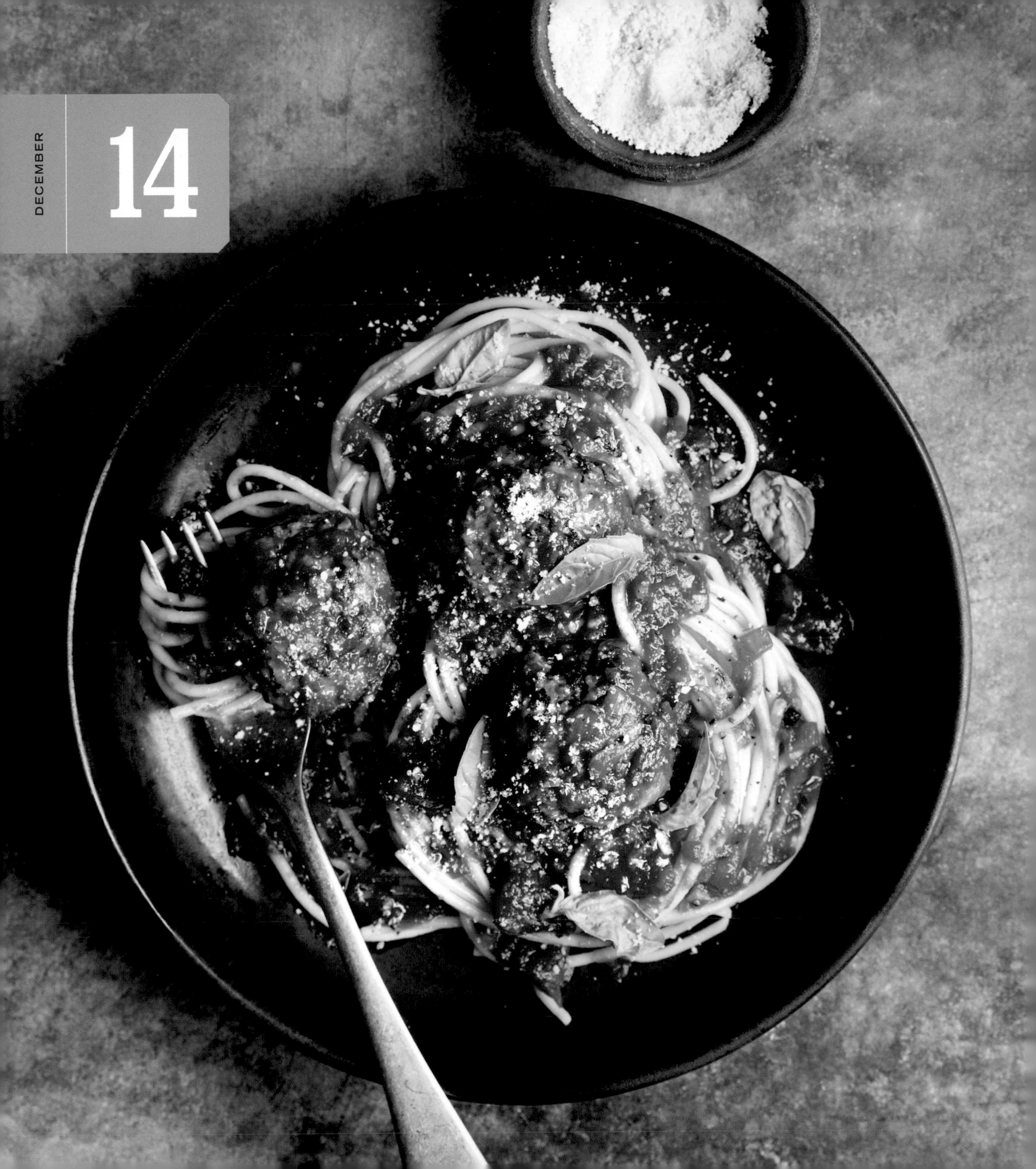

14

Meatballs are welcome during the cold days of December. This moist, flavorful version uses chicken instead of the more common beef or pork and mixes in spinach leaves for flavor and moisture. Red pepper flakes add just the right amount of spicy heat to the sauce. Serve the meatballs with bread for sopping up every last bit of the delicious sauce, or put some spaghetti on to cook and serve the meatballs and sauce on top.

CHICKEN MEATBALLS WITH SPICY TOMATO SAUCE

serves 4–6

FOR THE MEATBALLS

5 oz (155 g) spinach leaves

1 lb (500 g) ground chicken

6 Tbsp (1 oz/30 g) whole-wheat panko bread crumbs

3 Tbsp grated Parmesan cheese

2 cloves garlic, minced

1 large egg, slightly beaten

Salt and freshly ground black pepper

FOR THE SPICY TOMATO SAUCE

2 Tbsp olive oil

1 yellow onion, chopped

4 cloves garlic, chopped

¼ tsp *each* red pepper flakes and dried thyme

½ tsp dried oregano

Salt and freshly ground black pepper

⅓ cup (3 fl oz/80 ml) dry red wine

1 can (28 oz/875 g) diced tomatoes

¼ cup (¾ oz/20 g) chopped fresh basil

Bring a saucepan of water to a boil over high heat. Add the spinach and cook just until wilted, about 3 minutes. Drain well and then wrap in a clean kitchen towel to squeeze out any remaining moisture. Finely chop and transfer to a large bowl.

Preheat the oven to 375°F (190°C). To the bowl with the spinach, add the chicken, panko, Parmesan, garlic, and egg. Season well with salt and black pepper and stir to combine. Using 2 Tbsp of the chicken mixture at a time, form into meatballs and transfer to a baking sheet lightly coated with nonstick cooking spray. Bake until the meatballs are cooked through, about 15 minutes.

To make the tomato sauce, in a saucepan over medium-high heat, warm the oil. Add the onion and garlic and sauté until the onion is translucent, about 5 minutes. Add the red pepper flakes, thyme, and oregano. Season with salt and black pepper and sauté for about 30 seconds. Add the wine and »→

cook until the liquid is reduced by half, about 4 minutes. Add the tomatoes with their juices and bring to a boil. Reduce the heat to low and simmer for 25 minutes. Allow to cool slightly, then transfer half of the sauce to a blender in two batches. Purée the sauce and add it back into the saucepan. Season with salt and black pepper.

Ladle the sauce into shallow bowls and top with 3 or 4 meatballs. Garnish with the chopped basil and serve.

15

Dark soy sauce, Japanese rice wine, and thinly sliced shiitake mushrooms and green onions lend earthiness and depth to the salty-sweet sauce that laps these tender black cod fillets. Serve them with steamed rice for catching every drop of the richly flavored sauce.

BRAISED BLACK COD WITH SHIITAKE MUSHROOMS

serves 4

1 Tbsp canola oil

4 black cod fillets, skin removed

¼ cup (2 fl oz/60 ml) dark soy sauce

¼ cup (2 fl oz/60 ml) sake

2 Tbsp sugar

2 slices peeled fresh ginger, smashed

2 star anise

1 cinnamon stick

2 tsp cornstarch dissolved in 2 tsp cold water

12 shiitake mushrooms, stemmed and thinly sliced

4 green onions, white and tender green parts, cut into 1-inch (2.5 cm) pieces

In a large frying pan, heat the oil over medium-high heat. Add the fish and sear for 1–2 minutes. Turn and sear on the second side for 1–2 minutes. Transfer to a plate. Drain the oil from the pan.

Add the soy sauce, sake, sugar, ginger, star anise, cinnamon, cornstarch mixture, mushrooms, and green onions to the pan. Pour in ½ cup (4 fl oz/125 ml) water. Bring to a boil and simmer for about 2 minutes. Place the fish in the broth, cover, and simmer until opaque throughout, about 10 minutes. Discard the ginger, star anise, and cinnamon from the broth. Serve directly from the pan.

16

WARM MOLTEN CHOCOLATE CAKES

makes 6 cakes

8 oz (250 g) bittersweet chocolate, finely chopped

¼ cup (2 oz/60 g) unsalted butter, cut into pieces, plus more for greasing

1 tsp pure vanilla extract

Pinch of kosher salt

4 large egg yolks

6 Tbsp (3 oz/90 g) sugar

2 Tbsp unsweetened natural cocoa powder, sifted, plus more for dusting

3 large egg whites

Plunge a spoon into one of these warm, soft cakes and you'll find chocolate bliss. They are incredibly versatile, too. Dress them up with scoops of chocolate or vanilla ice cream, or top them with sliced poached pears or blood orange segments and a dollop of crème fraîche. In the summer months, serve with fresh raspberries or sliced strawberries.

Preheat the oven to 400°F (200°C). Lightly butter six ¾-cup (6–fl oz/180-ml) ramekins and dust with cocoa. Set the ramekins on a small baking sheet.

Place the chocolate and butter in the top of a double boiler over (not touching) barely simmering water, and melt, whisking until the mixture is glossy and smooth. Remove from over the water and stir in the vanilla and salt. Set aside to cool slightly.

In a large bowl, using a mixer, beat together the egg yolks, 3 Tbsp of the sugar, and the cocoa on medium-high speed until thick. Add the chocolate mixture to the yolk mixture and beat until blended. The mixture will be very thick.

In a bowl, using clean beaters, beat the egg whites on medium-high speed until very foamy and thick. Sprinkle in the remaining 3 Tbsp sugar and increase the speed to high. Continue beating until firm, glossy peaks form. Spoon half of the beaten whites onto the chocolate mixture and stir in just until blended. Gently fold in the remaining whites. Spoon into the prepared ramekins.

Bake the cakes until they are puffed and the tops are cracked, about 13 minutes. The inside of the cracks will look very wet. Remove from the oven and serve. Or, run a small knife around the inside of each ramekin and invert the cakes onto plates.

17

VIETNAMESE BEEF NOODLE SOUP

serves 4

7 oz (220 g) Asian rice stick noodles

8 cups (64 fl oz/2 l) low-sodium beef broth

5 whole cloves

4 thin slices fresh ginger

3 star anise

1 cinnamon stick

1 tsp black peppercorns

1 yellow onion, sliced

Salt and freshly ground pepper

¼ cup (2 fl oz/60 ml) peanut or canola oil

8 shallots, sliced

½ lb (250 g) beef eye-of-round, very thinly sliced, cut into 2-inch (5-cm) pieces

Leaves from 1 bunch *each* fresh cilantro, mint, and basil

1 cup (2 oz/60 g) bean sprouts

2 small Thai chiles, seeded, and thinly sliced

1 lime, cut into quarters

Sriracha sauce, for serving

In this adaptation of pho, Vietnam's popular beef noodle soup, cloves, ginger, star anise, and peppercorns flavor beef broth, creating an aromatic base for the rice noodles and meat. With the broth on hand, this is a quick winter meal, as the raw beef is cooked in the soup bowls by ladling the hot broth over it.

In a bowl, soak the noodles in warm water until very pliable, about 20 minutes. Meanwhile, in a soup pot, combine the broth, cloves, ginger, star anise, cinnamon stick, peppercorns, onion, and salt to taste. Bring to a boil over medium-high heat. Reduce the heat to low, cover, and simmer for 10 minutes. Meanwhile, in a frying pan over medium-high heat, warm the oil. Add the shallots and sauté until browned, about 4 minutes. Drain on paper towels. Strain the broth through a fine-mesh sieve, discarding the spices. Return the broth to the pot.

Have ready 4 large, deep soup bowls. Bring a large pot of water to a boil over high heat. Bring the broth to a boil over high heat. Drain the noodles. Place one-fourth of the noodles in a strainer and immerse in the boiling water until tender yet firm, about 10 seconds. Drain and place in one of the soup bowls. Repeat with the remaining noodles. Divide the beef slices among the bowls, then ladle over the hot broth. Divide the cilantro, mint, basil, bean sprouts, chiles, fried shallots, and lime wedges among the bowls. Serve, passing the Sriracha at the table.

CRISPY CHICKEN & CABBAGE SALAD WITH PEANUT DRESSING

serves 6

In this Asian-inspired recipe, the roasted flavor of the peanut butter infuses the salty-sweet dressing, while sesame seeds give the crispy chicken a nutty, rich finish. For an additional Asian touch, substitute shredded daikon for half of the shredded carrot.

½ cup (2½ oz/75 g) all-purpose flour

2 large eggs

1 cup (4 oz/125 g) panko bread crumbs

Salt and freshly ground pepper

3 skinless, boneless chicken breast halves (about 1½ lb/750 g total weight)

1 head napa cabbage

⅓ cup (3 fl oz/80 ml) peanut oil

2 Tbsp sesame seeds

FOR THE PEANUT DRESSING

¼ cup (2½ oz/75 g) natural peanut butter

¼ cup (2 fl oz/60 ml) rice vinegar

¼ cup (2 fl oz/60 ml) peanut oil

1 Tbsp toasted sesame oil

2 Tbsp brown sugar

1 tsp tamari sauce

3 large carrots, peeled and shredded

12 leaves green-leaf lettuce

Put the flour in a shallow bowl. In a second shallow bowl, whisk the eggs until blended. In a third shallow bowl, stir together the panko, ½ tsp salt, and several grindings of pepper. Season the chicken breasts on both sides with salt and pepper. One at a time, dip the breasts first in the flour, coating evenly and shaking off the excess, then in the egg, allowing the excess to drip off, and finally in the seasoned panko, coating evenly and shaking off the excess. Place on a large plate and refrigerate for 30 minutes.

Halve the cabbage lengthwise and core. Cut each half crosswise into thin slices. Set aside.

Preheat the oven to 350°F (180°C). In a large nonstick frying pan, warm the peanut oil over medium-high heat until hot but not smoking. Add the breaded chicken breasts and cook on the first side until golden brown, about 4 minutes. Turn and cook on the second side until golden brown, about 2 minutes. Transfer to a rimmed baking sheet and bake until an instant-read thermometer inserted into the thickest part of a breast registers 160°F (71°C), 15–20 minutes. »→

Meanwhile, in a dry frying pan, toast the sesame seeds over medium-low heat, stirring, until fragrant and starting to brown, about 2 minutes. Pour onto a plate and let cool.

To make the dressing, in a food processor or blender, combine the peanut butter, vinegar, peanut oil, sesame oil, brown sugar, tamari, ¾ tsp salt, and 2 Tbsp water and process until smooth. Taste and adjust the seasonings.

Remove the chicken from the oven, sprinkle lightly with salt, and tent with foil. Let rest, then cut crosswise into thin slices.

In a large bowl, toss the cabbage and carrots with 2 big pinches of salt and several grindings of pepper. Drizzle with about one-third of the dressing and toss well.

Line individual salad plates with 2 lettuce leaves. Top with the cabbage-carrot mixture and chicken slices. Drizzle with the remaining dressing, sprinkle with the sesame seeds, and serve.

19

Between holiday parties and cold-weather roasts, lighten up with a seafood supper. This famous San Francisco fisherman's stew has many variations. Most versions include local Dungeness crab, but the seafood additions beyond that depend on the catch of the day and the whim of the cook. Following this philosophy, use whatever seafood is best in your area.

CIOPPINO

serves 6

¼ cup (2 fl oz/60 ml) olive oil

2 yellow onions, chopped

2 red bell peppers, seeded and chopped

4 cloves garlic, minced

2 bay leaves, broken in half

1 can (28 oz/825 g) diced tomatoes

¾ cup (6 fl oz/180 ml) dry red wine

½ cup (4 fl oz/125 ml) dry white wine

2 Tbsp chopped fresh oregano

2 Tbsp chopped fresh thyme

¾ lb (375 g) firm white fish fillets such as halibut or monkfish, cut into 1-inch (2.5-cm) chunks

1 lb (500 g) littleneck or other small clams, scrubbed and soaked

1 lb (500 g) Dungeness crab claws, or ½ lb (250 g) Dungeness or other lump crabmeat, picked over for shell fragments

20 large shrimp, heads and legs removed, peeled and deveined if desired

¼–½ tsp hot-pepper sauce such as Tabasco

Salt and freshly ground pepper

In a large, heavy pot, warm the oil over medium heat. Add the onions and bell peppers and sauté until just tender, 4–5 minutes. Add the garlic and sauté for 30 seconds. Add the bay leaves, tomatoes and their juices, and red and white wines and bring to a simmer. Partially cover, reduce the heat to medium-low, and cook until thickened slightly, about 15 minutes.

Remove and discard the bay leaves. Add the oregano, thyme, fish, and clams, discarding any clams that do not close to the touch. Cover and cook over medium-low heat for 5 minutes. Add the crab and shrimp, cover, and cook until the shrimp and fish are opaque throughout and the clams have opened, 3–4 minutes. Discard any unopened clams. Stir in the hot-pepper sauce and season with salt and pepper. Serve.

20

Here, bright-tasting tangerines, which are at their best in winter, add a tart-sweet accent to the star anise–infused braising liquid. Their fragrant juice and zest perk up the deep flavors in the dish and cut through the richness of the tender braised chicken thighs.

BRAISED CHICKEN WITH TANGERINE & STAR ANISE

serves 4

2 tangerines

8 skin-on, bone-in chicken thighs, about 3¼ lb (1.6 kg) total

Salt and freshly ground pepper

2 Tbsp peanut oil

1 small yellow onion, finely chopped

2 cloves garlic, minced

1 tsp peeled and grated fresh ginger

1 cup (8 fl oz/250 ml) chicken broth

2 Tbsp soy sauce

1 tsp chile-garlic sauce, such as Sriracha

2–3 star anise

2 tsp cornstarch dissolved in 1 Tbsp water

Finely grate the zest from the tangerines, then squeeze ½ cup (4 fl oz/125 ml) juice. Season the chicken with 1 tsp salt and ½ tsp pepper.

In a large, heavy pot, heat the oil over medium-high heat. Working in batches, sear the chicken, turning once or twice, until browned on both sides, about 9 minutes. Transfer to a plate.

Pour off all but 1 Tbsp fat in the pot and return the pot to medium heat. Add the onion and cook, stirring occasionally, until softened, 3–4 minutes. Add the garlic, the ginger, and half of the tangerine zest and stir until fragrant, about 1 minute. Add the broth, tangerine juice, soy sauce, chile-garlic sauce, and star anise and bring to a boil, stirring to scrape up any browned bits from the bottom of the pot. Return the chicken to the pot, reduce the heat to low, cover, and simmer until the chicken is opaque throughout, about 25 minutes.

Transfer the chicken to a platter. Bring the liquid in the pot to a boil over medium-high heat. Stir in the cornstarch mixture and cook just until the sauce thickens slightly, about 30 seconds.

Pour the sauce over the chicken. Sprinkle with the remaining tangerine zest and serve.

21

In these elegant tartlets, the double dose of chocolate—in the cocoa crusts and the ganache filling—is complemented by an especially rich dark caramel. A sprinkle of briny sea salt to finish intensifies the flavors and adds sparkle and crunch.

BITTERSWEET CHOCOLATE & DARK CARAMEL TARTLETS

makes 6 tartlets

FOR THE COCOA TARTLET DOUGH

6 Tbsp (3 oz/90 g) unsalted butter, cut into pieces

½ cup (2 oz/60 g) plus 2 Tbsp confectioners' sugar, sifted

1¼ cups (6½ oz/200 g) all-purpose flour

⅓ cup (1 oz/30 g) unsweetened natural cocoa powder, plus more for dusting

½ tsp kosher salt

1 large egg, lightly beaten

1 cup (8 oz/250 g) granulated sugar

⅔ cup (5 fl oz/160 ml) heavy cream, plus ¾ cup (6 fl oz/180 ml)

3 Tbsp unsalted butter

¼ tsp kosher salt

6 oz (185 g) bittersweet chocolate, chopped

Flaky sea salt, such as Maldon

To make the dough, put the butter and confectioners' sugar in a food processor and process until combined. Sift the flour, cocoa, and salt over the butter mixture, then pulse until the mixture resembles coarse meal. Add the egg and process until the dough comes together. Turn out the dough onto a work surface and press into a disk.

In a saucepan, combine the sugar and 3 Tbsp water, cover, and bring to a simmer over medium-high heat. Once the sugar starts to melt, uncover and swirl the pan until the sugar dissolves, about 5 minutes. Continue to simmer, uncovered, until the sugar turns a deep amber-brown, 4–6 minutes. Remove from the heat, carefully add the ⅔ cup cream (the caramel will splatter), and whisk until smooth. Whisk in the butter and salt and let cool to room temperature.

Preheat the oven to 375°F (190°C). Divide the dough into 6 equal pieces. Place each piece into a 3-inch (7.5-cm) tartlet pan, then dip your fingertips in cocoa powder and press the dough into the bottom and up the sides. Use any scraps to fill cracks. Place the tartlet shells on a baking sheet and bake until set, about 10 minutes. Let cool on a wire rack.

Place the chocolate in a heatproof bowl. In a saucepan, bring the ¾ cup cream to a ⟫

simmer and pour over the chocolate. Let stand for about 5 minutes, then whisk until smooth.

Spread about 1 Tbsp of the caramel on each tart shell. Pour the chocolate mixture into the shells, smoothing the tops. Refrigerate until firm, at least 2 hours or up to 2 days, covering the tartlets with plastic wrap once the chocolate is set.

To serve, let the tartlets stand at room temperature for about 15 minutes to soften slightly. Remove the tartlets from the pans and sprinkle each with a little flaky sea salt.

22

High-quality ham contributes a smoky, meaty flavor that mimics long cooking in this quick braise of peppery kale. Creamy white beans and woodsy rosemary combine to create a hearty dish that can be served as a main course with just salad, bread, and perhaps a cheese plate on the side.

BRAISED DINOSAUR KALE WITH WHITE BEANS & SMOKED HAM

serves 4

2 bunches dinosaur kale, about 1 lb (500 g) total

2 tsp olive oil

2 cloves garlic, thinly sliced

4 oz (125 g) smoked ham such as Black Forest, diced

½ cup (4 fl oz/125 ml) chicken broth

Salt and freshly ground pepper

1 can (15 oz/470 g) cannellini beans, rinsed and drained

½ tsp minced fresh rosemary

Strip the stalks and ribs from the kale leaves, and then tear the leaves into 2-inch (5-cm) pieces.

In a frying pan, warm the oil over medium-low heat. Add the garlic and sauté until lightly browned, about 1 minute. Add the ham and sauté for 1 minute. Add the kale, cover, and cook, turning occasionally, until the kale leaves just begin to wilt, 2–3 minutes. Add the broth and a pinch each of salt and pepper and cook until the leaves are just tender and the liquid has almost evaporated, 4–5 minutes.

Add the beans and rosemary to the pan and raise the heat to medium-high. Cook, tossing gently, until the beans are heated through, 2–3 minutes. Adjust the seasoning if necessary and serve.

23

SWEET POTATO SOUP WITH CHEDDAR & CAVIAR CROUTONS

serves 8

8 baguette slices, each ¼ inch (6 mm) thick

2 Tbsp olive oil

2 large sweet potatoes (1½–2 lb/750 g–1 kg total)

4 cups (32 fl oz/1 l) chicken broth, plus 2–4 cups (16–32 fl oz/250 ml–1 l) more as needed

Salt and ground white pepper

¼ lb (125 g) white Cheddar cheese, shredded

2 oz (60 g) black caviar

This silky sweet potato purée boasts a striking presentation, as each bowl is crowned with a baguette slice topped with bubbling browned cheese. A dollop of inky black caviar added to each bowl just before serving elevates this dish to a special-occasion first course.

Preheat the oven to 350°F (180°C).

Arrange the baguette slices in a single layer on a baking sheet and brush with 1½ Tbsp of the oil. Toast in the oven until lightly golden, about 15 minutes. Turn and toast until lightly golden on the second side, about 8 minutes. Set aside.

Rub the sweet potatoes with the remaining ½ Tbsp oil and place on a baking sheet. Bake until the skin is wrinkled and the flesh is easily pierced with a fork, 1–1½ hours. Remove from the oven. When the potatoes are cool enough to handle, cut in half lengthwise and scoop the flesh into a large, heavy pot. Add 4 cups (32 fl oz/250 ml) of the broth and whisk until smooth, adding more broth as needed to achieve a creamy but soupy consistency. Place over medium-high heat and bring to just below a boil, stirring often. Add ½ tsp pepper and salt to taste. Reduce the heat to low and simmer while you finish making the croutons.

Preheat the broiler. Sprinkle the toasted baguette slices with the cheese and arrange on a baking sheet. Broil just until the cheese melts, about 3 minutes.

To serve, ladle the soup into bowls. Spoon a dollop of caviar on top of each crouton and float a crouton in each bowl of soup.

24

BEEF TENDERLOIN WITH SHALLOT & RED WINE REDUCTION

serves 8

1 beef tenderloin, 2½–3 lb (1.25–1.5 kg)

2 Tbsp extra-virgin olive oil

2 tsp minced fresh thyme

Salt and freshly ground pepper

2 Tbsp minced shallots

1 cup (8 fl oz/250 ml) full-bodied red wine such as Syrah or Cabernet Sauvignon

2½ Tbsp butter

The tenderloin is both the most tender and the most expensive cut of beef. It is also leaner than many other cuts, which means it needs relatively brief cooking and tastes best when cooked to no more than medium-rare. The red wine reduction, made from the flavorful pan juices, is quickly assembled while the roast rests.

Remove the tenderloin from the refrigerator about 1 hour before it is scheduled to go in the oven to allow it to lose its chill.

Preheat the oven to 450°F (230°C). Rub the beef all over with the oil, then rub with the thyme, 1½ teaspoons salt, and 1 teaspoon pepper.

Place the roast on a V-shaped rack in a shallow roasting pan just large enough to accommodate it. Roast until an instant-read thermometer inserted into the thickest part of the tenderloin registers 115°–120°F (46°–49°C) for rare, about 20 minutes; 125°–130°F (52°–54°C) for medium rare, about 25 minutes; or 130°–140°F (54°–60°C) for medium, about 30 minutes.

When the roast has reached the desired degree of doneness, transfer to a carving board and tent loosely with foil. Let rest for about 15 minutes.

Meanwhile, remove the rack from the roasting pan and place the pan on the stove top over medium heat. Add the shallots and sauté, stirring them into the pan juices, until translucent, about 2 minutes. Add the wine, a little at a time, stirring and scraping up any browned bits with a wooden spoon from the pan bottom. Continue to cook until the wine is reduced by nearly half. Stir in the butter. When the butter has melted, remove from the heat and cover to keep warm.

To serve, cut the beef across the grain into slices ½ inch (12 mm) thick. Arrange the slices on a platter, drizzle with the sauce, and serve.

DECEMBER

26

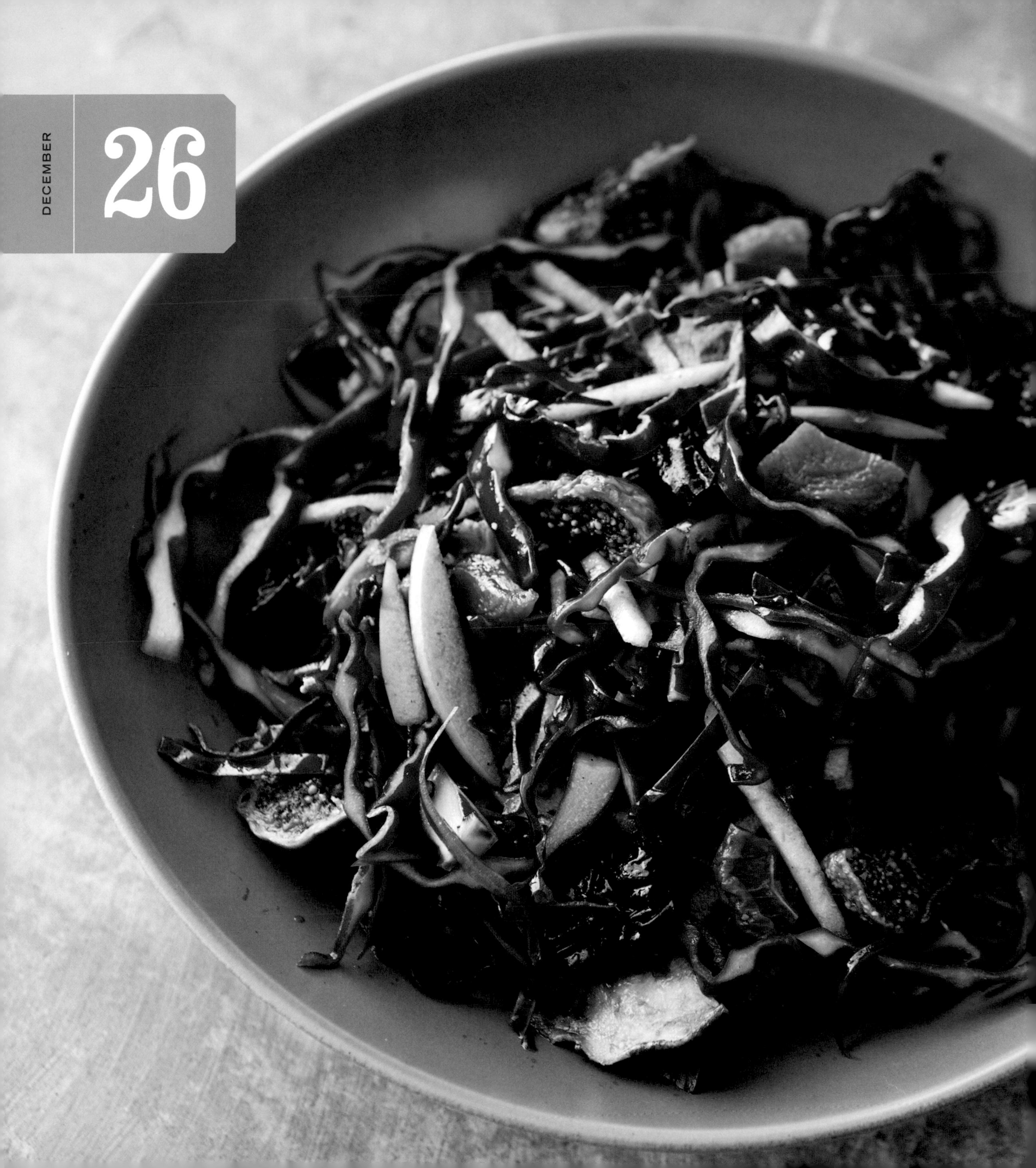

25

You can serve this elegant salad as a first course or a light main course. The fruit can vary with the season, such as cherries in spring, thinly sliced nectarines in summer, or pomegranate seeds in late fall. Parmigiano-Reggiano or fresh goat cheese is a nice addition.

DUCK BREAST SALAD WITH WALNUTS & ORANGES

serves 4

2 boneless duck breast halves (4–6 oz/125–185 g each)

Salt and freshly ground pepper

3 Tbsp sherry vinegar

7 Tbsp (3½ fl oz/110 ml) extra-virgin olive oil

1 head radicchio, torn into 1-inch (2.5-cm) strips

2 heads frisée, pale yellow inner leaves only

½ cup (2 oz/60 g) walnuts, toasted and coarsely chopped

2 oranges, peeled and segmented with a knife (see page 302)

Season the duck breasts with salt and pepper. Using a sharp knife, score the skin by making a crisscross pattern, being careful not to cut into the meat.

Warm a large sauté pan over medium-low heat. Place the duck, skin side down, in the pan and cook until the skin is very crisp and golden, 12–15 minutes. Turn the duck over and sear the other side, then continue cooking until the meat is just springy when pressed with a finger for rare to medium-rare, 3–5 minutes longer, or until cooked to your liking. Transfer to a cutting board, cover loosely with aluminum foil, and let rest for 3–5 minutes before slicing.

Pour the vinegar into a small bowl. Add the oil in a thin stream, whisking constantly until the vinaigrette is well blended. Season with salt and pepper.

In a large bowl, toss together the radicchio and frisée. Drizzle with half of the vinaigrette and toss to coat well. Divide the salad among individual plates and scatter the walnuts and orange segments on top.

Cut the duck across the grain into very thin slices and divide among the salads. Drizzle with the remaining vinaigrette and serve right away.

26

Tame cabbage with vinegar and seasonings, letting it sit and then draining it before proceeding. This will transform it from rough textured to silky and from strong flavored to mellow. The vinegar also turns the natural blue tinge of red cabbage a bright shade of scarlet.

WINTER SALAD OF RED CABBAGE & DRIED FRUITS

serves 4

½ head red cabbage, about 1 lb (500 g), cored and shredded or thinly sliced

Salt and freshly ground pepper

Red wine vinegar or cider vinegar

5 dried apricots, chopped

5 dried golden figs such as Calimyrna, chopped

5 dried pears, chopped

5 prunes, pitted and chopped

1 tart apple such as Granny Smith, cored and cut into matchsticks

1–2 Tbsp canola oil

Several pinches of ground cumin

½ tsp sugar, or to taste

2–3 Tbsp walnut pieces (optional)

In a bowl, combine the cabbage with salt, pepper, and vinegar to taste, and toss well. Cover and let stand for at least 2 hours at room temperature or, preferably, overnight in the refrigerator. Drain off all but 1 Tbsp of the liquid.

Add the apricots, figs, pears, prunes, and apple to the cabbage and toss well. Drizzle with 1 Tbsp of the oil and add the cumin and sugar. Season with salt and pepper and toss well. Adjust the seasoning with additional vinegar, cumin, sugar, salt, and pepper, if desired. Stir in additional oil if you feel it needs more moisture.

Add the walnuts, if using, toss to mix well, and serve.

27

*Spiced cakes are
an enduring
holiday tradition.
This gingery
version is dark and
fragrant, redolent
of molasses and
spice. Serve each
slice with a dollop
of whipped cream
(see page 53) or,
for a holiday meal,
with poached pears
and crème fraîche.*

SPICY DARK GINGERBREAD

serves 10–12

3 cups (15 oz/470 g) all-purpose flour

½ tsp kosher salt

1 tsp baking soda

1 tsp ground cinnamon

1 tsp ground allspice

2 Tbsp ground ginger

¼ cup (1½ oz/45 g) peeled and
grated fresh ginger

1 cup (8 oz/250 g) unsalted butter

1 cup (7 oz/220 g) firmly packed
light brown sugar

1 large egg

1 cup (11 oz/345 g) light molasses

1 cup (8 fl oz/250 ml) buttermilk

Preheat the oven to 350°F (180°C). Butter a
10-inch (25-cm) Bundt pan or two 9-by-5-inch
(23-by-13-inch) loaf pans. Dust lightly with
flour and shake out any excess.

In a large bowl, whisk together the flour,
salt, baking soda, cinnamon, allspice, ground
ginger, and fresh ginger. In another large
bowl, using an electric mixer, beat the butter
and brown sugar until light and creamy. Beat
in the egg. Add the molasses and beat until
well blended, about 2 minutes. Beat in the
dry ingredients in 3 additions alternately
with the buttermilk in 2 additions, beginning
and ending with the flour mixture. Pour
the batter into the prepared pan(s).

Bake until a toothpick inserted into the
center of the cake comes out clean, about
50 minutes. Let cool in the pan on a wire
rack for 10 minutes, then turn out of the
pan, slipping a knife between the cake and
the pan to loosen any stuck edges. Turn the
cake right side up and let cool for at least
15 minutes before serving.

28

*Look for a crusty
country loaf for this
recipe to ensure
good texture in
the finished dish,
and if your budget
allows, buy an
authentic creamy,
nutty fontina from
Italy's Aosta Valley
for the best flavor.
Accompany the
dish with a salad of
butter lettuce, sliced
pears, and toasted
walnuts and pour
a crisp Sauvignon
Blanc at the table.*

BREAD PUDDING WITH CHARD, SUN-DRIED TOMATOES & FONTINA

serves 4–6

2 cups (16 fl oz/500 ml) whole milk

4 eggs

Salt and freshly ground pepper

8 slices coarse country bread,
cut into 1-inch (2.5-cm) cubes

2 Tbsp unsalted butter

1 small yellow onion, chopped

2 cloves garlic, minced

1 bunch chard, tough stems removed,
leaves chopped

¼ cup (2 fl oz/60 ml) chicken or
vegetable broth

⅓ cup (3 oz/90 g) oil-packed sun-dried
tomatoes, chopped

½ cup (½ oz/15 g) packed fresh basil leaves

3 oz (90 g) fontina cheese, shredded

Preheat the oven to 350°F (180°C). Butter
a 2-qt (1-l) baking dish.

In a large bowl, whisk together the milk,
eggs, 1 tsp salt, and ½ tsp pepper. Add the
bread cubes and stir to combine. Let stand
for 15 minutes. Occasionally press down on
the bread cubes with a spatula to immerse
them in the liquid.

In a frying pan, melt the butter over medium-
high heat. Add the onion and garlic and
cook, stirring occasionally, until the onion
is translucent, about 5 minutes. Add the chard
and season with salt and pepper. Cook,
stirring, until it begins to wilt, about 2 minutes.
Add the broth and cook until most of the
liquid is absorbed, about 5 minutes.

Add the chard mixture, sun-dried tomatoes,
basil, and fontina to the bowl with the bread
and toss to combine. Season with salt and
pepper. Transfer the mixture to the prepared
dish. Bake the pudding until browned on
top, about 55 minutes. Remove from the
oven and serve.

Beef bourguignon represents French country cooking at its best. Long, slow cooking transforms a tough chuck roast into meat tender enough to cut with a fork. Don't stint when it comes to the wine: buy a good red Burgundy for both the kitchen and the table. Serve this iconic dish with steamed or roasted potatoes.

BEEF BOURGUIGNON

serves 6–8

3½ lb (1.75 kg) boneless beef chuck roast, or a combination of boneless chuck and beef shank, cut into 2–2½ inch (5–6 cm) chunks

Salt and freshly ground pepper

All-purpose flour

1 Tbsp olive oil

6 oz (185 g) pancetta, cut into 1-inch (2.5-cm) pieces

1 carrot, sliced

1 yellow onion, chopped

3 cups (24 fl oz/750 ml) hearty red wine

2 cloves garlic, minced

1 Tbsp fresh thyme leaves, or ½ Tbsp dried thyme

1 bay leaf

1 Tbsp tomato paste

3 Tbsp unsalted butter, plus more if needed

1 lb (500 g) mushrooms, thickly sliced

20–24 jarred or thawed frozen pearl onions

Sprinkle the beef chunks with ½ tsp salt and ¼ tsp pepper. Spread some flour on a large plate. Lightly coat the cubes with the flour, shaking off the excess.

In a large, heavy pot, warm the oil over low heat. Add the pancetta and cook until crisp and golden, 4–5 minutes. Using a slotted spoon, transfer to a large bowl. Raise the heat to medium-high and, working in batches, sear the beef, turning as needed, until browned on all sides, about 5 minutes. Transfer to the bowl with the pancetta. Add the carrot and onion to the pot and cook until browned, about 5 minutes. Transfer to the bowl with the pancetta and beef.

Pour off the fat from the pot. Reduce the heat to medium, add the wine, and stir to scrape up any browned bits on the pot bottom. Stir in the pancetta, beef, carrot, onion, garlic, thyme, bay leaf, and tomato paste. Season with ½ tsp salt and ¼ tsp pepper and bring to a simmer. Reduce the heat to low, cover, and cook until the beef is somewhat tender, about 2½ hours. »→

In a frying pan, melt the 3 Tbsp butter over medium heat. Add the mushrooms and sauté until lightly browned, 4–5 minutes.

Transfer to a bowl. Add the pearl onions to the pan and sauté, adding more butter if needed, until golden, about 10 minutes. After the beef has cooked for 2½ hours, add the mushrooms and pearl onions to the pot and continue to cook until the beef is fork-tender, about 1 hour more.

Transfer the beef, pancetta, and vegetables to a large serving bowl. Skim the fat from the surface of the sauce. Raise the heat to medium-high, bring to a boil, and cook until the sauce thickens slightly, 1–2 minutes. Pour the sauce over the beef mixture and serve.

30

RICOTTA WITH BLOOD ORANGE, PISTACHIOS & HONEY

serves 4

2 blood oranges

½ cup (4 oz/125 g) fresh whole-milk ricotta cheese

½ cup (2 oz/60 g) pistachios, chopped

Pomegranate seeds for garnish (optional)

¼ cup (3 oz/90 g) honey

December is full of cakes and cookies, so occasionally it's nice to keep dessert fresh, simple, and bright. Juicy winter citrus is delicious heaped onto soft ricotta and drizzled with honey. Scatter pistachios and pomegranate seeds over the top for both crunch and color.

Using a sharp knife, cut a slice off both ends of each blood orange to reveal the flesh. Place the orange upright on a cutting board and cut downward to remove all of the peel and white pith, following the contour of the fruit. You can segment or slice the fruit. To segment each fruit, hold it over a bowl to catch the juices, and cut on either side of each segment to free it from the membrane, letting it fall into the bowl. Pick out any seeds, then cut the segments in half crosswise. To slice the oranges, cut them crosswise into thin slices, then pick out any seeds.

Divide the ricotta among short glasses or bowls. Spoon the oranges over the cheese. Sprinkle evenly with the pistachios and the pomegranate seeds, if using. Drizzle with the honey and serve.

31

SHIITAKE BROTH WITH BUTTER-POACHED LOBSTER & CHIVES

serves 6

1 oz (30 g) dried shiitake mushrooms

2 Tbsp olive oil

1 small yellow onion, chopped

2 cloves garlic, minced

½ lb (250 g) fresh white mushrooms, diced

¼ cup (2 fl oz/60 ml) dry white wine

¼ cup (2 fl oz/60 ml) soy sauce

2 thyme sprigs

1 cup (8 oz/250 g) unsalted butter

2 lobster tails, in their shells

1 Tbsp chopped chives

This is an easygoing recipe when it comes to the ingredients list. It is absolutely fine to use frozen and thawed lobster tails. Be sure to keep the meat in the shells during poaching. This will ensure they hold their shape, making for a better presentation when you slice them.

Put the shiitakes in a small bowl, cover with very hot water, and soak for at least 30 minutes. Drain, reserving the soaking liquid. Remove the stems from the mushrooms and discard. Thinly slice the caps. Strain the soaking liquid through a coffee filter and reserve ¾ cup (6 fl oz/180 ml).

In a large, heavy pot, warm the oil over medium-high heat. Add the onion, garlic, and white mushrooms and sauté for 5 minutes. Add the wine, soy sauce, thyme, the reserved mushroom soaking liquid, and 2 cups (16 fl oz/500 ml) water and bring to a boil. Reduce the heat to low and simmer for 1 hour. Strain the liquid, discarding the solids, and return the broth to the saucepan. Add the sliced shiitakes and keep warm over low heat.

To poach the lobster, in a very small saucepan, melt the butter slowly over medium-low heat, skimming off any foam that rises to the top. Add the lobster tails and poach, turning the tails once and frequently spooning the butter over the exposed parts, until they are cooked all the way through, 5–7 minutes. Transfer the lobster tails to a cutting board, remove the meat from the shells, and cut into ½-inch (12-mm) slices.

To serve, ladle the broth and mushrooms into shallow bowls. Place the lobster slices in the center of each bowl, garnish with the chives, and serve.

INDEX

A

Albondigas, 145

Almonds
Apple Frangipane Tart, 233
Maple Almond Squares, 257
Oatmeal–Chocolate Chip Cookies with Almonds, 46
Penne with Grilled Summer Vegetables, Herbs & Almonds, 158
Raspberry-Almond Clafoutis, 127

Apples
Apple Frangipane Tart, 233
Cheddar & Hard Cider Soup with Fried Shallots, 239
Old-Fashioned Apple Pie, 270
Pulled Chicken Sliders with Apple-Jicama Relish, 259
Spiced Apple Cake with Maple Frosting, 215

Apricots
Apricot Clafoutis, 136
Moroccan-Spiced Roasted Vegetables & Quinoa, 50
Winter Salad of Red Cabbage & Dried Fruits, 299

Arroz con Pollo, 102

Artichokes
Artichokes with Warm Cannellini Bean Salad, 74
Four Seasons Pizza with Mushrooms, Bell Peppers, Artichokes & Olives, 70
Grilled Baby Artichokes with Spicy Garlic Butter, 127

Asian Pears, Grilled Pork Chops, Torpedo Onions &, 244

Asparagus
Asparagus Risotto, 97
Flank Steak Stuffed with Asparagus Pesto, 106
Grilled Asparagus & Endive with Favas, Orange & Mint, 123
Grilled Asparagus & Green Onion Soup with Poached Eggs, 101
Pizza with Asparagus, Leeks & Herbed Ricotta, 120
Red Quinoa with Asparagus, Portobellos & Feta, 59
Roasted Asparagus & Morels with Shallot Butter, 109
Salmon with Spring Vegetables, 63
Spring Vegetable Tart, 116
Thai Green Chicken Curry with Asparagus, 67

Avocados
Avocado Soup with Shrimp & Salsa, 136
Black Bean–Jalapeño Burgers with Avocado Mash, 77
Chorizo & Chicken Soup with Avocado Crema, 217
Fresh Corn Soup with Turkey & Avocado, 203
Grilled Steak Tacos with Chipotle Salsa & Avocado, 137
Lobster & Avocado Salad with Shaved Meyer Lemon, 115
Roasted Salmon with Avocado-Grapefruit Salsa, 37
Smoky Sea Scallops with Avocado-Corn Salsa, 162

B

Banana-Honey Cake, 71

Barley
Barley Risotto with Chicken, Mushrooms & Greens, 27
Kale, Turkey Sausage & Barley Stew, 285

Beans. See also Chickpeas; Edamame; Fava beans
Artichokes with Warm Cannellini Bean Salad, 74
Black Bean, Corn & Quinoa Salad, 161
Black Bean–Jalapeño Burgers with Avocado Mash, 77
Braised Beef Tips with Cranberry Beans, Cherry Tomatoes & Basil, 200
Braised Dinosaur Kale with White Beans & Smoked Ham, 296
Calamari & White Bean Salad, 85
Chicken Tostada Salad, 138
Fresh Shell Beans with Butternut Squash, Bacon & Sage, 225
Green Bean & Potato Salad with Herbs & Anchovies, 225
Halibut with Braised Escarole & White Beans, 112
Italian-Style Ribollita, 259
Mac & Cheese Chili, 18
Mexican Nacho Casserole, 126
Poblano Chiles Stuffed with Black Beans & Summer Vegetables, 189
Pumpkin with White Beans, Caramelized Onions & Roasted Garlic, 265
Roast Chicken & Bread Salad with Haricots Verts & Strawberries, 99
Spanish White Bean Soup with Chorizo & Piquillo Peppers, 192
Spicy Red Bean & Chorizo Stew, 22
Spinach & Black Bean Enchiladas, 39
Summer Chicken Braise with Wax Beans & Tomatoes, 161
Three-Bean Salad with Coriander Vinaigrette, 246
Two-Bean & Potato Salad, 144
Warm Kale & Tuna Niçoise, 218

Beef
Ale-Braised Short Ribs, 249
Barbecue-Style Brisket, 177
Beef & Basil Stir-Fry with Summer Vegetables, 165
Beef & Pumpkin Stew, 214
Beef Bourguignon, 301
Beef-Chipotle Chili, 68
Beef Tenderloin with Shallot & Red Wine Reduction, 297
Bibimbop with Brown Rice & Bulgogi, 241
Braised Beef Tips with Cranberry Beans, Cherry Tomatoes & Basil, 200
Corned Beef & Cabbage, 73
Cuban-Style Stuffed Flank Steak, 263
Flank Steak Stuffed with Asparagus Pesto, 106
Grilled Steak, Pepper & Onion Salad with Romesco Dressing, 170
Grilled Steak Tacos with Chipotle Salsa & Avocado, 137
Italian Braised Short Ribs, 18
Korean-Style Noodles with Marinated Steak & Kimchi, 43
Mac & Cheese Chili, 18
Spiced Tri-Tip with Roasted Brussels Sprouts, 12
Steak Pipérade, 149
Stir-Fried Beef & Bok Choy with Ginger, 286
Stir-Fried Soba Noodles with Beef & Cabbage, 25
Thai Beef Salad, 34
Vietnamese Beef Noodle Soup, 292

Beets
Roasted Beets with Baby Arugula & Ricotta Salata, 19
Spinach Salad with Oranges & Roasted Beets, 44

Belgian endive
Grilled Asparagus & Endive with Favas, Orange & Mint, 123
Roasted Snapper & Belgian Endive, 238

Bibimbop with Brown Rice & Bulgogi, 241

Blackberries
Blackberry Puree with Whipped Cream, 190
Mixed Berry Galette, 132

Blueberries
Blueberry Pie, 190
Cornmeal Shortcakes with Blueberries & Cream, 156
Mixed Berry Galette, 132

Bread. See also Sandwiches
Bread Pudding with Chard, Sun-Dried Tomatoes & Fontina, 300
Bread Salad with Charred Tomatoes, Cucumber & Olives, 195
Broccoli Rabe, Pesto & Smoked Mozzarella Strata, 275
Grilled Naan with Smoky Eggplant Purée & Grilled Red Onions, 203
Italian-Style Ribollita, 259
Roast Chicken & Bread Salad with Haricots Verts & Strawberries, 99
Summer Panzanella Soup with Tiny Pasta, 179

Broccoli
Broccoli & Cauliflower with Pickled Onions & Bacon, 238
Potato & Broccoli Soup with Blue Cheese, 21
Roasted Broccoli with Soy, Rice Vinegar & Sesame Seeds, 39

Broccoli rabe
Broccoli Rabe & Olive Pizza, 17
Broccoli Rabe & Parmesan Fritters, 99
Broccoli Rabe, Pesto & Smoked Mozzarella Strata, 275

Brownies, Cream Cheese Marble, 92

Brussels sprouts
Creamy Brussels Sprout Soup with Maple Bacon, 40
Seared Scallops with Warm Shredded Brussels Sprouts & Prosciutto, 284
Spiced Tri-Tip with Roasted Brussels Sprouts, 12

Vinegar-Glazed Brussels Sprouts with Chestnuts & Walnut Oil, 25

Bulgur with Persimmons, Pistachios & Pomegranate, 263

Burgers

Black Bean–Jalapeño Burgers with Avocado Mash, 77

Chickpea & Roasted Red Pepper Burgers with Smoked Paprika Mayonnaise, 151

Falafel Burgers with Lemon-Tahini Sauce, 60

Grilled Portobello Burgers, 184

Lamb Burgers with Spinach & Spiced Yogurt Sauce, 138

Red Lentil Burgers with Lemon-Herb Yogurt Sauce, 288

Tuna Burgers with Creamy Smoked Paprika Sauce, 92

Turkey Burgers with Cranberry Relish, 272

Turkey Burgers with Radicchio Slaw, 40

C

Cabbage

Asian-Style Cabbage Rolls, 269

Buttermilk Coleslaw with Carrots & Raisins, 143

Corned Beef & Cabbage, 73

Crispy Chicken & Cabbage Salad with Peanut Dressing, 293

Napa Cabbage & Kumquat Salad with Seared Scallops, 280

Salad of Asian Greens with Tamari-Glazed Pork Belly, 55

Spicy Shrimp Tacos with Red Cabbage Slaw, 246

Stir-Fried Soba Noodles with Beef & Cabbage, 25

Winter Salad of Red Cabbage & Dried Fruits, 299

Cakes. See also Cupcakes

Banana-Honey Cake, 71

Brown Butter Pound Cake with Strawberry-Rhubarb Compote, 89

Carrot Cake, 102

Chocolate Icebox Cake, 168

Classic Birthday Cake, 226

Devil's Food Layer Cake, 86

Glazed Cranberry-Lemon Cake, 242

Honey-Nectarine Cheesecake, 179

Spiced Apple Cake with Maple Frosting, 215

Spicy Dark Gingerbread, 300

Warm Molten Chocolate Cakes, 292

Calamari. See Squid

Cannelloni, Pumpkin-Sage, 212

Carnitas, 112

Carrots

Buttermilk Coleslaw with Carrots & Raisins, 143

Carrot Cake, 102

Curried Carrot Purée, 121

Fish Tagine with Carrots & Olives, 244

Kumquat-Carrot Purée with Toasted Fennel Seeds, 28

Sesame Noodles with Grilled Chicken, Carrots & Edamame, 249

Cauliflower

Broccoli & Cauliflower with Pickled Onions & Bacon, 238

Italian-Style Ribollita, 259

Roasted Cauliflower & Parmesan Soup, 241

Spicy Cauliflower Gratin, 218

Celery root

Braised Winter Vegetables with Coconut & Red Curry, 283

Fennel-Roasted Chicken with Celery Root Purée, 286

Porter-Braised Chicken with Root Vegetables, 265

Tofu Salad with Edamame & Shaved Root Vegetables, 17

Chai Tea Cupcakes with Honey Cream, 15

Chard

Barley Risotto with Chicken, Mushrooms & Greens, 27

Bread Pudding with Chard, Sun-Dried Tomatoes & Fontina, 300

Garlicky Shrimp & Chard Sauté, 66

Ginger Rice with Chicken, Chard & Shiitakes, 37

Indian-Spiced Char with Cucumber & Tomato Salad, 189

Italian-Style Ribollita, 259

Lentil & Chard Soup with Duck Confit, 38

Polenta with Wild Mushrooms, Chard & Cheddar Cheese, 22

Rainbow Chard Gratin with Ricotta & Gruyère, 38

Cheese

Cheddar & Hard Cider Soup with Fried Shallots, 239

Honey-Nectarine Cheesecake, 179

Mac & Cheese Chili, 18

Macaroni with Farmstead Cheddar & Bacon, 43

Ricotta with Blood Orange, Pistachios & Honey, 302

Ricotta with Honey & Figs, 247

Truffled Mac & Cheese, 285

Cherries

Braised Pork Chops with Cherries, 119

Cherry Lattice Pie, 129

Roasted Summer Fruits with Ricotta-Vanilla Cream, 152

Chicken

Arroz con Pollo, 102

Asian-Style Chicken Soup, 24

Barley Risotto with Chicken, Mushrooms & Greens, 27

Braised Chicken with Peppers, Olives & Capers, 234

Braised Chicken with Tangerine & Star Anise, 294

Chicken Agrodolce with Delicata Squash, 206

Chicken & Coconut Curry, 19

Chicken & Wild Rice Soup with Ginger, 74

Chicken Breasts with Fava Beans, 79

Chicken–Matzo Ball Soup, 83

Chicken Meatballs with Spicy Tomato Sauce, 291

Chicken Parmesan with Greens, 120

Chicken Potpie, 211

Chicken Stew with Buttermilk-Chive Dumplings, 47

Chicken Tacos with Radish Slaw, 91

Chicken Tagine with Preserved Lemons & Olives, 50

Chicken Tikka Masala, 284

Chicken Tostada Salad, 138

Chicken with Cilantro & Pumpkin Seed Pesto, 212

Chopped Chicken Salad with Lemon-Tarragon Dressing, 124

Chorizo & Chicken Soup with Avocado Crema, 217

Crispy Chicken & Cabbage Salad with Peanut Dressing, 293

Fava Greens with Chicken, Pecans & Kumquats, 70

Fennel-Crusted Chicken with Fennel & Herb Salad, 11

Fennel-Roasted Chicken with Celery Root Purée, 286

Ginger Rice with Chicken, Chard & Shiitakes, 37

Glass-Noodle Salad with Shrimp, Chicken & Mint, 88

Jerk Chicken with Pineapple Salsa, 209

Mediterranean-Style Chicken & Vegetable Kebabs, 174

Mexican Lime Soup with Chicken, 159

Mexican Nacho Casserole, 126

Porter-Braised Chicken with Root Vegetables, 265

Pulled Chicken Sliders with Apple-Jicama Relish, 259

Roast Chicken & Bread Salad with Haricots Verts & Strawberries, 99

Sesame Noodles with Grilled Chicken, Carrots & Edamame, 249

Smoky Grilled Chicken & Corn, 171

Spanish Chicken Stew, 247

Spicy Chicken & Basil Stir-Fry, 173

Stir-Fried Lemongrass Chicken, 196

Stir-Fried Rice Vermicelli with Chicken & Shrimp, 121

Summer Chicken Braise with Wax Beans & Tomatoes, 161

Tandoori-Style Chicken, 73

Thai Green Chicken Curry with Asparagus, 67

Thai Pumpkin & Chicken Curry, 270

Chickpeas

Chickpea & Roasted Red Pepper Burgers with Smoked Paprika Mayonnaise, 151

Chickpea & Roasted Tomato Soup with Fried Rosemary, 65

Chickpea & Sweet Potato Curry, 230

Chickpea & Turkey Meatball Soup with Mustard Greens, 250

Falafel Burgers with Lemon-Tahini Sauce, 60

Spanish Chicken Stew, 247

Two-Bean & Potato Salad, 144

Chiles
  Beef-Chipotle Chili, 68
  Black Bean–Jalapeño Burgers with
    Avocado Mash, 77
  Chile Verde, 242
  Fresh Corn, Jalapeño & Monterey Jack
    Tamales, 186
  Grilled Steak Tacos with Chipotle Salsa
    & Avocado, 137
  Poblano Chiles Stuffed with Black Beans
    & Summer Vegetables, 189
  Pork, Quinoa & Chile Casserole, 221
  Sweet Potato & Green Chile Quesadillas
    with Arugula, 34
Chili
  Beef-Chipotle Chili, 68
  Mac & Cheese Chili, 18
Chocolate
  Bittersweet Chocolate & Dark Caramel
    Tartlets, 296
  Chocolate Icebox Cake, 168
  Chocolate–Peanut Butter Ice Cream, 201
  Classic Birthday Cake, 226
  Classic Chocolate Chip Cookies, 224
  Cream Cheese Marble Brownies, 92
  Dark Chocolate Donut Holes, 114
  Dark Chocolate Pudding, 60
  Devil's Food Layer Cake, 86
  Mississippi Mud Pie, 239
  Oatmeal–Chocolate Chip Cookies
    with Almonds, 46
  Warm Molten Chocolate Cakes, 292
Cioppino, 294
Clafoutis
  Apricot Clafoutis, 136
  Raspberry-Almond Clafoutis, 127
Clams
  Cioppino, 294
  One-Pot Clambake, 166
  Pan-Roasted Clams with Potatoes & Fennel, 215
  Spanish Paella, 146
  Spanish Seafood Noodles, 191
Cobbler, White Peach, with Crystallized Ginger, 158
Cookies
  Classic Chocolate Chip Cookies, 224
  Lavender Shortbread, 66
  Maple Almond Squares, 257
  Oatmeal–Chocolate Chip Cookies
    with Almonds, 46
Corn. See also Polenta
  Black Bean, Corn & Quinoa Salad, 161
  Cajun Shrimp Boil, 190
  Chicken Tostada Salad, 138
  Corn & Pea Empanaditas, 119
  Cornmeal Shortcakes with Blueberries
    & Cream, 156
  Crispy Okra, Corn & Shrimp Salad
    with Harissa Dressing, 197

Fresh Corn, Jalapeño & Monterey Jack
    Tamales, 186
Fresh Corn Soup with Turkey & Avocado, 203
Mexican-Style Corn on the Cob, 166
One-Pot Clambake, 166
Pan-Roasted Pork Medallions with Summer
    Vegetables, 198
Smoky Grilled Chicken & Corn, 171
Smoky Sea Scallops with Avocado-Corn Salsa, 162
Spinach, Corn & Potato Enchiladas, 226
Tuna Kebabs with Summer Succotash, 159
Vegetable Enchiladas, 141
Crab
  Cioppino, 294
  Coconut Rice Noodles with Crab & Cilantro, 12
  Crab, Pea & Ricotta Frittata, 91
  Vietnamese-Style Rice Noodles with Crab
    & Black Pepper, 288
Cranberries
  Glazed Cranberry-Lemon Cake, 242
  Roasted Squash with Cranberries & Thyme, 271
  Turkey Burgers with Cranberry Relish, 272
  Wheat Berries with Roasted Parsnips,
    Butternut Squash & Dried Cranberries, 272
  Wild Rice Pilaf with Dried Cranberries
    & Pecans, 274
Crisps
  Gingered Rhubarb Crisp, 79
  Oatmeal Pear Crisp, 250
  Strawberry-Rhubarb Crisp, 140
Crostini, Polenta, with Chanterelles, 236
Crumble, Plum & Lime, 211
Cupcakes
  Chai Tea Cupcakes with Honey Cream, 15
  Frosted Lemon Cupcakes, 111

D, E

Devil's Food Layer Cake, 86
Donuts
  Buttermilk Donuts with Lemon Sugar, 49
  Dark Chocolate Donut Holes, 114
Duck
  Braised Duck Legs with Port & Figs, 220
  Duck Breast Salad with Walnuts & Oranges, 299
  Lentil & Chard Soup with Duck Confit, 38
Edamame
  Sesame Noodles with Grilled Chicken, Carrots
    & Edamame, 249
  Tofu Salad with Edamame & Shaved Root
    Vegetables, 17
Eggplant
  Charred Eggplant Soup with Cumin
    & Greek Yogurt, 177
  Crispy Eggplant, Miso Butter & Charred
    Sungold Tomato Salad, 176
  Eggplant Parmesan, 171

Grilled Naan with Smoky Eggplant Purée
    & Grilled Red Onions, 203
Lamb & Vegetable Kebabs with Indian Spices, 223
Miso-Glazed Grilled Asian Eggplant, 146
Soba Noodle Salad with Tofu & Marinated
    Eggplant, 208
Spicy Halibut with Ratatouille, 165
Spicy Stir-Fried Eggplant & Tofu, 187
Vietnamese Eggplant Curry, 197
Eggs
  Crab, Pea & Ricotta Frittata, 91
  Fava Bean & Ricotta Omelet with Spring
    Greens, 83
  Grilled Asparagus & Green Onion Soup
    with Poached Eggs, 101
  Shredded Kale Salad with Pancetta
    & Hard-Cooked Egg, 266
  Spanish Tortilla with Leeks, 11
  Spicy Simmered Eggs with Kale, 55
  Udon Noodle Soup with Pork Belly
    & Soft Eggs, 254
Empanaditas, Corn & Pea, 119
Enchiladas
  Spinach & Black Bean Enchiladas, 39
  Spinach, Corn & Potato Enchiladas, 226
  Turkey Mole Enchiladas, 271
  Vegetable Enchiladas, 141
Escarole, Braised, Halibut with White Beans &, 112

F

Falafel Burgers with Lemon-Tahini Sauce, 60
Farro Salad with Grape Tomatoes & Ricotta
    Salata, 136
Fava beans
  Chicken Breasts with Fava Beans, 79
  Fava Bean & Ricotta Omelet with Spring
    Greens, 83
  Fava Greens with Chicken, Pecans
    & Kumquats, 70
  Grilled Asparagus & Endive with Favas,
    Orange & Mint, 123
  Squid Salad with Oranges, Fava Beans
    & Fennel, 116
Fennel
  Arugula & Fennel Salad with Black
    Pepper-Crusted Tuna, 243
  Baked Rigatoni with Fennel, Sausage
    & Peperonata, 100
  Fennel-Crusted Chicken with Fennel
    & Herb Salad, 11
  Fennel-Roasted Chicken with Celery Root
    Purée, 286
  Fennel Salad with Blood Oranges & Arugula, 29
  Leg of Lamb with Roasted Fennel & Pan Sauce, 52
  Pan-Roasted Clams with Potatoes & Fennel, 215
  Sautéed Sole with Fennel & Lemon Compote, 46
  Spaghetti with Shrimp, Fennel, Tomatoes
    & Olives, 53

Squid Salad with Oranges, Fava Beans
& Fennel, 116
Figs
Braised Duck Legs with Port & Figs, 220
Grilled Fig & Bacon Kebabs with Shaved
Parmesan, 214
Pork Tenderloin with Thyme & Figs, 217
Ricotta with Honey & Figs, 247
Roasted Summer Fruits with Ricotta-Vanilla
Cream, 152
Winter Salad of Red Cabbage & Dried Fruits, 299
Fish. *See also* Halibut; Salmon; Tuna
Baked Cod with Leeks, Morels & Bacon, 68
Braised Black Cod with Shiitake Mushrooms, 291
Cioppino, 294
Fish Tagine with Carrots & Olives, 244
Indian-Spiced Char with Cucumber & Tomato
Salad, 189
Roasted Snapper & Belgian Endive, 238
Sautéed Sole with Fennel & Lemon Compote, 46
Spanish Seafood Noodles, 191
Frittata, Crab, Pea & Ricotta, 91
Fritters, Broccoli Rabe & Parmesan Fritters, 99

G, H

Galette, Mixed Berry, 132
Gazpacho, Yellow, with Lemon-Basil Ricotta, 198
Gingerbread, Spicy Dark, 300
Gnocchi, Baked, with Taleggio, Pancetta & Sage, 235
Grapefruit
Roasted Salmon with Avocado-Grapefruit
Salsa, 37
Ruby Grapefruit Sorbet, 14
Gyros, Grilled Vegetable, with Cucumber-Mint
Sauce, 144
Halibut
Cioppino, 294
Halibut Provençal, 201
Halibut with Braised Escarole & White Beans, 112
Spanish Seafood Noodles, 191
Spicy Halibut with Ratatouille, 165
Ham
Bourbon-Glazed Ham, 97
Braised Dinosaur Kale with White Beans
& Smoked Ham, 296
Roasted Tomato Soup with Serrano Ham
& Burrata, 135

I, K

Ice cream
Chocolate–Peanut Butter Ice Cream, 201
Ice Cream Sandwiches, 196
Lemon Crème Milkshakes, 62
Mississippi Mud Pie, 239
Kale
Braised Dinosaur Kale with White Beans
& Smoked Ham, 296

Chicken Parmesan with Greens, 120
Kale, Cremini Mushroom & Goat Cheese
Hand Pies, 84
Kale, Turkey Sausage & Barley Stew, 285
Pastina & Kale Soup with Andouille, 208
Shredded Kale Salad with Pancetta
& Hard-Cooked Egg, 266
Spicy Simmered Eggs with Kale, 55
Warm Kale & Tuna Niçoise, 218
Warm Lentil & Kale Salad with Bacon, 30
Kumquats
Fava Greens with Chicken, Pecans
& Kumquats, 70
Kumquat-Carrot Purée with Toasted
Fennel Seeds, 28
Napa Cabbage & Kumquat Salad with
Seared Scallops, 280

L

Lamb
Citrus-Braised Lamb Shanks, 280
Grilled Lamb Chops with Fresh Peach Salsa, 174
Grilled Lamb Chops with Pea, Feta
& Mint Salad, 86
Lamb & Vegetable Kebabs with Indian Spices, 223
Lamb Burgers with Spinach & Spiced Yogurt
Sauce, 138
Lamb Shoulder with Salsa Verde, 236
Lamb Tagine with Olives & Preserved Lemon, 94
Leg of Lamb with Roasted Fennel & Pan Sauce, 52
Pasta with Rosemary-Lamb Sugo, 141
Pomegranate-Glazed Lamb & Vegetable
Skewers, 195
Lasagna, Butternut Squash, 262
Lavender Shortbread, 66
Leeks
Baked Cod with Leeks, Morels & Bacon, 68
Baked Leeks with Bread Crumbs, 96
Leek & Yukon Gold Potato Soup with Fried
Prosciutto, 76
Leek, Pancetta & Gruyère Tart, 67
Morel & Leek Ravioli with English Pea Purée, 62
Pizza with Asparagus, Leeks & Herbed Ricotta, 120
Spanish Tortilla with Leeks, 11
Lemons
Fresh Lemon Mousse, 93
Frosted Lemon Cupcakes, 111
Glazed Cranberry-Lemon Cake, 242
Lemon Chiffon Gingersnap Pie, 24
Lemon Crème Milkshakes, 62
Meyer Lemon Squares, 44
Pink Lemonade Ice Pops, 183
Lentils
Lentil & Andouille Soup, 85
Lentil & Chard Soup with Duck Confit, 38
Red Lentil Burgers with Lemon-Herb
Yogurt Sauce, 288

Warm Lentil & Kale Salad with Bacon, 30
Limes
Mexican Lime Soup with Chicken, 159
Plum & Lime Crumble, 211
Lobster
Creamy Pasta Salad with Lobster, 187
Lobster & Avocado Salad with Shaved
Meyer Lemon, 115
One-Pot Clambake, 166
Shiitake Broth with Butter-Poached
Lobster & Chives, 302

M, N

Macadamia Tartlets, Caramel-, 29
Macaroni. See Pasta and noodles
Mandarin oranges
Spicy Coconut-Mandarin Soup with
Mushrooms, 266
Matzo Ball Soup, Chicken–, 83
Milkshakes, Lemon Crème, 62
Mousse, Fresh Lemon, 93
Mushrooms
Baked Cod with Leeks, Morels & Bacon, 68
Barley Risotto with Chicken, Mushrooms
& Greens, 27
Beef Bourguignon, 301
Braised Black Cod with Shiitake Mushrooms, 291
Four Seasons Pizza with Mushrooms, Bell
Peppers, Artichokes & Olives, 70
Ginger Rice with Chicken, Chard & Shiitakes, 37
Grilled Portobello Burgers, 184
Kale, Cremini Mushroom & Goat Cheese
Hand Pies, 84
Morel & Leek Ravioli with English Pea Purée, 62
Mushrooms with Garlic Butter & Pine Nuts, 65
Pea Shoots & Shiitake Mushrooms with Soba
Noodles, 93
Polenta Crostini with Chanterelles, 236
Polenta with Wild Mushrooms, Chard
& Cheddar Cheese, 22
Red Quinoa with Asparagus, Portobellos
& Feta, 59
Roasted Asparagus & Morels with Shallot
Butter, 109
Shiitake Broth with Butter-Poached Lobster
& Chives, 302
Soba with Shiitakes & Mustard Greens, 269
Spicy Coconut-Mandarin Soup with
Mushrooms, 266
Turkey Tetrazzini, 260
Mussels
Mussels in Thai Coconut Broth, 260
One-Pot Clambake, 166
Mustard greens
Chickpea & Turkey Meatball Soup with
Mustard Greens, 250
Soba with Shiitakes & Mustard Greens, 269
Napoleons, Strawberry, 124

Nectarines
  Brined Pork Chops with Grilled Stone Fruit, 143
  Honey-Nectarine Cheesecake, 179
  Roasted Summer Fruits with Ricotta-Vanilla
    Cream, 152
Noodles. *See* Pasta and noodles

O

Oats
  Maple Almond Squares, 257
  Oatmeal–Chocolate Chip Cookies
    with Almonds, 46
  Oatmeal Pear Crisp, 250
Okra, Corn & Shrimp Salad, Crispy, with
  Harissa Dressing, 197
Onion Soup, Three-, with Cambozola Grilled
  Cheese, 77
Oranges
  Blood Orange Tartlets, 53
  Duck Breast Salad with Walnuts & Oranges, 299
  Fennel Salad with Blood Oranges & Arugula, 29
  Grilled Asparagus & Endive with Favas, Orange
    & Mint, 123
  Ricotta with Blood Orange, Pistachios
    & Honey, 302
  Seared Scallop, Orange & Red Onion Salad, 94
  Spinach Salad with Oranges & Roasted Beets, 44
  Squid Salad with Oranges, Fava Beans
    & Fennel, 116
Osso Buco with Gremolata, 256

P

Paella, Spanish, 146
Parsnips
  Moroccan-Spiced Roasted Vegetables
    & Quinoa, 50
  Root Vegetable Tacos with Lime-Cilantro
    Cream, 230
  Wheat Berries with Roasted Parsnips,
    Butternut Squash & Dried Cranberries, 272
Pasta and noodles
  Asian-Style Chicken Soup, 24
  Baked Pasta with Prosciutto & Peas, 14
  Baked Rigatoni with Fennel, Sausage &
    Peperonata, 100
  Butternut Squash Lasagna, 262
  Coconut Rice Noodles with Crab & Cilantro, 12
  Creamy Pasta Salad with Lobster, 187
  Glass-Noodle Salad with Shrimp, Chicken
    & Mint, 88
  Korean-Style Noodles with Marinated Steak
    & Kimchi, 43
  Mac & Cheese Chili, 18
  Macaroni with Farmstead Cheddar & Bacon, 43
  Morel & Leek Ravioli with English Pea Purée, 62
  Noodle Salad with Pork & Asian Lime
    Vinaigrette, 27
  Pasta with Rosemary-Lamb Sugo, 141

Pastina & Kale Soup with Andouille, 208
Peanut-Braised Tofu with Noodles, 47
Pea Shoots & Shiitake Mushrooms with Soba
  Noodles, 93
Penne with Grilled Summer Vegetables,
  Herbs & Almonds, 158
Pumpkin-Sage Cannelloni, 212
Ramen Noodle Soup with Sugar Snap Peas, 114
Sesame Noodles with Grilled Chicken,
  Carrots & Edamame, 249
Shrimp Summer Rolls, 126
Soba Noodle Salad with Sugar Snap Peas
  & Soy-Peanut Dressing, 63
Soba Noodle Salad with Tofu & Marinated
  Eggplant, 208
Soba with Shiitakes & Mustard Greens, 269
Spaghetti with Shrimp, Fennel, Tomatoes
  & Olives, 53
Spanish Seafood Noodles, 191
Stir-Fried Pork & Sugar Snaps with Soba
  Noodles, 59
Stir-Fried Rice Vermicelli with Chicken
  & Shrimp, 121
Stir-Fried Soba Noodles with Beef & Cabbage, 25
Summer Panzanella Soup with Tiny Pasta, 179
Tortellini in Herbaceous Broth with Snow Peas, 88
Truffled Mac & Cheese, 285
Turkey Tetrazzini, 260
Udon Noodle Soup with Pork Belly
  & Soft Eggs, 254
Udon Noodles with Poached Shrimp, Baby
  Spinach & Miso, 96
Vietnamese Beef Noodle Soup, 292
Vietnamese-Style Rice Noodles with Crab
  & Black Pepper, 288
Peaches
  Brined Pork Chops with Grilled Stone Fruit, 143
  Grilled Lamb Chops with Fresh Peach Salsa, 174
  Pulled Pork with Spicy Peach-Mustard Sauce, 183
  Roasted Summer Fruits with Ricotta-Vanilla
    Cream, 152
  White Peach Cobbler with Crystallized
    Ginger, 158
Peanut butter
  Chocolate–Peanut Butter Ice Cream, 201
  Crispy Chicken & Cabbage Salad with
    Peanut Dressing, 293
  Peanut-Braised Tofu with Noodles, 47
  Soba Noodle Salad with Sugar Snap Peas
    & Soy-Peanut Dressing, 63
Pears
  Oatmeal Pear Crisp, 250
  Salad of Grilled Pork, Pears & Toasted
    Pecans, 206
  Spiced Pear Tarte Tatin, 30
  Winter Salad of Red Cabbage & Dried Fruits, 299
Peas. *See also* Pea shoots
  Baked Pasta with Prosciutto & Peas, 14
  Corn & Pea Empanaditas, 119
  Crab, Pea & Ricotta Frittata, 91

Curried Yellow Split Pea Soup with Kabocha
  Squash, 234
Fresh Pea Soup with Chives & Crème Fraîche, 111
Grilled Lamb Chops with Pea, Feta
  & Mint Salad, 86
Morel & Leek Ravioli with English Pea Purée, 62
Ramen Noodle Soup with Sugar Snap Peas, 114
Salad of New Potatoes, Spring Peas & Mint, 76
Soba Noodle Salad with Sugar Snap Peas
  & Soy-Peanut Dressing, 63
Stir-Fried Pork & Sugar Snaps with Soba
  Noodles, 59
Tortellini in Herbaceous Broth with Snow Peas, 88
Pea shoots
  Miso Soup with Shrimp & Pea Shoots, 70
  Pea Shoots & Shiitake Mushrooms with
    Soba Noodles, 93
  Stir-Fried Calamari & Pea Shoots, 109
Pecans
  Fava Greens with Chicken, Pecans
    & Kumquats, 70
  Honey-Glazed Sweet Potato & Curried
    Pecan Salad, 257
  Salad of Grilled Pork, Pears & Toasted
    Pecans, 206
  Southern Pecan Pie, 283
  Wild Rice Pilaf with Dried Cranberries
    & Pecans, 274
Peppers. *See also* Chiles
  Baked Rigatoni with Fennel, Sausage
    & Peperonata, 100
  Braised Chicken with Peppers, Olives
    & Capers, 234
  Chef's Salad with Sopressata, Fontina
    & Pickled Peppers, 106
  Chickpea & Roasted Red Pepper Burgers with
    Smoked Paprika Mayonnaise, 151
  Four Seasons Pizza with Mushrooms, Bell
    Peppers, Artichokes & Olives, 70
  Grilled Steak, Pepper & Onion Salad with
    Romesco Dressing, 170
  Lamb & Vegetable Kebabs with Indian Spices, 223
  Penne with Grilled Summer Vegetables,
    Herbs & Almonds, 158
  Romesco Sauce, 191
  Spanish White Bean Soup with Chorizo
    & Piquillo Peppers, 192
  Steak Pipérade, 149
  Stuffed Piquillo Peppers, 115
  Yellow Gazpacho with Lemon-Basil Ricotta, 198
Persimmons, Bulgur with Pistachios, Pomegranate
  &, 263
Pies
  Blueberry Pie, 190
  Brown Sugar Pumpkin Pie, 274
  Cherry Lattice Pie, 129
  Chicken Potpie, 211
  Deep-Dish Plum Pie, 148
  Kale, Cremini Mushroom & Goat Cheese
    Hand Pies, 84

Lemon Chiffon Gingersnap Pie, 24
Mississippi Mud Pie, 239
Old-Fashioned Apple Pie, 270
Southern Pecan Pie, 283
Pineapple
Jerk Chicken with Pineapple Salsa, 209
Pineapple Skewers with Rum & Molasses, 167
Pizza
Broccoli Rabe & Olive Pizza, 17
Butternut Squash Pizza, 247
Four Seasons Pizza with Mushrooms, Bell
Peppers, Artichokes & Olives, 70
Pizza with Asparagus, Leeks & Herbed Ricotta, 120
Pizza with Pesto, Cherry Tomatoes
& Mozzarella, 156
Plums
Brined Pork Chops with Grilled Stone Fruit, 143
Deep-Dish Plum Pie, 148
Plum & Lime Crumble, 211
Roasted Summer Fruits with Ricotta-Vanilla
Cream, 152
Polenta
Polenta Crostini with Chanterelles, 236
Polenta with Wild Mushrooms, Chard
& Cheddar Cheese, 22
Pomegranate
Bulgur with Persimmons, Pistachios
& Pomegranate, 263
Pomegranate-Glazed Lamb & Vegetable
Skewers, 195
Pops, Pink Lemonade Ice, 183
Pork. See also Ham; Sausage
Albondigas, 145
Asian-Style Cabbage Rolls, 269
Baby Back Ribs, 167
Braised Pork Chops with Cherries, 119
Brined Pork Chops with Grilled Stone Fruit, 143
Carnitas, 112
Chile Verde, 242
Grilled Pork Chops with Asian Pears & Torpedo
Onions, 244
Grilled Pork Chops with Potato Salad
& Romesco, 191
Molasses-Glazed Roast Pork & Sweet
Potatoes, 275
Noodle Salad with Pork & Asian Lime
Vinaigrette, 27
Pan-Roasted Pork Medallions with Summer
Vegetables, 198
Pork, Quinoa & Chile Casserole, 221
Pork Tenderloin with Rhubarb Chutney, 100
Pork Tenderloin with Thyme & Figs, 217
Pulled Pork with Spicy Peach-Mustard Sauce, 183
Salad of Asian Greens with Tamari-Glazed
Pork Belly, 55
Salad of Grilled Pork, Pears & Toasted
Pecans, 206
Spicy Braised Tofu with Pork, 71
Spicy Pork Kebabs, 149

Stir-Fried Pork & Sugar Snaps with
Soba Noodles, 59
Udon Noodle Soup with Pork Belly
& Soft Eggs, 254
Potatoes
Green Bean & Potato Salad with Herbs
& Anchovies, 225
Grilled Pork Chops with Potato Salad
& Romesco, 191
Leek & Yukon Gold Potato Soup with Fried
Prosciutto, 76
Mustard-Crusted Salmon with Red Potatoes, 101
Pan-Roasted Clams with Potatoes & Fennel, 215
Porter-Braised Chicken with Root Vegetables, 265
Potato & Broccoli Soup with Blue Cheese, 21
Potato Galettes with Smoked Salmon, 52
Roasted Potato Salad with Green Onion
Dressing, 151
Salad of New Potatoes, Spring Peas & Mint, 76
Sautéed Potatoes with Chorizo & Parsley, 14
Spinach, Corn & Potato Enchiladas, 226
Two-Bean & Potato Salad, 144
Potpie, Chicken, 211
Puddings
Bread Pudding with Chard, Sun-Dried Tomatoes
& Fontina, 300
Dark Chocolate Pudding, 60
Pumpkin
Beef & Pumpkin Stew, 214
Brown Sugar Pumpkin Pie, 274
Pumpkin Purée with Toasted Pumpkin Seeds, 243
Pumpkin-Sage Cannelloni, 212
Pumpkin Tortilla Soup, 221
Pumpkin with White Beans, Caramelized
Onions & Roasted Garlic, 265
Thai Pumpkin & Chicken Curry, 270

Q, R

Quesadillas, Sweet Potato & Green Chile, with
Arugula, 34
Quiche, Spinach-Feta, 223
Quinoa
Black Bean, Corn & Quinoa Salad, 161
Moroccan-Spiced Roasted Vegetables
& Quinoa, 50
Pork, Quinoa & Chile Casserole, 221
Quinoa Salad with Grilled Vegetables & Feta, 162
Quinoa Tabbouleh with Lemony Grilled
Shrimp, 28
Red Quinoa with Asparagus, Portobellos
& Feta, 59
Raspberry-Almond Clafoutis, 127
Ravioli, Morel & Leek, with English Pea Purée, 62
Rhubarb
Brown Butter Pound Cake with
Strawberry-Rhubarb Compote, 89
Gingered Rhubarb Crisp, 79
Pork Tenderloin with Rhubarb Chutney, 100

Strawberry-Rhubarb Crisp, 140
Ribollita, Italian-Style, 259
Rice
Arroz con Pollo, 102
Asparagus Risotto, 97
Bibimbop with Brown Rice & Bulgogi, 241
Butternut Squash Risotto with Sage, 256
Chicken & Wild Rice Soup with Ginger, 74
Ginger Rice with Chicken, Chard & Shiitakes, 37
Poblano Chiles Stuffed with Black Beans
& Summer Vegetables, 189
Risotto with Sautéed Scallops, 145
Spanish Paella, 146
Spicy Coconut-Mandarin Soup with
Mushrooms, 266
Turkey & Jasmine Rice Soup with Lemongrass, 262

S

Salmon
Mustard-Crusted Salmon with Red Potatoes, 101
Potato Galettes with Smoked Salmon, 52
Roasted Salmon with Avocado-Grapefruit
Salsa, 37
Salmon Cakes with Ginger & Green Onion, 21
Salmon with Spring Vegetables, 63
Sesame-Crusted Salmon with Chermoula, 135
White Wine–Braised Salmon with Tarragon, 123
Zucchini-Pecorino Purée with Roasted
Salmon, 220
Samosas, Curried, with Tamarind Chutney, 110
Sandwiches. See also Burgers
Pulled Chicken Sliders with Apple-Jicama
Relish, 259
Pulled Pork with Spicy Peach-Mustard Sauce, 183
Three-Onion Soup with Cambozola Grilled
Cheese, 77
Sausage
Acorn Squash & Chorizo Tart, 235
Baked Rigatoni with Fennel, Sausage
& Peperonata, 100
Cajun Shrimp Boil, 190
Chef's Salad with Sopressata, Fontina
& Pickled Peppers, 106
Chorizo & Chicken Soup with Avocado Crema, 217
Cuban-Style Stuffed Flank Steak, 263
Kale, Turkey Sausage & Barley Stew, 285
Lentil & Andouille Soup, 85
One-Pot Clambake, 166
Pastina & Kale Soup with Andouille, 208
Sautéed Potatoes with Chorizo & Parsley, 14
Spanish Paella, 146
Spanish White Bean Soup with Chorizo
& Piquillo Peppers, 192
Spicy Red Bean & Chorizo Stew, 22
Scallops
Napa Cabbage & Kumquat Salad with
Seared Scallops, 280

Provençal Seafood Stew, 224
Risotto with Sautéed Scallops, 145
Seared Scallop, Orange & Red Onion Salad, 94
Seared Scallops with Warm Shredded Brussels
   Sprouts & Prosciutto, 284
Smoky Sea Scallops with Avocado-Corn Salsa, 162
Shortbread, Lavender, 66
Shortcakes, Cornmeal, with Blueberries
   & Cream, 156
Shrimp
   Avocado Soup with Shrimp & Salsa, 136
   Cajun Shrimp Boil, 190
   Cioppino, 294
   Crispy Okra, Corn & Shrimp Salad with
      Harissa Dressing, 197
   Garlicky Shrimp & Chard Sauté, 66
   Garlicky Shrimp Scampi, 49
   Glass-Noodle Salad with Shrimp, Chicken
      & Mint, 88
   Grilled Lemon Shrimp & Summer Squash, 176
   Miso Soup with Shrimp & Pea Shoots, 70
   One-Pot Clambake, 166
   Quinoa Tabbouleh with Lemony Grilled
      Shrimp, 28
   Shrimp Summer Rolls, 126
   Spaghetti with Shrimp, Fennel, Tomatoes
      & Olives, 53
   Spanish Garlic Shrimp, 129
   Spanish Paella, 146
   Spanish Seafood Noodles, 191
   Spicy Shrimp Tacos with Red Cabbage Slaw, 246
   Stir-Fried Rice Vermicelli with Chicken
      & Shrimp, 121
   Udon Noodles with Poached Shrimp,
      Baby Spinach & Miso, 96
Sorbet
   Lemon Crème Milkshakes, 62
   Ruby Grapefruit Sorbet, 14
Soups
   Albondigas, 145
   Asian-Style Chicken Soup, 24
   Avocado Soup with Shrimp & Salsa, 136
   Charred Eggplant Soup with Cumin
      & Greek Yogurt, 177
   Cheddar & Hard Cider Soup with
      Fried Shallots, 239
   Chicken & Wild Rice Soup with Ginger, 74
   Chicken–Matzo Ball Soup, 83
   Chickpea & Roasted Tomato Soup with Fried
      Rosemary, 65
   Chickpea & Turkey Meatball Soup with Mustard
      Greens, 250
   Chorizo & Chicken Soup with Avocado Crema, 217
   Creamy Brussels Sprout Soup with Maple
      Bacon, 40
   Curried Yellow Split Pea Soup with Kabocha
      Squash, 234
   Fresh Corn Soup with Turkey & Avocado, 203

Fresh Pea Soup with Chives & Crème Fraîche, 111
Garlicky Zucchini Soup with Basil Gremolata, 140
Grilled Asparagus & Green Onion Soup with
   Poached Eggs, 101
Italian-Style Ribollita, 259
Leek & Yukon Gold Potato Soup with Fried
   Prosciutto, 76
Lentil & Andouille Soup, 85
Lentil & Chard Soup with Duck Confit, 38
Mexican Lime Soup with Chicken, 159
Miso Soup with Shrimp & Pea Shoots, 70
Mussels in Thai Coconut Broth, 260
Pastina & Kale Soup with Andouille, 208
Potato & Broccoli Soup with Blue Cheese, 21
Pumpkin Tortilla Soup, 221
Ramen Noodle Soup with Sugar Snap Peas, 114
Roasted Tomato Soup with Serrano Ham
   & Burrata, 135
Soba with Shiitakes & Mustard Greens, 269
Spanish White Bean Soup with Chorizo
   & Piquillo Peppers, 192
Spicy Coconut-Mandarin Soup with
   Mushrooms, 266
Summer Panzanella Soup with Tiny Pasta, 179
Sweet Potato Soup with Cheddar & Caviar
   Croutons, 297
Three-Onion Soup with Cambozola Grilled
   Cheese, 77
Tortellini in Herbaceous Broth with Snow Peas, 88
Turkey & Jasmine Rice Soup with Lemongrass, 262
Udon Noodle Soup with Pork Belly
   & Soft Eggs, 254
Vietnamese Beef Noodle Soup, 292
Yellow Gazpacho with Lemon-Basil Ricotta, 198
Spinach
   Lamb Burgers with Spinach & Spiced Yogurt
      Sauce, 138
   Spinach & Black Bean Enchiladas, 39
   Spinach, Corn & Potato Enchiladas, 226
   Spinach-Feta Quiche, 223
   Spinach Salad with Oranges & Roasted Beets, 44
   Udon Noodles with Poached Shrimp, Baby
      Spinach & Miso, 96
Squash, summer
   Beef & Basil Stir-Fry with Summer Vegetables, 165
   Farmers' Market Salad with Tomato-Basil
      Vinaigrette, 132
   Fried Ricotta-Stuffed Zucchini Blossoms, 168
   Fried Zucchini with Curry Dip, 200
   Garlicky Zucchini Soup with Basil Gremolata, 140
   Grilled Lemon Shrimp & Summer Squash, 176
   Grilled Summer Squash Parmesan, 152
   Grilled Vegetable Gyros with Cucumber-Mint
      Sauce, 144
   Italian-Style Ribollita, 259
   Mediterranean-Style Chicken & Vegetable
      Kebabs, 174
   Pan-Roasted Pork Medallions with Summer

Vegetables, 198
Pasta with Rosemary-Lamb Sugo, 141
Penne with Grilled Summer Vegetables,
   Herbs & Almonds, 158
Poblano Chiles Stuffed with Black Beans
   & Summer Vegetables, 189
Pomegranate-Glazed Lamb & Vegetable
   Skewers, 195
Quinoa Salad with Grilled Vegetables & Feta, 162
Spicy Halibut with Ratatouille, 165
Summer Squash Noodles with Mint Pesto, 173
Tomato, Zucchini & Goat Cheese Tart, 192
Vegetable Enchiladas, 141
Zucchini-Pecorino Purée with Roasted
   Salmon, 220
Squash, winter
   Acorn Squash & Chorizo Tart, 235
   Braised Winter Vegetables with Coconut
      & Red Curry, 283
   Butternut Squash Lasagna, 262
   Butternut Squash Pizza, 247
   Butternut Squash Risotto with Sage, 256
   Chicken Agrodolce with Delicata Squash, 206
   Curried Samosas with Tamarind Chutney, 110
   Curried Yellow Split Pea Soup with Kabocha
      Squash, 234
   Fresh Shell Beans with Butternut Squash,
      Bacon & Sage, 225
   Roasted Squash with Cranberries & Thyme, 271
   Spiced Butternut Squash Tagine, 233
   Wheat Berries with Roasted Parsnips, Butternut
      Squash & Dried Cranberries, 272
   Winter Squash & Pecorino Tart, 289
Squid
   Calamari & White Bean Salad, 85
   Grilled Calamari Steaks with Mediterranean
      Salsa, 184
   Provençal Seafood Stew, 224
   Squid Salad with Oranges, Fava Beans
      & Fennel, 116
   Stir-Fried Calamari & Pea Shoots, 109
Strawberries
   Brown Butter Pound Cake with
      Strawberry-Rhubarb Compote, 89
   Pink Lemonade Ice Pops, 183
   Roast Chicken & Bread Salad with Haricots
      Verts & Strawberries, 99
   Strawberry Napoleons, 124
   Strawberry-Rhubarb Crisp, 140
Sweet potatoes
   Braised Winter Vegetables with Coconut
      & Red Curry, 283
   Chicken & Coconut Curry, 19
   Chickpea & Sweet Potato Curry, 230
   Honey-Glazed Sweet Potato & Curried
      Pecan Salad, 257
   Molasses-Glazed Roast Pork & Sweet
      Potatoes, 275

Root-Vegetable Tacos with Lime-Cilantro Cream, 230
Spiced Butternut Squash Tagine, 233
Spicy Pork Kebabs, 149
Sweet Potato & Green Chile Quesadillas with Arugula, 34
Sweet Potato Fries with Garlic & Herbs, 209
Sweet Potato Soup with Cheddar & Caviar Croutons, 297

T

Tabbouleh, Quinoa, with Lemony Grilled Shrimp, 28
Tacos
 Chicken Tacos with Radish Slaw, 91
 Grilled Steak Tacos with Chipotle Salsa & Avocado, 137
 Root Vegetable Tacos with Lime-Cilantro Cream, 230
 Spicy Shrimp Tacos with Red Cabbage Slaw, 246
Tamales, Fresh Corn, Jalapeño & Monterey Jack, 186
Tangerine, Braised Chicken with Star Anise &, 294
Tarts and tartlets
 Acorn Squash & Chorizo Tart, 235
 Apple Frangipane Tart, 233
 Bittersweet Chocolate & Dark Caramel Tartlets, 296
 Blood Orange Tartlets, 53
 Caramel-Macadamia Tartlets, 29
 Leek, Pancetta & Gruyère Tart, 67
 Mixed Berry Galette, 132
 Spiced Pear Tarte Tatin, 30
 Spring Vegetable Tart, 116
 Tomato, Zucchini & Goat Cheese Tart, 192
 Winter Squash & Pecorino Tart, 289
Tiramisù, 277
Tofu
 Peanut-Braised Tofu with Noodles, 47
 Soba Noodle Salad with Tofu & Marinated Eggplant, 208
 Spicy Braised Tofu with Pork, 71
 Spicy Stir-Fried Eggplant & Tofu, 187
 Tofu Salad with Edamame & Shaved Root Vegetables, 17
 Vietnamese Eggplant Curry, 197
Tomatoes
 Braised Beef Tips with Cranberry Beans, Cherry Tomatoes & Basil, 200
 Bread Pudding with Chard, Sun-Dried Tomatoes & Fontina, 300
 Bread Salad with Charred Tomatoes, Cucumber & Olives, 195
 Chicken Meatballs with Spicy Tomato Sauce, 291
 Chickpea & Roasted Tomato Soup with Fried Rosemary, 65
 Crispy Eggplant, Miso Butter & Charred Sungold Tomato Salad, 176
 Farmers' Market Salad with Tomato-Basil Vinaigrette, 132

Farro Salad with Grape Tomatoes & Ricotta Salata, 136
Fried Green Tomatoes with Rémoulade, 148
Indian-Spiced Char with Cucumber & Tomato Salad, 189
Pizza with Pesto, Cherry Tomatoes & Mozzarella, 156
Roasted Tomato Soup with Serrano Ham & Burrata, 135
Spaghetti with Shrimp, Fennel, Tomatoes & Olives, 53
Summer Chicken Braise with Wax Beans & Tomatoes, 161
Tomato, Zucchini & Goat Cheese Tart, 192
Yellow Gazpacho with Lemon-Basil Ricotta, 198
Tortellini in Herbaceous Broth with Snow Peas, 88
Tortilla, Spanish, with Leeks, 11
Tortilla chips
 Mexican Nacho Casserole, 126
Tortillas. See also Enchiladas; Tacos
 Chicken Tostada Salad, 138
 Pumpkin Tortilla Soup, 221
 Sweet Potato & Green Chile Quesadillas with Arugula, 34
Tostada Salad, Chicken, 138
Tuna
 Arugula & Fennel Salad with Black Pepper–Crusted Tuna, 243
 Tuna Burgers with Creamy Smoked Paprika Sauce, 92
 Tuna in Escabeche, 15
 Tuna Kebabs with Summer Succotash, 159
 Warm Kale & Tuna Niçoise, 218
Turkey
 Chickpea & Turkey Meatball Soup with Mustard Greens, 250
 Fresh Corn Soup with Turkey & Avocado, 203
 Kale, Turkey Sausage & Barley Stew, 285
 Turkey & Jasmine Rice Soup with Lemongrass, 262
 Turkey Burgers with Cranberry Relish, 272
 Turkey Burgers with Radicchio Slaw, 40
 Turkey Mole Enchiladas, 271
 Turkey Tetrazzini, 260

V, W, Z

Veal
 Osso Buco with Gremolata, 256
Watermelon, Feta & Mint Salad, 186
Wheat Berries with Roasted Parsnips, Butternut Squash & Dried Cranberries, 272
Wild rice
 Chicken & Wild Rice Soup with Ginger, 74
 Wild Rice Pilaf with Dried Cranberries & Pecans, 274
Zucchini. See Squash, summer

weldonowen

1045 Sansome Street, Suite 100, San Francisco, CA 94111
www.weldonowen.com
Weldon Owen is a division of Bonnier Publishing USA

DISH OF THE DAY
Conceived and produced by Weldon Owen, Inc.
In collaboration with Williams Sonoma, Inc.
3250 Van Ness Avenue, San Francisco, CA 94109

A WELDON OWEN PRODUCTION
Copyright © 2017 Weldon Owen, Inc.
and Williams Sonoma, Inc.
All rights reserved, including the right of reproduction
in whole or in part in any form.

Printed and bound in China

First printed in 2017
10 9 8 7 6 5 4 3 2 1

Library of Congress Cataloging in Publication
data is available.

ISBN: 978-1-68188-243-7

WELDON OWEN, INC.
President & Publisher Roger Shaw
SVP, Sales & Marketing Amy Kaneko
Finance & Operations Director Philip Paulick

Associate Publisher Amy Marr
Associate Editor Emma Rudolph

Creative Director Kelly Booth
Associate Art Director Lisa Berman
Senior Production Designer Rachel Lopez Metzger

Production Director Chris Hemesath
Associate Production Director Michelle Duggan

Imaging Manager Don Hill

Photographer Erin Kunkel
Food Stylists Robyn Valarik, Lillian Kang
Prop Stylists Leigh Noe, Emma Star Jensen, Glenn Jenkins

ACKNOWLEDGMENTS
Weldon Owen wishes to thank the following people for their generous support in producing this book:
Lisa Atwood, Donita Boles, David Bornfriend, Georgeanne Brennan, Lesley Bruynesteyn, Joe Budd, Sarah Putman Clegg,
Alicia Deal, Ken DellaPenta, Judith Dunham, David Evans, Gloria Geller, Alexa Hyman, Kim Laidlaw, Veronica Laramie,
Rachel Markowitz, Alexis Mersel, Carolyn Miller, Kala Minko, Julie Nelson, Jennifer Newens, Elizabeth Parson,
Hannah Rahill, Tracy White Taylor, Jason Wheeler, and Sharron Wood.